6 X 11/09 √11/09

THE
BOOK
of
CALAMITIES

ALSO BY PETER TRACHTENBERG

7 Tattoos:
A Memoir in the Flesh

THE

BOOK

of

CALAMITIES

FIVE QUESTIONS *about*
SUFFERING *and* ITS MEANING

PETER TRACHTENBERG

Little, Brown and Company
New York Boston London

Little, Brown and Company
Hachette Book Group USA
237 Park Avenue, New York, NY 10017
Visit our Web site at www.HachetteBookGroupUSA.com

First Edition: August 2008

Copyright acknowledgments appear on page 449.

Little, Brown and Company is a division of Hachette Book Group USA, Inc. The Little, Brown name and logo are trademarks of Hachette Book Group USA, Inc.

Library of Congress Cataloging-in-Publication Data
Trachtenberg, Peter.
  The book of calamities : five questions about suffering and its meaning / Peter Trachtenberg. — 1st ed.
    p. cm.
ISBN 978-0-316-15879-4 / 0-316-15879-8
1. Suffering.   I. Title.
BF789.S8T73 2008
128'.4 — dc22   2008013351

10 9 8 7 6 5 4 3 2 1

RRD-IN

Printed in the United States of America

To MG, LC, and GM,

THE LIVING AND THE DEAD

We do not see and we do not hear those who suffer, and what is terrible in life goes on somewhere behind the scenes. . . . Everything is quiet and peaceful, and nothing protests but mute statistics: so many people gone out of their minds, so many gallons of vodka drunk, so many children dead from malnutrition. . . . And this order of things is evidently necessary; evidently the happy man only feels at ease because the unhappy bear their burdens in silence, and without that silence happiness would be impossible. It's a case of general hypnotism. There ought to be behind the door of every happy, contented man some one standing with a hammer continually reminding him with a tap that there are unhappy people; that however happy he may be, life will show him her laws sooner or later, trouble will come for him — disease, poverty, losses, and no one will hear or see, just as now he neither hears nor sees others.

— ANTON CHEKHOV, "GOOSEBERRIES"[1]

CONTENTS

THE
BOOK
of
CALAMITIES

INTRODUCTION

Birth is suffering, sickness is suffering, old age is suffering, death is suffering, union with a person one does not love is suffering, separation from the one whom one loves is suffering, not to obtain what one desires is suffering, the five aggregates of appropriation . . . are suffering.

— The Samyutta Nikāya[1]

Cursed is the ground for thy sake; in sorrow shalt thou eat of it all the days of thy life.

— Genesis 3:17

Were a stranger to drop on a sudden into this world, I would show him, as a specimen of its ills, an hospital full of diseases, a prison crowded with malefactors and debtors, a field of battle strewed with carcases, a fleet foundering in the ocean, a nation languishing under tyranny, famine or pestilence. To turn the gay side of life to him and give him a notion of its pleasures — whither should I conduct

him? To a ball, to an opera, to a court? He might justly
think that I was only showing him a diversity of distress
and sorrow.

— David Hume, *Dialogues Concerning Natural Religion*[2]

Everybody suffers: War, sickness, poverty, hunger, oppression, prison, exile, bigotry, loss, madness, rape, addiction, age, loneliness. We suffer, depending on our religious or ideological convictions, because we are born in sin; because God has chosen us; because he is punishing us; because we are bound by craving and illusion; because suffering makes us better. We suffer because some of our cells are programmed, when exposed to certain biological stressors, to turn cancerous. We suffer because some of us have nothing and others have everything and those with everything want even more. We suffer because some reptilian portion of the brain delights in murder and sways not only individuals but entire nations to its purposes. We suffer because at a very early age we learn that we are going to die and spend the rest of our lives in dread of it.

Everybody suffers, but Americans have the peculiar delusion that they're exempt from suffering. In support of that statement one might cite everything from the rate of medical malpractice claims to the national epidemic of incomprehension and rage that followed the terrorist attacks of 9/11, when in a matter of moments the distant, negligible world was revealed to be no longer *there* but *here,* its breath hot in our faces. This book is meant to address that delusion. It explores suffering as a spiritual phenomenon, a condition that afflicts the spirit as well as the body; this is true of both the pain we endure and the pain we only witness. It explores the ways that people try to make sense of suffering, in order not to be destroyed.

I think of myself as a stranger to suffering. Although I was an active drug addict and alcoholic for twenty years and during that time experienced the usual dope sickness, over-doses, scams, and muggings, such unhappiness as I knew back then was voluntary; I courted it. Apart from that and my parents' deaths, I've led an insulated life, a privileged life, and I once shared the placid national fantasy that trag-edy is something that happens elsewhere or to people with bad habits: to designated sufferers. Then a friend, a woman my own age, with no bad habits to speak of, died of breast cancer. She was a good person. She was what I had in mind whenever I described anyone as good. Her death had been preceded by years of surgery and chemo and radiation, of experimental treatments, of false remissions, of metastases, of bones so decayed that a short car trip on a rough road might cause them to splinter like dry twigs, of pain. At the end she may not have been afraid to die.

In much of the literature about suffering, a protagonist is awakened by a catastrophe. Sometimes the catastrophe falls on him; sometimes it strikes another, but close enough that some blood spills on him. Gilgamesh's best friend sickens and dies in his arms. The prince Siddhartha sees three im-possible things in his father's garden — an old man, a sick man, and a corpse — and his peace is shattered. Between sunrise and sunset the blameless Job loses everything he loves. The scholar Boethius, who once counseled the king and translated Aristotle, is accused of treachery and flung into prison to await his death. Simone Weil, the brilliant, cosseted child of assimilated French Jews, takes a job in a factory, where the wretchedness of the work and the degradation of her fellow workers "marked me in so lasting a manner," she will write later, "that still today when any human being, whomever he may be and in whatever circumstances, speaks to me without brutality, I cannot help having the impression that there must be a mistake."[3]

The same thing has happened to ordinary people, and to base ones. It happened to me. The death of my friend awakened me. Afterward I became conscious of human misery in a way I hadn't been before, acutely, viscerally; I became enraged by it. (Of course the rage was childish, but I don't regret it, only the long stupor that came before.) And I began to ask the same questions that occur to almost everyone who suffers or beholds the suffering of others. Most of these are unanswerable.

THE WORLD'S OLDEST poem may be the Babylonian *Epic of Gilgamesh,* written some two thousand years before Christ. It's the story of a loss of immunity. Gilgamesh (the name means either "He Who Discovered the Source" or "He Who Saw All")[4] is king of Erech. He is two-thirds god and one-third man, terrible in strength, implacable in his appetites, a rapacious oppressor of his people. Then the gods create a rival for him, the wild man Enkidu. He and Gilgamesh struggle, become friends, undertake heroic errands. They slay the demon Humbaba and the Bull of Heaven, which the goddess Ishtar sends against them when Gilgamesh scorns her favors. But Enkidu falls ill. For twelve days and nights he lies shaking with fever; on the morning of the thirteenth day he dies.

Deranged with grief and fear, Gilgamesh flees his palace. He laments:

> *Enkidu, my friend, my little brother, who chased the*
> *panther of the desert,*
> *My friend who with me killed lions,*
> *My friend who faced with me all difficulties,*
> *His fate has overtaken him.*
> *Six days and six nights have I wept over him.*
> *Then I was afraid of death and I fled through the land.*
> *My friend whom I loved has become like unto mud.*
> *And I, must I too, lie down like him and never rise*
> *again?*[5]

His only desire now is to escape death. He travels to the end of the earth, through the country of impenetrable night, in search of Utanapishtim, the last survivor of the Great Flood. This is someone whom the gods have made immortal. When at last Gilgamesh finds him, he begs him to share his gift. Utanapishtim gives him a test: let Gilgamesh stay awake for six days and seven nights, and he will grant him eternal life. But Gilgamesh falls asleep. Still, out of pity the immortal tells him of a plant growing at the bottom of the sea that makes those who eat it young again. Gilgamesh fastens heavy stones to his feet, dives into the ocean, and plucks a sprig of the plant from the muddy floor. But before he can eat, a snake steals it. Perhaps this serpent — the text calls it "the lion of the ground" [6] — is kin to the one in Eden, which also robbed men of their chance for eternal life. Henceforth all snakes will shed their skins, and Gilgamesh will die.

> *For whom have my arms labored . . . !*
> *For whom has my heart's blood roiled!*
> *I have not secured any good deed for myself,*
> *but done a good deed for the "lion of the ground"!* [7]

It is a story that lies at the core of all religions, even those that, like the worship of ancient Babylon, have passed out of observance: first the terrifying discovery of pain and death and then, even more terrible, the discovery that they cannot be escaped.

The rest of religion is an attempt to break that rule.

Enkidu dies as the result of a curse. In other words, his death is unnatural, and that is how both he and Gilgamesh experience it. Although they have faced the prospect of death in battle, such a death — swift, exalted, dealt by enemies who could be seen and touched — was one they could understand. In a sense they sought it out. But now death has come to Enkidu unsought; it has overtaken him. And Gilgamesh's courage, which withstood monsters, fails. He runs. It's not just that he has witnessed this other kind of death for the first time; it's as if in the entire history of the world, no one had ever died this way. *Must I too lie down like him and never rise again?*

A child usually discovers death in two stages. First he sees the thing that was once a bird or a cat or a grandmother but is now something else, a simulacrum, cold and very still; then he realizes that what has happened will one day happen to him. I had no pets as a child, and as Jews we buried our dead in closed coffins, so I was in my twenties before I saw my first dead body. It was my grandfather, who had died a moment before of the last in a daylong arpeggio of coronaries. The respirator that had distended his mouth into a soundless howl had been taken out, and the eyes that had stared up at me with hopeless entreaty were empty. Beside me my mother was weeping. But I felt calm and — guiltily — relieved. It was better than watching him suffer.

By the end of *Gilgamesh* death is no longer an unnatural event. The hero has stopped running. He knows that one day he will die, and this knowledge no longer fills him with horror, only an ashen sadness. The movement of the epic is a movement from immortality to mortality, the human third of Gilgamesh's blood winning out at last. In psychological terms, this movement reenacts the individual's passage from the omnipotent fantasies of infancy to the mature recognition of his inevitable end. There's some debate as to when this recognition normally occurs. A psychoanalyst I spoke with thinks most people put it off until just before they die, and I suspect that a lot of people never get around to it at all. These are the ones who die with their mouths open, so to speak, agog at what has happened to them.

In its evolving view of mortality, *Gilgamesh* also suggests the transition from archaic, tribal religions to more sophisticated theologies, for among the former, death is often regarded as a violation of the natural order. The Ngaju Dayak people of southern Borneo, for example, believe that most deaths are the consequence of breaches of spiritual etiquette, of cutting down the wrong tree, say, or neglecting one of the funerary rites, of which the Ngaju have many. There are vestiges of this view in the Bible. In Leviticus we read that the sons of Aaron, who, like him, were consecrated as priests, are consumed by divine fire for a ritual infraction involving incense. One commentary refers to this episode as "Systems Failure." [8]

Today Gilgamesh's city, Erech, is known as Warka. It lies inside Iraq, which in 2003 was occupied — "liberated," in the official rhetoric — by my country's armed forces, which at this writing are still there. Columns of Abrams tanks weighing seventy tons apiece steamrolled across the plains where the king of Erech had once tried to outrace death. Their guns fired, and miles away men fell. Like Gilgamesh, Saddam Hussein was a notorious oppressor of his subjects, an analogy that might have been used to provide a context for the U.S. invasion if anyone in our government had known who Gilgamesh was, or cared. But the gods preferred to work indirectly. Instead of overthrowing Gilgamesh, they gave him a rival; moreover, a rival whom he would come to love. The gods understood that love would accomplish what death could not.

Covering the war in Baghdad, the journalist Jon Lee Anderson recounted a conversation he had with an Iraqi doctor. In the desert outside the city, a sandstorm was raging, and the air smelled of earth. "Whenever I smell this, it reminds me of dead people," the doctor told Anderson. "Think about it. Think of Iraq's history. What is that history but thousands of years of wars and killing? This is something we have always done rather well, and a lot of, right back to Sumerian and Babylonian times. Millions of people have died on this earth and become part of it. Their bodies are part of the land, the earth we are breathing." [9]

. . .

WE LIVE IN a country whose politics and culture sometimes resemble a vast machine designed to deny the inevitability of suffering. The machine works by promoting the fiction that suffering is something that happens to other people, under circumstances so exotic and bizarre as to be statistically impossible. In this manner suffering becomes entertainment. The disease of the week isn't cancer or heart attack but Bubble Boy syndrome. On television more people die of terrorism than in car accidents. The new conventional medical wisdom seems to be that with proper diet, exercise, and lifestyle, nobody has to get sick; maybe nobody has to die except for some fat chain-smokers in trailer parks. Our public policies amount to a symbolic exorcism in which crime, illness, and ignorance are drawn out of the general population and projected into the Gadarene herds of the poor, the black and colored poor especially. Throughout there's the implication that those who suffer somehow deserve their suffering. *Do not ask for whom the bell tolls; it tolls for Stupid.*

This fantasy of immunity arose out of traditional American exceptionalism but became prevalent only amid the euphoric abundance of the postwar years. It is a child's fantasy, and it has made us a nation of children. I believe it accounts for our collective helplessness in the face of illness, our paranoia about crime, our contempt for the disadvantaged. It's why we have no national health policy and vote for politicians who slash medical aid to the poor. It's why antidepressants are among the most widely prescribed drugs in the United States. It's why the attacks of September 11 plunged us into a paroxysm of incredulous rage and self-pity that, instead of being allayed by the successful invasion of Afghanistan, keeps seeking new cathartic outlets: today Iraq, tomorrow who knows? It's why our government wouldn't let us see the coffins of the soldiers killed in those cathartic wars, and why we didn't want to see them. Because Americans don't know how to suffer, we are inflicting great suffering on others, and in all likelihood we will bring further suffering upon ourselves. I don't want to speculate about what form this suffering will take. However it comes, I'm willing to bet we'll be unprepared for it, unprepared in the deepest psychic and spiritual sense. Clueless.

This book is an investigation of the ways in which people try to find meaning in suffering, or try not to be driven mad by the possibility that it means nothing. What explanation can possibly make sense of the chain of calamities that ends in a young woman's death from cancer? What sort of justice can even begin to address the crime of genocide or grant redress to its survivors? Why do some people cheerfully refuse to see the misery around them while others fetishize it, treating each AIDS patient or victim of sexual abuse as an opportunity for moral uplift? What sort of response does misfortune require from the fortunate, other than simply to *see* it? Or is that just another way of saying that it's okay to do nothing?

I've structured this investigation as a narrative, with myself as narrator, a middle-aged, middle-class American layman who's had the preposterous good luck to live half a lifetime without knowing hunger or homelessness, life-threatening violence or serious illness, only the garden-variety sorrow of his parents' deaths and the self-inflicted wretchedness of his bad habits. For most of this time my view of suffering was occluded and complacent. There was the suffering I saw on the TV news, flashing past as a prelude to the next commercial and happening mostly to populations that seemed created to suffer, penned in their refugee camps like animals in preserves. There were the people I knew who'd died of AIDS and overdoses, but their deaths barely registered on me. Given the anesthetizing and solipsizing effects of the drugs I took, they probably couldn't register. I'd overdosed myself a few times and had come to — or been reeled back, by irritated emergency room personnel — feeling more sheepish than anything else, and angry at losing my high. My explanation for the difference between my acquaintances and myself was that I'd been lucky and they hadn't.

My friend Linda was a poet who wrote shapely sestinas about the Heisenberg uncertainty principle. She was good in all the ways I wasn't. She was temperate and loyal; she loved her family. She was good to me. It's quite likely that I owed her my life, though in all the years I knew her, she never reminded me of my debt to her. But things kept happening to her: that "but" is my interjection. Her father died suddenly; her marriage ended. She got sick, once and then a second time, and at last with something fatal. On the day I learned that she wouldn't be getting better, I passed a man and a woman talking on the front steps of my apartment building. Maybe I didn't hear correctly, but I'm pretty sure the woman was saying, "The thing you've got to understand about God is that he's not *nice*. He's not nice at all."

This is hardly an original discovery (see Job: "He destroyeth the perfect and the wicked" [9:22]), and it's mortifying to admit that it took me until my mid-forties to realize, with the same walleyed astonishment that someone realizes he's been shot, how arbitrary and irremediable suffering can be. Linda's death peeled a skin off the world, and where that skin had been I seemed to see a vast, flayed corpus of human wretchedness: so many millions of cells rotten with cancer; so many hundreds of thousands butchered in Rwanda; so many more torn apart by bombs in Sarajevo; so many hundreds of millions starving everywhere from Uttar Pradesh to Mozambique; so many imprisoned, so many mad, so many homeless. I had been so blind.

Linda and I were no longer close; the violence of my reaction wasn't due to personal bereavement. Usually one experiences something like this only when he himself is suffering, but I wasn't suffering. I was healthy and strong and well fed, and my consciousness of the gulf that separated me from Linda — of the gulf that had separated me from my own mother when she lay dying before me — was as acute as my consciousness of Linda's pain. I couldn't know what she was feeling. She couldn't tell me, and I was afraid to ask. At some point nearly every account of suffering mentions this gulf or lacuna, and bows down before it.

Linda's death and my response to it are a point of entry. What follows unfolds in several locations and from multiple points of view, but its primary coordinates are moral and spiritual. This is a book about what suffering *means:* to its victims, onlookers, and attendants. Suffering may not inherently mean anything, but I believe that giving it meaning is the only way people can escape being ultimately destroyed by it. Faith in God is one source of meaning, the most ancient and maybe the most powerful. To people in extremity,

God may be a protector, healer, or avenger; failing all else, he may be a witness. But even when he seems to be indifferent to human tragedy — even when we suspect him of being its author — this is somehow preferable to the possibility that the tragedy took place by itself, *for no reason.*

Still, there are other sources of meaning. Primo Levi tells how, while a prisoner at Auschwitz and dispatched to collect that day's ration — a pot of soup that weighed a hundred pounds and required two men to carry it the half mile to the camp — he began reciting the Ulysses canto from the *Inferno* to the inmate trudging beside him. It was an impossible task. His companion, an Alsatian boy called Pikolo, spoke no Italian, and Levi's memory was full of holes, so that he had to skip entire passages and keep stopping to explain what was missing, as well as to translate Dante's fleet Italian into leaden French. Yet at one point it was "as if I also was hearing it for the first time: like the blast of a trumpet, like the voice of God. For a moment I forget who I am and where I am." Pikolo begged him to repeat the verse. Incredulously, Levi realized that in spite of his broken recitation, his companion understood that the story "has to do with him, that it has to do with all men who toil, and with us in particular; and that it has to do with us two, who dare to reason of these things with the poles for the soup on our shoulders."

Even as they approached the camp, Levi writes:

> I keep Pikolo back, it is vitally necessary and urgent that he listen, that he understand . . . before it is too late; tomorrow he or I might be dead, or we might never see each other again. I must tell

him, I must explain to him about the Middle Ages, about the so human and so necessary and yet unexpected anachronism, but still more, something gigantic that I myself have only just seen, in a flash of intuition, perhaps the reason for our fate, for our being here today.[10]

This book tells the stories of people who have been stricken by grave misfortune or witnessed it firsthand: life-threatening illness, unjust imprisonment, the death of a loved one, the Rwandan genocide, the tsunami in Sri Lanka, the terrorist attacks of 9/11. It is by no means a taxonomy of all the ways human beings can suffer. Rather, it examines the ways in which its subjects, its protagonists, tried to make sense of their suffering, to explain it or derive lessons from it or otherwise incorporate it into a conceptual and moral order. Suffering is often experienced as chaotic, and so to impose order on that suffering — even order of the most skewed and subjective sort — is in a sense to overcome it, if only for a little while.

I believe that ordering suffering is in part what enables some human beings to survive it. I say this even of suffering that proves fatal to the body. There is a death of the body and a death of the psyche or the spirit, and just as in the Nazi concentration camps many prisoners underwent a psychic death while they were still physically alive, so it is possible for people to remain whole in spirit up until the moment they give up their last breath. The psychoanalyst Viktor Frankl, himself a survivor of the death camps, wrote, "When a man finds that it is his destiny to suffer, he will have to accept his suffering as his task; his single and unique task."[11] You could argue with parts of this statement, particularly the word "destiny," which the Nazis loved. Still, it comes close to what I have in mind.

Before suffering people can form a coherent picture of their suffering, they must first ask questions about it, or maybe of it. In doing so, they are performing the work of science and philosophy, interrogating their reality in order to derive a thesis about it. But they are working at a terrible disadvantage, as if hobbled and gagged. They pose their questions in the silence of a hospital room or the murmuring heat of a refugee camp, in a house where someone has died; his clothes still hang in the closet, bearing a trace of his smell. Often they ask their questions without words, without even knowing that they are asking them.

- Why did this happen to me?
- How do I go on?
- If my suffering is the result of other people's malice, what do I require in the way of justice?
- What does my suffering say about me? What does it say about God?
- If I have been spared suffering, what obligation do I have toward those who haven't?

I came to this undertaking without much background in the fields on which it touches, and in the course of writing I felt my ignorance acutely; at times I was almost paralyzed by it. I am what I was when I started out, a layman, and this book should be read as a layman's response to the mass murder of Rwandan Tutsi, the state of Texas's philosophy of capital punishment, the psychology of the early Christian

martyrs, and the Buddhist ideal of the bodhisattva. Looking back, I especially regret how little attention I gave to Islamic attitudes toward suffering, suffering — the inflicting
of it, the bearing of it, the convulsive attempts to avenge it
or stave it off — having now become the dominant theme of
most of America's transactions with the Muslim world. A
while ago, while watching a documentary on a Baghdad
hospital, I was struck by the matter-of-factness with which
doctors and patients — many of the latter had just been
treated for terrible wounds and were still bleeding through
their dressings — spoke of their dead, and by the word they
all used in reference to them: "martyred." "He was martyred." "She was martyred." "My son was martyred." In the
West the word was used to denote people who had died
willingly, sometimes even joyously, in testimony to the
truths of their religion, thousands of years ago. The Iraqis
were saying it of children who had been killed while playing
ball in the street the day before.

When I began researching this book, I was afraid I might
end up as one of those journalistic voyeurs who waylay the
broken and grieving to ask them how they feel. And so I decided instead to ask people what they thought. Thinking is
less private than feeling, representing the mantle of the interior life rather than its molten core, which perhaps should
remain off-limits to strangers. Further, an interviewer who
confines his questioning to his subjects' emotions is creating a lopsided transaction in which one party feels while the
other decides what those feelings mean. Such a transaction
seemed like an awful lot of work to me, and more moral responsibility than I was comfortable taking on. In asking
people to think about what their suffering meant, I hoped

to lessen my burden and at the same time invite my respondents to reclaim some of the agency their condition had robbed them of.

One characteristic common to all the suffering I write about is that it entails a loss of power, at times even the power to frame one's anguish in words. And so to say not just what suffering had made of them but what they had made of it — true meaning being not so much found as made, maybe made the same way God is supposed to have made Adam, from earth and breath and spit — might represent a small, tentative lifting of its dominion. I would like to think so.

CHAPTER I

Your Eyes Are upon Me, and I Am Not

Why Me?

She was sick a long time, but at the time I knew her best she was healthy, a beautiful young woman with translucent olive skin and the eyes of a Sienese Madonna, slanted but flashing majolica blue, and broad shoulders that kept the beauty from being too delicate. Yet when I think of her, it is as she was in her illness. I don't understand why this should be so. I didn't see Linda much when she was ill, I was afraid to see her, I didn't know what to say, and Linda herself was withdrawing from everybody but her family and close friends. By then we were no longer close. We still called each other by the nicknames we'd made up years before, but this was a sign that our relationship was essentially nostalgic. If she hadn't died when she did, we probably would have gone on drifting apart, gently, with an occasional fond backward glance and a wave that in time would be meaningless because we could no longer see whom we were waving to.

In the late 1970s we were coworkers at a threadbare but

spunky arts organization that paid staff a starting salary of $3.50 an hour and expected them, among other things, to restock the bathrooms with toilet paper. Our friendship was a work friendship. It was the friendship of people who share a desk and pass each other the Wite-Out, who finish each other's paperwork and field each other's phone calls. "Linda's not here right now, but maybe I can help you? I'm her associate." Actually Linda *would* be there, holding up a tracking sheet on which she'd written NO MORE $$!! And after I'd gotten off the phone without offering the client a dime more than what we'd already given him, she'd say, "I like the way you helped that guy," and I'd say, "Hey, that's what I'm here for. I love helping people."

Of course she was more likely to write $3K, since she had nothing against the fellow on the other end, just wanted to eat her lunch in peace. Our clients were poets and novelists and librarians and social workers, heads of college English departments and administrators at senior centers in forlorn northern towns where the snow was gray with ash. Many of them were difficult people — angry, crafty, wheedling, given to tantrums of outraged self-importance — but Linda was always patient with them and kinder than she had to be. She was a good person.

I'm not sure she'd be happy with my describing her that way, goodness being to virtues what beige is to colors. But she was, in a casual, unself-conscious, unfanatical way, her goodness not cultivated but growing wild, like a weed. Once I was making fun of a poet we knew, a thundering, oracular pest who was always hassling us for fifty-dollar gigs and whose style of reading was to declaim something meaningless with a long pause in the middle and a hypnotic widening of his eyes: *I myself . . . am . . . myself!* When I was done imitating him, Linda laughed, but then she shook her head sadly. "Poor Andrew, he can't help it. He's got problems." A while later she recommended him for a reading series that paid especially well. Maybe a truly good person wouldn't have laughed, but I'm talking about the goodness of persons and not of angels.

As kind as she was, she was no pushover. A stubborn, contrarian vein ran through her personality. She'd probably gotten it from her father. He was a doctor, a brilliant, tactless overachiever who'd bulldozed his way into medical school before he could shave, bulldozed his way into practice, and then set about bulldozing his children onto the various paths he'd chosen for them. Linda was the only one who pushed back. She didn't want to be a doctor; she wanted to be a poet. She didn't care if it meant putting herself through graduate school on her own dime or having to listen to the acid scorn with which the old man pronounced the initials "MFA." Nothing could move her against her will, not even the universal bulldozer of cool. Like practically everybody else in our office, she wrote poems, but hers weren't about her genitals or her feelings. They were about the Heisenberg uncertainty principle, and they were sestinas.

Maybe Linda seemed so good to me because I was so conscious of what I was, which wasn't bad so much as spineless, flailed by appetites I was always apologizing for but never really tried to resist. Back then I used to take a vial of meth with me to work, like a little thermos, and sip from it through the day. Once, halfway through the morning, I realized that the vial had come open in the inside pocket of my sport coat. It was drenched. Racing into the bathroom, I tore off the jacket and began frantically, abjectly sucking the lining. But even as I sucked, I imagined Linda coming in and finding me like that. I pictured her shaking her head with a small, sad smile. "Oh, poor Peter, he can't help it," she'd say to anyone who tried to pick on me. "He's got problems."

I don't really know how we became friends. People rarely make friends with their superegos. Maybe I befriended Linda in order to disarm her. I liked to make her laugh and to that end used to regale her with imitations of everybody from our more irritating clients to Idi Amin. The payoff was that moment when her watchful stillness broke and she abandoned herself to laughter, her head tossed back, her stomach quaking. Watching that laughter, I felt the relief of a comic who's managed to break up a roomful of stiffs. But why was I so relieved? Linda wasn't my boss; she had no power over me. She wasn't even that much better a worker than I was. Anyway, I wasn't that much of a fuckup. Hungover or not, most mornings I made it into the office before she did. She was a comically deep sleeper. You could surround her with alarm clocks set to go off a minute apart, you could pop a paper bag in her ear, and still she'd sleep on. A few times she came in with her hair wet and explained that, finding no other way to wake her and being late for work himself, her husband had dumped a pot of water on her head.

We'd been working together for about six months when she got a phone call. I didn't notice her answer it. At some point, though, I became aware that an unfamiliar note had entered her voice. I looked up. She'd turned away from me and was holding the phone so tightly that her knuckles had gone white. "Yes," she said, and then, "When?" and then, "God." The last came out tonelessly, as if she were reading from a script, not her script but somebody else's. I came up behind her and placed my hands on her shoulders. It was the first time I'd ever touched her. Only after she hung up did she start to cry. Her father had just died of a heart attack. I looked at her in wonder. I had never seen someone so close to death. Its glow surrounded her. Later I realized it was not just death but loss, unmitigated and unalloyed. She'd loved her father without the usual grudges. She'd once told me that she gave him her poems to read. I hadn't shown my father anything I'd written since junior high. We called her husband, he came to get her, and the two of them drove up to New England for the funeral. This was the first misfortune.

A while after that I left the job. I left it of my own free will but under a cloud. My bad habits had gotten worse; there'd been an episode involving the emergency room at St. Vincent's, and it had gotten back to my office — unavoidably, since two of my coworkers had had to take me in. Everybody was tactful; I don't remember getting so much as a warning. But still, it was embarrassing to go to work every day with people who had possibly saved my life — and at the very least seen me half-naked and half-unconscious, with vomit on my chin. When a chance for another job came up, I took it.

Naturally, Linda and I didn't see each other as much; maybe we had coffee once in a while. And so I was surprised

when she called and asked me to dinner. We met at a discon-
certingly nice restaurant off Sixth Avenue; I wasn't sure I
could afford it. There was some scuffling about whether I
would order something to eat along with my drinks, and
then over dinner, in that same cautious, airport announcer's
voice I'd heard before, her improbably large hands folded
primly on the table before her, she told me that she and her
husband were getting a divorce.

I looked at her expectantly, waiting for the story. There
had to be a story. It would have something to do with sex.
For all that I thought of myself as worldly, deep down I assumed that people divorced only because of that. But there
was no story, or rather the things Linda told me wouldn't
cohere into the kind of story I recognized. She'd taken her
marriage vows seriously, which in the 1970s was a wildly eccentric thing to do, especially for someone still in her twenties. It was like being a Luddite. I don't remember what
reason she gave for the breakup. Maybe she and her husband
didn't communicate; maybe they no longer wanted the same
things. Marriages are fragile constructions, perhaps none
more so than the ones that are based on love. It was the second misfortune.

We saw even less of each other, the things we had in common dropping away. The next I knew she had a new boyfriend. He was very tall and elegant, with a matinee idol's
mustache. "Is he good to you?" I asked her. I could tell the
question embarrassed her. I was turning into a blurter.
Sometime after that I married a woman I'd met while on my
way to cop heroin. Linda brought Star to the wedding. I
can't imagine what they made of it. It was the wedding of

two people who'd met in the course of a drug buy and were trying to pretend otherwise, not all that persuasively.

A year and a half later Linda and Star got married, too. I don't remember if they invited me. Linda looks very happy in her wedding pictures. They moved into an apartment that was the kind of place people used to have in mind when they came to New York to become famous. It had high ceilings and parquet floors, and on warm nights they could stand on the terrace and look down at Central Park, a calm dim pool amid frantically lit streets where cars coursed and jostled. Linda still worked for the arts organization, although instead of giving out grants she now designed its magazine. The endless procession of favor seekers had begun to make her misanthropic. She liked fonts and layouts; they satisfied her taste for order. Her drafting table stood beside a window, arrayed with pencils and X-Acto knives even after Macs made the old tools obsolete, even after she became too ill to use them. I pictured her working there, with Star slouched on the love seat in the next room, writing on a yellow pad, a Bach prelude on the stereo. In the silence between movements you could hear the scratch of pencils.

My marriage ended. For a while I lived in a converted pickle factory a few blocks from the East River. In damp weather its crumbling brick still gave off a smell of brine. My roommate was a proofreader who worked the lobster shift. Most mornings he'd come home as I was doing my wake-up shot and stand outside the bathroom until I was finished, then trudge in to do his own. Each of us suspected the other of stealing from him, and we disliked each other so much that we refused to shoot up with the same tie. I moved, moved again. My joints hurt all the time. Once or twice I came to on a gurney.

During this time a number of people I knew died: of overdoses, in car wrecks, one in a fire that started when he nodded out with a lit cigarette between his fingers. A few of them were presenting with the coughs and night sweats of what would turn out to be AIDS. Some of these people I liked and some of them I despised, but I viewed what happened to them in an actuarial spirit, as a predictable risk of the life we shared. "Really, we all ought to be dead," I used to tell friends, but I was usually loaded when I said it. Deep down, of course, I was afraid. Fear should have made me cautious, but instead it made me reckless, like some timid nocturnal animal that suddenly hurls itself into the glare of approaching headlights. The time I felt safest was the moment before I pitched forward on the toilet seat. Like many heroin addicts, I consumed the drug in a place normally consecrated to shitting.

I moved to another city, where I knew few people. Here I was relieved of my habit. I did not give it up so much as it was lifted while my attention was elsewhere. I would compare it to being awakened by someone bursting a paper bag in my ear: an explosion that did no damage but for a moment stopped my heart. The prospect of unmediated life baffled me. For a while I lived low to the ground, seeing the same people night after night, eating in the same coffee shops where cigarette smoke hung blue in the air. It was only when I believed that the change might take that I called Linda. She was so happy for me. When I asked to see her, though, she became evasive. It wasn't a good time. Her voice was muffled and remote, and I was suddenly afraid that she didn't believe I'd really changed. So great was the faith I placed in her judgment that I was afraid she was right.

Perhaps two years passed before we finally met again. Somewhere during that time I learned that she'd been ill, but I didn't realize how bad it was until she sat down across from me in the café. She was barely recognizable. Even beneath the heavy coat — and the heavy sweater she wore under it, though it was early spring and no longer cold — her body looked thick and misshapen. Her face was a bloated mask, as yellow as a callus. Her folded hands were swollen as well. She was wearing dark glasses and a headband, and my initial thought was that their purpose was to conceal her disfigurement. But the headband served as a kind of truss. Without it, her cheeks and eyelids would have sagged like an old woman's. She was still in her early thirties. Her condition was called Hashimoto's thyroiditis. This is an auto-immune disease that attacks the thyroid and eventually destroys it. Symptoms include goiter, a dull facial expression, puffiness and swelling around the eyes, drooping eyelids, thinning hair, excessive fatigue, and weight gain. Her old difficulty waking up had been an early warning sign.

What bothered her most wasn't the change in her appearance. She wasn't vain that way. She hated the loss of her strength. It took her an hour to get dressed in the morning. Most days she couldn't leave the apartment by herself. She'd lie on the sofa watching sunlight circle the living room, falling onto the Oriental rug, the coffee table with its dirty saucers, the photographs on the sideboard. It got so that she could tell the time that way. I told myself that this might not be the worst impediment for a poet. I was trying to be optimistic, and my optimism had something brutal about it, as if my friend's suffering was a blank wall that I was trying to ram through.

Perhaps I was denying that the wall was in fact suffering. Suffering can be difficult to define, especially for those who stand on its other side, guessing at the feelings of the immured. Spinoza, the most precise and systematic of philosophers, defined pain as "that passion by which the mind passes to a lesser perfection" — that is, by which its powers of acting are lessened or impeded.[1] Certainly, Linda was in pain. Along with disfiguring her face and body, the Hashimoto's had caused her brain to swell against her skull like the brain of someone who has been savagely beaten. It meant the end of sestinas about quantum physics; it meant the end of poetry. This was the third misfortune.

THE TSUNAMI OF December 26, 2004, struck Sri Lanka with varying force and violence, depending on the affected area's distance from the epicenter of the initial earthquake, the depth of water offshore, and the presence of islands, reefs, or sandbars that might slow the wave's thundering rush toward land. Among the worst affected places was Mullaittivu, the northern stronghold of the Liberation Tigers of Tamil Eelam (LTTE), where three thousand people died.[2] When I went there a few months later, the shore was a field of rubble extending as far as the eye could see, the rubble ground so fine that one could scarcely tell what it had once been part of. The only recognizable ruins were religious structures. Here was a *kovil,* or Hindu temple, with its outer walls crumpled and its courtyard strewn with debris. Nearby was a Catholic church whose canary yellow facade was virtually unscathed but whose back and side walls had been plowed away. A few hundred yards away stood an intact shrine to the Virgin Mary, every stone and seashell still in place and the Virgin's statue stationed primly in its niche, gazing skyward as if calling heaven to witness what had happened here.

What could you infer from this hierarchy of destruction? That God, or the god of the tsunami anyway, was a Catholic? Or that he preferred plaster effigies to live human beings, no matter how devout? Whoever had been inside that church when the wave crashed down on it must have been drowned or crushed, I thought. But later I learned that on December 26 the priest had chosen not to celebrate Mass at the church but at a chapel a mile inland, effectively saving his entire congregation.[3]

Elsewhere the tsunami had been more capricious. In the tourist towns along the Galle Road on the southwest coast, a few perfectly preserved hotels stood beside ones that had been leveled. Intact fishermen's huts rose above the splinters of their neighbors. The ATM in the bank in Ambalangoda was dispensing cash. Every so often you saw a foreigner, his skin the red of terra-cotta or a luxurious cocoa, driving by on a rented scooter. They might be relief workers or tourists. Either way, the remaining hotels would be happy to have them.

On the landward side of the highway between Bentota and Hikkaduwa were the tent villages of the relief agencies. In this more prosperous and predominantly Sinhalese part of the country, they were villages rather than cities, a testament to the speed with which aid had come from Colombo and survivors had resettled with their relatives.[4] The tents were the low, teardrop-shaped kind used by alpinists and were decorated with the flags or ensigns of their donor countries, a colony of red crosses followed by a colony of blue, then yellow, then a little England where every dwelling was gaily emblazoned with the Union Jack. The tents were tiny and stifling, and their occupants preferred to spend most of their time outside them. The luckier survivors — the ones who hadn't lost everything — were already rebuilding houses along the beach, disregarding the official edict that barred construction within a hundred meters of the water. The less fortunate hunkered in whatever shade they could find.

I was with a group of Sri Lankan volunteers who were taking a census of orphans — "tsunami orphans" was the phrase everyone kept using, the way aid workers in South Africa spoke of "AIDS orphans" and the ones in Rwanda of "genocide orphans" — for a children's village that was being built nearby by a consortium of Buddhist temples. This part of Sri Lanka is predominantly Buddhist, and temples loom over the landscape, their blinding white stupas looking like enormous bells or, if you know your iconography, the Buddha sitting in meditation. Most of the children were now staying with family members in hamlets situated a little distance from the sea. Their location had once been a sign of their poverty — anybody who had any money wanted to build by the water — but it had saved the lives of their residents.

In the hamlet of Duwa Malavenna a thin, anxious-looking woman named K. W. Lenora was living with her daughter and twin sons in a small house near a lumberyard; the whole time we were visiting, we could hear the whine of its saw. Her husband, Nishendra, had been killed in the marketplace, where he'd gone to buy a cake for the boys' twelfth birthday. His photo was displayed on a cupboard: a slight man with large ears and a severe gaze. Mrs. Lenora had placed a plate of bananas before it as an offering, as she might before the statue of the Buddha in her temple. The only other image in the house was a picture one of the boys had drawn. It was a tableau of the tsunami that showed palm trees bending and snapping and human stick figures being tossed like leaves in the wind.

The twins were named Lakmal and Dazun. They were as sleek as ferrets and at least outwardly cheerful, eager to show the visitors the new cricket bats they were pasting with decals. But I noticed how roughly Dazun played with the family dog. At one point it did something that displeased him, and he picked it up, then dropped it heavily with a smack on its bony rump. The dog shook itself and slunk from the room. I was always touched by the kindness with which Sri Lankans treat animals, especially dogs, which are so despised in other parts of Asia. Although they run more or less wild throughout the country and lie on the roads as they please, their mangy fur the color of dust, and although Sri Lankans are reckless drivers, the dogs are rarely run over.

We drove on to Pereliya. On December 26 the *Sea Queen*, a train carrying passengers from Galle to Colombo, had been broadsided here as it traveled on the coastal railroad, its cars swept off the tracks as if by a contemptuous hand, the tracks themselves uprooted. Fifteen hundred people had been killed, including some two hundred villagers who had clambered on board in an attempt to find shelter. Many of them had passed their children through the windows, thinking they'd be safe inside. There must have been an awful, protracted moment in which all on board watched the wave race toward them.

Three cars had been retrieved from the swamp and placed back on the tracks as a memorial. They were half-crushed, their windows shattered. As expressive as this damage was, it gave only a partial sense of what had happened here. For weeks after the catastrophe these beaches and villages had been charnel grounds. At each incoming tide the sea had spewed more bloated bodies back onshore. Everything smelled of death.

We climbed a sandy ridge and entered Totagamuwa Bridge, a hamlet of wooden houses with low thatched roofs. One house was overflowing with children minded by two middle-aged women. For the next half hour I frantically tried to write down everything the project director, a bustling entrepreneurial fellow named Dolitha told me: the kids' names — which I kept misspelling — and ages and grades in school, the names of their deceased relatives, and their relation to the grown-ups who were presenting them to us with varying degrees of pride, tenderness, and suspicion.

The child who caught my attention was a grave sixteen-year-old girl named Achini. "Child" is not what I'd call an American sixteen-year-old, for whom the word "teenager" was invented, but like many Sri Lankans, Achini seemed younger than her age, as if the carapace of young adulthood hadn't fully closed around her. Both dawn and dusk are brief in this part of the world. The sun shoots out of the sea and twelve hours later plunges back into it, and perhaps it is like that for human time as well, children bursting into young adulthood and adults falling into the pit of old age in the blink of an eye. In Sri Lanka this has less to do with latitude than with economics. How many families can afford an idle teenager? How many can pay for the medical and cosmetic truss-work that keeps Americans looking youthful into their fifties and sixties? Many of the old people I met in Sri Lanka had no teeth, or even dentures. Their collapsed profiles reminded me of the faces I'd made when I was imitating old people as a child, long before I actually saw an old person who was toothless.

Achini's mother had died in the tsunami, and she was now living with her aunt Sandiya and her children. There was a cousin her age to whom she was particularly attached. The whole time I was there, Achini held on to her arm. The sight of the two girls, both tall and slender with long necks and deep, lambent eyes, always moving in tandem, was heartrending. Their faces were as expressive as the faces in silent films. Part of what made them seem so young, I realized, was their anachronistic willingness to do what was expected of them. Docilely they greeted the visiting grownups, pulled out plastic stools for us to sit on, served us glasses of sweet tea. They knelt before the yellow-robed nun who had come along to comfort the grieving and touched her sandaled feet. Invited to help themselves from a box of donated clothing from the United States, they hesitated until the nun motioned them to go ahead; then they meekly sorted through the contents. I have a photograph of them holding up a pair of jeans so grotesquely huge that one girl could fit in each leg.

Dolitha signaled me to write something down. "This child's father left when she was little, and now her mother is dead, too." He lowered his voice, though it was unlikely that Achini or her relatives spoke any English. "Many people are teasing her because she is an unlucky girl."[5]

For a moment I thought it was a morbid joke. How do you single out the unlucky child in a village of orphans, on an entire coast of the bereaved? But I needed to accommodate a different notion of luck. Like most Americans, I think of luck as a temporary condition, a streak of wins or losses that eventually comes to an end: hence the expression "My luck ran out." This model of fortune corresponds to mathematical reality, probability theory being essentially a theory of instances, one toss of a coin or roll of the dice repeated over and over until a tendency is revealed.

But the belief that luck is temporary also reflects a democratic outlook. A lucky person is an aristocrat; an unlucky one belongs to fate's lumpen. Americans like to think of themselves as egalitarians, so we see luck as malleable and imagine that even the lowliest schmo can get lucky. It's why we idolize self-made millionaires and turn up our noses at other people's hard-luck stories. We believe that we can transform ourselves, that we can make our luck. It's the idea that motivated anyone who ever sent away for a salesman's kit or signed up for a correspondence course or decided to move halfway across the country to a place where there was no job waiting and he knew no one, but where the odds might be better. "Those who live in the midst of democratic fluctuations," Alexis de Tocqueville wrote, "have always before their eyes the image of chance."[6]

In Pereliya luck wasn't plastic, as it is in the United States. It was stone. Achini's luck was seen as part of her character, as intrinsic as courage or a quick temper. I would have liked to know when people had started calling her unlucky. Was it when her father left or only after her mother was killed, or had her unfortunate nature been recognized even in the cradle? Achini wasn't the only child I met that day whose father had abandoned her. Men left because there were no jobs or because the jobs they had, in the tourist industry especially, brought too much temptation. All along this stretch of coast I heard stories of the corrupting effects of foreign wealth and immorality on previously upright Sinhalese. There were people who thought they were the reason for the tsunami. But what bearing did that have on a modest girl who probably bathed on the shore in her sari? And why did people find her bad luck cause for scorn, as if it were a degrading vice?

Of course the very idea of luck is problematic to Buddhists. They acknowledge its existence but prefer to speak of karma, or, in Pali, the language of the first Buddhist scriptures, *kamma*. The word literally means "action," but in Buddhist usage it carries the connotation of deliberate action and its appropriate results, a moral quantum packet of cause and effect.[7] Wholesome acts bear pleasant consequences, unwholesome acts unpleasant ones. Those consequences, of course, may not become apparent for several lifetimes. Someone withholds alms from a monk or gratuitously kills an animal, and a generation later a different iteration of the malefactor — his moral descendant — finds himself hungry and penniless or trapped in a small, bewildered body on which stronger, cleverer creatures are inflicting inexplicable torments. In this manner most of what happens to human beings can be accounted for. Nobody suffers by accident or for someone else's misbehavior: "By self alone is evil done; by self alone is one defiled; by self alone is evil not done; by self alone is one purified." [8]

The Western cliché about Buddhism is that it's pessimistic, but the religion's cheerful central teaching is that liberation is available to any human being at any moment. Even in the most wretched circumstances you can begin to unravel the knot of bad karma through meritorious actions that will in time secure you a better rebirth. If sufficiently motivated, you can follow the example of the Buddha and seek not just to unravel the knot but sever it, willing nothing, craving nothing, free from ignorance and suffering alike. This is what's meant by "nirvana."

But tempering that optimistic scenario is the ineluctable fact that whatever your affliction is, it has not been wrongly addressed. It is yours. You have, in a sense, sent it to yourself. Buddhism doesn't, strictly speaking, believe in a self, but that's a hard idea to wrap one's head around, and I wondered how consoling it would be to Achini. Sometime in the past she or some karmic predecessor had done something terrible, must have done so to merit this bad luck that was not luck at all. Perhaps not even that far in the past. A Sri Lankan abbot in the States had told me that one-seventh of our karma is accrued in the present lifetime. Asked what kind of karma could possibly account for the thousands of deaths in his homeland, he answered imperturbably: "All that has washed in has washed out." [9]

When I watched Achini, though, she didn't strike me as guilty, only as sad and anxious, clinging to her cousin's side like a beginning swimmer clinging to the side of the pool. The Buddha was practical-minded. Having identified ignorance and craving as the universal causes of suffering, he saw no need to trace its individual etiology, the path that leads from specific acts to specific misfortunes.

> It's just as if a man were wounded with an arrow thickly smeared with poison. His friends and companions, kinsmen and relatives would provide him with a surgeon, and the man would say, "I won't have this arrow removed until I know whether the man who wounded me was a noble warrior, a priest, a merchant, or a worker." He would say, "I won't have this arrow removed until I know the given name and clan name of the man who wounded me . . . until I know whether he was tall, medium, or short . . . until I know whether he was dark, ruddy-brown, or golden-colored . . . until I know his home village, town, or city . . . until I know whether the bow with which I was wounded was a long bow or a cross-bow. . . . The man would die and those things would still remain unknown to him." [10]

Maybe my problem was that I was viewing Achini's misfortune through Western — that is, Judeo-Christian — eyes, which are so attuned to the spectrum of sin and retribution, or of weakness and testing, that they can't apprehend suffering in any other light.

• • •

IN CALAMITY THE most common question is why? Why me or why us or why them instead of us? Survivors of the South Asian tsunami were asking it even before the waters receded. The people in this part of the world are devout, and many explained the tragedy in the language of their faith. "In Muslim society, God only gives us his goodness and we have to learn lessons from a disaster like this," a man in Aceh, Indonesia, told a reporter. "This may be God saying he is angry with human conduct in the world."[11] Some Sri Lankan Buddhists saw the tsunami as evidence of the primacy of *dukkha,* suffering or awry-ness, its imperviousness to all human attempts to ward it off. A monk cautioned, "If you think something will happen, it never will. If you think it never will happen, it will."[12]

"God makes the world," said a Muslim imam in devastated Hambantota. "He can give, he can take. Sometimes he gives more. Sometimes he takes."[13] The Roman Catholic bishop of Kandy[14] struggled with the contradiction between a God who loves mankind and a God who kills thousands of human beings in the space of a long breath: "It is a question, a problem, a mystery. Though I don't believe that God wants to destroy human life in that sense, but, biblically, also we find that along sometimes with evil people, some innocent people also perish."[15] It wasn't an explanation so much as a shrug of exhaustion.

These were instances of higher religion, informed by centuries of systematic contemplation of the divine. On the ground people looked for practical reasons why the gods had chosen them or passed them over, reasons that had less to do with the gods than with their own character and actions. They weren't engaging in theology; they were making a personal reckoning with the force that had torn their lives asunder. A baker whose fourteen family members had escaped the destruction thought it was because he kept all the Buddhist precepts: not lying, stealing, drinking, philandering, or killing animals. "We earn money the correct way. That's why it didn't happen to us."[16] As we went about our census work, Dolitha assured me that the wave had targeted villages of fishermen and coral divers (the latter especially suspect for the damage they inflicted on the environment), all those generations of bad karma functioning as a sort of moral lightning rod that instead of bringing down destruction from the sky called it up from the ocean. People looked for consolation. An elderly Christian named Patricia Jayasuriya had vanished when the sea foamed into her church in Hambantota, but her surviving sister was sure she'd died in a state of grace, for she had just taken Communion.[17]

And they looked for someone to blame. It might be the foreigners fornicating and getting high in their resorts or the locals who had begun to emulate them or an apocryphal Christian who was said to have baked a cake in the shape of the Buddha and stuck a knife in it.[18] A thin, luxuriantly bearded Hindu holy man in a refugee camp in Batticaloa ticked off the responsible parties on his fingers: "People looked to different gods. Some people didn't respect their parents. If people got a job, they'd think 'I'm a big man.' The stock of bad habits got full."[19] An Achenese man named Yusmadi Sulaiman had tried to save his four-year-old son, only to watch helplessly as the child was pried from his arms and carried away by the churning waters. Now he was weeping and a visitor was patting his shoulder. "It's not your fault, it's not your fault," the visitor kept saying. Here was the immemorial division between power and affliction, authority and shame. You don't tell someone that what has happened to him is not his fault unless the suspicion has arisen — in his mind or your own — that it is.[20]

Similar speculation was taking place on the other side of the world, though there the tone was generally calmer. The catastrophe was far away; you could talk about it without having to hold your nose against the ripeness of the unburied dead. England's royal family heard the bishop of Norwich preach that "God has given us an Earth that lives and moves. It is not inert, it is alive — that is why we can live. Last week's events were the starkest possible reminder that what gives life can also take it away."[21] Other Christian commentators shifted the emphasis from the first person of the Trinity to the second: "God does not prevent suffering but promises to redeem it. And it is this promise that we see fulfilled in the death and resurrection of Jesus Christ."[22]

Although few of the speakers explicitly addressed one another's claims, you had the sense that you were listening to a debate, one whose decorum sometimes gave way to outbursts of peevishness and fist-shaking prophetic wrath. "God does not micromanage the universe," insisted a Reform rabbi in the United States, recoiling at the thought of a deity who lets small children drown before the eyes of their parents. "It's not a notion I can live with. . . . And if I need to stand here and say that I think that God does not control everything in order to clear God of such a crime, I will do so."[23] This echoed an argument made years earlier by Rabbi

Harold Kushner, who had lost a teenage son to a rare congenital disease: "I can worship a God who hates suffering but cannot eliminate it more easily than I can worship a God who chooses to make children suffer and die, for whatever exalted reason." [24]

The idea that God might be judged guilty of anything seemed to inflame the Baptist minister and author John Piper, who scolded an interviewer: "When I hear of a calamity like this, my deepest interpretation is God is calling John Piper to repent. God is breaking my heart. God is pointing out my sin. God is telling me, 'Be amazed you weren't under the wave,' and so my biggest interpretation is God is calling the world to repent. We put God on trial every time something big happens, and I think what repentance would mean is that we stop making God a whipping boy and blaming him for every pain and not praising him for any pleasure." [25]

What lay behind the vehemence of these arguments? Elsewhere in the world some 100,000 people had died in the American occupation of Iraq. One could argue about those dead — about who had killed them and why and whether those reasons justified their deaths — but who could argue about the dead of Sri Lanka and Aceh? Unless the argument wasn't really about them but about God. Everywhere people were rushing to — in Kushner's memorable phrase — "defend [his] honor." [26] It was as if the earthquake off the coast of Sumatra had opened a rift not just in the earth but in the sphere of belief, and all those priests and ministers, rabbis and imams, those paid and unpaid vendors of judgment, were scurrying to mend it, feverishly trying to stuff God back into a world that suddenly seemed empty of him. [27]

⌒

How many are mine iniquities and sins?

— JOB 13:23

The story is told by Jews, Christians, and Muslims, the last of whom call its protagonist Ayyub. It owes some of its ecumenism to the fact that Job belongs to no clear faith. The god he appeals to may not be the God of Abraham; Abraham may not yet be born. Some commentators claim that Job is the oldest book in the Bible, though most modern scholarship dates it to the Babylonian exile or the age of the Maccabees.[28] Like Proverbs and Ecclesiastes, it represents an interlude in the biblical narrative and as such is not bound by that narrative's conventions of chronology, place, and character.

Job lives in Uz, in Edom, at some unspecified time after the Fall.[29] He is not a Hebrew. In the course of his trial he never invokes the Mosaic law that is so central to the Old Testament, the hinge that joins man to God, binding both. All he has is the general, almost instinctual conviction that God doesn't destroy his creations without cause, or ought not to. Perhaps this conviction is founded on the ancient covenant with Noah, though that covenant extended to the whole world. Well, in calamity each person becomes the world: that is what Job discovers. "There was a man in the land of Uz, whose name was Job; and that man was perfect and upright, and one that feared God and eschewed evil" (1:1). Note the word "feared." This is a story from the time before man learned to love God, before he came to think of God as his best friend.

What do we know about Job? Only that he is upright and prosperous, "the greatest of all the men of the east" (1:3). Of his wealth we get a detailed inventory: so many sons, so many daughters, so many sheep, camels, oxen, she-asses. But of Job's virtue we at first know only this: he makes sacrificial offerings not only on his own behalf but on his sons', lest any of them have sinned and cursed God in their hearts. The immediate import is that the field of his conscience is wider than ordinary virtue requires, wide enough to encompass his children as well as himself. But his conscience is also finer than most people's, registering not only actions but thoughts, the fleeting shadow of the inward curse.

You could argue that what Job practices isn't morality so much as it is conscientiousness in ritual. But isn't that where all morality begins, with ritual? Evidence elsewhere in the Bible, especially in Leviticus, suggests this, as does much anthropology. Morality prescribes how we should behave toward other humans, ritual how we should behave toward God, and in the parched, skeletal lands of the Middle East, God took precedence over man as a gnomon takes precedence over the shadow it casts. Only after they've stipulated what human beings owe their maker do the Commandments get around to detailing their obligations to each other, the fine print about adultery and murder.

Job's good fortune sets the stage for his misfortune. His goodness, to paraphrase one writer, is a bull's-eye painted on his forehead.[30] Because he is both wealthy and virtuous, he becomes the object of a wager. More accurately, he becomes the wager's marker, the coin that is tossed, the die that is cast, the card that's turned over and over until its face is all but worn away. The wager's active parties are God and

Satan. This isn't the serpent who whispered to Eve in the Garden. This isn't the fallen Son of the Morning Star. Nor is he the old enemy whose power is almost equal to that of God himself, so that in some theologies he is the source of every evil that befalls mankind.[31]

Satan is Hebrew for "adversary," the one who blocks or opposes. Similarly, the Greek *diabolos* means "one who throws something across someone's path." In the Bible he's always called "ha-Satan," *the* Satan, *the* adversary. This isn't a name but a title, that of an angel who scours the earth, accusing evildoers: a prosecutor. He's God's prosecutor, of course, a subordinate, but one of sufficiently high rank to operate on his own initiative, going up and down in the earth and back and forth in it. He speaks to God in the voice of a familiar. This isn't the place to ask who or what God is, but it bears considering why an all-powerful being who contains roles and functions that in other traditions are parceled out to entire pantheons — creator, destroyer, bringer of storm and flood, warrior, king, lawgiver, comforter, and, in the end, sacrifice — would see fit to subcontract the office of adversary.

The story proper begins with these two in conference, in what looks to be the heavenly throne room. God asks Satan where he's been, and Satan tells him, and then the conversation shifts to Job. The argument has been made that Satan has already chosen Job as his victim, but the fact is that it's God who brings him up. "Hast thou considered my servant Job?" (1:8). Why does he do this? Because of where Satan has come from. He hasn't been idly wandering the earth but patrolling its slums and sinkholes — some of which are located in palaces — peering at the figures that precipitate out of the darkness and deliquesce back into it, not interfering with their abominations, just wanting to *see,* though it goes without saying that what Satan sees is always and only baseness. He is adapted to his role perfectly but narrowly. That is what makes him less than God. When God asks him, "Whence comest thou?" (1:7), his true meaning is "Whom do you accuse?" Satan accuses Job. But only after God has, in a sense, invited him to. In courtroom tactics this is called asking a leading question.

Interestingly, given what we know of Job's piety, the devil accuses him of being superficial. Job, he says, loves God only because of what God has given him. Except, as we recall, the word isn't "love" but "fear." "Doth Job fear God for nought?" (1:9). Like so much in the Bible, the question is open to interpretation. Is Satan being sarcastic, or is he chiding God for being too soft on his servant — for not putting the fear of God in him? The Old Testament has many stories of sibling rivalry, and in a sense Job is one of them, Satan's accusations suggesting nothing so much as an unloved child's envy of the family favorite.

Satan proposes a wager. Let God put forth his hand and withdraw his blessings, and Job will curse him to his face. Thousands of years of literature and folklore have taught us never to bet with the devil, but maybe the warning applies only to human beings, whose souls are so small and defenseless and so easily lost. God is tempted; he takes the bet: "Behold, all that he hath is in thy power" (1:12). I don't know if he says it magnanimously, being certain of Job's loyalty, or in a burst of anger, because Satan, that master of mind-fuck and insinuation, has opened a small fissure in his trust. But either way, from that moment on Job is doomed.

• • •

THE AIR FORCE stationed him in Arizona, and he liked it so much — the winters that were like summers, the fierce blue ax blade of the sky, the flat roads unspooling through wavering brakes of cholla and ocotillo — that after his tour was up, he stayed on. The heat took getting used to, but he could drive two hours north and go skiing in the mountains around Flagstaff. He got a job as a postal worker. In 1991 he was making $30,000 a year and paying $500 a month for his mortgage. He'd started a towing business on the side that he planned to get into more seriously after he retired. He raced motorcycles and stock cars; he'd just bought himself a 1974 Corvette. He went hunting in season and played in the post office softball league; he'd been invited to join the A team. Ray Krone told me this quickly and matter-of-factly, as if he were reading an inventory. These were the things he'd done. These were the things he'd had. These were the things he'd been looking forward to. They were gone now; it was better not to dwell on them.[32]

There was a bar in downtown Phoenix where he liked to go after ball games to drink beer and play darts. A waitress named Kim Ancona worked there; he'd once given her a lift to a party. On the morning of December 29, 1991, her naked body was found lying in a pool of blood in the men's bathroom. The police thought she'd been stabbed from behind — stabbed eleven times — and then raped while she drowned in her own blood. On her left breast there were bite marks made by somebody with uneven teeth. Local news stations would later speak of a "snaggletooth killer."

A friend of Ancona's reported seeing a short, thickset

Native American man with long black hair sitting at the bar that night, so drunk that Kim had refused to serve him. Other witnesses had spotted someone of that description loitering outside the club in the early hours of the morning. Had the police made a thorough search of their database, they would have found a man who looked like that living less than half a mile from the crime scene. His name was Kenneth Phillips, and he was on probation for having broken into the house of a neighborhood woman and "choking her while threatening to kill her." Twenty days later he would be arrested for sexually assaulting a seven-year-old girl.[33]

Ray Krone is a sparely built white man with thinning brown hair. He had no criminal record. His roommate would vouch that on the night of the murder, he had been at home.

Two things first brought him to the attention of police: he lived a few blocks from the bar, and his name was written in the victim's address book. The detective who came to interview him on the afternoon of December 29 noticed that his upper teeth were conspicuously uneven. This was the beginning of a theory. He asked Ray if he and Kim had been lovers and, when Ray denied it, accused him of lying. He brushed aside the roommate's alibi. He took Ray down to police headquarters, where strands of hair were pulled from his head and he was made to bite on a piece of Styrofoam. His blood was drawn; the detective wanted to do it himself, but Ray wouldn't let him. They were in a pissing contest, the kind that usually ends harmlessly if nobody is drunk or if one man isn't a cop in urgent need of a murder suspect. The detective told Ray that he knew he was guilty and demanded that he confess. "I got back in his face," Ray said. "I told him, 'Go find the guy who did this!' And the next day, December 31, I was arrested."

He was charged with murder, kidnapping, and sexual assault. Three weeks passed before he saw a public defender, who told him that he would probably be convicted but reassured him that he could expect a reversal on appeal. The day before the trial, the prosecution announced that it would introduce dental evidence, and the next day Ray watched an elaborately produced videotaped presentation in which a forensic expert testified that the impressions of his teeth matched the marks on the victim's breast. There'd been no time to prepare a defense.

Such a defense might have dwelt on the earlier career of the state's witness, a Nevada dentist who had once matched a murder suspect's teeth with wounds that turned out not to have been made by teeth at all. It might have cited the report of a forensic expert the Maricopa County district attorney's office had consulted before it turned to the dentist from Nevada: that expert had rejected the prosecution's evidence out of hand, saying that Krone's teeth could not have made the marks on Ancona's body. Unfortunately, his report was never shown to the defense.[34] Alternatively, Krone's attorney might have emphasized the controversy that surrounds the entire field of bite-mark analysis, which, according to one study, yields false positives in 66 percent of cases and false negatives in 22 percent more.[35] A charitable conclusion is that bite-mark evidence is accurate only 12 percent of the time. The jury that convicted Krone of murder was probably also unacquainted with this statistic, but even if it had been, it might have reached the same verdict, as juries once found men guilty on the basis of phrenological evidence.

Today Ray can tick off the holes in the case against him. He can talk about tooth marks, bloodstains, and hair samples with the virtuosity of a jailhouse lawyer. It's hard to fault him for showing off a little, it being one thing to have learned the law and another to have done so while pinned beneath its full weight. But his present knowingness makes it hard to reconstruct what he was thinking during the murder investigation and trial. Listening to him, I could make out the artifacts of his former mental state distributed through his story like the shards and bone fragments at an archaeological site, not chronologically but scattered by the upheavals of time and memory.

There was incredulity, for instance: "Who's gonna believe I killed her? I was home in bed; I had a roommate who knew I was home." There was irony: "There's no reason or logic to it, but the prosecution says there's been a horrible crime committed and this is [who] we know is guilty." There was bitterness: "The truth won't protect you. There's no integrity, there's no honor. Three months later, it comes time for sentencing, they want me to show remorse. I'm thinking, 'You do this to me and you want me to show remorse?'" Because the murder had been committed in an especially "heinous or depraved manner" — at a presentencing hearing, the prosecutor demonstrated just how heinous and depraved by rolling out a dressmaker's dummy meant to represent the victim and, as Ray put it, "going ballistic on it" with a knife — the judge sentenced Krone to death by lethal injection and remanded him to the state penitentiary to await execution.[36] He was thirty-five years old.

• • •

IN TIME AND with proper medication Linda's symptoms improved. The greatcoat of fat slid from her body; her face lost its masklike quality; her strength returned. She was still too weak to go to the office every day but could do much of her work from home. I believe that similar impulses drew her to graphic design and to the kind of poetry she wrote. She needed to make things fit. The grid of the magazine page was like the grid of the poem, a field measuring eight and a half by eleven inches or six lines by six stanzas. The art lay in disguising the grid or in making its order seem natural and spontaneous rather than willed.

I don't know if Linda went back to writing poetry after she got better. The illness had been long and debilitating, affecting not just her body but also her mind. On bad days, she would actually become deaf from the pressure on the auditory cortex. The prolonged violence of years of swelling and compression may be more than the brain can recover from; many people with Hashimoto's disease can no longer remember common words.

Regarding order: on the ceiling of Linda and Star's dining room, stenciled above the molding in a medieval font, was a phrase that for a long time I remembered as being from a Latin hymn by the twelfth-century German mystic Hildegard von Bingen: *O spiraculum sanctitatis, o ignis caritatis,* "O breath of holiness, O fire of loving." Linda had hired a painter to do it, specifying that the words form a circle, or really a lozenge, around the perimeter of the ceiling. She'd been particularly insistent that the letters be uniformly spaced — or really, because some letters take up more space than others, *appear* uniformly spaced. The printer's term for this is kerning, after that part of the letter that projects beyond the body — for example, the curled head of an *f* or the tail of a *j*. Linda and the painter used to talk about kerning for hours with the fine-toothed, burrowing interest of academics. Just listening to their conversations, Star said, had made him a minor authority on the subject.

I don't recall Linda being that finicky when we were working together; if she was, I must have driven her crazy. Maybe she became that way because of what had happened to her. Even when it has a slow onset, severe illness feels chaotic to its sufferer, breaching from the somber depths of the body to shatter the body's order: *goiter, puffiness and swelling around the eyes, drooping eyelids, thinning hair, excessive fatigue, weight gain.* In time it will institute its own order, the order of sickness ("It's not like I *have* cancer," a man I interviewed explained. "I'm *in* cancer"),[37] but in the beginning there's just anarchy. And so it would be natural for Linda to seek order elsewhere, if only in the arrangement of painted letters on a ceiling. I imagine her looking up and feeling soothed by their even progress around the molding.

Linda and Star used to spend weekends at a country house that had been in his family for decades. He likes to garden, and for a while he tried to get Linda interested in it, too. One spring he enlisted her in the planting. He gave her a packet of carrot seeds and told her to plant one seed every quarter inch. When he came back from turning over the lettuce beds, she was still on her second row. She'd been using a tape measure. It's a funny story, especially when you realize how tiny carrot seeds are, and I laughed when Star told it to me. But I neglected to ask him when the incident took place, before or after Linda was diagnosed with breast cancer. This was the fourth misfortune. She got her diagnosis on the day Star was celebrating the publication of his first book. They had been talking about having a child. It was only when I heard of it, months after the fact, that I began to see my friend the way Achini's neighbors saw her: as unlucky.

I came to this belief without consulting statistics: in 1993 the odds of a woman Linda's age developing breast cancer were approximately 93 in 100,000;[38] the odds of her getting Hashimoto's syndrome were between 0.3 and 1.5 in 1,000.[39] (I can't determine the odds of her having both, either concurrently or consecutively.) I came to it without knowing what factors (genetics, smoking, consumption of alcohol and animal fats, taking birth control pills, exposure to environmental toxins) might have made Linda susceptible to cancer. If you'd asked me, I would have said that there were no factors, not because I knew that to be the case but because I saw Linda as someone devoid of bad habits or even the vulnerable corporeality that is prone to sickness. She was blameless. That, implicitly, was part of what made her unlucky, rather than . . . what is the word I want? The word that describes a sailor who drowns at sea or a drug addict who dies of an overdose? Those people, too, are unlucky. But Linda's blamelessness made her bad luck seem freakish to me, as opposed to the pedestrian bad luck of the sailor or the junkie, freakish and therefore more frightening and pitiable.

Bad luck, like good, is relative, and Linda's wasn't as bad as it might have been. They caught the cancer early. She and Star had some money, and they had health insurance, which meant she could actually afford proper care. As the child of a prominent physician, she had an introduction to the upper tier of oncologists and surgeons. She could speak their language, and that predisposed them in her favor. She had the necessary surgery, followed by radiation.

By the time I visited her, she could joke about it. "You're not the only one who's got tattoos," she told me, tapping the one on my wrist. The radiologists had put some on her chest to mark the treatment field, the area subject to bombardment. There were six, she said, four in the corners and two in the center, each mark no larger than a freckle. She didn't offer to show them to me, but what struck me about our exchange is that for the first time I could remember, she sounded almost flirtatious. I didn't know how extensive the surgery had been — how much had been cut away — and couldn't bring myself to ask. Later it occurred to me that the tattoos represented another kind of grid, one that other people had inscribed on Linda's body to keep her alive.

It was a good visit. She looked well, much better than she had when she was ill with Hashimoto's. She was lively and full of good humor; she laughed easily. She and Star told a funny story about a friend of theirs, an august English writer, encrusted with literary honors, who'd gotten misrouted during an American reading tour and ended up having to travel from Washington to Charleston, South Carolina, by taxi. Briefly I regarded the scene as a stranger might: three well-dressed people laughing in a handsomely appointed living room high above the glittering, abundant streets and shops with $5,000 dresses preening in their windows. Ten years before, I would have had to excuse myself to rifle the bathroom medicine cabinets. I stole drugs from a few people with cancer back then, including my father, who was dying slowly of multiple myeloma. I have a photo that was taken of the two of us a few months before he died, my father gaunt and staring, his eyes sunken so deeply in his head that they might be those of a hunted animal peering exhaustedly from its cave, and me beside him, an arm resting uneasily on his shoulder, as if I were afraid its full weight would crush him. I can barely stand to look at it.

In 1979, five years before that photograph was taken, I'd been unhappy enough to try to kill myself. At the time I thought my unhappiness had to do with being an unpublished writer getting paid $4.25 an hour (the arts organization had raised my salary) to give larger amounts of money to writers I felt were no better than I (though most of them were, the recognition of which constituted another, keener source of unhappiness), or with feeling guilty for breaking up with my last girlfriend or despondent at being dumped by another one. I thought it had to do with my crummy relationship with my mother. In retrospect I doubt there was any real cause beyond the three days I'd gone without sleep and the drugs that had stung and harried me through them.

The attempt was improvisational and required no more forethought than it takes to cook a pot of spaghetti. On the afternoon of the fourth day, I left my job and stopped at a laundry on Seventh Avenue to pick up the clothes I'd dropped off that morning, and when I got home the prospect of taking them out of the bag and refolding them — the laundry had folded them, but of course they would have come unfolded in the course of being carried back to my apartment, and I had a speed freak's horror of disorder, or of certain kinds of disorder, say the disorder of unmade beds and cluttered kitchen drawers and badly folded clothing — was too much for me. Lying on the floor, the bag of laundry looked like a toppled pillar. I was pinned beneath it. Lifting the pillar was one more of the ten thousand things I couldn't do, and suicide suddenly appealed to me as something I *could* do, though, being high, I didn't consider the consequences of doing it badly.

I used about fifty Fiorinal and a razor blade that I was too squeamish to do very much with. The attempt cost me a visit to the St. Vincent's emergency room and a day off work that I didn't get paid for. On the evening after the attempt, I was supposed to have dinner with my father and stepmother. I begged off with a cold, but nothing could dissuade them from coming over with several bags of prepared food. The whole time they were in the apartment, I had to remember to keep the sleeves of my bathrobe covering my wrists. The cuts weren't deep, but the ER had bandaged them anyway. My father didn't notice. He was too busy making sure I ate. He thought I was too thin.

Sometime during that evening at Linda and Star's, perhaps while laughing at the story of the misrouted literary eminence, I looked up and noticed the verse painted on their ceiling. I have a distinct memory of seeing Latin and recognizing the words as Hildegard von Bingen's; back then I was proud of knowing that kind of thing. But when I visited the apartment later, after Linda's death, I saw that I had remembered incorrectly. The verse on the ceiling was English: "For health and strength and daily food we praise thy name O Lord." It was, Star told me, an old English grace that his family used to sing at festive dinners. To this day I can't explain how I mistook a line in English for one in Latin. Maybe I had once seen the Latin words somewhere else, in a church in Europe or on one of those pieces of medieval sheet music you find in antiquarians' shops. Maybe I unconsciously preferred the reckless ardor of the hymn to the more modest sentiments of the singing grace, its simple gratitude for health and strength.

On rereading the Hildegard von Bingen hymn, I'm struck by the verse that precedes the one I saw — or thought I saw:

You are a holy ointment
for perilous injuries
You are holy in cleansing
the fetid wound [40]

I wonder whether that explains my defective memory. The verse is like the caption to my mental image of the three of us sitting around the dining table. What injury, after all, could be more perilous than Linda's? As to why I remember the less descriptive words, "O breath of holiness, O fire of loving," perhaps they fall into the category of the Freudian screen memory, a false memory that simultaneously conceals and points to a genuine one too painful to be fully admitted to consciousness. I want to remember that night as happy; I want to remember Linda and Star that way. And so I have edited the caption so that all graphic references to the chaotic, endangered body, so vulnerable to tumor and metastasis and mysterious fetid wound, are absent, suggested only by the words "breath" and "fire."

JOB'S AFFLICTIONS COME in two stages. First he is stripped of his goods and his children; the latter are killed when a great wind comes out of the wilderness and smites the four corners of the house, bringing it down on top of them. Still he refuses to turn against God, and so he is stricken — "from the sole of his foot unto his crown" (2:7) — with burning sores; his only relief is to scratch himself with a piece of broken pottery as a dog with mange might scrape itself against a fence. A modern writer might have reversed the order of these calamities on grounds that physical suffering is less ruinously complex than psychological loss, especially the loss of a child. But it's hard for us to imagine what illness meant in an age before morphine and penicillin. It's difficult, too, to enter fully into the Old Testament's cringing horror of diseases of the skin, its sense that every lesion is both the source and register of spiritual pollution. "Touch all that he hath" (1:11), Satan challenges the Lord, and when that touch fails to break Job, Satan dares God to touch all that he *is.*

There's some ambiguity about who does the actual touching. Satan to God: "Put forth thine hand" (2:5). God to Satan: "Behold, he is in *thine* hand" (2:6). How is one to interpret this game of hot potato? Does God feel misgivings? Does Satan? The Hebrews believed that God himself does no evil, instead employing intermediary angels like the ones who lay waste to Sodom and harrow Israel. From a believer's standpoint it's a powerful and convenient idea, and it finds its way into Christian doctrine, where the troops of obedient destroyers are consolidated into a single towering devil. (Except the Christian Satan is no longer God's agent but his enemy; the entire New Testament may be read as the account of their struggle for mastery of creation.) The same division of judgment and execution enters the temporal realm. During the Inquisition the Church seized and tortured suspected heretics, but once they confessed, it passed them on to the state. It was the state that burned them.

Structurally, the book of Job is a folktale (chapters 1–2 and 42) wrapped around a long poem. As in other folktales, things in the first part of Job happen in threes. Three friends come to comfort him; three times the initially silent Job is provoked into speech. The first time it's by the servant who brings him the news of his children's deaths; then by his wife, who rails at him for his seemingly inhuman forbearance at the destruction of everything they loved. I don't know why Job speaks the third time. By then he hasn't said a thing for seven days; maybe he's just ready. But if his earlier words expressed dutiful, uncomplaining faith, what comes out now is a cry of sorrow and outrage that continues through thirty chapters of the ensuing poem. His lament is bitter and inexhaustible. Rather than diminish with time, the way tantrums do, it gathers force and majesty. It is like the unspooling of a gigantic scroll that records the grievances of everyone who ever suffered unjustly, a scroll long enough to bind up the entire world. All the comforters' objections barely interrupt it.

Whoever first described Job as patient can't have read this part of the book, or preferred to forget it. That may be literally true, since the likeliest scenario of Job's composition is that its author used the ancient folktale of Job the patient as the frame for a long dramatic poem about Job the *impatient*.[41] Part of the drama arises from the poem's limited point of view, the fact that its human characters are unaware of the wager that took place in the folktale. Because they are unaware, they ask, Why has Job — that is, Job of all people — been made to suffer?

When the poem begins, Job isn't yet able to ask this question. He can only reject what has happened to him, viscerally, as one vomits up poison. All he wants is to die, or, rather, not to have lived. He would have the day of his birth excised from time. It's a blasphemous wish, and his three conventionally pious friends, Eliphaz, Bildad, and Zophar, are horrified by it. They aren't bad people. They've traveled a long way to be with Job, have wept with him and sat silently at his side in an attempt to share his grief. But his outburst exposes the limits of their sympathy, and their angry response to it turns them from comforters into adversaries. He speaks of heartsickness, and they speak of doctrine.

By turns unctuous and scolding, bullying and condescending, Job's friends tell him that no evil can come from God; that God is always just, upholding the righteous ("Whoever perished, being innocent?" [4:7]) and punishing the wicked ("Though his excellency mount up to the heavens, and his head reach into the clouds; Yet [the wicked man] shall perish forever like his own dung" [20:6]). That, given the general vileness of the species ("What is man that he should be clean?" [15:14]) and the glaring character of Job's afflictions, he almost certainly falls into the latter category. He must, they say, have done *something* to deserve his misery ("Know that God exacteth of thee less than thine iniquity deserveth" [11:6]), as remedy for which they propose that Job accept this misery, even welcome it, as a necessary chastisement, as discipline ("Behold, happy is the man whom God correcteth" [5:17]), and repent his sin, whatever it was, so that God may restore him ("Thy seed shall be great, and thine offspring as the grass of the earth. Thou shalt come to thy grave in a full age, like as a shock of corn cometh to in his season" [5:25–26]). Among the many things that make the book of Job feel like a modern work is its irony, and few instances of that irony are sharper than Eliphaz's promise of a ripe old age to a man who has been yearning for death.

The trouble with Eliphaz, Bildad, and Zophar is that they are generalists. They have an abstract notion of who God is and how he is supposed to behave. Drawing on earlier theologians, Harold Kushner sums up their beliefs as follows:

A. God is infinitely powerful, the cause of everything that happens in the world.
B. God is infallibly just, distributing good to the good and evil to evildoers.
C. Job is good.[42]

But the last belief falls casualty to the manifest facts of Job's misery — the fresh graves of his children and the sores that cover his face — and his refusal to bear his misery without protest. It falls casualty to the comforters' blind adherence to the first two propositions. I say "blind" because the infinitude of the Lord's power and justice cannot be proved, whereas Job's goodness can at least be observed. The comforters ought to have observed it; they were, after all, his friends. Instead, faced with the conflict between propositions A, B, and C, they abandon C. They abandon Job. They aren't satisfied with accusing him of blasphemy. He's been hypocritical and stiff-necked. His children have died for his sins. In the heat of argument the charges mount. Before long they'll be claiming that he tramples on widows and snatches bread from the mouths of the hungry.

Even today, a number of religious commentators have trouble with Job's innocence. It's startling to see how many suggest that he isn't really blameless, or that "blamelessness" is only a relative virtue, the best available to ordinary humans.

> The Revised Standard Version says he was blameless, and many who have read that thought it meant that Job was sinless. But it is not the same thing. You can be sinful and still be blameless if you have learned how to handle your sin the way God tells you to. Evidently Job had learned how to handle sin, so, in that sense, he was blameless.[43]

> *Perfect:* That is, perfect in his life at the time. Still, he needed more development of his character.[44]

> The Scriptures say Job's problem was that "he was righteous in his own eyes" and that "he justified himself rather than God" (32:1–2).[45]

It's as though Job's comforters were still standing beside the ash heap, casting judgment on its miserable tenant. Unable to reconcile their faith in God's infinite power and justice with the spectacle of unmerited suffering, they insist that the suffering must be merited. The citations above are all drawn from fundamentalist Christian sources that treat the Bible as literal and inerrant in its smallest utterances, and there is no little irony in the authors' attempts to introduce some give into the biblical words "perfect," "righteous," and "blameless." Among the points I've seen marshaled against Job are the sacrifices he made on his children's behalf, back when he still had children. Some commentators accuse him of trying to bribe the Lord into staying judgment, a complaint that seems to echo the old Protestant distrust of Roman Catholic rites of penance. And then there are the ones who say that instead of quietly paying the tab for his children's sins, he should have "corrected" them.

For the most part Job doesn't bother to answer his critics' charges. He speaks over them rather than against them. The comforters claim that his suffering says something about him. He insists that it says something about God, and also about man. If the comforters' large, nebulous beliefs about God keep them from seeing the small, huddled fact of a suffering human being, Job's particular experience of suffering brings him to a global — really, a cosmic — understanding of the human predicament, its arbitrariness and dizzying powerlessness. "Is there not an appointed time to man upon earth? Are not his days also like the days of a hireling?" (7:1); "Man that is born of a woman is full of trouble" (14:1).

At such moments Job seems to have intuitively seen beyond the frame of the dramatic poem and into the folktale, into that celestial throne room where God and Satan haggle over his fate. Still, he can't help circling back to the subject of his guilt. "How many are mine iniquities and sins? Make me to know my transgression and my sin" (13:23). The comforters are more than happy to tell him, but here again he speaks past them, knowing that in a courtroom one doesn't address the witnesses but the judge. It's almost as if he wants to learn that he deserves his calamity. Better to be proved guilty than to be destroyed without cause: to be made nothing, for nothing. The bitterest of Job's losses, writes one biblical scholar, is his loss of faith in God's providence.[46]

Ray Krone's cell on death row was six by eight feet, the size of a bathroom. Inmates were controlled with physical force, solitary confinement, and Thorazine, a drug used primarily for the treatment of psychosis. Some people enjoyed it; Ray used to hoard his pills and trade them for seventy-cent packs of tobacco. He became adept at faking the zombielike Thorazine shuffle. The shock of the last year wore off, and for the first time he became fully conscious of what had happened to him. "Only when I'm on death row do I think, 'Did you do something wrong? Did you do something to deserve this?' "

Fourteen years later, he seemed to address the question all over again, maybe not for my benefit so much as for his own. "I was the one you could call at two in the A.M. when your truck got stuck. I was the guy you'd ask to call your girlfriend for you when you'd had a fight; you knew I wouldn't try to take advantage. I was someone who could help people. I didn't need help." His voice was urgent and plaintive. "The only thing I hadn't done, I hadn't kept with my faith. We were Lutherans. Every Sunday morning we'd go to church, and then we'd go to my grandparents' house. The grown-ups would be drinking coffee and reading the funny papers. It was great. But by the time I came to Phoenix, I didn't go to church at all."

Ray Krone spent almost three years on death row. In 1995 his sentence was overturned, but the following year he was convicted on retrial and sentenced to life in prison. On hearing the verdict, his mother and sister screamed. The judge who sentenced him wrote, "This is one of those cases that will haunt me for the rest of my life, wondering whether I have done the right thing."[47] Seven years passed. In 2002 he was released after DNA tests performed on traces of saliva found on the victim's tank top not only excluded him but strongly incriminated (by odds of 1.3 quadrillion to one) Kenneth Phillips, who was by then doing time for child molestation at the Florence State Prison,[48] where Krone had first been incarcerated. In June 2006 Phillips pleaded guilty to the first-degree murder of Kim Ancona. The court sentenced him to life in prison.[49]

Krone was the hundredth person in this country to have been sentenced to death and subsequently exonerated since executions resumed in the mid-1970s.[50] That, along with lawsuits against the Maricopa County DA's office and the city of Phoenix that netted him more than $4 million,[51] have made him a celebrity, and he regularly travels around the country to speak against the death penalty. Today he lives in southeastern Pennsylvania, near the town where he grew up. He bought a farm with his settlement. In another instance of the surreal largesse that is sometimes showered on victims of public tragedy or injustice, Krone also has a new set of very white, very straight teeth, courtesy of the TV show *Extreme Makeover*, which had him on as a guest following his release.

Four million dollars is a lot of money, but I don't know if it compensates for ten lost years of a man's life, especially if

those years weren't lost but stolen, taken from him by subterfuge and force, out of a slouching bureaucratic expedi-
ency that would rather strap an innocent man to a gurney
and stop his heart with potassium chloride than go to the
trouble of scrapping faulty evidence. During his time on
death row Krone saw men who had been his friends led
away to the holding area that would be their last domicile
before execution. In general population he was stabbed three
times and had his arm broken. He lost his fear of dying.
Once, after another convict attacked him, he found himself
daring — maybe begging — the man to kill him. "I felt like
there's nothing more that can happen to me," he explained.
"I'm already dead in this world. You already killed me."

Listening to him, I noticed that he still spoke like an
inmate — not just the slang, but the quick, half-swallowed
delivery of somebody furtively passing on a message to the
man beside him in the yard and an emotional guardedness
that could easily be mistaken for deadness. I don't know if
he is able to fully enjoy his freedom. Some months after he
got out, he told me, one of his friends jokingly called him a
punk, and without thinking he slammed his friend against a
wall. The only way he could survive inside prison was by allowing it to deform him. It was still too early to tell whether
he could be made straight again.

Krone's story bears striking resemblances to those of
other men who've been unjustly sentenced to death, with
one exception. He was innocent not only of the crime of
which he'd been convicted but of any crime. From the
standpoint of the law, he'd never done anything worse than
drive while drinking. On one level Krone's innocence
worked in his favor. It made him an attractive cause, some-

one people could rally around. Friends he hadn't seen since childhood contributed to his defense fund. Even a corrections officer he'd known on death row wrote a mitigation letter on his behalf, something that still moves him when he speaks about it today. (Conversely, even the laughably mean-spirited Web site maintained by the pro–death penalty organization Justice for All, which purports to prove on a case-by-case basis that most of the 128 innocent men and women released from death row in the past thirty years were in fact guilty, conspicuously has nothing to say about his case.)[52]

But Krone's innocence also made him vulnerable, fatally slow to grasp the forces that were gathering against him and why people he'd never crossed would want to have him killed. In that way he was a little like Job, with his deadly bull's-eye of righteousness. A hardened lawbreaker wouldn't have lost his temper at a detective who accused him, wrongly or not, of murder. He wouldn't have been dumbfounded by a prosecutor's underhandedness; he would on some level have anticipated it. He would have known what he was guilty of. And so once he was convicted, he wouldn't have been so desperate to account for what had happened to him that he would shovel his way past legal, and even moral, explanations to magical ones, according to which people are damned for what they didn't do as well as for what they did. "I felt guilty that I didn't keep up with my religion. Right before I was arrested, I'd been out with some friends at a drinking party, and one of them asked me, 'Do you believe in God?' I said, 'Sure, I believe in God, but I don't think you have to go to church.' It was the first time I'd thought about God in years."

. . .

People who are struck by calamity often feel that they have been singled out, chosen. This in turn implies the existence of an agent that does the choosing, whose gaze has fallen on you, whose intelligence has claimed you as an object. Job says to God, "Thine eyes are upon me, and I am not." I interviewed a woman who as a graduate student had been badly wounded by a deranged man who walked into the restaurant where she was sitting and began stabbing patrons with a knife. She'd done nothing to provoke him; she hadn't even looked at him. Nearly twenty years and many surgeries later — for the doctors who first treated her had misjudged the extent of her injuries, and the wounds had developed adhesions — she was still haunted by the randomness of the attack, the ease with which a stranger's malign intention had alighted on her as she quietly ate her dinner.[53]

As she spoke, I thought of the Nick Cave song "Henry Lee," the story of a young man murdered by a woman he spurned. The chorus ends with the line, "A little bird lit down on Henry Lee." It occurred to me that the bird isn't just death but the evil intention that summons it to you. We hear of people ascribing such intimate ill will to bombs (this even before the invention of smart bombs) and artillery shells fired from a distance, to viruses, to cancer cells, to earthquakes, to fires, to floods. Sometimes they feel singled out not as individuals but as members of a marked population. My father, a Russian Jew who managed to escape the exterminations but whose mother died on a train to Auschwitz, felt like that, and of course he was right. So, too, did many of the Tutsi *rescapés* (survivors) I met in Rwanda. It was why they often compared themselves to the Jews. It wasn't just other people who had singled them out — Nazis in Europe or the Interahamwe in Rwanda. It was some larger force, inscrutable in everything but its malignity. When my father's younger sister, who'd fled Europe around the same time he had, learned that her cancer was terminal, she told me, "It's funny, what comes to my mind is Auschwitz," and I think she meant that whatever had failed to kill her forty-odd years before was at last succeeding.

Implicit in these accounts of selection is the idea of order. There must, we think, be some pattern that determines who is chosen for suffering, one that is revealed by the distribution of the dead, the maimed, and the destitute as a magnetic field is revealed by the arcs of iron filings at its poles. The most obvious interpretation is that the victims are being punished. A measure of that obviousness is that it's the explanation most often given by children — for example, by a ten-year-old Russian girl whose misfortune it was to be in attendance at a school in Beslan on the day it was seized by Chechen terrorists: "I was taught you get punished for sins. But what kind of sins have I committed to be punished that way?"[54]

An alternate explanation is that suffering isn't evidence of a higher power's disfavor but of its esteem, its love. This is more or less what Eliphaz has in mind when he tells Job, "Happy is the man whom God correcteth" (5:17). The most sophisticated expression of the idea may be John Hick's "soul-making theodicy," which treats suffering as the agency by which the spiritually and morally immature animals that are human beings evolve into genuine children of God.[55] But Hick has in mind something as impersonal as natural selection, and we've already seen that people take their suffering personally. Witness the following verse, attributed to various authors or, more commonly, to "Anonymous" and posted on more than twelve thousand Web sites, many of them having to do with illness.[56] I first saw it on an online discussion board for people with stage IV breast cancer:

> *I asked God to spare me pain*
> *God said No.*
> *Suffering draws you apart from worldly cares*
> *And brings you closer to me.*

The old stereotype about cancer was that it was a disease of repression and self-hatred.[57] The logical consequence was that it could be dangerous to view one's cancer as a punishment. As one of the support group's regulars, a woman named Sue, told me, "Guilt is something I can't afford." And so it made sense that someone like Sue, who had undergone a double mastectomy and several rounds of chemotherapy, whose cumulative side effects included hair loss, burning skin, nausea, vomiting, and blisters on her hands that made it impossible for her to open a jar of the baby food that was the only nutrition she could keep down, might choose to believe that God was making her life unendurable in order to draw her away from it and toward him, and that he was doing this because he loved her.

But suppose there is no because? If suffering is about anything, it's about chaos, or the *experience* of chaos, the path chaos cleaves in the mind. Its common denominator is the loss or destruction of some prior order, which may be that of the organism or the family or society. Cancer is literally a chaos inside the body, the tidy growth and division of cells accelerating into a boiling frenzy of reproduction. Cancer sufferers speak of feeling the body transformed into a hostile wilderness where once familiar processes turn ominous and grotesque. Why are you getting those backaches? What's that taste in your mouth? Was your period always this heavy? It's as if the body has been invaded, but not by a bacterium or a virus — not by something outside it. Rather, the invader is something spawned inside the body; the body has invaded itself. "*Seven* areas," the writer Katherine Russell Rich marveled, after learning that her breast cancer had metastasized to her bones (and consider the chaotic implications of cancerous breast cells showing up in one's skeleton, as if all the distinctions between different organs had been obliterated). "All through my spine and ribs. One spot in my calf. Even one in the back of my head. . . . The cancer was in my skull! What if it grew and broke the skull bone? Seven places, half my skeleton." [58]

In chaos things lose their familiar meanings; they cease to mean anything at all. A man enters his teenage son's bedroom to find the boy lying crumpled on the floor; he has shot himself in the head. On one level the father knows exactly what has happened. But he will later describe the experience as "stepping into a room and none of your five senses work. It was like seeing the snow falling upward." [59]

THE BOOK OF Job may be the first text to explicitly acknowledge the chaotic nature of suffering. Suffering is the door through which chaos enters the world, the human world and maybe the divine one as well. The chaos in question isn't physical — Job's sun goes on rising in the east and setting in the west — but moral, a rupture in the order of meaning and justice. Job's friends accuse him because his suffering doesn't make sense. Job accuses God for the same reason. He may question his innocence, but he can't accept that he deserves his wretchedness. Nor can he believe — as Kushner thousands of years later does — that God is powerless over his suffering, didn't cause it and cannot lift it.

By default, then, he has to discard the idea that God is just. It is like lopping off a limb. What could be more terrible than limitless power unconstrained by justice, as indifferent to human wishes as an earthquake, yet drawn to assert itself among men?

> *He discovereth deep things out of darkness, and bringeth them out to light the shadow of death.*
> *He increaseth the nations, and destroyeth them: he enlargeth the nations, and straiteneth them again.*
> *He taketh away the heart of the chief of the people of the earth, and causeth them to wander in a wilderness where there is no way.*
> *They grope in the dark without light, and he maketh them to stagger like a drunken man* (12:22–25).

The true heartbreak of Job's position is that he can't fully cast off his old belief. In spite of everything he knows, he still wants the Lord to treat him justly. This is the heartbreak of the beaten child who keeps climbing back into the lap of the parent who beats him. Job doesn't ask God to make him whole. He asks only to argue his case before him, for some part of him still believes that if he does, God will have to vindicate him, as if the fanatical prosecutor's mask would drop away to reveal the face of a fair and compassionate judge. Vindication is another word for the restoration of one's good name, the first thing one loses when one is falsely accused. Ask Ray Krone.

A moment later, of course, Job remembers that God *has* to do nothing: "But he is one mind, and who can turn him? and what his soul desireth, even that he doeth" (23:13). All these rhetorical strategies — the entreaties, the sarcasm, the complaint that expands concentrically outward from the self to take in the motiveless torment of a world of blameless casualties — have a single aim: to charge God with breaking the order of justice, to confront him with its shards.

A new contestant enters the debate, a self-confident young man named Elihu. He upbraids Job's friends for what is essentially their failure of imagination, since the only answer they have for Job is that he has to be guilty of something. He scolds Job for justifying himself against the Lord. His chief contribution is less dramatic than theological: the argument, later elaborated by Saint Augustine, that God, being perfect, cannot act unjustly and that all misery originates in the evil of men. The one dramatic function he has is to be a herald. No sooner has he finished speaking of God than a whirlwind appears and a voice calls out of it. The voice belongs to the personage who has been the subject of every word spoken by Job and his interlocutors but until now has remained offstage. Among the infinitude of things the personage knows is when to make an entrance.

There are those who say that God's answer to Job, which

continues through the next four chapters, isn't an answer at all but a show of force, as of a judge pounding his gavel over the ranting of an angry defendant.

> *Where wast thou when I laid the measures of the*
> *earth? . . .*
> *Who hath laid the measures thereof, if thou knowest? or*
> *who hath stretched the line upon it?*
> *Whereupon are the foundations thereof fastened? or who*
> *laid the corner stones thereof;*
> *When the morning stars sang together, and all the sons of*
> *God shouted out for joy?*
> *Or who shut up the sea with doors, when it brake forth,*
> *as if it had issued out of the womb?. (38:4–7)*

But God, too, is speaking about order, of a kind so vast and connotative that beside it justice seems small and sterile. The justice Job longs for is only a subset of that order, a human subset. And in the entire triumphant catalog of his creation, God scarcely mentions human beings. He speaks of the lion and the unicorn and the wild goat, of behemoth and leviathan, those immense, kingly relics of a time when the earth was still void and without form and darkness moved upon the face of the deep.[60] He might be speaking of chaos, except that it's a chaos he's subjected to his will, binding and fencing it, commanding its lightning, shutting up its seas. Accused of breaking the order of justice, God shows Job the larger order of providence. He slaps it down like a hand of cards. Who can see such a bet? Job can't. He folds: "Who is he that hideth counsel without knowledge? Therefore have I uttered that I understood not; things too wonderful for me, which I knew not" (42:3).

Throughout the preceding text, the reader has had the advantage of knowing the true reason for Job's wretchedness: he is not being punished but tested. It's a stringent test, bearing certain resemblances to the stress tests to which cars are subjected in the factory in order to determine their roadworthiness and that sometimes culminate with the vehicles being driven at high speed into a concrete wall. Only the testing of Abraham may surpass it in cruelty. I don't think it excessive to characterize it as torture. As in the later tortures of Jewish and Christian martyrs, the apparent aim is to make the victim renounce God: in Satan's words, "curse [him] to [his] face" (1:11). The difference is that Job's torture is inflicted not by men but by God, or by Satan with God's consent. And it's only the devil who wants the victim to break. The Lord wants Job to hold on to his integrity, to remain spiritually intact. But because this is a test, he remains silent.

IT'S PROBABLY JOB more than any other biblical story that has led people throughout history to imagine their suffering as a test or trial. Ray Krone read the book many times when he was in prison, feeling a profound identification with its story of an innocent man persecuted for reasons he could never grasp. I picture him lying in his cell at night. He has spent the day being moved about by bells, herded from his cell to the dining hall to his job in the law library to the yard and back to his cell. He has done this for years. He can anticipate doing it for the rest of his life.

In prison the word "life" has drastically different connotations than it does elsewhere. These are succinctly expressed by the "time comp" letters inmates receive every six months, informing them of how long they still have to serve. Krone's letters always say "until death." Outside are men who would put a knife in him to relieve their boredom. During a week's stay in the Maricopa County jail, where inmates are fed spoiled bologna and housed in tents whose temperature reaches 120 degrees, he was in seven fights. His cell is the only place where he feels safe, but even there he has trouble sleeping, some part of him always listening for the sound of someone coming through the door. He picks up the Bible his mother sent him. He turns to Job.

"It taught me to rejoice in my tribulations," Krone says today. "I had to ask myself, 'Am I going to blame the Lord?' Me blaming him was the wrong way around." Over time he came to see his imprisonment as a test of faith and humility and of his ability to survive in an alien and hostile environment with his dignity intact. To some extent that meant living by the environment's unstated rules. Although he was innocent, he didn't cooperate with the corrections officers. "Corrections officers," he sniffs. "You ain't correcting nothing. You're just here to guard me." Although he attended chapel, he didn't join a Christian group. "When you're in a dog-eat-dog situation, you come out of a room with guys with taped-together glasses, and people say, 'You're going to *what?* '" He tried to stay out of trouble but refused to back down from fights. "You don't have to stand tall there, but you sure as hell got to stand up." It was one of the reasons he refused to take psychiatric meds. A man on meds was too foggy and slow-moving to stand up for himself.

Stories of prison conversions often hinge on a sudden, joyful encounter with a loving God, who announces his arrival with a flood of tears. What happened to Krone, though, wasn't a conversion in any traditional sense; he's emphatic about this. He believes in God but can't believe that God chose to put him in prison, whether to punish him or to try him. He can't say whether it was God who set him free. If he credits a higher power with anything, it's with sustaining the hope that ten years in prison almost crushed. He saw it crushed in many of the men around him. "I had to be like an anxious four-year-old learning to read in kindergarten," he says. "I had to be grateful for what I had. I had to be patient with delays. I had to learn to accept failure. Everything was insignificant compared to what I was dealing with now."

THE TIBETAN BUDDHIST nun Ngawang Sangdrol spent even more time in prison than Krone did: twelve years, which at the time I met her was almost half her life. Unlike Krone, she was guilty of the crimes she was charged with, and she committed them knowingly. She was jailed for the first time at the age of ten, not long after entering the convent, for taking part in an independence demonstration in Lhasa; this detention lasted only a few weeks.[61]

Two years later, in August 1990, she and some twelve other novices shouted nationalist slogans during a festival on the grounds of the Norbulingka palace. Within minutes they were surrounded by Chinese troops, beaten, and thrown into trucks that conveyed them to Gutsa prison on the outskirts of Lhasa. There she was subjected to more methodical beatings and torture by electric shock, the latter administered with a cattle prod and a smaller device that was thrust inside the victim's mouth." Some of the women who were abused in this manner went into convulsions. At one point a female prison employee looked at Sangdrol and exclaimed, "Why, she's just a girl!" The man who was working on her snapped, "She's not *just* a girl," and gave her another shock.

In retrospect she believes that her age caused some guards to abuse her more severely, in the expectation that she would break and denounce the adults who had influenced her. The torturers were sure that girls so young could have acted as they had only because grown-ups had told them to, and they demanded to know who those grown-ups were. Their other obsession was their victims' "ingratitude." They kept scolding them for it, like angry mothers.

She spent nine months at Gutsa, confined for the most part in an unheated cell whose only furnishings were a concrete sleeping pallet and a bucket for a toilet. In consideration of her age, she was released without formal charges. During this time her father and one of her brothers were jailed for subversive activities and her mother died, so that on her release she was essentially an orphan.

In June 1992 Sangdrol mounted another public protest against the Chinese occupation and was again arrested. This time she was sentenced to three years in Drapchi, the most feared penal institution in the Tibetan gulag. Days in the women's unit began with a blast of whistles at 4:30 a.m. From 5:00 to 6:00 prisoners exercised in the courtyard. If they moved too slowly, the guards thrashed them with bamboo canes. As part of their rehabilitation they were made to chant, "We confess our faults!" or "We oppose the separatists!" Following a meal of steamed bread and tea, they were put to work in the prison greenhouses, whose air was hot and rank with a pesticide that made them sick if they breathed it too long. Later, back in their cells, the women were made to knit caps or slippers that prison authorities sold for five yuan apiece. Each inmate had a quota of twenty-four pieces a year.

At night they slept twelve to a cell on metal bunks, politicals alongside common-law criminals. It was taken for granted that some of the latter were informers.[62] The prisoners were given very little to drink, and what Sangdrol remembers most of this time was the constant torment of thirst. One guard used to taunt them by turning on the tap in the courtyard and making them watch while its water trickled into the earth.

In 1993, using a smuggled tape recorder, Sangdrol and some other nuns secretly recorded protest songs they sang to popular Tibetan or Chinese melodies. They were about the sadness of incarceration, the indignity of beatings and bad food, the longing for freedom. A sample lyric goes like this:

> Song of sadness in our hearts
> We sing this to our brothers and friends
> What we Tibetans feel in this darkness will pass
> The food does not sustain body or soul
> Beatings impossible to forget
> This suffering inflicted upon us
> May no others suffer like this.[63]

The tape was spirited outside Drapchi and duplicated; exiles brought copies across the Himalayas to Dharamsala, from which they were circulated to Europe and America. But the singers were betrayed, and Sangdrol's sentence was extended by six years. Conditions grew harsher. She might be made to stand for hours with a book balanced on her head for the offense of slouching, and punched and kicked if she let the book drop. On grounds of having folded her blankets improperly, she was placed in solitary confinement for six months.[64]

The maltreatment only provoked her. She began to openly flout prison discipline. In the mandatory history class she mocked the instructor's claim that China had liberated Tibet. She refused to join in the ceremonial renunciations of "errors" and "bad attitudes." Eventually she repeated the crime for which she had first been incarcerated, leading the other inmates in a defiant chant of pro-independence slogans during a prison ceremony. For this she was beaten so savagely that witnesses feared for her life. "It was like she was dead," one said. "They told her to stand up but she couldn't. . . . When she did, she was bleeding heavily, blood was literally streaming from her. She walked with great difficulty, as they had trampled all over her body. Earlier, there were so many people beating her that we couldn't see her when she fell down."[65]

Eight more years were added to her sentence. Had it not been for the efforts of several foreign governments and humanitarian organizations, Ngawang Sangdrol would have remained a prisoner until 2014, at which time she would have been thirty-five years old. But in 2002, in consideration of her failing health — and perhaps self-conscious about China's dismal human rights record — authorities released the young nun from Drapchi and allowed her to leave the country.

I met her two years later, at the Washington, D.C., headquarters of the International Campaign for Tibet. I expected to find her in the brilliant maroon and goldenrod yellow habit of a Tibetan religious, but she wore ordinary Western clothing, including a light ski jacket that she kept on, although we were sitting indoors. That and her slightness gave her the appearance of a child parked on a bench in an airport lounge — a child who won't take off her jacket because she knows she'll have to put it back on when she boards. The years in prison had marked her. She suffered from headaches, and from time to time she would fall silent and let her head drop as if she could no longer support its weight. I watched her anxiously, wondering whether to cut the interview short, but her translator assured me that Sangdrol was all right, and a few moments later she'd rouse herself and continue.

She'd grown up in a household of activists. Her father, uncles, and older brothers were all involved in the resistance, and an older sister was a nun. This was essentially another form of resistance, since for most of the occupation the Chinese have sought to control — and at times suppress — Tibetan Buddhism and have often persecuted its clergy. The girl had absorbed her elders' values, their love of their country, their hatred of its new masters. I don't think it minimizes her heroism to say that when she first protested against Chinese rule, she didn't really understand what she was doing. She was, after all, a child. She passed her first night at Gutsa in terror, for her jailers had put her in a dark cell by herself and she still believed in ghosts.

But over the years, in different penal institutions, she developed a fuller understanding of her situation and, correspondingly, of her country's. She was a prisoner, and Tibet was enslaved. The regime inside the prison was only a harsher version of the regime outside it, with its informers and secret police, its gutted temples, its shuttered monasteries, the schools where Tibetan children kept falling farther and farther behind because they were made to do their lessons in Chinese, the soldiers who clubbed those children for the crime of yelling *"Po Rangzen!"* — "Independence!" — in public. The smallest act of resistance was therefore a defense of a free Tibet, the least capitulation a betrayal of it. When one of her brothers, who had gone into exile in India, sent her a letter urging her to be careful, she was briefly furious, convinced that he was trying to make her give up her struggle.

Like Ray Krone, Sangdrol saw her suffering as a test, but she didn't think that test had been imposed on her by God. Strictly speaking, Buddhists don't believe in one. If she held anything responsible, it was karma. For the virtuous or unwholesome acts of past lives, she had been born in a country that lay under the yoke, and she was required — not so much by her conscience as by a deeply Tibetan sense of the appropriate — to resist that yoke using the small means available to her. They were very small. Given all the catastrophic measures subject peoples have resorted to in the pursuit of freedom, what subversive power attaches to a child's shout in a public square or a prisoner's refusal to apologize for crimes for which she is already being wretchedly punished?

But to the Chinese even symbolic protests were dangerous. Being totalitarians, they were not content with controlling their captives' bodies; they wanted to reform their minds. This was a bad tactic to use with Tibetans, who, as Robert Thurman reminds us, have devoted so many centuries to the exploration of the mind that they qualify as astronauts of consciousness.[66] It was a bad one to use with Sangdrol, who even as a little girl is said to have been very stubborn. By packing significance into the slightest details of the penal routine, by turning that routine into political theater, Sangdrol's jailers guaranteed that she would find comparable significance in thwarting them. She, too, could make theater, even at the risk of her life. That theater had an audience in the other prisoners, some of whom were children like herself. Even during her months in solitary she was conscious of them. At those times when her strength was weakest, she reminded herself that they were watching her and that any surrender would be devastating to them.

THERE IS A vast psychological difference between suffering that is inflicted as punishment and suffering that is inflicted as a test. Because it presupposes some offense, punishment is inherently shameful, and those who are punished feel this shame piled on top of their other hurts like the stones that were once heaped on the chests of people accused of witchcraft. This may be even more the case when such punishment is visited on the innocent. For them, writes Simone Weil, "everything happens as though the state of soul suitable for criminals had been separated from crime and attached to affliction."[67] Apologists for torture often argue that it is only used on guilty persons (Senator James Inhofe of Oklahoma, dismissing photographs of the cowering, naked inmates at Abu Ghraib: "You know they're not there for traffic violations. . . . Many of them probably have American blood on their hands"),[68] and in a sense they're right: such treatment renders its victims guilty in their souls. Weil also writes about Job: "If Job cries out that he is innocent in such despairing accents, it is because he himself is beginning not to believe in it."[69]

In contrast, there is nothing shameful about being tested. A test belongs not to the realm of sin and retribution but to that of experiment and knowledge. It is meant to discover what its subject is or knows, what it can do or what it can bear. People who view their suffering as a test often feel paradoxically honored by it. It isn't everyone who gets chosen in this fashion. Job isn't made to suffer because he is flawed; he is chosen because he is perfect. In the words of the Christian philosopher Paul Ciholas, he has "become too conspicuous in his search for a righteous life."[70]

In keeping with their sacralized model of history, early Christians saw Job's suffering as a precursor of Christ's passion on the cross.[71] Similarly, they viewed Christ's agony as the pattern for the later ordeals of the martyrs. The Romans may have designed their grotesque tortures as mechanisms of degradation — what could be more degrading than crucifixion except crucifixion upside down? — but their victims reinterpreted those tortures as a test, and some who were not yet victims looked forward to being tested. "You are about to enter a noble contest," Tertullian enjoined the martyrs, "in which the living God acts the part of superintendent and the Holy Spirit is your trainer, a contest whose crown is eternity. And so your Master, Jesus Christ, who has anointed you with His Spirit and has brought you to this training ground, has resolved . . . to take you from a softer way of life to a harsher treatment that your strength may be increased." [72]

Ngawang Sangdrol struck me as extremely self-effacing. Throughout our interview she kept insisting on how ordinary she is. But as she described some of what her captors had done to her, a note of pride entered her voice, and when she told the story of the interrogator who had sneered at her youth and then gone back to torturing her, she smiled broadly. Maybe she was only amused by the incongruity, but I thought her smile bore a trace of demure exultation. It was as if she were saying, "Look what I endured!"

It's natural to interpret ordeals of torture and imprisonment as tests. They are, after all, administered by human beings and are informed by human will and intelligence — the will to inflict harm and an intelligence that seeks the most effective way of doing so. But the idea of a trial has migrated into accounts of suffering that has no human cause. A member of a stage IV breast cancer online discussion board posts a message saying that the disease has been sent into her life (she doesn't say by whom) to turn her into a "woman warrior." What does it mean to be a warrior? Presumably it means to be strong, maybe strong enough to "beat" cancer, an expression you hear fairly often among cancer patients as well as their doctors and loved ones.

"My opinion of this thing is that only the tough really persevere," a man with advanced lung cancer told me. His name was Lenny, and I'd describe him as a tough guy. A year after his diagnosis he was still big and strapping in spite of surgery, chemo, and radiation treatments that had made him sweat so heavily that the only way he could sleep through the night was by swathing himself in towels. But he was no longer sure that mere strength could keep him alive. After a while he ventured that what his cancer was really testing was his ability to face death. "Most of them don't face it too well," he said of the other people in his support group. "They're all freaking out." A moment later, with macabre satisfaction, he added, "I face it pretty easy."

I DON'T KNOW if Linda ever saw her cancer as a test, and if so, what she might have thought was being tested. I doubt she thought of cancer as something that could be beaten. That would have been her bulldozing father's way of seeing things. The last time I saw her healthy, she joked about her treatment — that was when she made the remark about our respective tattoos — but the joke probably expressed hope rather than certainty. It's considered inaccurate, if not dangerously irresponsible, to say that someone has been "cured" of breast cancer. Still, shortly after she'd finished treatment, a doctor looked at Linda's blood markers and told her that she could stop worrying. She had no more chance of developing a recurrence than any woman walking down the street.

But just a few months later she began to get backaches. She went to chiropractors and a physical therapist, but the pain kept returning, and finally she had some tests that may have included a CAT scan or an MRI. This was in 1997. One day a friend of ours called to tell me that Linda's cancer had come back; it had spread to her bones. By now I know enough about the disease to know the questions I might have asked: what stage was it and what kind of metastases were involved, what drugs were the doctors considering giving her. But I was still a novice then, having lost no one to cancer but my father and mother, who were relatively old, their lives almost spent, and not inclined to use scorched-earth tactics to hold on to them a little longer. I didn't ask any questions. I hung up the phone in a daze.

At the time I was living down by the meat market in a drafty, high-ceilinged loft that I was subletting from another old friend, a guy I'd known even longer than Linda. It was thirteen stories up and distinguished by its view and the continual, tormented howling of the wind outside its windows. I'd stayed there many times before, both during my active addiction and after. Especially during. I have a memory of disgustedly squirting the blood left in my syringe onto the bathroom mirror, wasting whatever drug was still suspended in it, a wildly profligate thing for an addict to do. The face that sneered back at me through a veil of red blobs and rivulets was the face of a zitty high school kid playing air guitar in his bedroom mirror. Kids like that are always searching for something to be repelled by. I had found it.

By that time, the early 1980s, I was mostly a solitary user. I'd told so many people so many times that I was cleaning up that I was ashamed even in the company of other addicts, maybe especially in their company, since they were the ones I usually told I was cleaning up. "You ain't gonna see me around this joint anymore, my friend. I'm getting straight." "You do that, man." "I am, dude, I'm putting that shit down." "I know you will." "Damn straight, bro." "I hear you." It could go on like that for fifteen minutes, like the ceremonious greetings of desert nomads: "Is it peace with you?" "It is peace." "And with your mother and father?" "With my mother and father it is peace." Nobody ever told me that I was full of shit, unless it was the dealer who smirked at me as I filed once more past his checkpoint on the tenement stairs with my wrinkled passport of tens or twenties, depending on whether I'd stayed away long enough to put a dent in my habit: "Mr. *Recovery!* Where you been?"

These events transpired in relative privilege, the privilege of a middle-class white man with a good education and marketable skills and an overdraft account at Chase. I never spent a night in jail. I didn't get AIDS or hepatitis C. I overdosed a few times but without lasting damage, and practically the first thing I did after climbing off the gurney was go out looking for more of what had landed me there, feeling entitled to it now because of what I'd been through. I had the same response the times I was robbed. And yet for the last few years of my using, I was unhappy, not because of what might happen to me — like most addicts, I had only a tenuous sense of the future and an even vaguer one of the conditional — but because of what already had happened.

By the time I got the phone call about Linda, I'd been clean twelve years, long enough that the apartment was no longer stained by old associations, and I was happy to be living in it, high above the lonely, shining band of the river. Yet after I hung up, the place felt cold and oppressive, its proportions those of an oubliette. I took an elevator downstairs and began walking east. On the building's front steps a middle-aged man and woman were talking over their shopping carts, and as I passed I heard the woman say, "The thing you've got to understand about God is he's not *nice.* He's not nice at all." Maybe I only thought I heard this.

⌐⌐⌐

Behold, I am vile; what shall I answer thee?
I will lay mine hand upon my mouth. (40:4)

Job utters these words in response to God's challenge: "Shall he that contendeth with the Almighty instruct him?" (40:2). In an orthodox reading they signal the man's surrender to the Creator's majesty and wisdom. To some commentators, the very fact that God has revealed himself to Job is sufficient proof of God's providence. Nothing stops an argument like a theophany. But is surrender the same thing as assent? What Job is really telling God is "I can't answer you." Actually he says it twice. In the tenth century the biblical scholar Saadya Gaon noted that this phrase can have two meanings, depending on whether one is acknowledging the truth of an adversary's position or the fact that the adversary is too powerful to argue with.[73] "I can't answer you" would be an appropriate response to someone who was holding a gun to one's head. Job isn't a Jew in the modern sense, but in his speeches he displays a highly Jewish sense of irony. This may be another instance of it. To lay one's hand upon one's mouth isn't all that different from shrugging one's shoulders, and we know how eloquently Jews can do that.

But what about Satan? By any strict accounting, he's the true author of Job's misery, not just the hand that snatches and smites but the initiator of the heartless wager over Job's integrity. Even all those thousands of years ago he has the inveigling manner of a three-card monte dealer. "You can see him sauntering about among the angels," a pastor says of him, "hands in his pockets, or picking his teeth, disdainful of all the rest." [74] Once he has blasted Job with sores, the adversary steps offstage, but if this were a conventional story, the kind where an early mention of a gun guarantees that a gun will eventually be fired, he would reappear, downcast and shamefaced, at its end. He has, after all, lost the bet: Job has remained faithful.

Still, Satan's reentry would remind us that the Almighty agreed to bet with him in the first place, a supremely unnecessary thing for an omniscient being to do. Jung cites their wager, and the general forbearance with which God treats Satan, as evidence that the devil has "bamboozled" God. [75] Perhaps Job — who at moments seems to have guessed the true cause of his suffering — has this in mind when he demurs in answering God. Maybe he's thinking of it later when he apologizes: "Therefore have I uttered that I understood not" (42:3). Here, too, he may be speaking ironically. [76] Just before this, God has boasted of being "a king over all the children of pride" (41:34).

But this is probably unfair to God, who, whatever else he may be, isn't foolish. It's also unfair to Job. All along he's been desperate to know the meaning of his suffering, desperate to believe that it means anything at all. How terrible it would be for him to learn that he has suffered because God was duped. I prefer to think that Satan has vanished because the Lord has no further use for him. He has sent him away. If we want to know where he's gone, we might ask God to show us his face. This is widely supposed to be fatal (Exod. 33:20), and I wonder whether that's because that face is really a multitude of faces.

As a child in the nunnery, Ngawang Sangdrol must have seen tankas depicting thousand-faced Chenrezig, the patron bodhisattva of Tibet. All those faces are compassionate. That is one of the advantages of polytheism, or of the pluralistic atheism that is Tibetan Buddhism: each divine being can be wholly and purely itself. But the God of Job is one God, possessed of contradictory traits, possessed by contradictory impulses. Each has its own face, grave, joyful, fierce, consoling, beautiful, or grotesque. This ambivalence is what Job intuited when he appealed to God to defend him from himself, invoking the merciful judge against the ruthless prosecutor.

Although traditional religious commentaries, whether Jewish or Christian, are divided as to whether to pin Job's calamities on God or Satan,[77] Job himself always ascribes them to God. He may not even know that Satan exists. He may be too much a monotheist (perhaps more of a monotheist than either the conservative clerics who insist on God's omnipotence or the liberal ones who want him to be good) to believe that such a being could have an existence apart from God, that it could be anything more than the face God turns toward those whom he has marked for destructive testing. It looks on them for a while, its gaze fixed and pitiless, and then it turns away, to be supplanted by another face or by the radical facelessness of death.

There's a long and fecund tradition of thought that posits chaos — or orderlessness — as the fundamental state of existence. The tradition extends from the Buddha to the pre-Socratics and from Nietzsche to Lacan, varying its nomenclature and emphasis. Buddhism speaks of phenomena as being "empty," devoid of any permanent essence, and Lacan reconfigures chaos as the "real," the staticky primal layer of experience that is beyond the reach of language. But human beings are order-seeking animals. Order is the nest we make for our minds. When we cannot find it, we invent it. We prefer even a nest of thorns and nettles to the terror of the open.

Job's comforters will sooner deny his goodness than admit that his suffering may have no cause. A part of Job himself will deny his goodness. And perhaps the author of Job felt the same way, for no sooner has God rebuked Job for expecting him to conform to a human model of justice than he turns around and behaves justly. In the final chapter he restores Job. The false comforters are brought low; the lost flocks are redeemed. The dead children are replaced by other children, and only a modern reader, made sentimental by modern philosophies of parenting and modern pediatrics, would complain that no child is replaceable.

The poem of Job the impatient, spine-chilling, anarchic, and tragic, gives way to the folktale of Job the patient. The folktale is essentially a comedic form, since in it order is threatened and then restored. "Which Job do you remember?" is another way of asking "Which God do you believe in?" And so it may be inevitable that a certain type of reader will insist that order was there all along and that Job fell foul of it for a reason. Still, the biblical scholar Jack Miles notes that in the Tanakh, or Hebrew Bible, Job is the last book in which God speaks directly. And he ventures that this may be so because Job has reduced him to silence.[78] Maybe he has shamed him into it.

LINDA'S CANCER WAS inoperable, and none of the other treatments her doctors tried did more than slow its advance.

After a time she could no longer go out to the country house because the drive on the rough back roads might cause her weakened bones to fracture. Once she became mysteriously weak and drowsy, almost falling into a coma, so that they thought she might be having a recurrence of the Hashimoto's. Blood tests showed that her system was flooded with free calcium, which was leaching out of her bones. Her skeleton was disintegrating.

The last time I saw her, I came expecting to find the worst, but she greeted me at the door and led me back to her office without the help of her walker. I could see it standing against the wall, spindly and rubber-footed, evoking both the fragility of old age and the soft, toppling clumsiness of toddlerhood. Every time my eye fell on it, I reminded myself that she didn't seem to need it, which could mean that she was getting better.

She was thin and her skin was very pale, with blue-green veins showing in her neck and forehead. Her hair had grown back thickly; it was colored an ethereal silver that made me think of one of Tolkien's elf queens. By that token Linda wouldn't die but simply pass into a better world, where death had no dominion. But maybe she'd just dyed her hair.

We talked about our past in that office with its chipping paint and overflowing boxes of index cards. To please her I did my old imitation of our thundering pest of a poet. *I myself . . . am . . . myself!* She laughed. Her laughter was wonderful to see. I'd had a molar pulled the week before — the only lasting consequence of my addiction was lousy teeth — and was in the middle of complaining about how it looked when I caught myself. I felt my face redden.

Linda shook her hand dismissively. "Smile," she said. I did. "Don't worry. You can't even see it."

I'd come for a number of reasons: to say good-bye, of course, and also to thank her, and lastly to apologize. Almost twenty years had passed since I'd tried to kill myself. The way I remembered it, I'd swallowed the pills and then, once the grogginess set in, cut my wrists and lay down to wait for my life to drain like motor oil from a crankcase. As another friend would later tell me, I just wanted to wake up dead. But during the night, maybe because I'd washed down the Fiorinal with some vile wine, I was sick, and although I vomited in bed rather than in the toilet, it was enough to save my life.

The next morning the phone rang and I reflexively picked it up to hear someone from my office asking me if I was ill, and I said yes I was. Something in my voice must have indicated otherwise. Before long two of my coworkers showed up at my apartment. One of them was Linda, the other a gentle fellow named Leonard. Leonard was always faultlessly groomed, the buttons of his shirt lined up, as if by a ruler, with the fly of his trousers, and the sight and smell of me must have been repellent to him. I believe I knew they were coming, for I'd pulled on some pants and when they stepped out of the elevator I was trying to cram my soiled bedclothes down the incinerator in the hall.

The first thing they did for me was make me stop, kindly, with care not to make me feel any more foolish than I already felt, for who feels more foolish than a failed suicide? Clamped inside his ass's head, he has blundered off the stage set of a tragedy and onto that of a comedy, a sour comedy that nobody really laughs at. I remember the two of them wrangling me into a sweatshirt while I apologized over and over for my breath. I don't remember the expressions on their faces, but of course I was ashamed to look at them. Later, as they were helping me out of the taxi, I looked up and saw the sun, very small and pale in the cold white sky. It was just before Easter.

In the emergency room a nurse asked me for my insurance card. I may have been too stoned to remember what it looked like or just trying to turn my shame into a joke. In my wallet I found a *Star Wars* trading card with a picture of those two robots, the ones you saw everywhere that year, and I solemnly handed this to the nurse as if it were the calling card of someone illustrious. "That's not your insurance card," Linda said. Was she angry at me? I looked at her anxiously, but her attention was focused on my wallet, and all I could make out was the effortful line of her lips as she drew them back over her teeth, like a laundress with a mouthful of clothespins. She flipped through the cards inside until she found the proper one and gave it to the nurse. "He still has his sense of humor," she said.

I remember little more. I'm told that they pumped my stomach. When I returned to work, I apologized to both the people who had rescued me, but the apology was mumbling and perfunctory. At the time I understood how messy and inconvenient it must have been for them to be forced to save my life, but not how terrible. How terrible it is to have to do that for anyone.

I meant to say it now, but Linda stopped me. "That's not what happened," she said. She told me that no one from the office had called me that morning. It was I who'd called, and I had asked to talk to her, and when she answered, I told her what I'd done.

I was horrified. "I *told* you?"

"Yes."

"And then what?"

"You asked me to come."

I looked at her and I knew that she was about to die. I was lucky enough to see her on a good day — she wasn't in too much pain — but there was no use hoping that the next treatment would work any better than the others had. "Why me?" she asked. We'd been working together only a little while back then, had barely known each other. Maybe I hadn't even gotten around to deciding I was in love with her. I couldn't say why I'd chosen her. I couldn't say why she'd been chosen.

CHAPTER 2

A Place to Be Heartbroken

How Do I Endure?

All his life Peter was afraid of flying," Sally Good-rich said. "He was afraid of being hijacked. He just had it in his head. I used to make fun of him. And that's how he died. I could not have picked a worse death."[1] It was the worst thing I've ever heard a mother say about her child. Sally, a sixty-one-year-old teacher and reading specialist from Bennington, Vermont, has had to speak about her son many times in the years since he was killed and she was pressed into the ranks of the celebrity bereaved. The second time I met her, she'd just come back from taping a segment of a morning talk show, where a producer had kept scolding her for not smiling enough. "Bigger!" she'd urged, baring her teeth to show what she had in mind. Finally, exasperated, the producer had a makeup artist plaster Sally's mouth with a garish clown's grin of lipstick so that viewers would know she was happy.

"Peter watched somebody dying on the plane," Sally went on. This would have been a flight attendant whom the terrorists stabbed on their way into the cockpit. "And he was Maced." She motioned to her husband, Don, sixty-four, who was sitting quietly beside her on the living room sofa. "It's Don's brother that makes Mace." I thought I was hearing her wrong, but her brother-in-law, Jon E. Goodrich, really is president and CEO of Mace Security International, whose incapacitating chemical spray is marketed as a nonlethal alternative to firearms.[2] Peter Goodrich was tall and athletic and had been an all-American shot-putter in college. But the Mace left him blind and gasping for breath, and while some of the other passengers were able to call their loved ones in their final minutes, he could not. "He was on the second flight, and on the second flight the hijackers told them right off the bat that they were going to die. They were told they were going to fly into a building in Chicago." This turned out to be untrue. United Airlines (UA) Flight 175 instead hit the south tower of the World Trade Center. It was 9:03 on the morning of September 11, 2001. Peter was thirty-three.

He'd spent his last weekend helping his parents move from their home in Williamstown, Massachusetts, to Bennington, Vermont, where Sally had grown up and where her elderly father was ill with Alzheimer's. They were coming back to care for him rather than entrust him to a nursing home. Originally they'd hired movers, but at the last minute Peter's younger brother, Foster, insisted on making it a family activity. And although the move wasn't easy — Sally's father was having a bad day, and Peter's car broke down — it took on a celebratory air, as if it were part of the Labor Day holiday just past. As a family, the Goodriches were tightly wired, improvisational, a little raffish. They were like the Four Musketeers. A lot of that had to do with Peter. "He was just a scurrying-around, loving, in-our-lives person," Sally says. "He was the centerpiece of the family. He was the hub. He was the giver." It was Peter's idea that the family take in his best friend Kimberly Barney Reese at the end of her freshman year in college when she had broken with her mother and had no place to live. When she was thirty, they formally adopted her. And it was Peter who used to promise that he'd take care of Sally in her old age, his plan being to move her into a little house near the one in Sudbury, Massachusetts, where he lived with his wife, Rachel. "He'd say, 'That's where I'm gonna put you, Ma,' " Sally remembers. "And truthfully he would have."

In childhood photographs he looks grave and fragile, with a visor of blond bangs overhanging a small, uncertain face. He was dyslexic and did poorly in grade school, where his learning impediment made him a target of bullies. "This was a kid who respected every bug that ever lived and couldn't bring himself to kill a thing from the time I made him kill a snake as a little boy," Sally remembers. Then she adds ruefully, "Apparently I did that." She's a small, energetic woman with rosy cheeks and eyes that are at once humorous and watchful, and while you can imagine her bossing a child — cheerfully, clapping her hands at him with mock officiousness — it's hard to picture her ordering one to kill something, even a snake.

The first thing Peter learned to do well was play chess. "It was his way of fighting back," she says. As he got more skilled, his parents started taking him to a chess club in Schenectady, New York, to play opponents two or three times his age. In high school he shot up and filled out. He ran track and cross-country, solitary sports that allowed him to compete with himself without the risk of public failure. Each new area of mastery added to his confidence. By the time he graduated, the former underachiever was at the top of his class.

In college he was a six-time all-American and captain of the track team. He was a good student but rarely ventured beyond the subjects that already interested him, signing up for a German class in the hope of being able to read the great chess books in their original language but attending only a few sessions and never bothering to drop the course. After graduating magna cum laude in math, he moved to Cambridge, Massachusetts, to get a job as a computer programmer. He married Rachel Carr, his college girlfriend. In time he became manager of product software development at a company called Software Emancipation Technology, which later changed its name to Upspring. He made friends with his foreign-born coworkers — Russian Jews, Indians, and Serbs — who fascinated him with their babble of languages and cultures and religions. He studied Judaism; he read the Bible and the Qur'an, studding their pages with brass book darts to mark passages he found meaningful.

A passage from the Qur'an was read at his memorial service. It's from the chapter called "The Dinner Table":

> In the name of Allah, the Beneficent, the Merciful. O you who believe! Be upright for Allah, bearers of witness with justice, and let not hatred of a people incite you not to act equitably; act equitably, that is nearer to piety, and be careful of your duty to Allah; surely Allah is aware of what

you do. Allah has promised to those who believe
and do good deeds that they shall have forgiveness and a mighty reward.[3]

For all his interest in other religions, he had none of his
own. This is something that still troubles Sally, who used to
attend a Congregational church: the thought that he had
nothing to console him in the last moments of his life, no
sense of another world awaiting him. In place of religion
Peter had a reverent, omnivorous curiosity, a feeling, in Don's
words, "that in the mystery of all this, there has to be something beyond mere physics." It was what drew him to string
theory and sacred texts. It was why he respected bugs.

Don is a trial lawyer, and his son would often call him
with professional questions: "Not just about legal issues but
fairness issues. Stuff would come up at work where they had
this language or that licensing agreement, or he'd be out in
the field where people were unhappy with this product and
he'd ask me, 'What do I do with this?' He was intrinsically
curious not so much about who was going to win or lose
from a legal perspective, but about what was right." Peter's
ethics were deeply held and occasionally impractical. In
2000 Upspring had a bad year, and he was ordered to cut
$200,000 from his budget. Rather than lay off his program-
mers, he eliminated his own job. A while later Upspring was
purchased by MKS, another software firm, and one of the
company's first actions was to rehire him.

Sally and Don show me more photos of him. In one taken
in Peter's senior year in college, he crouches on a Maine
beach, sculpting a meticulously lifelike dinosaur in the sand
while Don looks on admiringly. A picture taken on his wed-

ding day shows him standing at the center of a family group, his bow tie jauntily askew. He looks like a strapping prince welcoming guests to the feast after the hunt. Sally is standing next to him; they have the same magnanimous smile. In the first days after the 9/11 attacks, photos like this were posted by the hundreds outside St. Vincent's Hospital or in Union Square in New York City, usually bearing the heading "Missing." Later the same photos would appear in impromptu outdoor memorials, and still later in the pages of the *New York Times,* alongside short obituaries of their subjects under the heading "Portraits of Grief." It was as if the photos were being developed a second time, not as images but as meaning. In the photo I like best, Peter and Don are playing chess, facing each other but gazing down at the board. Don's well-trimmed beard gives him the look of a Victorian gentleman in his study. It's a classic illustration of the masculine style of relating, with both parties tactfully diverting their attention toward a neutral third object. There's something incongruous and touching about the sight of Peter's powerful body hunched over the small board. You get a sense of the child he once was, a boy whose response to the cruelty of other kids was to become expert at a stylized, cerebral form of combat in which no one was ever hurt.

The best way for me to understand how Peter Goodrich died, his parents tell me, would be to read *The 9/11 Commission Report.* He isn't named in it, but neither are most of the people who died that day. For the report's purposes they are simply "the passengers" or "all on board," as in "all on board were killed instantly." That morning he was flying from Boston to Los Angeles on company business, one of fifty-six passengers on board a Boeing 767. Five of them were members of Al Qaeda, led by Marwan al-Shehhi, a native of the United Arab Emirates who'd learned the rudiments of flying at a school in Florida. The plane took off at 8:14 a.m. and reached cruising altitude at 8:33. At 8:42 the flight crew reported overhearing an unspecified "suspicious transmission" from another aircraft. This would have been American Airlines Flight 11, which had been hijacked approximately thirty minutes before. Between 8:42 and 8:46 it was UA 175's turn. Armed with knives, box cutters, and Mace, al-Shehhi and his team stabbed a member of the flight crew, burst into the cockpit, and killed both pilots. This may have been when they Maced Peter. They then herded passengers to the back of the plane. At 8:51 the aircraft altered course, ignoring increasingly frantic messages from New York air traffic control. At 8:52 a passenger named Peter Hanson called his father on his cell phone and told him that the flight had been hijacked. A flight attendant called the United Airlines office in San Francisco. At 8:58 the plane took a heading toward New York City. The passengers debated storming the cockpit. At 9:00 Hanson called his father again: "It's getting bad," he said. "A stewardess was stabbed — They seem to have knives and Mace — They said they have a bomb — It's getting very bad on the plane — Passengers are throwing up and getting sick — The plane is making jerky movements — I don't think the pilot is flying the plane — I think we are going down — I think they intend to go to Chicago or someplace and fly into a building — Don't worry, Dad — If it happens, it'll be very fast." There was a scream, and then the line went dead.[4]

The phone rang as Sally was leaving the house that morning, but whoever it was hung up before she could answer. For a long time afterward she was tormented by the thought that it might have been Peter. Looking back, she thinks that the main reason she kept going to the FBI's briefings for family members was to find out if somewhere amid the mounting heaps of evidence lay one piece that would confirm that her son had tried to speak with her before he died. Only months later, after the time line of the hijacking had become clear, was she persuaded that it would have been physically impossible: "I imagine him as being so anxious and impaired by fear that he couldn't call. He couldn't understand what was happening. What was happening had no place in his consciousness. He would've tried to protect the other passengers, but it would've been another instance in which he was helpless before other people's brutality. When he used to get bullied in school, he'd tell me, 'My arms won't work.' It would have been like that all over again."

At the time the phone rang, she was on her way to Massachusetts to finish cleaning her former home for its new owners. When she was done there, she drove back to Vermont through the gently climbing hills, past houses built close to the road and barns that had once held sheep or cattle but were now filled with pottery or antiques. In another few weeks it would be leaf season. Although she had the radio on, she doesn't remember hearing anything about the attacks then, only Samuel Barber's *Adagio for Strings*, playing endlessly "like something from science fiction." When she got home, her father and his attendant were watching TV. On the screen a plane — it must have been the second one — was smashing into a building that she did not yet understand was the World Trade Center. She felt a "horrific" flash of anger. It's the last thing she remembers feeling for many hours.

On reading my notes of her story, I'm struck by how long it took, how much evidence was laid out before her, before she realized the significance of what she had seen, how long she drifted in the limbo of not knowing. But she was still tired from the move of the day before, and she had to take her father to the doctor and then to the emergency room for some X-rays. By a little before noon Don knew and had gone to the hospital to tell her, but he didn't find her, so it wasn't until she returned home later that afternoon that Sally finally learned what had happened — learning it, as in Job or *Oedipus Rex*, from messengers. "Don and our minister came into the kitchen, and my brother and his wife were walking down the driveway, and I was trapped."

In the hierarchy of loss, nothing is said to be worse than a parent's loss of a child. A study of 9/11 family members conducted by the psychologist Yuval Neria found that people whose children had died in the attacks were the worst affected of all survivors.[5] It must be even more awful when the parent witnesses the child's death, for then grief is compounded by trauma, the visceral shock of seeing something that the conscious mind may not — in some theories, *cannot* — understand. What is particularly strange and terrible about Sally Goodrich's loss is that she saw her son die without realizing it. On one level this makes sense, given the sheer improbability of what she was seeing: a jet plane crashing into a skyscraper amid a globe of flames. The only image more improbable might be that building subsequently collapsing, sliding like water over a cliff, its smooth, vertical plunge so uncanny that it would inspire theories that the tower had been brought down by shaped charges secreted at its base. Both images belong to the category of snow falling upward. A transit cop who was at the scene said, "I basically just thought it was not real."[6]

Both images involve not the deaths of human beings but the destruction of inanimate objects. For all their improbability, they are also familiar in a generic way, images of this sort being a staple of our movies and TV shows, many of which are literally plotted around scenes that feature the spectacular demolition of machines and real estate. "The first, irrational thought that came into my staggered mind," one witness wrote, "was that someone was making a blockbuster disaster movie. What I thought, in fact, was this: In this day and age, with its sophisticated digital effects, why would anyone use *real* planes?"[7]

Airplanes and buildings usually have people inside them, and when we watch a scene in which one is destroyed, we assume that we are also witnessing the violent deaths of its occupants. An exploding airplane or a falling skyscraper is a metonymy for human death, a sanitary metonymy in which burning flesh is hidden behind a veil of flames and smoke and the cries of the dying vanish in the roar of cascading rubble. A movie can include many scenes like this without losing its PG rating. The true horror of those scenes is tacit, contingent on what we know about airplanes and skyscrapers, about the lives they contain and what happens to those lives when their containers are burned or crushed or turned to vapor.

The most disturbing footage of 9/11 is that which tracks the second plane's — Peter's plane's — collision with the south tower. Unlike the footage of the first plane, which was captured almost by accident, this was taken by someone who plainly knew that something was wrong. That building shouldn't be burning. That plane shouldn't be flying so low. (It shears across the frame like the blade of a knife.) But the cameraman is distraught, and in the next shot the aircraft has disappeared, leaving only an empty blue sky in which some smoke is rising. That would never happen in a thriller, unless the empty frame were immediately followed by a shot of a screaming face. But the screams one hears in the 9/11 footage are attached to no face. They come from the air.

A common feature of many theories of trauma is the idea that the causative — the wounding — event is not remembered but relived, as it is in the flashbacks of combat veterans, experienced anew with a visceral immediacy that affords no critical distance. To remember something, you have to consign it to the past — put it behind you — but trauma remains in the present; it fills that present entirely. You are inside it. Your mouth is always filled with the taste of blood. The killers are always crashing through the brush behind you. Some researchers believe that trauma bypasses the normal mechanisms of memory and engraves itself directly on some portion of the brain, like a brand. Cattle are branded to signify that they are someone's property, and so, too, were slaves. The brand of trauma signifies that henceforth you yourself are property, the property of that which has injured you. The psychoanalyst Sándor Ferenczi believed that trauma is characterized by the victim's helpless identification with the perpetrator, and elsewhere in the literature one often comes across the word "possession." The moment of trauma marks an event horizon after which memory ceases. Or else memory breaks down, so that the victim can reconstruct the event but not the feeling that accompanied it, or alternatively only the feeling.

A bolt of horrific anger, followed by nothing.

⁓

Nothing is miserable except when you think it so, and vice versa, all luck is good luck to the man who bears it with equanimity.

— BOETHIUS, *THE CONSOLATION OF PHILOSOPHY*[8]

Sometime between A.D. 524 and 526 (the sources disagree about the year) Anicius Manlius Severinus Boethius, an imperial official, philosopher, and member of an illustrious Roman family, was bludgeoned to death in Pavia on the orders of Theodoric, the Ostrogothic king he had served as minister. He was forty-four or forty-five. His fall had been sudden. Only a few years before, he had looked on proudly as his two sons were appointed consuls together. Before that Theodoric had made him *magister officiorum,* head of the entire Roman civil service and chief of palace officials. Alongside his official career, Boethius had translated or written commentaries on Aristotle and Porphyry, as well as his own highly regarded works of logic and theology. His life's goal was to translate Plato's complete dialogues. In spite of the honors that were heaped on him at court, he longed for a life of undistracted scholarship, envisioning himself, in the words of a later commentator, "as the schoolmaster of the West."[9] It was the ambition of a man of great learning and intellectual scope living in a downgraded imperial capital that was sinking into barbarism under a foreign ruler, like a grand house that falls into disrepair when new owners move in.

Boethius achieved his goal posthumously. His writing became the foundation for much of the thought of the Middle Ages. It was translated into Old French by Jean de Meun, Old English by King Alfred, Middle English by Chaucer, and Elizabethan English by Queen Elizabeth herself, who is supposed to have dashed off her version of *The Consolation of Philosophy* in a day. When Chaucer writes philosophically, his philosophy is usually Boethius's. Dante places him among the twelve lights in the heaven of the Sun. To Boethius we owe the image of Fortune as a wheel on whose rim men are randomly borne up and helplessly carried down. Paradoxically, to him we also owe some part of our idea of a universe ordered by God, its events unfolding in accordance with his purposes. Boethius thought that we could know these purposes; he thought that God himself could be known through the application of human reason. Of all his ideas, this may be the one that seems the most exotic to us, who dwell in an age in which God's partisans have more or less taken out orders of protection to make sure that reason keeps its filthy hands off him.

Boethius's Rome was diminished and backward-looking. In 476, not long before his birth, Theodoric's predecessor, Odoacer, had deposed the last Roman emperor, leaving Constantinople the sole remaining seat of the empire. Rather than confront Byzantium, the Ostrogoths declared loyalty to its ruler and governed as his viceroys. As they grew more confident, however, they began to have second thoughts. In 484 a doctrinal schism opened between the

Roman and Eastern churches, a precursor of the one that would eventually split Christendom in two a little less than six hundred years later. Boethius, who revered the unity of the empire, tried in his donnish way to heal the rift. But a rift may have been what Theodoric wanted. He was no longer content to be a viceroy. Further, he and his magister officiorum had religious differences. The king was an Arian Christian who believed that Christ was a separate being from God the Father and inferior to him. Boethius was an orthodox Christian, that is, a Catholic.[10] Only a few years after his triumphs at court, Boethius's enemies produced — or maybe fabricated — evidence that he was intriguing against Theodoric. They added the charge of sorcery. He was arrested, condemned, and imprisoned pending execution. The senate confirmed his sentence. No history tells us how much time transpired between his sentencing and the hour of his death, which was preceded by torture.

While waiting to die, he wrote *De Consolatione Philosophiae (The Consolation of Philosophy)*. The *consolatio* was a popular literary genre of antiquity, an extended philosophical argument that was employed as "a kind of moral medication"[11] for various illnesses of thought. It was a self-help book, written by a man who by his own admission was sick with despair. Part of what makes the *Consolation* moving is our sense of what it must have taken its author to write it. He must have had to tunnel out of his hopelessness as if through meters of rock, for the book's mood is not despairing but serene and optimistic, at times even playful.

As he laments his misfortune in his cell, Boethius — a tearful, "worn out bone-bag hung with flesh" — is visited

by Philosophy. She is a woman of "awe-inspiring appearance," very old but full of vitality, who sometimes seems to
be of normal height and at others so tall that her head pierces
the sky. Her garments are splendid but filmed, as if by "long
neglect, like statues covered in dust,"[12] and pieces of them
have been torn off by marauders. It's an image of idolatry
turned to vandalism, signifying the violence Philosophy's
false admirers have done to her. Even before Boethius iden-
tifies her as his former nurse, you recognize something nan-
nylike about her. She's starchy and possessive, and she
bristles if unqualified persons mess with her charge. When
she arrives, Boethius is being attended by some Muses, who
are dictating poetry to him. Philosophy calls them hysterical sluts and shoos them away. Once she and Boethius are
alone, her mood softens; he really is in terrible shape.

> *So sinks the mind in deep despair*
> *And sight grows dim; when storms of life*
> *Inflate the weight of earthly care.*
> *The mind forgets its inward light*
> *And turns in trust to the dark without.*[13]

We are used to looking for light outside, in the world or
in heaven above it. The chief of Egypt's gods was the sun,
and among the first things the God of the Hebrews is said to
have done was hang lights in the sky. By extension, the outer
world is also where we look for truth. Boethius reverses
that. Light dwells inside, in the mind; it's the outside world
that is dark. Or, rather, we see the world darkly, occluded
by its appearances and our own desires. This is an old idea.
Boethius probably got it from Plato, as he did so many of

the ideas in the *Consolation,* but we also find a variant of it in Buddhism, whose founder preceded Plato by a hundred years. Plato believed that the visible world is a copy — an inferior copy, blotched and degraded, like a bad Xerox — of an imperishable realm of ideas. The Buddha believed that there is no original — or, put another way, no enduring essence — just a jury-rigged arrangement of conditioned things that are constantly decaying and transforming. This includes the mind, which is as wispy and changeable as anything it perceives. None of these thinkers was exactly contemptuous of the world, just skeptical of it, like someone rapping on a stone wall that he suspects is really papier-mâché. And yes, it does sound hollow.

As befits a self-help book, the *Consolation* abounds in medical metaphors. Philosophy tells Boethius that he's suffering from amnesia. He has forgotten her, the one who reared him. More to the point, he's forgotten who he is. Like Plato and the Neoplatonists who came after him, Boethius had an optimistic view of human nature. He believed that we are not born ignorant but possessed of knowledge, especially knowledge of the good. Goodness is our natural inclination, and our happiness lies in following it. When we deviate from the good, we betray our own nature and suffer accordingly: "Indeed, the condition of human nature is just this: man towers above the rest of creation as long as he recognizes his own nature, and when he forgets it, he sinks lower than the beasts. For other living things to be ignorant of themselves is natural, but for man it is a defect." [14]

Philosophy begins to heal her charge the same way Jesus healed the sick, with a touch. The moment she does, Boethius writes, "the clouds of my grief dissolved and I drank in the light." [15] This is the light that has been shining inside him all along, unattended and forgotten. Another way of describing this is to say that Philosophy has *restored* Boethius, returning him to the original state of well-being from which he has strayed. Throughout the ensuing dialogue, Philosophy's role is not so much to teach as to remind. Again and again she will rein her ward back from the glittering shop window of what he lacks and instead direct his attention toward the truth he already knows, the happiness he already has. Nurses do this with children all the time.

Job's comforters tell him that his afflictions are a punishment for his sins. Philosophy tells Boethius that his are the consequence of error. He hasn't done anything wrong, only perceived wrongly. Most thinking about suffering can be divided along these lines. We suffer either because of what we believe or because of what we do. In most Christian thought, which holds that we are born sinful and can barely refrain from committing more sins with every breath, it would be more accurate to say that we suffer because of what we *are*. The idea that unhappiness arises from our habits of thought appears in Buddhism and the Enlightenment, in Christian Science, which treats even cancer as an error, and the cognitive psychotherapies. On the surface it seems a kindlier way of looking at suffering than the haunted vision of Christianity. People can be educated out of erroneous beliefs, but what does it take to rid them of sin, especially if you believe that sin is a strand of humanity's moral DNA, woven into it since the Fall? For comparable pessimism you have to look to Freud, who replaced sin with tyrannical drives that bellow at us to fornicate and murder and that we can neither be rid of nor truly satisfy.

Boethius's error has been to place his trust in Fortune. Fortune is the closest thing this book has to an antagonist, though one that remains offstage and unseen, knowable only through what Philosophy has to say about her. She's portrayed as a beautiful woman turning a wheel, and you might imagine her as a sexy croupier, whose lowered eyes and languid half smile seem like a message meant only for you: *I'm crazy about you.* And because you believe her, you keep doubling your bet long after your run is over and your little pile of chips has been raked away. But who is she smiling at, really? Philosophy calls Fortune a monster but places the greater blame on Boethius for wanting what she has to offer. It is, after all, just chips. "Not one of those things which you count among your blessings is in fact any blessing of your own at all. And if, then, they don't contain a spark of beauty worth seeking, why weep over their loss or rejoice at their preservation?"[16]

Against these ephemeral, ornamental goods, Philosophy holds up happiness, not the provisional happiness afforded by wealth, beauty, or prestige, but the real thing, whose reality is demonstrated by the fact that it can't be taken away. The other characteristic of happiness is sufficiency. To have it is to want nothing else, even if you've lost everything. This, says Philosophy, is what all human beings desire; even the most wicked and benighted people seek it in their blundering way, and we ought to pity them because they will never have it. Their error lies in believing that such contentment can be obtained outside the self, at the table where

Fortune turns her wheel and dispenses her snack-box prizes. The movement toward happiness, then, is an inward movement, a contraction. You turn away, first from the tumult and darkness of the world, then from the passions that draw you toward it. You seek refuge in the good you were born knowing. Inside that refuge is another one still stronger, since all goodness has its origin in God and leads to him. The point of all those withdrawals is not to make you smaller but infinitely larger, completely identified with the immeasurable vastness and sufficiency of God.

It makes sense that a man who had been suddenly toppled from his place in the world would come to distrust the world and view its goods with suspicion. It makes sense that a man in prison would look inward for consolation. I think of Ngawang Sangdrol meditating in her cell, oblivious to the way her breath steams in the cold. I think of an Iranian woman named Farinaz Amirsehi, who, as a twenty-year-old student nurse, was arrested for distributing leftist flyers in Tehran. Khomeini had recently come to power, and she might have been released if she had agreed to name her accomplices in the student movement, as the religious police wanted, and seal her repentance by praying. But she refused, and so she was sentenced to ten years in Evin prison. She was tortured regularly.

The worst torture, she told me, was being made to sit hunched and blindfolded in a narrow compartment called a "grave," because it was scarcely bigger than one, to sit silently and without budging on pain of being whipped with cables, while prayer chants were piped into the room. It went on all day. Many prisoners broke down. Many went mad. What Amirsehi believes enabled her to withstand this ordeal was a mental exercise she used to perform. She would build a hospital in her head, calculating how many bricks she would need, how many meters of pipe, what kinds of medicines. "I kept my mind busy," she says. "I tried to make use of my time until they came to execute me. Because I never believed I would be released."[17]

Meditation is often described as emptying the mind (though this isn't strictly true), while what Amirsehi was doing was filling hers, stuffing it with bricks and pipe and rolls of gauze. What the practices have in common is the deliberate exercise of consciousness, the insistence on *remaining* conscious in circumstances in which consciousness is so often ground out. The *Consolation* contains a poem that appears to describe meditation. In it the soul rises above the earth and through the spheres of the four elements, past the moon and planets and stars, until at last it comes face-to-face with God. The journey anticipates the one Dante takes in the *Paradiso*. The sense of great distances effortlessly traveled is especially striking, as the poem's author may have written it while confined to a single room that he would leave only on the day he was taken forth to be killed.

THE REST OF September 11, 2001, is sketchy in Sally's memory. She and Don found themselves driving down to Peter and Rachel's house in Sudbury, half-expecting to find him there, as earlier they had half-expected him to call to tell them he was all right. At one point she reached for a bag of her son's clothing that was still lying on the living room floor, where he must have dropped it after coming home from moving her the day before. Rachel snapped at her not to touch it. Later that night, after they'd checked into a motel, Sally got very drunk, so drunk she couldn't walk, and cried out that she was being punished for her sins.

"Of course the first question you ask yourself after you absorb the shock is why?" she says. "Why did they hate us so much? And why did my good kid have to die such a horrible death. And just why?" The next morning they went with Rachel and Foster to Logan Airport, where the FBI was beginning to brief the families of the passengers. Sitting across from them was the family of a young girl who'd been on Peter's plane. They were loudly blaming God for her death.

Don could tell that the FBI agents were trying to be helpful, but they were working under constraints. Where Sally is outspoken and so quick to reveal herself that you sometimes want to shush her for her own protection, her husband speaks slowly and cautiously. A lot of attorneys speak that way, but in Don the effect is deliberative rather than evasive. He'll make a statement, then qualify it, then elaborate on the qualification, and following him is like watching an ice-skater's sinuous progress across a frozen pond. "The FBI is interested in gathering information without compromising anything, and so they don't disclose anything," he says. "And so we couldn't find out what happened. And that was very difficult for me, not being able to get answers. Now there weren't a lot of answers out there, but even the scant ones that existed we couldn't get, like what seat he was sitting in or who he was sitting next to. We couldn't get any of that, not even from the airline. And that was very difficult."

"We had *no* access to information," Sally says. "It was inexcusable."

It would be a year and a half before the Goodriches were allowed to see the seating chart of Peter's flight.

They responded to the lack of information differently. Sally couldn't stop watching the news and reading the *New York Times*: "I had a complete fixation on it. Maybe it was just hope that the news was going to change and my kid was going to come back, or [fear] that there was going to be more calamity." But Don couldn't bear to do either. Between them, they were enacting the dichotomy of the traumatized, the split between the desire — the obsession — to know the truth and the deep, visceral defenses against obtaining such knowledge. The psychiatrist Jonathan Shay treated a Vietnam vet who spent years after his return from the war photocopying documents in the Marine Corps archive so as to have a record of his unit's actions during his tour. He carried this record around with him in a gym bag, fearful that it might otherwise be lost or stolen. But he couldn't bring himself to read any of it.[18]

The absence of information was emblematic of other kinds of absence. There was no body.[19] Peter had simply vanished in a fire that burned hot enough and long enough to melt the south tower's steel support core like taffy. Most of the people who died at the World Trade Center died like that, burned to ash or crushed beneath more than a million tons of rubble, and in another time their disappearance would have been nonnegotiable. But that was before high-tech sifting machines and DNA analysis. It was before we stopped believing in irretrievable loss. A little over a month after the attacks, when New York City's chief medical examiner cautioned families of police officers and firefighters that most of the bodies would not be recovered, the audience rebelled. One woman screamed, "You're a liar!"[20]

The reclamation of victims' remains became one of the great public works projects of post-9/11 New York, a macabre gold rush in which armies of firefighters and police, their faces masked by respirators, methodically combed the gray heaps of debris at Ground Zero and the Fresh Kills Landfill for scraps of human tissue.[21] Dust itself became sacred. At the World Trade Center it was blessed on-site by a chaplain, shoveled into fifty-five-pound drums, and then conveyed to police headquarters under full guard to be ceremoniously presented to the victims' families in polished mahogany urns.[22]

A year and a half later, aided by samples of Sally's DNA, searchers would identify a fragment of Peter's bone. The Goodriches feel lucky that this happened only once. Some families would get phone call after phone call notifying them that another piece of their loved one had been brought up out of the dust. Al Petrocelli, whose son was killed in the north tower, had this happen five times in two years. "This time from his left knee down to the top of his foot," he described one find. "Right femur with right lower leg and kneecap. Some skin. A piece of skull bone. Soft tissue. Muscle." His wife, Ginger, added, "They found his heart. What do you say?"[23]

The concern for retrieving the remains of the dead is ancient and widespread. Think of Priam, falling to his knees before Achilles to beg for his son's corpse. One of the enduring scars of the Vietnam War is the fact that so many of its victims died far from home, their bodies so grievously disorganized by bombs or claymore mines or napalm that there was nothing left to bury. But the Vietnamese, who call that war "the American war," believe that the dead have to be buried in their native villages if they are to rest, and so the entire country is haunted, crowded with the unquiet spirits of its unburied dead. After the war the communist government built military cemeteries, but only for fallen soldiers of the North Vietnamese Army (NVA) and Vietcong. Nothing was done for the men who had died fighting for the South, and the Army of the Republic of Vietnam (ARVN) cemeteries that had been built during the war soon fell into disrepair, their tombstones defaced, their plots overgrown with weeds for goats to graze on.[24]

Maybe the Americans who fought in Vietnam also were haunted. So many vets became obsessed with the fate of POWs and MIAs. The obsession took outward form in the flags and bumper stickers that thirty years after the war's end can still be seen in every part of the United States. The flags are black, with a white medallion at their center bearing the silhouette of a dejected soldier, a guard tower looming behind him. The emblem calls up the stories of secret prison camps housing starving and abused Americans whom the Vietnamese were rumored to be holding for reasons that became more elusive with every passing year.[25] (Viewed from twenty-five years later, those stories seem uncannily to predict what America would be doing with *its* enemy prisoners at Guantánamo and at "black sites" in eastern Europe.) The search for the Southeast Asian camps evolved into a cottage industry, led by freelance entrepreneurs in cammies and black berets.[26]

But take another look at the MIA flag. Does its human

figure, a featureless shadow with bowed head, suggest a prisoner or one of the dead? It might be one of the ghosts Odysseus visited in Hades, those "after images of used-up men."[27] Beneath the grim insistence on bringing the missing warriors home — and the fury directed at all the powers that seemed to impede their return — there must have been some tacit understanding that they were dead. And as if to prove they were (and signal their goodwill toward their powerful former enemy), the Vietnamese began digging up their remains and repatriating them.[28] As relations between the countries improved, they allowed teams of American military investigators to come search for the bodies themselves.[29]

The Goodriches were never that preoccupied with the whereabouts of their son's remains. A chip of bone was just a chip of bone. What Sally missed was Peter's overpowering physical presence: "He would embrace you fully and keep you in his arms until you tried to struggle to get out, past that comfort point. That was his signature hug." For Don it was their phone conversations and chess games. No matter what the search crews might bring them, Peter himself — what his parents might have called "the real Peter" — was gone, and for a while everything conspired to remind them of that. Because his son had loved insects, Don would think of him every time he saw a dragonfly, and he couldn't think of him without remembering how he'd died. Every memory led inescapably to the image of the burning towers. This is one of the paradoxes of mourning: the beloved is gone, but his memory is everywhere, suffusing the world, coating its surfaces like ash. Here is Gilgamesh, grieving for his lost friend Enkidu in words written some four thousand years ago:

> *May the peoples who gave their blessings after us*
> *mourn you*
> *May the men of the mountains and hills mourn you . . .*
> *May the pasture lands shriek in mourning as if it were*
> *your mother*
> *May the cypress and the cedar which we destroyed in*
> *our anger mourn you*
> *May the bear, hyena, panther, tiger, water buffalo,*
> *jackal, lion, wild bull, stag, ibex, all the creatures of the*
> *plains mourn you.*
> *May the holy River Ulaja, along whose banks we*
> *grandly used to stroll, mourn you.*
> *May the pure Euphrates, to which we would libate water*
> *from our waterskins, mourn you.*
> *May the men of Uruk-Haven, whom we saw in our bat-*
> *tle when we killed the Bull of Heaven, mourn you.*[30]

In some ways the dead person is more present than he was when he was alive and confined to a single place, a single body. The only corollary to this state is the state of being in love. And yet even as the world is filled with memories of the loved one, it is also emptied. His death has made it empty. And the mourner, too, is made empty because an essential part of her, a part so completely identified with the dead person as to be indistinguishable from him, has been torn out. "I couldn't feel a thing. I just could not . . ." Sally begins, then fumbles for words. "It was a really shut-down kind of . . ."

Don completes her thought. "Like a black hole. It's just so hard to one day have a living, loving body and spirit, and then it's just gone, and [what's left are] some visual images that are extremely disturbing and hard to see, and beyond that an emptiness."

For months after her son's death, Sally couldn't bear to go to the supermarket for fear of running into a neighbor, who might ask her how she was. "I was afraid that if I answered, I would fall apart. You think, 'If I cry, I will never stop crying; I will not exist. I *will* try to kill myself.' How can I answer that question, 'How are you?' And that's not what they're really asking. They're really saying, 'I'm sorry. I'm concerned about you.' But just to go into a grocery store feels like an assault. To have to go from aisle to aisle, not knowing who you're going to see, who that person was in your last life. You can't even get lost in the simple process of buying food."

She also had to be especially careful while she was driving, because she was so often seized by the impulse to swerve into oncoming traffic.

After a while the Goodriches returned to a semblance of their former routines. Don went back to his law office and Sally to her job at the North Adams, Massachusetts, school board. "In the initial days it was just breathing," she says. "I would just try to get through a day and then a night and then another day. I would just tell myself to breathe, and we divided the days into the light and the dark. In those early days I don't really remember much. I remember going home and drinking a bottle of wine at night, and then going to work and spending the next seven hours looking at budgets.

I had a very tight path. It would be work, church, home, work, church, home."

I asked her if she'd found church comforting. The question seemed to displease her. "I wouldn't say it was a comfort. It's safe. It's a beautiful building. It has lovely architecture." She ticked off the amenities mechanically and with what felt like a grudging air, as if I suddenly reminded her of the TV producer who'd wanted her to smile more. The truth, she told me later, was that she no longer believed in any of the things she'd once believed in. Everything had been swept away. Mostly, she says, she went to church for her father's sake. She was grateful for anything that gave him pleasure now that he was deteriorating so quickly. Some days she'd come home and have to clean his room of urine and feces. "Still, it was a blessing he was here. He knew that something was bad. He loved us; he was a fabulous father. And I needed to have somebody need me and make demands on my time and keep me going." She had planned to take care of him until the end of his life, but in November, weighed down by their loss and the strange new responsibilities that arose from it, she and Don placed him in a nursing home, where he died six months and a day after his grandson.

By that time the informal group of family members that had converged on Logan Airport as the first reports came in had coalesced into the nonprofit Families of September 11. At the group's first meeting, Sally volunteered to serve on the board. Later, when the stress of channeling aid to needy survivors became too much for her, Don took over her position. Early in 2004, he became the group's chairman. The organization's Web site describes it as being open "to any-one affected by the events of September 11." From the be-ginning, though, it was implicitly a group for people who had lost loved ones on the two flights that had hit the World Trade Center.[31] Most of the fourteen organizations that formed in the aftermath of the attacks served specific popu-lations: a group for families of New York City police and firefighters; a Pentagon group; a group for UA Flight 93; a group for survivors of the more than seven hundred em-ployees of the securities broker Cantor Fitzgerald who died in the north tower. It was as if the immensity of the disaster forced mourners back to basic tribal affiliations: where their people had lived, the kind of work they had done, where they had died.

The groups' original purpose was to provide their mem-bers with emotional and practical support, but they soon developed more ambitious objectives. They wanted things from the government: information and material aid, but also policies that would prevent a catastrophe like 9/11 from oc-curring again. Nearly all of them wanted an independent commission set up to investigate the attacks, but the Bush administration resisted. Only after months of public pres-sure did it grudgingly agree to authorize one. Then it nomi-nated Henry Kissinger as the commission's chair. Whatever relief the families had begun to feel gave way to shock and disgust. For the position of national truth teller, the White House had chosen a self-proclaimed master of diplomatic subterfuge, who since leaving government service had set up shop as a consultant to a roster of foreign clients rumored to include the Saudi royal family. (There was no way to be sure, since Kissinger refused to make the list public.) The families dug in their heels, and so did a growing number of legislators, and Kissinger ended up resigning a month after he was appointed. He was replaced by former New Jersey governor Thomas Kean, with Lee H. Hamilton, a former Democratic congressman from Indiana, as cochair.[32] When asked what role Families of September 11 may have played in shaping the commission's final makeup, Don Goodrich is modest: "We just insisted on being a voice."

Because he was not just an officer of a leading survivors' group but also a trial lawyer, Don was asked to draw up recommendations to the September 11th Victim Compensation Fund concerning its rules for distributing aid to families. Today, when the fund is widely seen as an instrument of government charity and its recipients viewed through the cracked lens of compassion and resentment that Americans turn toward charity cases, it's easy to forget that it was created to protect the airlines. The bill that authorized the fund is titled the Air Transportation Safety and System Stabilization Act. In it the victims' families are literally an afterthought, mentioned for the first time only in the fourth of six sections.[33] The bulk of the legislation outlines the $15 billion bailout of an industry that was already in trouble before September 11 and that afterward was at risk of disintegrating beneath a torrent of anticipated lawsuits. In its original version the bill simply placed a cap on the airlines' liability in such suits. Only after Senate Democrats (who, as part of the tireless courtship dance of Washington, had been lobbied by the Association of Trial Lawyers of America) insisted that the victims' families ought not to be left empty-handed was the fund tacked onto the legislation. It was less a means of restitution than hush money. Any family that applies to the fund must waive its right to sue the airlines.

Don based his proposals on the sort of judgments he makes all the time in his work, where he routinely assesses the value of lost lives and the suffering of bereaved survivors. The law recognizes two kinds of loss. One is economic — for example, the income the young vice-president of a thriving software company might be expected to earn in a normal lifetime, that is, a lifetime not radically cut short; the loss of other employment and business opportunities; the cost of his burial. The other kind of loss is noneconomic. It is encompassed by terms such as "loss of consortium" and "hedonic damages": the loss of the companionship of a spouse or lover, the loss of joy itself. Noneconomic loss is harder to calculate than economic loss, but the law is filled with precedents. Don found one ready to hand. Three weeks before September 11, the Federal Aviation Administration had promulgated a ruling that estimated the value of a typical airline passenger's life at $2.7 million, regardless of his or her projected income.[34] This was the amount the agency deemed it reasonable for an airline to spend to keep a passenger alive while on board one of its flights. By extension, it might be what the airline would be expected to pay his survivors if he died.

Another historical fixture of American tort law is the idea that noneconomic loss varies with time. If we think of pleasure as something finite, a vessel from which the individual drinks in the course of a lifetime until it is at last drained, a victim who dies at the age of thirty-three is deprived of more pleasure, say, than the sixty-eight-year-old in the airplane seat beside him, who has already drunk most of his fill. The first man's young widow faces more years of loneliness than a widow who is already old. Both the $2.7 million compensation figure and the model of time-dependent loss were part of the proposed regulations Don took down to Washington in the late fall of 2001 to present to the Department of Justice, the authorizing agency for the victims' fund. Once there he discovered that the DOJ had quietly decided to sweep away decades of tort law. There would be a fixed sum for noneconomic loss, its negotiators told him: $250,000. "I couldn't understand why it was that we were receiving an absolutely deaf ear and a stone-faced response," he says. "And I was sitting in my motel room, and I had all these papers and all this stuff, and I realized, the resistance here is tort reform!"

Tort reform was one of the Bush administration's idées fixes. George W. Bush had run on it in the 2000 election; he would again in 2004. As used by the president and his allies in the business community, "tort reform" was a term almost as vague and inclusive as "the global war on terror." It might mean placing limits on class-action suits or moving damage suits out of the state courts, with their cranky, openhanded juries, and into the federal system. But any Bush administration discussion of tort reform inevitably included a $250,000 cap on noneconomic loss. "They saw this as a precedent," Don believes. "If they could get these regulations to memorialize a noneconomic loss recovery of $250,000 that would apply to the worst disaster in the history of this country, then they would have memorialized a number that applied to the worst possible circumstance. And it dawned on me that it's hopeless for us to [try to] change this. We had shifted to the enforcement of an ideological, political agenda in which we were pawns. It wasn't us," he says, his voice curdling with scorn. "It was the *agenda*."

In spite of every argument he could put forward, the $250,000 cap remained in place, and the Association of Trial Lawyers of America refused to challenge it, fearing that a Supreme Court dominated by conservative justices would rule in favor of the DOJ and enshrine the cap in law. Some two years later Congress passed a widely touted tort reform bill; one of its key features was a $250,000 limit on compensation for noneconomic loss.[35]

Of course, in a catastrophe as massive as September 11, the lines between different types of loss are bound to be blurred, sometimes to the point of erasure. Consider this exchange between Kenneth Feinberg, the Victim Compensation Fund's virtually omnipotent special master, and the mother of a firefighter protesting the government's offer of $500,000 — one-sixth of what it might award the family of a bond trader: "I cannot make you happy," Feinberg tells her.[36] There's no way of knowing whether his tone is sympathetic or dismissive; the reporter relaying the conversation doesn't say. "I cannot bring people back."

"It's not about the money," the woman answers. "This is not ever about the money."

Then why is she being so vehement? And why does the special master feel driven to tell her that he can't bring back the dead, as if that was what she had asked him for? Why do they keep speaking past each other? The reporter explains: "Tragedy, particularly American tragedy, is always and inevitably about the money."[37]

Well, Americans like to measure things, and money is one of the ways — maybe the chief way — that tragedy is measured. And perhaps, given the human tendency to confuse objective and subjective states, money has become its inward registry as well, being easier to count than tears. It is, at any rate, how suffering people reassure themselves that their suffering has been recognized. Even Sally Goodrich, whose early experience with Families of September 11 gave her an insider's understanding of how disaster aid gets distributed, is still angry that she and Don, like other parents of married children, didn't qualify as claimants under the Victim Compensation Fund. They didn't need the money or even especially want it, but whoever qualified was officially a victim. Because only Peter's wife, Rachel, qualified, it meant that she was a victim and they were not. This happened repeatedly under the fund's zero-sum calculus: a wife might be eligible for assistance but not a fiancée, a husband of three months but not a boyfriend who had lived with the deceased for ten years. There was no category at all for same-sex partners. In recognizing only some of the victims, the fund had negated the rest. As one congressman who had voted for the fund explained, "Some unlucky victims are more unlucky than others."[38]

Sally shot off a bitter note to Feinberg, calling him "the most amoral person I have ever met." The next morning she repented: "I am deeply sorry for my inappropriate personal remarks last night. Your job is impossible and I promise not to write again. I have lost all judgment. What you saw in those remarks does not reflect who I used to be. I can barely stand being what I have become."

Because this is the United States, there was plenty of

money to go around. Within months of the 9/11 attacks, some $2.7 billion in aid from government and private sources had descended on the amorphous entity called "the victims."[39] Sometimes it overwhelmed the recipients, like a firefighter's widow who tried to cheer up her kids by buying a $50,000 Escalade.[40] Sometimes it overwhelmed the benefactors. A man named Chris Burke, whose brother had been killed while working for Cantor Fitzgerald, started a charity that sent victims' children to New York Yankees games and Broadway shows. One group traveled as far as Dollywood, Dolly Parton's theme park in Tennessee, where they were greeted by the singer herself. The charity's budget grew from $673,000 in 2002 to $2 million in 2005, and with it Burke's sense of mission. No longer content with arranging morale-boosting outings for his charges, he began pressing them into therapy and social services. He paid for their household expenses and then for a specially outfitted van for a friend of his who wasn't a 9/11 victim but was a paraplegic. Amid an ocean of need, who cared about the origin of any droplet? To meet these exigencies, Burke set up a secret account that he alone controlled, and maybe it was inevitable that he would end up diverting a portion of that money — some $311,000 — for his own use. There was so much of it (at one point he claimed to have found an unsolicited check for $250,000 in a stack of Christmas cards), and he was a victim, too. After the embezzling came to light and Burke's heartbroken parents had paid back the money, he explained both his frenzy of giving and the theft as a misguided attempt to delay grieving: "The building of Tuesday's Children allowed me to hide from 9/11 in 9/11."[41]

• • •

TO FULLY IDENTIFY one's happiness with God, one must on some level trust him. Fifteen centuries after his death, Boethius is remembered chiefly for his method of proving that such trust wasn't just necessary but rational. Putting it another way, he demonstrated that faith needn't be blind, that it could be consistent with reason. Job comes to accept his suffering as the result of divine revelation. God speaks to him, and he believes (though the book's ending is sufficiently mysterious as to leave room for doubt as to *what* he believes). Boethius's answers come from Philosophy, whose preferred modes of argument have Greek, rather than Hebrew, origins. Instead of revelation, she offers logic and proofs, and given his grounding in classical scholarship, it's these that Boethius finds most congenial.

He wants to know not just why terrible things have happened to him but why they should happen to any moral person in a world ruled by an omnipotent, benevolent god. Philosophy's explanation hinges on the ideas of Fate and Providence. Fate is the force that controls individuals. It places a Theodoric on the throne and a Boethius in prison, though at some future point it may set Boethius free and dispatch assassins to the king's bedchamber. It governs things that change and is itself always changing. But Fate is only an aspect, a subsidiary, of Providence, the vast, unchanging plan in the unchanging mind of God that "is set at the head of all things and disposes all things."[42]

Fate is local; Providence is universal. Fate operates instance by instance, in different places at different times. It's a series of close-ups: a faithless king, a dishonored civil servant, a torturer with a club. Providence is a wide-angle shot that encompasses everything simultaneously, not just individuals but all created beings, arrayed like the figures in a Spielberg crowd scene. Providence is known only to the Creator. An argument could be made that Fate is known only to the human beings it happens to, since only a human being can fully understand what it means to be *happened to.*[43] Boethius doesn't say this, of course. His God is omniscient, and this would presumably include a knowledge of powerlessness and abjection.

The final difference between these forces is that Fate is amoral, while Providence works unerringly toward the good. Logically speaking, it has to since it is a part of God — Philosophy says it is "the divine reason itself"[44] — and God wills only good. The paradox is that we experience Providence exclusively through its local effects — that is, through bloody-handed Fate. It's Fate that happens to us, and we, the happened-to, have to trust that even the cruelest of its operations are part of God's Providence. We have to trust that our suffering serves his purposes. According to Boethius,

> Providence stings some people to avoid giving them happiness for too long, and others she allows to be vexed by hard fortune to strengthen their virtues of mind by the use and exercise of patience. Some people are excessively afraid of suffering for which they actually have the endurance; others are full of scorn for suffering they cannot in fact bear. Both kinds she brings to self

discovery through hardship. Some men at the price of a glorious death have won a fame that generations will venerate; some indomitable in the face of punishment have given others an example that evil cannot defeat virtue. There is no doubt that it is right that these things happen, that they are planned.[45]

Fifteen centuries later, this idea is still part of Catholic doctrine, illustrated in the Catechism by Genesis's story of Joseph's joyful reunion with the brothers who once sold him into slavery:

In time we can discover that God in his almighty providence can bring a good from the consequences of an evil, even a moral evil, caused by his creatures: "It was not you," said Joseph to his brothers, "who sent me here, but God. . . . You meant evil against me; but God meant it for good." From the greatest moral evil ever committed — the rejection and murder of God's only Son, caused by the sins of all men — God, by his grace that "abounded all the more," brought the greatest of goods.[46]

Boethius's God is as mighty as Job's, but instead of moving the universe by main strength, with an occasional assist from Satan, he uses pulleys, levers, gears. Boethius would have been familiar with these mechanisms, since they were invented by his forebears, though to power theirs the Romans used slaves. God has only to think and the machinery turns. All human beings revolve around him; they are his mechanisms. Some stay close to the divine hub and partake of its serene stillness; some stray and succumb to the heartless gravity of Fate. God controls everything but does nothing *to* anyone. He could do his job in white gloves. "If you could see the plan of Providence," Philosophy reassures her pupil, "you would not think there was evil anywhere."[47]

I don't know if I find this uplifting or terrifying. I think of Leibniz's argument that since God is both infinitely good and has the wherewithal to create any kind of world he pleases, this world must necessarily be the best one possible. It was Leibniz whom Voltaire had in mind when he created the preposterously cheerful Pangloss in *Candide*. It must be a cracked idea of Providence that moves some Christian fundamentalists to applaud the butchery in the Middle East as confirmation of biblical prophecy, as others cheered the tsunami of December 26, 2004, because its principal victims were Muslims, Buddhists, and Hindus. One congregant at the New Life Church in Colorado Springs declared himself "psyched" about what God was doing with "his ocean."[48]

Peter Goodrich's murderers may have had something similar in mind when they nerved themselves for the attacks with the thought that they would be killing infidels and that if any good people were to die, they would immediately be transported into paradise. The view you have of Providence must differ according to whether you are one of the suffering or one of the sheltered. Boethius, who had once been among the most honored men in Rome, was now one of the suffering. He tried to make sense of his suffering using the tools he knew, logic and rhetoric, the ordering of thought and the ordering of language. In the course of the *Consola-*

tion his argument grows ever more complex, more intricately buttressed. It's like Farinaz Amirsehi's hospital, with each proposition taking the place of a row of bricks, the rows rising higher the closer death approaches. Was the hospital ever completed? The last lines of the *Consolation* suggest that it was.

> Hope is not placed in God in vain and prayers are not made in vain, for if they are the right kind they cannot but be efficacious. Avoid vice, therefore, and cultivate virtue; lift up your mind to the right kind of hope, and put forth humble prayers on high. A great necessity is laid upon you, if you will be honest with yourself, a great necessity to be good, since you live in the sight of a judge who sees all things.[49]

It's hard not to be moved by the image of a man alone in prison, wretched and self-pitying as he contemplates the end of his life. It is almost here; he knows it will be brutal. They will spill his brains upon the ground. To compose himself, he marshals the arguments that faith and reason have taught him; he embodies them in the figure of a woman in robust old age, someone he knew in childhood. Although at first she is severe with him, on seeing his plight she is filled with pity. And when she wipes the tears from his eyes, using a fold of her dress, his grief ceases.

In the hour of their death, even grown men call out for their mothers.

• • •

Sally Goodrich left the board of Families of September 11 after a few months. She was no longer willing to play by the Victim Compensation Fund's arbitrary rules of what constituted a victim. On top of that, she'd begun to drink heavily and was beginning to suffer the consequences: she wrote her first letter to Kenneth Feinberg while drunk. She stopped drinking for good in April 2002, a month after her father's death. That August she was diagnosed with ovarian cancer and started chemotherapy. The following year, in remission, she entered graduate school to study language and learning disabilities. During this time she and Don worked constantly, Sally at the school board and Don at his law firm and, increasingly, on the business of Families of September 11. There were weekly board meetings for the group requiring hours of preparation and follow-up. There were funds to raise and donations to distribute. There were memorials to attend.

The Goodriches had become part of a deeply, if relatively recent, American phenomenon: the community of suffering. Such communities are spread across our landscape now like encampments on a plain, each organized around its central trauma: the attacks of September 11, the bombing in Oklahoma City, the bombings of the U.S. embassies in Nairobi and Dar es Salaam, airplane crashes, Agent Orange, Vietnam. And, increasingly, the war in Iraq. Their proliferation may say something about the splintering of American society or about the rift that separates those who have known violent loss from their more fortunate neighbors. "Large populations with no personal attachment to the deceased do not 'grieve,'" Don specifies. "They may sympathize, empathize, regret, retaliate, or in most cases not know what to do, but they do not grieve. Those around us here in this country see us as a curiosity because they know little of suffering. Well, no one wants to be a curiosity."

The community to which the Goodriches now belonged was as diverse as any other, and on several occasions — especially during the buildup to the 2004 presidential election — it would be nearly torn apart by political disagreements. What held it together was not a set of beliefs but a kind of knowledge, one so remote from the experience of most Americans that it was essentially incommunicable, a secret hidden in plain sight. This was the knowledge of what it was like to sit in a crowded airport lounge waiting to find out how your loved one had died on a routine flight from Boston to Los Angeles — how it was *possible* that he had died; waiting, moreover, while stunned by the lights and shouted questions of reporters and TV crews, because your bafflement and your grief were public property now, as, by extension, were you.

In its own dreadful way, membership in this community carried benefits. We are generous to suffering people, or to people whose suffering we think we can understand, and although the suffering of the families of 9/11 was in many ways a new thing, it conformed to the classic American narrative of innocents victimized by foreign treachery. (One reason there was no compensation fund for victims of the 1995 Oklahoma City bombing may have been that the terrorists there were Americans.)

Like other 9/11 families, the Goodriches were the recipients of many acts of compassion, both official and private. Four days after the attacks an honor guard of police escorted them through Ground Zero, past the broken latticework that suggested the interior of a ruined cathedral, between the deformed girders to the Delphically smoking pit.

Around that time Don was representing the plaintiff in a high-stakes lawsuit. The defendants' attorneys had just filed a motion of summary judgment to have the case thrown out. Don was supposed to respond that month. But although he diligently showed up at his office, once there he could do little more than leaf halfheartedly through thousands of pages of documents. He was paralyzed. "I remember picking up the phone, and I called the defense attorneys and I said, 'I just can't do this; I can't get this response in.' And in each instance there was no question. 'Sure, sign my name to it, whatever you want.' I didn't file my response to that motion till February."

Because they were victims of a public tragedy, the families now had a public voice. People listened to them. Many Americans were uneasy with the choice of Henry Kissinger as chair of the 9/11 Commission, but only the families' objections could carry far enough to make a difference. Without the families there might have been no 9/11 Commission at all. In the following months and years the victims' relatives and friends made their opinions felt in contingent realms from foreign policy to public architecture. In a society dominated by false feeling — expedient grief, calculated outrage, scripted uplift — that of the families was unmistakably authentic, and it gave them a moral authority that few public figures today possess.[50] Some people objected to the elevation of these ordinary men and women to the status of prophets — objected to the elevation of mourners in general, whom one columnist called a "new politically invulnerable class."[51] The right-wing haranguer Ann Coulter denounced "the Jersey girls" — a group of firefighters' widows who harshly criticized Congress and the Bush administration for failing to enact the 9/11 Commission's recommendations — as "harpies." She wrote, "These broads are millionaires, lionized on TV and in articles about them, reveling in their status as celebrities and stalked by grief-arazzis. I have never seen people enjoying their husbands' death so much."[52]

What really bothered Coulter may have been that the Jersey girls were speaking up for themselves. Nobody said a word when other family members were drafted to serve as silent extras at speeches and bill signings. None of them, not even the Jersey girls, was recognizable as an individual, but collectively they were icons, and to introduce them at a political event — looking stunned and sheepish in good dresses that might have been bought especially for the occasion — was to lend that event the gravity of their sorrow. Further, their mere presence established a connection between it and the events of September 11. It made sense that when President Bush addressed Congress nine days after the attacks, a widow named Lisa Beamer would be sitting in the audience, in the sight lines of the TV cameras. When she stood, the chamber exploded in applause. Her husband, Todd, had died on UA Flight 93, where passengers had fought back against the terrorists, and George W. Bush was now declaring that the entire country was fighting back, not just against terrorists but against terror itself.

More widows were on hand during the president's "axis of evil" speech on January 29, 2002, implicitly accusing the member states of having murdered their husbands, and other victims were brought forward during the run-up to the Iraq invasion, an invasion that, depending on your point of view, September 11 had either made necessary or made possible. Few victims were more heartbreaking than a teenager named Ashley Faulkner, whose mother had died at the World Trade Center and who three years later was shown being hugged by the president in an ad for his reelection campaign. "He's the most powerful man in the world," she told the camera, "and all he wants to do is make sure I'm safe."[53] For once it was all right for a victim to speak. At all other public appearances it was understood that the victims of 9/11, who were usually women, would abide by the same rules that used to apply to children: they were to be seen and not heard.

For the most part, the Goodriches tried to keep a low profile. Don spoke before Congress (on the need to preserve America's civil liberties in the midst of an unending war on terror), and Sally, to her bemusement, appeared on at least one TV talk show, but they never were as visible as the Jersey girls. Don is naturally reticent, and Sally developed an almost phobic distaste for the ritualized solicitousness that seemed to follow her like a tracking spot. "There was never ever any way of escaping," she says. "Just when you thought you might start to feel okay — you know, the memorial services are over — something else would happen. You'd try to do things that were normal, like watch the Super Bowl. But then at halftime Peter's name came up on the [scoreboard]. So it was a constant resurrection of these painful feelings. And because the rest of society was as devastated by the event as we were, we understood intellectually why that had to be. But emotionally I felt like I had the scarlet letters

'9/11' on my forehead. I hated being the mother of a 9/11 victim."

There's only one event from that time that she remembers with any fondness — the night a week after the attacks that people across the United States lit candles for the victims. Bennington is a small town, and the lights were everywhere. They burned on every porch and in every window. And because no one sought her out that evening, and because people have been lighting candles as symbols of grief and hope for hundreds of years, she felt that what she was seeing wasn't necessarily about her, that she was just a witness to it. After a while, however, she began to feel overwhelmed and she went back to her house, whose picture window looked out on nothing but the distant shapes of the mountains, where no lights burned.

In the aftermath of 9/11 such rites of mourning took place in every part of the country. Some were elaborate, almost pharaonic, ceremonies staged by federal, state, and local governments. Some were spontaneous. There was the service at the Washington National Cathedral three days after the attacks, which began with the president declaring, "We are in the middle hour of our grief" and ended with him pledging to rid the world of evil, a rhetorical shift whose nearest antecedent may be Mark Antony's funeral oration in Shakespeare's *Tragedy of Julius Caesar*.[54] There were the towers of light that materialized in the sky over lower Manhattan on the six-month anniversary like ghosts of the fallen buildings. There was the first-anniversary memorial, at which none of the attending officials — not the governor or the mayor or the ex-mayor, whom the catastrophe had transformed into a national hero — gave an original speech.

They simply read the names of the dead, the Gettys-
burg Address, the Four Freedoms, and an excerpt from the
Declaration of Independence, their reticence being variously interpreted as a sober refusal to politicize the occasion
or an admission that none of them could find words appropriate for it.[55]

Once the trance of the first few weeks wore off, every
ceremony and monument contained the potential for dis-
cord. None contained more than the proposed memorial at
Ground Zero that in 2007 was projected to cost $600 mil-
lion.[56] It wasn't the price tag that most people were angry
about. Instead they fought over how the victims' names
would be displayed, over whether there would be separate
plaques for the north and south towers, whether police and
firefighters would be designated with shields. Kai Thompson, whose husband, Glenn, had died while trying to help
coworkers at Cantor Fitzgerald, argued that "everyone who
was killed that day was attacked equally. Was Glenn
Thompson not, in his own selfless way, as heroic as any of
the brave firefighters and police officers who attempted
similar rescues?"[57] Even the word "heroes" became suspect.
For one thing, it created a class distinction between cops
and firefighters, who became a sort of aristocracy, and all
the other dead. And in the view of some family members, it
also minimized the horror of the day, using the language of
war for what had in fact been a mass murder. The widow of
one office worker bitterly observed, "If you have 3,000 people slaughtered, you have to say who's responsible for the
slaughter. But you don't have to look at who's responsible if
they're heroes, do you?"[58]

The anger had multiple sources. Of course people were

angry at the terrorists: the terrorists had killed their loved ones and countrymen. But because their identity was so nebulous (they had been trained in Afghanistan, but they were not Afghan; a lot of them had come from Saudi Arabia, but Saudi Arabia was an American ally, and in the days after 9/11 the government had gone to the trouble of spiriting several high-ranking Saudi visitors — including a few members of the bin Laden family — back to their country), the anger had no object, or too many objects. It darted from sinister foreigners to native-born traitors, from Islamofascists to secular liberals, and from liberals to politicians and bureaucrats. Not even comedians were exempt. One lost his job for questioning the official designation of the terrorists as "cowards."

The anger surged up most violently around the public commemorations of the attacks precisely because they were public, bringing together different constituencies with different expectations and agendas. An architect would want a memorial to be one thing, and a governor looking ahead to reelection would want it to be something else, and the developer who owned the site would have yet a third idea. And a man who had lost his wife in the north tower would have his own vision of how her death should be honored, and if the architect's sketch didn't jibe with it, it would seem to him as if her death were being *dis*honored.

This was, as I said, a solicitous time: the wishes of the victims' families would be given greater weight than those of any mourner since Queen Victoria. Still, the final decision lay elsewhere; others would make it. So the anger of the mourners arose from their powerlessness, which was not just powerlessness over how the dead would be commemorated but also powerlessness over death. And they were angry at the representatives of the other constituencies they had to deal with. Probably they couldn't help seeing them as one constituency — preening, entitled, unfeeling — the constituency of those who had lost no one, the constituency of the intact.

Walter Benjamin said that history passes before our eyes as a series of separate events but appears to its angel as "one single catastrophe which keeps piling wreckage upon wreckage."[59] We think of history as bidirectional, extending back to the earliest human past and forward to the vanishing point of the future. But those people who looked for a history behind the attacks, who wanted to trace the rage of an Osama bin Laden or an Ayman al-Zawahri to antecedents such as the first Gulf War or the U.S.-financed guerrilla campaign in Afghanistan, found themselves accused of making excuses for terror. The *New York Times,* for instance, wrote contemptuously of "excuseniks."[60] In opposition to those explanations there arose a history of 9/11 that ran in one direction only. In that history the attacks had no antecedent apart from the malice of the perpetrators, who hated us for our freedom. September 11 came from nowhere, out of nothing, like the beating of a great wing in the darkness.

There are many reasons why people might choose to believe that 9/11 came out of nothing. If the attacks had no cause, it meant that their victims were truly, unequivocally innocent, less like unsuspecting adults cut down by the malice of strangers than like children, who can't even conceive that strangers might want to kill them. What crime is more monstrous than the murder of children? Such an atrocity justifies any kind of vengeance, no matter how overreaching or wild, even a vengeance that misses its proper target and falls on a third party, say a nation with no links to the murder.

In 2005 a conservative columnist brushed aside qualms about the unraveling occupation of Iraq: "On September 12, 2001, no one in America cared about whether there would be enough Sunni participation in a fledgling Iraqi democracy if Saddam were ever toppled. No one in lower Manhattan cared whether the electricity would work in Baghdad, or whether Muqtada al-Sadr's Shiite militia could be coaxed into a political process. They cared about smashing terrorists and the states that supported them."[61] A few years earlier, on the eve of the invasion, a firefighter in Alabama put it more simply: "They're all in it together — all of them hate this country."[62]

If the attacks had no cause, it meant they couldn't have been anticipated, and if they couldn't have been anticipated, no one could be blamed for having failed to prevent them, not the CIA or the FBI or the Department of Justice. Not even the White House. And if the events of 9/11 belonged to a new kind of history, a history untethered from the past, *exempt* from the past, then maybe it was exempt from other things as well, including the law decreeing that death is final. One of the first novels to deal with the destruction of the World Trade Center, Jonathan Safran Foer's *Extremely Loud and Incredibly Close,* features a scene in which the towers miraculously reassemble and rise back into the sky, followed by the tiny, despairing human beings who had plunged from them. If history had only begun on September 11, maybe such a thing could really happen. Maybe time had been more fluid then, and the boundary between life and death easier to cross, and the dead might really rise again, as we are promised they will on the Last Day.

Early in Sally Goodrich's bereavement — she thinks it was the night after her father died — she wrote a letter to the Saudi Arabian embassy, asking if she could meet the parents of one of the hijackers. "I wanted to ask them, 'What do you have left of him? Your kid is dead, my kid is dead, our lives are ruined. Where do we go from here? Why did this thing happen?' " There was no official response. Months later she heard from one of the embassy's information officers, who agreed to meet with her informally. She wouldn't tell me his name, not wanting to compromise his career. She went down to Washington; they had lunch together. He was young and ill at ease. He was probably unused to talking with women, especially one who wasn't wearing a veil. And Sally thinks that he was so intent on defending his country's honor that he couldn't respond to her grief. "He gave me what he could give me," she says. "And it was a great thing just to be acknowledged. It would allow me to go forward. But the end result was still the same. There was still a brick wall."

The notion of going forward comes up repeatedly in the stories of 9/11 families, usually paired with that of closure, which Merriam-Webster defines as "an often comforting or satisfying sense of finality." The point of scouring the Pit at Ground Zero and the Hill at Fresh Kills for the most minuscule remnants of the dead was so that the families could have closure and go forward. The point of the payments from the Victim Compensation Fund was not money but closure. The point of the Ground Zero memorial was closure; hence the distress of those family members who found the plans for one too modest or too commercial or too focused on heroes rather than the ordinary, plebeian dead. If the bodies weren't found, if restitution wasn't made, if the memorial was wrong, something would remain open, unfinished. That something might reside in the mourners or in the dead themselves.

In the early 1990s, in a Ngaju Dayak village in central Borneo, I attended a funerary rite that went on for three days and culminated in the disinterment of someone who had been buried twenty-odd years before — or, really, of his bones, which were all that was left in his unmarked grave in the forest. Now his surviving relatives dug them up and washed them with great tenderness before placing them in an ancestral ossuary called a *sandung* that sat behind the family residence like a gaily carved children's playhouse, complete with roof beams that ended in jocular, grinning dragons' heads. It had stairs, but they were notched the wrong way because the dead do everything backward. Up until that time the remains had been considered so dangerous — or so *unstable*, the way radioactive waste is unstable — that the deceased's entire family was thought to be contaminated. Any death or severe illness among its members — even the death or illness of their livestock — was treated as a supernatural event, the working out of a curse. The Ngaju define "natural death" more narrowly than most other people. Or it may be that no death feels natural to its mourners. Early in 2004, a few months after her husband's sudden death from a coronary, Joan Didion found herself unable to get rid of his shoes. "I stood there for a moment," she writes, "then realized why: he would need the shoes if he was to return."[63] How long must the dead remain dead before we understand that they're not coming back?

Had Peter Goodrich died in the nineteenth century, his mother would have observed a formal mourning period of at least a year, divided into stages of full, regular, and half mourning. A black wreath would have hung on the Goodriches' door, black drapes in their windows. The clocks in the house would have been stopped. During this period Sally would rarely have ventured outside, and when she did, she would have been dressed in black crepe and bombazine and her head draped in a black weeping veil. What jewelry she wore would have been made of jet and human hair, preferably the hair of the deceased, which she herself had woven into earrings or a brooch. In *The Godey's Lady's Book* of May 1855, one reads that "hair is at once the most delicate and lasting of our materials, and survives us, like love. It is so light, so gentle, so escaping from the idea of death, that with a lock of hair belonging to a child or friend, we may almost look up to heaven and compare notes with the angelic nature — may almost say, 'I have a piece of thee here, not unworthy of thy being now.' "[64] Don would have continued working, but he would have written his correspondence on black-edged mourning stationery and when making calls would have announced himself with a mourning card edged in black.

Mourning was characterized not only by somberness but by seclusion and stillness. The bereaved withdrew from the world; they retired from active life. Their social metabolism dropped to zero. They did not form associations with other bereaved; they did not make statements to the news media;

they did not petition their government, nor did their government recruit them as celebrity endorsers. The bereaved, assuming they were of the upper or middle class, were not expected to pursue their own interests. Other people did that for them. This seclusion may have reflected their society's anxieties about death: the Ngaju aren't the only people to think of it as contaminating. But our ancestors' mourning habits also served a psychological purpose. They gave the bereaved the liberty to do nothing but attend to their loss: to sigh, to weep, to stare into space remembering. For that time they became anchorites of grief, walled up in their sorrow. Freud, who understood the Victorian era better than anybody else and did more than anybody to bring it to an end, spoke of this as "the work which mourning performs."[65] The psychiatrist Erich Lindemann would later coin the term "the grief work."[66]

A curious feature of the enterprises that occupied the mourners of September 11, the ones that were meant to bring about closure, is how many of them were inherently open-ended. What, for instance, would it mean to retrieve the last piece of the last victim? Or to distribute money in a way that would leave both a firefighter's mother and the widow of the bond trader he'd died trying to save with a satisfying or comforting sense of finality? How could any memorial satisfy mourners who disagreed so bitterly about what ought to be remembered? The open-endedness has a parallel in the repetitive and inconclusive nature of so much of the war on terror: the color-coded alerts; the highly publicized arrests of master plotters whose charges are subsequently reduced or dropped for lack of evidence; the flights grounded because of the "odd" behavior of certain passengers or because someone, later revealed to be a small boy, was heard to say something "inappropriate."

Such open-endedness may be inherent in a war that is not waged against a state or an ideology but against a method of warfare. Repetitiveness and open-endedness are also hallmarks of traumatic flashbacks. But what I am reminded of most are the tasks that you read about in fairy tales, the ones that someone, a witch or a wicked stepmother, imposes on the heroine. The hair must be spun into gold; the lake must be emptied with a sieve. The point of the tasks is their impossibility. The heroine is meant to fail, either because the person who assigned the task wants to keep her in bondage or to furnish a pretext for killing her.

Yuval Neria's study of 9/11 families found that three and a half years after the attacks, 43 percent of those surveyed exhibited symptoms of "complicated grief." This is a disorder, "distinct from depression and PTSD," that is characterized by "yearning for the deceased" and "preoccupation with thoughts about the deceased that interrupt functioning." [67] In a letter to Dr. Neria, Don Goodrich wrote:

> The use of the expression "Complicated Grief" appears to me to beg the question that needs answering in the context of your research: i.e., what is it that distinguishes the grief of September 11 families from culturally normative grief following a death of natural causes. Is it the innocence of the victims, the malevolence of the attackers, the size of the population of the dead, the sud-

denness of the event, its public nature, the intense and prolonged media attention given it, or some combination of one or more of these considerations and perhaps others as well? . . . Can a condition (e.g., bereavement) that is the normal consequence of abnormal human behavior (i.e., terrorism) ever be a "mental disorder"?

For close to a year after Peter's death, Don and Sally saw a grief counselor, commuting an hour each way to her office. For Don the point of these sessions was "to define for me the normalness of my abnormality" — to be reassured that what he was feeling, and sometimes how he was acting, was not a symptom of madness. He ends his letter to Neria with a quote from Shakespeare's *Life and Death of King John*:

I am not mad: I would to heaven I were!
For then 'tis like I should forget myself:
O! If I could, what grief should I forget,
Preach some philosophy to make me mad.

The speaker is a woman who has lost her child.

Once the meaning of suffering had been revealed to us, we refused to minimize or alleviate the camp's tortures by ignoring them or harboring false illusions and entertaining artificial optimism. Suffering had become a task on which we did not want to turn our backs.

— Viktor E. Frankl, *Man's Search for Meaning*[68]

In September 1943, Viktor Frankl, a young psychiatrist and neurologist, was arrested in Vienna along with his mother, father, brother, and wife. What happened to him requires less explanation than what happened to Boethius: Frankl was a Jew; his parents, brother, and wife were Jews. The Third Reich, of which Austria had been a part since 1938, was pursuing a final solution to its Jewish question, which consisted of systematically killing those Jews under its control. (Or perhaps there is no explanation. As a guard in one of the camps once told Primo Levi, *"Hier ist kein warum."* "There is no why here.")[69] Frankl had obtained a visa to go to the United States in 1939, but unwilling to leave his aging parents behind, he had let it expire. Now he and they were taken to Theresienstadt. His father would die of starvation there. Over the next year and a half Frankl, who had been tattooed with the number 119,104, was transferred to Auschwitz and then Dachau. His mother and brother, who also had been transferred to Auschwitz, were killed there in 1944. His wife was killed at Dachau in 1945.

In *Man's Search for Meaning,* his record of his imprisonment and the book for which he is best known, Frankl doesn't mention his parents' deaths and passes lightly over his wife's, but he describes at some length the loss of the one precious thing he brought with him into the camps. This was the manuscript of a scientific text he'd been working on for some years and carried with him, rolled up in the inside pocket of his coat. On being made to strip and surrender his possessions, he tried to persuade a veteran prisoner to let him keep the book. The man heard him out, a contemptuous grin spreading across his face. Then he snarled, "Shit!" Frankl writes, "At that moment I saw the plain truth and did what marked the culminating point of the first phase of my psychological reaction: I struck out my whole former life." [70]

Such clinical reserve regarding his own suffering informs the entire book. It is not merely a literary strategy. It is a strategy of survival.

> Cold curiosity predominated even in Auschwitz, somehow detaching the mind from its surroundings, which came to be regarded with a kind of objectivity. At that time one cultivated this state of mind as a means of protection. We were anxious to know what would happen next, and what would be the consequence, for example, of our standing in the open air in the chill of late autumn, stark naked and still wet from the shower. In the next few days our curiosity evolved into surprise; surprise that we did not catch cold. [71]

In Frankl such curiosity was also a professional habit. He had been trained as a psychiatrist. Psychiatric training — at least as it was conducted in Vienna in the 1920s and 1930s, under the Freudian aegis — seeks to make the student not only more observant but also more self-conscious, on the theory that he can better identify his patient's submerged intentions by monitoring his own responses to them: the demisemiquavers of attraction, revulsion, anxiety, warmth, and pity that resound inside him as he listens to the speaker on the couch. During his imprisonment Frankl paid a lot of attention to his fellow inmates, but his primary material was himself. He understood the delusions of reprieve that the condemned are prone to, because he himself had had them, taking false hope in the robust appearance of the kapos who took newcomers off the freight cars. For the same reason he understood the giddiness that overcomes men after they have been stripped naked and shaved from head to toe and driven into a little hut containing what they are told are showers, only to discover that they are in fact showers, *only* showers, that spray them with nothing but cold water.

He understood that the inmate's initial shock gives way to apathy, because he had felt that, too, watching calmly as another doctor debrided the gangrenous black toes of a boy who had been made to stand barefoot for hours in the snow. In time he reached a stage where beatings hurt only because of the insult implicit in them. He knew that that apathy stemmed partly from the feelings of worthlessness common to men who had once been something but were now nothing — for example, the promising young clinician who had had the manuscript that constituted his life's work taken from him and then dismissed as shit.

Apathy was the prisoner's defense against the squalor and brutality of the camps, but it also could be fatal, especially when exacerbated by malnutrition. With the extinction of desire there could come the extinction of will, affect, and finally consciousness, or of its outward signs. Then one became a "Moslem." One of Frankl's mentors in the camp described this as "a man who looks miserable, down and out, sick and emaciated, and who cannot manage hard physical labor any longer." He warned Frankl, "Sooner or later, usually sooner, every 'Moslem' goes to the gas chambers."[72]

Other authors go into more detail:

The so-called *Musselmann,* as the camp language termed the prisoner who was giving up and was given up by his comrades, no longer had room in his consciousness for the contrasts good or bad, noble or base, intellectual or unintellectual. He was a staggering corpse, a bundle of physical functions in its last convulsions.[73]

They became indifferent to everything around them. They excluded themselves from all relations to their environment. If they could still move around, they did so in slow motion, without bending their knees. They shivered since their body temperature usually fell below 98.7 degrees. Seeing them from afar, one had the impression of seeing Arabs praying. This image was the origin of the term used at Auschwitz for people dying of malnutrition: Muslims.[74]

To become a Moslem was to undergo a psychic and spiritual death as a prelude to a physical one. "The divine spark," Primo Levi writes of the Moslems, "is dead within them."[75] Frankl understood that there was nothing he could do to guarantee his physical survival, but there were measures he could take to keep from becoming one of those walking corpses. A Moslem was a person whose consciousness had been crushed, and so one had to struggle to keep one's consciousness intact, even through the marginal exercise of tallying the isolated pleasures of the week: a ladle of soup from the bottom of the pot, where it was thick with peas; the chance to delouse before bed; a glimpse of a sunset. "As the inner life of the prisoner tended to become more intense," Frankl writes, "he also experienced the beauty of art and nature as never before."[76] I find this the most startling sentence in *Man's Search for Meaning,* and perhaps the most terrible.

A more strenuous exercise in recollection was the one by which Frankl set out to reconstruct his lost manuscript, scribbling its key phrases on scraps of paper as they came back to him. Even as he deployed his consciousness retrospectively, he was also training it on his present environment. The book is evidence of that. Like other firsthand accounts of the camps, *Man's Search for Meaning* turns observation into an act of survival. The reader understands that seeing — and making sense of what he saw — was the author's way of staying alive in a world so inimical that the automatic response to it was to shut one's eyes.

Observation was also a moral act. The goal of the death camps was to kill their inmates after extracting whatever value could be extracted from them, though in actuality the last increment of value was gouged out posthumously, in the form of the victims' gold teeth. Maybe "kill" is the wrong word. Survivors note that in the camps it was forbidden to refer to the dead as corpses. One could be beaten for that. The term of preference was *figuren,* "dolls" or "figures."[77] A human being can be killed, and so can an animal, but neither can be made into a figure. That can happen only to a Moslem.

The Moslem, then, represented an essential stage in the industrial process by which humans were transformed into figures. He was an ex–human being in the same way that a figure was an ex–living one. Perhaps he embodied the true

purpose of the *Lager* — the camp — system: a living corpse
that didn't protest when it was beaten and made no outcry
when it was finally disanimated in the gas chambers. It was
Goebbels who boasted that Nazi politics was "the art of
making possible what seems impossible."[78] In addition, the
Moslem may have represented the Nazis' hideous practical
joke on their Jewish captives. What more apt a torture could
one inflict on a people who worshipped consciousness than
to cut it out of them like some rotting vestigial organ? And
if this was true, how could a man like Frankl more effectively thwart his tormentors than by refusing to become one
of their hollowed-out automata?

Automata: along with consciousness, the Moslems had
given up their will. Most prisoners did this to a degree; it
was inevitable. The great stones of camp routine — waking,
working, eating, shitting, delousing — were fitted together
so closely that they permitted virtually no space for individual choice. Whatever choices the individual might make
could be negated in an instant by the choices of others. This
was brought home during the initial process of selection, a
process that suggests a demonic version of the Last Judgment. On entering the camp, new inmates passed before an
SS man who bade them turn either right or left.

> Somebody whispered to me that to be sent to the
> right side would mean work, the way to the left
> being for the sick and those incapable of work,
> who would be sent to a special camp. I just waited
> for things to take their course, the first of many
> such times to come. My haversack weighed me
> down a bit to the left, but I made an effort to walk

upright. The SS man looked me over, appeared to hesitate, then put both his hands on my shoulders. I tried very hard to look smart, and he turned my shoulders very slowly until I faced right, and I moved over to that side.[79]

Yet at critical junctures in his imprisonment, Frankl exercised free will. On at least one occasion he did so even when it seemed to fly in the face of survival. In the closing months of the war another inmate invited him to join him in an escape. Frankl agreed. Before the break, however, he made a final round of his patients in sick bay. Most of them were ill with typhus, and all he had to treat them with was a pathetically small quantity of aspirin. As he knelt over one of them, the only other Austrian in the group, the man asked him, "You too are getting out?" His voice was tired, and the look he gave Frankl was tragic. Frankl completed his rounds in an agony of guilt.

> Suddenly I decided to take fate into my own hands for once. I ran out of the hut and told my friend that I could not go with him. As soon as I had told him with finality that I had made up my mind to stay with my patients, the unhappy feeling left me. I did not know what the following days would bring, but I had gained an inward peace that I had never experienced before. I returned to the hut, sat down on the boards at my countryman's feet and tried to comfort him.[80]

The escape was aborted. Before they could try again, the camp was visited by a delegation from the International Red

Cross, which announced that all inmates were under its protection. Escaping was now beside the point. That night the SS began loading prisoners onto trucks, telling them that they were being transported to Switzerland to be exchanged for German POWs. At the last moment Frankl was left off the convoy. The trucks rumbled off without him. In the night, in a tumult of gunfire, the camp was liberated. Later Frankl learned that the prisoners who had been evacuated for Switzerland had in fact been taken to another camp. There their custodians had barricaded them inside huts and set the huts on fire. They had burned to death.

The Moslem in the death camps had no reason for living. Many prisoners who were better off had none except life itself. They wanted nothing more than to stay alive. To do so they would violate any contract of dignity or decency. The more altruistic extended their efforts to their friends. The more broken became kapos or *Sonderkommando,* members of the "special squad" that ran the gas chambers and crematoriums, for which service they were granted a few more months of life. Beyond life there was the common goal of avoiding suffering. It was a nonsensical goal, since suffering was the fetid air of the camps, which one took in with every breath.

But what else was there? Much of what sustained Frankl was his sense of responsibility as a physician. This was what kept him from joining his friend's escape attempt, just as earlier it had caused him to volunteer to work with typhus patients, which even his colleagues dreaded as a virtual death sentence. His other purpose was to be reunited with his wife. They were young and newly married, and he thought of her often during the long, silent marches to the work site, visualizing her so intently that he seemed to see her face amid the fading stars in the predawn sky and conducting an entire conversation with her in the privacy of his thoughts even as a man farther up the line stumbled and fell, bringing down the men behind him, and a guard rushed over to ply his whip on them all. "But soon my soul found its way back from the prisoner's existence to another world, and I resumed talk with my loved one," Frankl writes. "I asked her questions, and she answered; she questioned me in return, and I answered." [81]

Only after this passage does Frankl tell the reader what he subsequently learned: that at the time of their imagined conversation, his wife was dead. He does it in an offhand manner that suggests either callousness or a weight of grief so immense that it can only be borne briefly; then it must be set down, and the one it belongs to must walk away. Someone might say that his exalted feelings meant nothing because they were directed toward an object that no longer existed. A crueler Boethius — or one who was a more slavish disciple of Plato's — might have dismissed Frankl's wife as a secondary or inferior good, a good that had been taken away. Perhaps Frankl is answering such arguments when he writes:

> I did not know whether my wife was alive, and I had no means of knowing...; but at that moment it ceased to matter. There was no need for me to know; nothing could touch the strength of my love, my thoughts, and the image of my beloved. Had I known then that my wife was dead, I think that I would still have given myself, un-

disturbed by that knowledge, to the contemplation of her image, and that my mental conversation
with her would have been just as vivid and just as
satisfying.[82]

Like Boethius, Frankl finds value in what cannot be taken
away. Chief among those things, he says, is meaning. Its
permanence arises from the fact that it is not located in its
objects — to an unbeliever a cross is only two pieces of wood
tacked together at right angles, and to the men who drove
her into the gas chamber Frankl's wife was only a future
"figure" — nor solely in its subjects — those who assign
meaning to one thing while denying it to another — but in
the psychic space between subject and object. Meaning can,
however, be forfeited, as the Moslems forfeited it. It may be
the most precious of the treasures they gave up.

Frankl believes that the search for meaning is the winding stem of human existence, a force as primary as sex or
aggression. One can derive meaning from actions or experience, from the things one does in the present (or wants to do
in the future) or from the things one did in the past. To find
meaning in the experience of many years before is one of the
consolations of old age. In the camps, though, there was no
freedom of action, and memory was an ambiguous gift that
reminded people of all they had lost. Boethius writes that
"in all adversity of fortune, the most wretched kind is once
to have been happy."[83] And so people discovered another
source of meaning: It was their suffering. "When a man
finds that it is his destiny to suffer, he will have to accept his
suffering as his task: his single and unique task." What is the
right way to suffer? Frankl doesn't specify, though he cites

with approval both men who laughed at their misfortune and men who wept at it. If he thinks that the task was mandated by God, he doesn't say so.

Boethius would have spoken of Fate, and against it he would have held up Providence, or pointed up at it, as a man on a blasted and denuded planet might point up at the stars. There, he would say, is where the meaning is, meaning for Boethius occurring only in the singular since it comes from a single good, a single God. Frankl speaks in the plural: of meanings, of destinies. He believes that each human being is responsible for discovering the one that is his. His use of the plural reflects his experience in the camps, where people who had been pressed by suffering into an anonymous, claylike mass kept reverting back to individuals, even when it meant that they would suffer more. It reflects a kind of propriety, for who could attribute the obscene scrawl of Auschwitz — a finger painting done in blood and shit and ashes — to a divine hand? Frankl is not a theologian; he's a psychiatrist and a moral philosopher. He is concerned with human beings and what they need to remain human in an environment designed to turn them into figures. And noting the ingenuity of his fellow prisoners, their ability to turn the camp's discards into tools or clothing, he declares that when everything else is gone, suffering itself remains, the dull stone that one clutches to one's heart and calls treasure.

In August 2004 Sally Goodrich was approached by the parents of Rush Filson, a childhood friend of Peter's who was now a marine major serving in Afghanistan. In Logar province, forty miles south of Kabul, he'd met a schoolteacher who was trying to collect supplies for his pupils. The man had impressed Filson, and his parents wondered whether Sally, who worked for a school board, might be able to help out. It was just before the third anniversary of Peter's death, and she had a strong feeling that it was something he would have wanted her to do. "It was a door opening," she says. "We just followed Peter's lead."

She and Don formed the Peter M. Goodrich Memorial Foundation and began raising money to build a new school in Logar. It would be a school for girls. This is a risky enterprise in Afghanistan. Under the Taliban, girls' schools were banned as un-Islamic, and the few that have opened since they were driven from power have been targets of violence. (Early in 2006 Taliban insurgents beheaded the principal of one girls' school while forcing his wife to watch.) Sally raised most of the money locally, relying on small donations. Students at the prep school Peter had attended held a bake sale. A church contributed its Christmas Eve offering. Some Eagle Scouts collected two hundred backpacks filled with school supplies. At the end of 2005 she had $160,000. That and an additional $136,000 (some of it from Peter's estate and the rest from contributions to the foundation) were enough to construct a twenty-five-room K–8 school serving some five hundred students.

Sally made her first trip to Afghanistan in April 2005. She's been there four times since. The word that keeps recurring in her descriptions of the country is "biblical." It encompasses the jagged, parched terrain; the baked-mud buildings that seem to grow out of the earth; the grave, turbaned men bound by an intractable code of honor. Among the Pashtun majority, that code is known as Pashtunwali.

Biblical, too, is the country's grinding, unreasoning violence. Afghanistan has been at war almost constantly for thirty years. One and a half million of its people have been killed. It is tragically poor and sedimented with corruption. Sally complains that the amount of money spent on the foreign contract soldiers in President Hamid Karzai's security detail surpasses the total outlay for humanitarian projects in the country. In spite of these soldiers' presence, and that of some 42,000 U.S. and NATO troops,[84] Afghanistan remains dangerous, especially for foreigners. In 2007 the Taliban and Al Qaeda were said to be offering $10,000 for a video of a foreigner's killing and $20,000 for a foreigner captured alive. Sally's e-mail messages from Kabul calmly note bombings and rocket attacks. When she was first in country, every time her convoy approached a checkpoint, her Afghan hosts would have to remind her to take off her sunglasses and cover her hair so as not to be recognized as a Westerner. Since then she has learned to do it automatically.

Her official contact is Shahmahmood Miakhel, a former deputy minister of the interior who is now an adviser to the United Nations Assistance Mission in Afghanistan. It's through his intercession and (given the fate of much of the foreign aid that enters Afghanistan) hawkeyed vigilance that the school in Logar was built and a second one is now being planned for Kunar province. He represents the best of the new generation of Afghan officials: upright, enlightened, and compulsively hardworking. He spent the years of the Russian occupation and the ensuing civil war in exile, first as a refugee in Pakistan, later in the United States.

When Shahmahmood was still working in the government, Sally would travel with him in fast-moving armored vehicles and be surrounded by petitioners the moment they came to a stop. Casual visits became state occasions, accompanied by speeches and imams' blessings. Children showered them with flower petals. Shahmahmood had trained teachers before entering the government, and on an early visit to Logar's old school, he startled and delighted Sally by conducting an impromptu art class. The building was grim and overcrowded, and many of the classrooms lacked desks or chairs. In the warmer months the younger children did their lessons in tents set up in a courtyard.

The next time she went to Logar, it was for the dedication of the school that had been built with her funds. It looked, she thought, like a Comfort Inn, but one that had no heat or plumbing. All the doorknobs were inexplicably broken. Still, it was roomy and clean, and the girls no longer had to sit outside. Sally brought the backpacks and school supplies the Scouts back home had donated, unimaginable largesse to children who might not have their own pencils. She also brought a gift for the principal: an English-Arabic Qur'an like the one Peter used to read. It was an object of immense interest to her hosts. Many of them didn't know that the Qur'an existed in any language apart from Arabic, the language in which the angel Gabriel is said to have dictated it to Mohammed. And they were moved to hear that their guest's son had read it faithfully, with scholarly attention, especially because they knew how he had died.

If Shahmahmood is Sally's facilitator in Afghanistan, Seraj Wardak is her protector and her liaison to its ordinary people. He's a former mujahideen commander and "ruffian" who fought on several sides in the civil war, switching allegiances according to what he thought Pashtunwali required of him on the occasion. Both the Taliban and the Americans jailed him arbitrarily and arbitrarily set him free. Now he's the khan — Sally calls him "the commander, mayor, Pied Piper, father of all" — of a mountain village in Wardak, the province adjoining Logar. Although he has exchanged fighting for securing development money and caring for his widowed and orphaned constituents, he remains an object of interest and suspicion to both the Karzai government and the insurgents. His independence makes them nervous.

Once, after insurgents burned a nearby school, Seraj made the villagers promise to personally guard the building. To date the school is standing. Under the terms of Pashtunwali, he is absolutely responsible for the safety of his guests. When, on her second morning in his village, Sally, exhausted from travel and hobbled by her chador, fell on one of its stony footpaths and badly bruised her face, he was livid. "This is werry, werry bad, Sarrrah," she says, imitating him. "All you do is fall." He had failed to protect her.

"He'd had a little interpreter right at my elbow watching over me," she says. "I was just feeling a little too suffocated by the hospitality, and this poor kid ended getting chewed up because I was unsteady emotionally. 'All you ever do is fall.' And I'm sure that's true. My knees were weak that very first voyage. I remember telling myself after that, 'Sally, whatever you do, do not fall.' "

By the time her first visit to Afghanistan was over, Sally had come to trust this man completely, but after returning to the United States she discovered that in the late 1990s he had been involved with the Taliban. In an indirect way he had been part of the force that had killed her son, part of a vengeful, demon-haunted religiosity that would raise human beings to heaven on a tower of corpses. When she next went to Wardak, it was close to the fourth anniversary of Peter's death. Seraj was running for parliament. Sally understood that it would be disastrous for him to be seen squiring an American, and so she spent the next few days in conditions similar to those in which most Afghan women spend their entire lives — sequestered in a guesthouse, "in purdah."

On the night of September 10, she got a chance to see Seraj, and she asked him why he had joined the Taliban. He answered her calmly, without apologizing or defending himself. He simply told her the story of his actions eight years before, when he had gone from serving the government of President Burhanuddin Rabbani to serving its enemies. "There was a moment in time when his honor and the honor of his tribe was challenged," Sally says, summing up. "Seraj did what he did to right an offense and restore that honor." His conversion had nothing to do with ideology. "Seraj is religious without being . . . He's not going to make it to hajj; he's not going to pray five times a day. It's more like he watches out for widows and orphans, and he does what he has to do. Initially he thought the Taliban would offer relief from the slaughter and the insanity of the civil conflict."

As it turned out, they didn't. A while after he threw in his lot with them, they imprisoned him for the offense of trimming his beard.

Sally says, "After he told me, I felt no sense of betrayal. He'd provided so well for my needs and my security. When you're in Afghanistan and see how fluid that situation is, you realize that people have to hedge their bets. Seraj's life and mine were changed in different ways by the same set of circumstances."

It's easy to understand the excitement and passion Sally feels about Afghanistan. You feel passionate about places where people live on a precipice, clinging to life with all their strength. What used to puzzle me, though, was the ease she says she feels there. She's blunt, forceful, and charismatic, quintessentially American, and in Afghanistan she must have to hold herself in check every minute. Women there aren't just veiled but invisible, and their invisibility is enforced. Under the Taliban they risked being beaten if they ventured outside without a burka, a garment that is best described as a body bag for the living. Many women still wear them. A necessary addition to Sally's school was a wall high enough to keep the girls concealed from passersby. (Some pupils' families asked that they also be driven to and from school by van in deference to religious sensitivities, but Sally quickly learned that that would be impossible unless she first supplied a van for the students at a neighboring boys' school.) But being invisible doesn't free women from having to do much of the hard work. They must be as aridly stoical as their men, enduring loss upon loss without weeping.

Perhaps they are even more stoical, since in Afghan culture men are given other ways of expressing feeling. They pray in public, prostrating themselves before God and their fellow men. They fire their guns often and exuberantly. And they dance together in the martial circle dance called the *attan,* a dance so physically demanding that participants sometimes faint in mid-stride.

This is the country where Peter's murder was planned.

One day, after a visit to the school in Logar, Sally's party stopped in a village that had an apple orchard. Their hosts laid rugs on the ground, and they sat down to eat. There were apples, of course, and corn, a coarse variety that would be fed to cattle in the States. Sally was feeling ill and took only a few bites. When she put down the corn, the man beside her picked it up and began to eat it. It was, someone told her, a gesture of great respect. Like other Afghans, this man had been touched by his country's bloodletting. He owned a gas station, where he worked with his twenty-two-year-old son. One day a car full of strangers had pulled in and taken fuel. They may have been Taliban or mujahideen; so many people in Afghanistan go about with guns. The son asked them for payment. They shot him dead. Then they drove off.

"A friend of mine says that Afghanistan attracts mercenaries, missionaries, misfits, and the brokenhearted — just those four categories," Sally explains. "And if you go to Afghanistan, you fall into at least one of them. I'm one of the brokenhearted ones. When I'm in Afghanistan, I'm in Peter mode. I'm fortunate to be there. I'm fortunate to be where people are good to me. They're so warm. What a great place to be heartbroken. Anyone who's in pain should have the experience of being plunked down in a place where everyone is heartbroken."

CHAPTER 3

The Purpose of the Blindfold

What Is Just?

Before there was justice, there was only vengeance, the unmediated reciprocity of offense and counter-offense, outrage and retribution. If your neighbor stole some of your sheep, you felt entitled to steal some back. If he killed one of your children, you killed one of his (if you didn't decide to take care of the neighbor himself). Your other neighbors might frown on theft and murder, might consider them immoral or at least unseemly, but they wouldn't interfere as long as they didn't feel personally injured. It was all personal back then, the fuming intimacy of grievance. In time people realized how treacherous such intimacy could be and began to want a little distance. Good fences make good neighbors. From the time of the Code of Hammurabi, justice did more than specify which acts were criminal and how they were to be punished. It made society a buffer between the wrongdoer and his victim, whom it now had the responsibility of protecting or, if its protective measures failed, avenging. Society became the victim's guardian; beyond that, his surrogate. In the United States today criminal trials are designated "*The State v. . . .*"

The substitution has an obvious value. Absent some intervention, vengeance might burn on indefinitely, consuming not just the original combatants but their children and grandchildren. And vengeance doesn't just propagate vertically, across generations, but laterally, through the surrounding population. It makes no exception for neutral bystanders. Stripped of their ideology and profiteering, what are Ulster and Bosnia, Sierra Leone and Iraq (factoring in the prior destruction of most of the last country's institutions and thousands of its people by a foreign occupier), but vendettas that jumped the fuel break and became firestorms, sucking everything into themselves, no matter how old or young or inoffensive or defenseless, using babies as tinder and children barely big enough to carry a gun as soldiers, prizing such soldiers above all others because they are too young to repress their cruelest impulses? In this manner, entire societies regress into a state of maddened, bereaved childhood from which they may never emerge. But once the community steps in to break the cycle of outrage and retribution, it imposes a code of justice that is at least ostensibly fair and objective, as a code must be if people are to accept it. Under that code, outrage and retribution become crime and punishment. Society is the sole judge of the first and the sole administrator of the second.

Vengeance is focused on the value of victims and the needs of survivors. Its rules permit the retaliatory killing of people who are technically blameless, as long as they are related to the perpetrator and their social status is on a par with the decedent's, as in some imaginary chess game in which the capture of a black bishop can be balanced only by the capture of a white one. But justice, in order to pass as objective, must concentrate on the crime while more or less ignoring the victim. Rather, it must turn the victim into an ethereal abstraction — a Platonic, statistical victim. Justice must fix a penalty for sheep theft, say, without considering whether the sheep in question belongs to a rich man or a poor one; it's just somebody's sheep. It must set a punishment for murder that remains the same regardless of the victim. (Of course justice, like everything else, plays out differently in practice than in theory.) The intention is to arrive at a system so nicely calibrated as to reckon the precise weights of murder with or without lethal intent; robbery armed or unarmed; fraud or kidnapping or arson. The system is supposed to combine the neutrality of a machine with the discernment of God, and it's fitting that the modern system of justice came into being during the Enlightenment, an age that envisioned God as a geometer or watchmaker. But victims — real victims as opposed to Platonic ones — are neither gods nor machines. And although justice purports to do what it does in their name and to function as the perfect instrument of their outrage, victims feel other things as well: grief, shame, even, at times, sympathy for the ones who injured them. These may be beyond justice's power to express.

> *We'd heard the announcement on the radio that people weren't allowed to leave their homes, and we thought, "Okay, no problem." We heard gunshots around the neighborhood; we heard yelling. The house was surrounded by soldiers. I saw the com-*

manding officer; he was one of our neighbors. He beat down the door. He said, "You, K." — my husband's name was K. — "what are you doing here when everybody else is outside being checked by security? Come out with your identity card." My husband went outside with his card, and then from April 7 till the fourteenth they held him at the roadblock, right nearby. So he would have seen them torturing other men and young people, young boys. They cut off men's genitals and fed them to the dogs. They hacked people to death with machetes. He watched all of it. And at two or three one morning it was his misfortune to be tortured, too. He died on the fifteenth, very early in the morning.

Not "he was killed" but "he died." Rwandans often used that innocuous phrase when speaking of loved ones they'd lost in the genocide. I took it for an attempt at normalization. During World War II the Nazis committed most of their crimes away from eyewitnesses, herding their victims to remote killing grounds or sequestering them in death camps whose function was betrayed only by the pillars of smoke that rose from their chimneys. Afterward it was possible — if not particularly credible — for people to say they hadn't known. In Rwanda, though, the killing took place in public. Everybody saw it. You had only to look out through your garden gate. All over Kigali bodies lay piled on the roadside like sacks of refuse until, like refuse, they were carted away by garbage trucks. Hutu office girls in white dresses picked their way to work between spreading puddles of blood. The Canadian general Roméo Dallaire describes seeing one such girl slip and fall. She got up quickly, but still, he writes, "it was as if someone had painted her body and her dress with a dark red oil. She became hysterical looking at it, and the more she screamed, the more attention she drew."[1] What need was there for anyone to be more explicit? I hadn't been in Rwanda long before I was taking it for granted that when anyone spoke of a death ten years before, he meant a death by violence. Murder had become a natural death.

> *On the eighteenth, at nine in the morning, a group of soldiers and militiamen came to my house. They told me, "Give us the money your husband left you." My husband's body was being dragged through the street, no one had buried him. They formed mountains, the bodies of all the men and boys they'd killed. And I said, "I don't have any money. We don't have any money." They carried me from the living room and took me into a bedroom; my mother-in-law was shut up in another room. And from that day until the end of the war, the soldiers raped me. They were at it day and night, day and night, all of them. They came in all together, they dropped their pants at the same moment, and they raped me, jostling each other. There was always another group waiting in the living room. If one man left, another one came in to take his place, one after another. In the fifth month of my pregnancy, I aborted. They took me to the hospital for the abortion, and they told me, "We killed your brothers and sisters with machetes, but you, we're just going to*

rape you till you're dead." That whole time I was
naked; I never had clothes on. I was completely swol-
len. I had infections. I kept vomiting. I couldn't even
cry because I wanted to die and I couldn't die.

In the midst of violence, especially if that violence is prolonged, a relationship sometimes forms between perpetrators and victims. It is not a true relationship, in the sense of a
free association of individuals, only the simulacrum of one
or, more accurately, a parody. It may come into being because the victims implicitly understand that their survival
depends on winning the goodwill of their captors or because even killers — maybe *especially* killers — need to feel
that they are good people and will seek validation of their
goodness from the very ones they are about to kill. It may
simply be that when human beings are forced together over
time, they fall by inertia into the lulling rhythms and proto-
cols of society. For such reasons a group of soldiers and militiamen might interrupt months of rape and sexual torture
to take their victim to the hospital for an abortion. It's startling to realize that at the height of the genocide, Rwanda's
hospitals were still functioning, treating old people with
pneumonia, children with broken arms. And, of course, de-
livering babies.

What was the meaning of that gesture? On one level the
abortion was a continuation of the violence these men were
inflicting on their captive, an intensification of it, a rape
committed in the deepest parts of her body. As a Catholic,
the woman would experience it as a murder of the life within
her, of her husband's life, because it was his baby they were

killing; they were killing him all over again. And at the same time she would know that she was being spared, since it wasn't uncommon for *génocidaires* to terminate the pregnancies of Tutsi women in other ways. And so at some point in the procedure, perhaps only for a moment, she might feel a tremor of gratitude, and in recollection this gratitude would be the most terrible thing of all.

> *If I go before the court, if I tell them what happened, if I say what was done to my body, people will mock me. All I want to say is that they made me suffer. I want to tell the story of my suffering. And I want the one who raped me to understand that he tortured me, that he's guilty. I want him to understand what he did — freely, without being forced. I want him to admit his blame.*

The woman who told me this story was named Anastasie K.[2] She was forty-five, with a handsome oval face that had begun to soften with age and very large dark eyes that looked even larger because of the dark circles beneath them. The whole time she spoke, she held my eyes with hers. Once she had been a girl on one of the thousands of haystack-shaped hills that make up the Rwandan landscape — *Rwanda, pays des milles collines* (Rwanda, land of a thousand hills) — destined for a life of farming beans and sorghum. Against all expectations, she had gotten an education and become a secretary at a government ministry in Kigali. She had married, borne children. And then the life she had won for herself had been torn asunder, and she had been turned into a sort of domestic animal, naked and speechless, kept alive only to be abused until it was time to kill her. It seemed a miracle that she could speak. But she could, and could write as well; she had a journal that she had written about her ordeal. "Each page," she said, "is a thousand tears."

I met Anastasie at a women's center that provided counseling to other survivors of rape and sexual torture, many of whom were sick with AIDS. In this regard, she considered herself fortunate. As a result of what had been done to her, she could no longer perform any kind of physical labor, not even sweep a floor, but she didn't have the virus and could look forward to a long life. Perhaps it's better to say that she could anticipate a normal life span, which for a Rwandan woman in 2004 was forty-seven years.[3] I had been referred to Anastasie by someone in the States, and when our interview was over she told me, "When you see David, you must remember to tell him how fat I've gotten." The pride in her voice took me aback until I remembered the possible connotations of thinness.

The clinic was a complex of low, gray cinder block buildings decorated inside with the drawings of the clients and their children — crude productions of crayon, glitter, and construction paper mounted on the walls with yellowing tape. In one building a large woman with a jagged scar on her forehead greeted me with a sardonic roll of her eyes. "You've come to look at the woman with AIDS," she said. I hadn't come to look at her. I didn't know she had AIDS, and if I had, I wouldn't have considered that any reason to look at her, given how prevalent AIDS had become among a generation of Rwandan women. Still, I turned away in shame. My whole time in Rwanda, shame was what I felt most.

When I left the clinic a few hours later, a group of women were dancing in the yard. They were welcoming some visitors from a Canadian aid organization. The dancers' movements were fierce and strutting; they held their arms out from their sides, their fingers splayed and quivering, and lifted their knees high, like wading birds. Drums sounded. The women dipped, took a step forward, a step to the side, a step back, each pent inside her square of an invisible grid drawn on the red earth. Some of them looked very old, their faces seamed, their eyes dim. Their limbs might have been made of twisted rope. One woman had only one leg, on which she hopped unceasingly, as if trying to pound a stake into the ground. Up and down she leapt, grinning and triumphant and terrible. I suppose she was trying to proclaim victory over her disfigurement, but to me she seemed like a reproach to the world of the whole.

A FEW WEEKS before this, at a cocktail party at the American Club in Kigali, I'd been introduced to an American who worked for a Christian conflict management organization. He was running reconciliation workshops. "Reconciliation" was a word you heard a great deal in Rwanda. You heard it from government officials, including employees of the National Unity and Reconciliation Commission, and the spokespersons of victims' groups, from *ex-détenus* (former prisoners) and, more rarely, from *rescapés* (survivors). You heard it from taxi drivers. Depending on your point of view, the unanimity with which the word emerged under certain lines of questioning could be moving or creepy. I

was curious as to how one would go about teaching reconciliation in a country that was already pursuing it as single-
mindedly as China had once pursued five-year plans. My
acquaintance said that his workshops were based on scrip-
ture and geared toward local pastors, who were then supposed to pass on what they'd learned to their
congregations.

"Which is what?" I asked. "I mean, what are you teaching them?"

Insects were keening in the brush. I had walked a half
mile up the steep slope of Avenue des Grands Lacs in the
heat of the late afternoon and was disheveled and sweaty,
while the man I was talking with looked as well pressed as a
cruise ship captain. But when I asked my question, his face
flushed. Maybe he thought I was trying to start something.
"We tell them to think of Rwanda in terms of a family
quarrel."

OF COURSE RWANDANS needed to reconcile. Ten years
before, they had suffered a genocide comparable to the destruction of the Jews of Europe. Hundreds of thousands of
Tutsi and moderate Hutu had been killed; thousands more
had been raped, tortured, maimed, made destitute. Because
these horrors had been perpetrated by members of the Hutu
majority, ostensibly in the name of their ethnic brethren,
surviving Tutsi viewed almost all Hutu with bitterness and
suspicion. But the official rhetoric treated reconciliation as
something that could be brought about by fiat, hurried
along by government bureaus and pastoral committees.

And it skipped over certain essential preliminaries. Before Rwanda's people could reconcile, some of them would have to be held accountable for the crimes they had committed against the others and make penance for them. "Held accountable," "make penance": the very insufficiency of these phrases suggested how hard it would be to do either. For their part, the survivors needed assurance that they wouldn't be victimized again. The soldiers of the current government constituted one kind of assurance, but one that was only partial and provisional; unaided force always is. True reconciliation depended on an alliance of force and principle, on justice. Such justice would have to satisfy the genocide's victims without irreparably alienating the majority population, which feared that, as administered by a regime that was dominated by Tutsi, justice would turn out to be nothing more than revenge. At civil rights demonstrations in the United States, we used to hear the chant, "No justice, no peace." In Rwanda, at last, it made sense.

From a purely material perspective, other needs were more pressing. Rwanda was poor, and nobody there was poorer than the rescapés. They had lost everything; looters had stripped the very roofs from their houses. (Those corrugated metal roofs had been one of the currencies of the genocide: easy to pry off, easy to sell or trade, and relatively easy to carry. During their mass exodus to Congo at the war's end, many Hutu refugees brought along the roofs they had looted from Tutsi houses and used them to pay their way across the border.)[4] Thousands of Tutsi women were dying of AIDS, which the rape squads had deployed as a weapon of delayed biological warfare.[5] There were families — and this was a country where families were big and endlessly ramified, everybody related to everybody else — made up entirely of children, the older children caring for the younger ones, valiantly, hopelessly. What could these children know about raising children? Their parents had died before they could teach them.

And yet it often seemed that what survivors wanted most was justice. In Rwanda the word had even more connotations than it does elsewhere. A spokeswoman for Avega, the Association of Widows of the Genocide, defined it as being able to bury your own dead,[6] a right especially resonant in a country where the most common memorial was a heap of unclaimed bones.[7] Many of these crushingly impoverished people equated justice with financial reparations. As one widow put it, "How can I forgive when my livelihood was destroyed and I cannot even pay for the schooling of my children?"[8] But beyond that I sensed a widespread desire for something that resisted definition. It was as if, in the back of their minds, the survivors held the idea of a Platonic justice, of which all known instrumentalities — all laws, statutes, courts, tribunals, settlements, penalties — were only shadows. "What I need is justice itself," Anastasie told me. "True justice."

I thought I understood this, and not just because what had happened in Rwanda suggested a Platonic archetype of *in*justice, a crime so immense as to make any response to it seem pathetically, even insultingly, inadequate. Hannah Arendt was speaking of genocide when she said that we "are unable to forgive what [we] cannot punish [and] we are unable to punish what has turned out to be unforgivable."[9] What all justice does, however cruelly or inequitably, is to impose order on the pandemonium of acts, declaring that certain of those acts are transgressions, warranting particular kinds of punishment. Ten years after the genocide, Rwanda was in many ways an orderly society, with passable roads and fairly reliable water and electric grids. But beneath that order lay the memory of moral chaos; maybe more than just the memory. "Do you think it is going to stop because we are safe now?" one rescapée asked a foreign observer. "So much death, so much grief, so many families wiped out, and we are to forget about it. The fire is out; but not the fear. And what about the fire inside?"[10]

Human justice is *human:* it applies to relations between human beings or between human beings and the man-made artifact of the state. The afflictions sent by God or nature don't trouble us the same way wrongs committed by other people do. The word "wrongs" is indicative, since it isn't used of nature. A tidal wave may kill a quarter of a million people and a man with a knife only one, yet it's the murderer who inspires not just horror but outrage, and it's the murderer we seek to punish.

I do not think this difference stems solely from the human capacity for malice. Adolf Eichmann appears to have sent millions to the gas chambers without feeling much of it. People know that God and nature are bigger and more powerful than they are (though in our time this knowledge may be fading). But we think of other humans as our equals, not in the social but in the creaturely sense, as beings moved by the same desires and aversions as ourselves and subject to the same laws of pain and death. Every crime shatters this equality. When one man kills another man, he declares that he is big and the other is small, is nothing. If the victim's wife and children are forced to witness this, they, too, are made nothing. When a chemical plant discharges poison gas that wipes out a village, all of its people are made nothing, and their annihilation is compounded when the officers of the chemical company are allowed to live on without consequence.

Among the things I heard during my time in Rwanda, one of the most painful was uttered almost incidentally by a rescapée in a village near Rugarama after I asked her if she believed Tutsi and Hutu could ever truly reconcile. "It is impossible," she began, and I think she meant to explain, methodically, impersonally, why this should be so. But suddenly she clutched her head and blurted, *"J'étais très abaissée."*[11] I would translate it as "I was so degraded" or "I was so abased," except the French more clearly expresses the idea of being lowered. At that moment everything that had been done to this woman snapped into focus with such clarity that I could no more stand to look at her directly than if she had been the sun.

From the state's perspective, justice has multiple functions, from ensuring that the criminal cannot harm others to deterring future wrongdoers. (When the latter is carried beyond a certain point, it becomes a form of mass terrorism, with the threat of jail or execution held at the throat of an entire suspect population.) To victims of crimes, however, or to their survivors, the purpose of justice is to restore the equality between themselves and the persons who wronged them.[12] That this equality is spiritual is evident from the fact that it may be restored even to the dead. It's precisely when justice is denied that people most long for it, even if they can only imagine the world in which it exists. Hell was invented because on earth men commit crime after crime and grow fat while their victims' children go hungry.

To assuage the survivors' need for justice — and to address the plight of some 120,000 detainees crushed inside its prisons — the Rwandan government had embarked on a legal experiment. The experiment owed something to South Africa's Truth and Reconciliation Commission and something to traditional Rwandan jurisprudence — or, really, to the *idea* of such jurisprudence as it had come down through the accounts of European civil servants and anthropologists and the stories of old people. It would dispense with most of the mechanisms of adversarial law. It would, for instance, move the settlement of the genocide from courtrooms to the villages where so much of the slaughter had actually taken place. Instead of legal professionals, the alternative system would use volunteer judges elected from the general population, contemporary counterparts of the elders who had once been the arbiters of the nation's moral life. In place of the skirmishing of rival attorneys, the impugning of witnesses, the dismantling of facts, there would be the stately unscrolling of collective memory. Who knows this man? What are his crimes? Who saw him commit them? And if, in the Western model of criminal procedure, the defendant is mostly silent, here he would have a chance — would be urged — to speak; his fate would hinge on his speaking. In a sense the new procedure would be a dialogue between the survivors and the accused, with a role, too, for the witnesses: an entire country telling the story of its wound and coming to agreement about who and what had made it. This agreement would be the prelude to the wound's healing. That, at least, was what was supposed to happen. The name for this experiment was *gacaca* (ga-CHA-cha), a Kinyarwanda word meaning "lawn" or "grass."

• • •

KIGALI IS SHAPED like a bowl, or rather a group of bowls, the hills forming a rim around a central basin. As in other cities, the heights belong to the wealthy, while the low ground is occupied by the poor. The streets in that part of town are unpaved and ungraded. They yaw and pitch and subside into craters that might have been made by bombs. Four-wheel drive is obligatory. Amid the omnipresent red dust, even new structures resemble ruins. (One exception was an incongruous glass-fronted office tower that was said to be the property of Félicien Kabuga, a prosperous génoci-daire[13] who fled Rwanda when the Rwandan Patriotic Army, or RPA, took Kigali; he is rumored to be hiding in Kenya.)[14] The combination of topography and history yields a meta-phor: the city as mass grave, as offering bowl filled with bones and blood.

Yet at the time of my visit, Kigali was a boomtown. For this it could thank the genocide. Everywhere, I saw the Land Cruisers and Pajeros of the donors: UNICEF, Oxfam, the World Food Programme, Save the Children, Christian Aid (whose vehicles bore the slogan "We believe in life be-fore death"). The aid organizations had snapped up the choicest real estate in the Nyarugenge district, big walled compounds shaded by violet-blossomed jacaranda and pa-trolled by guards with AK-47s. The sidewalks outside were often planted with a surreally purple ground cover whose triangular leaves made me think of the tips of devils' tails — cartoon devils, maybe. The journalists had spilled out of the InterContinental and the Mille Collines into the cheaper hotels, like the one I was staying in on the Rue du Deputé

Kamuzinzi, which had no fax service or Internet connection and power that blinked out several times a day.

Rwanda was still mostly Catholic, but ten years after the atrocities, the old loyalty was frayed. Too many clergy had collaborated. The UN's ICTR, or International Criminal Tribunal for Rwanda had charged the former rector of Christ-Roi College in Butare province with "genocide, conspiracy to commit genocide, and crimes against humanity for murder and extermination." [15] A priest in Kibuye was accused of having murdered two thousand Tutsi by bulldozing the church in which they had taken refuge. [16] (The holocaust was ecumenical, the list of génocidaires also including a prominent Seventh-Day Adventist minister.) [17] As a result, Rwandans were migrating to the *nouvelles églises* (new churches), which were intimate, boisterous, and egalitarian and whose doctrines stressed not just the remission of sins but the sloughing off of the self. Well, who wanted to stay the same person who had seen his sisters gang-raped and sawed in half and then had hidden for days beneath their corpses? [18] Who wanted to stay the same person who had committed such crimes? Given a choice between being absolved and being reborn, who wouldn't choose to be reborn? (The desire for radical self-renewal may also explain why so many Rwandans were converting to Islam, which, according to the *New York Times*, was the country's fastest-growing religion.) [19] To assist the new churches, American evangelicals had poured into the country, bearing cartons of Bibles, hymnals, and religious coloring books for the children. They were easy to spot, and not just because they were white. They were usually heavier than the aid workers, and on the whole they seemed happier. It was the evangelicals who kept telling you how much they loved the Rwandan people.

April 7, 2004, would mark the tenth anniversary of the onset of the genocide, and a number of events had been planned in commemoration. The government was holding a march through the center of Kigali, and for a while it was rumored that the UN was planning to sponsor one, too. (Given the often strained relations between the ruling Rwandan Patriotic Front, or RPF — the Rwandan Patriotic Army was its military wing — and the UN, the second march might be seen as a gesture of solidarity, even of atonement, or as one-upmanship. As it turned out, however, the UN held its commemoration at its headquarters in New York; it did not include a march.) There would be conferences and symposia. There would be concerts and art exhibits. At midday the entire nation would observe three minutes of silence. The remains of an unspecified number of victims would be unearthed from mass graves and formally reinterred on the grounds of the new genocide monument in Gisozi. On a preopening visit I had seen the rows of coffins that would receive them, stacked like crates in a warehouse but decorously covered with strips of lace. Both here and at other memorials around the country there was an ongoing controversy as to whether victims' remains ought to be kept on view or properly buried, and as a compromise the Kigali site contained a room in which the bones of hundreds of grown-ups and children were displayed behind dark glass.[20] Anyone who looked at those bones would also see his own reflection floating above them like a soul somehow tethered to the broken remnants of its former life.

Official guests would include delegates from dozens of

countries, 250 from Belgium alone; Pierre Richard Prosper, a former ICTR prosecutor now serving as the U.S. Ambassador-at-Large for War Crimes Issues; Philip Gourevitch, the author of the best-known account of the genocide; and General Dallaire, who as commanding officer of the UN's peacekeeping contingent had tried to avert the catastrophe and, failing, had stayed on to witness it. Failure and witnessing had weighed on him so heavily that since leaving Rwanda, he had on at least one occasion tried to kill himself.[21] Kofi Annan may also have been invited but chose instead to attend the UN ceremony in New York, which, all things considered, was probably a good decision. In the spring of 1994 he had been in overall charge of the UN's peacekeeping operations, in which capacity he had vetoed Dallaire's plans to intervene in the bloodletting. If the general could be seen as one of the genocide's collateral casualties, Annan could be seen as one of its many negligent stepfathers.

The world's tendency to treat the genocide as a one-time occurrence irritated many Rwandans. They reminded visitors that Hutu political parties and Hutu-led governments had been orchestrating the mass murder of Tutsi as early as 1959 — maybe not continuously, but with sufficient frequency that somebody should have spotted a trend. Instead, confronted with mounting evidence that certain elements (politicians, military officers, ideologues, street thugs) were preparing a final solution to what someone in those circles might have called "the Tutsi question" — confronted with General Dallaire's chillingly detailed intelligence of how that solution would be set in motion — the UN had not only failed to act but had barred Dallaire from acting, cutting his forces from 2,600 to 450.

There was plenty of blame to go around. One could blame the United States, which, dreading a reprise of its humiliation in Somalia the year before, had pressured the UN into withdrawing troops. One could blame France, which, having succored, equipped, and on occasion fought beside the Rwandan army through years of human rights abuses, had continued to protect the génocidaires. Reminding the world of past derelictions was something Rwanda's new leaders were very good at. The exploitation of guilt is a classic Rwandan political skill, denoted by the phrase *akibu kajya iwamungarurire* — "one makes the borrowed basket return." [22] And perhaps, knowing that anniversaries are occasions for strong feelings, including feelings of guilt, the RPF had chosen to clean up the story for foreign consumption and mark the genocide as if it were a single, bounded event that had begun on April 7, 1994, and ended that July — one hundred days in which 800,000 Tutsi and moderate Hutu were killed at approximately five times the rate at which Europe's Jews had been exterminated under the Third Reich.

A few weeks before, I had gone to a village an hour and a half from Kigali to interview a rescapée named Jeanne d'Arc M. — Joan of Arc M. One of the striking things about the country was how steadfastly it preserved certain remnants of its colonial past, particularly names. Jeanne d'Arc, Dieudonné, Anastasie, Faustin — had anybody in Belgium or France given children such names since World War II? The village was bleached and dusty, and walking through it was like walking through a faded photograph. Even the banana trees seemed leached of color. Jeanne d'Arc's house was built of dried mud and cow dung and was surprisingly cool inside. It had no windows; light streamed through open doors at the front and back. The only furniture was a bench, a low table, and three high-backed chairs. On one wall was a sampler embroidered with a Kinyarwanda phrase, "Zaburi 143:1."

Jeanne d'Arc had large, deep-set eyes that were the chief source of energy in her face, which was narrow, triangular, and distorted by tension, as if it were being pulled in several directions at once. She was forty years old but had the unlined skin of someone much younger. That and her smallness, which was exaggerated by her outsize T-shirt, gave her the look of a pinched child, a child forced to live like a grown-up in a world without protectors, and angry about it. We think of people as being aged by suffering, but I've found that the opposite is often true, perhaps because in extreme pain, as in severe illness, time seems to slow down. Ten years before, this woman had seen the genocide sweep through her village. Her husband had been killed; her in-laws had been killed; her sisters had been raped and then killed. She and her two children had survived by fleeing into the marshes, where she had hidden until RPA soldiers had rescued her. She said this matter-of-factly, but afterward I realized that she had lived in hiding for three months, amid mud and reeds, tormented by stinging insects, not knowing whether she and her children were the only Tutsi left alive. This happened often during the genocide. At a symposium in the States, I met a woman who had spent those hundred days huddled with thirty others in the tiny bathroom of an Anglican church. She, too, seemed oddly youthful.

Jeanne d'Arc lived in an isolation that was almost absolute. Apart from her children and brother, who had hidden separately in the bush, there were no other Tutsi left in the village. Her relations with her neighbors were minimal. The people across the road, which was barely ten feet wide, were "criminals." That is, the husband was in jail for things he'd done during the genocide, and in Jeanne d'Arc's eyes his guilt extended to his wife. Still, she tried to get along with her for the children's sake; if anything were to happen to her, she'd need someone to take her to the hospital.

It had been suggested in official circles that the ten-year commemorations would help provide the country's thousands of rescapés with "closure." I don't remember what word Rwandans were using. Jeanne d'Arc had no plans to attend any of the ceremonies. "It just brings everything back," she told me. "The thoughts turn in my head. I look at pictures of my family, and I relive all those years before. I'd like to tell the government to stop the celebrations. They're for the people who are happy, not for the ones who still grieve."

I was working with a translator named Geneviève and a Dutch journalist named Lola, and the latter asked Jeanne d'Arc how she envisioned her future. "I can't say anything about my future. The only thing that's important to me is my children. Let them grow up safe and healthy. As for me, there is nothing." She folded her arms defiantly across her chest, as if someone had suggested otherwise, then said it again, almost spitting. "Nothing."

Zaburi means "Psalms." It wasn't until I got back to the States that I had a chance to open a Bible and read the verse in question: "Hear my prayer, O Lord, give ear to my supplications; in thy faithfulness answer me, and in thy righteousness." The next verse goes, "And enter not into judgment with thy servant: for in thy sight shall no man living be justified."

To see the contours of the genocide, you had to squint through a haze of misrepresentations so dense as to make the underlying facts seem gauzy and unconvincing. Some of the misrepresentations were products of ignorance and laziness, and some were deliberate. It was ignorance and laziness, together with racism, that led the American press to initially characterize the killings as "ancient" and "tribal," words that connoted a spontaneous upwelling of essential African savagery, drums beating in the background. Of course, such characterizations proved useful to interests (mainly but not exclusively American) that opposed intervening in Rwanda. This was just what those people did to each other every few years. What could anybody do about it? The aforementioned interests sometimes argued that the killings weren't really genocide; they just looked like genocide. (Until recently, much the same arguments were being made about the atrocities in Darfur.)

This distinction was necessary in view of the 1948 UN convention that treats genocide as a trip wire requiring an immediate response from all member states. To watch footage in which a Clinton administration spokeswoman tortuously skirts the g word is to get a premonition of Clinton himself, four years later, saying, "It depends on what the meaning of the word 'is' is."[23] It's also to have proof that history really does replay tragedy as farce. The French, for their part, seized on the RPA's killing of Hutu civilians to make the peevish case for a "double genocide,"[24] a term they were still using ten years later.

In this manner the whole of Rwandan history became debatable, as did the very nature of categories such as Hutu and Tutsi. (A third group, the Twa, is too small and marginalized to figure significantly here.) Their ancestors had probably once inhabited different parts of Africa and arrived in what is now Rwanda centuries apart. The Tutsi were tall, attenuated, and elegantly sharp of feature; the Hutu were short and thickset. To the German colonists and their Belgian successors, these differences were so striking as to suggest entirely different races, Eloi and Morlocks. Dazzled by the Tutsi's physical beauty and their tidily centralized kingdom, Europeans insisted that they had to come from somewhere else — Ethiopia (which may actually have been the case) or Tibet or, most daffily, Israel, an origin suggested by their intelligence and "love of money."[25] (Years later, recalling the Ethiopian theory, a Hutu propagandist would promise to send the Tutsi back there "via the Nyabarongo," a river that flows north.)[26] Wherever they came from, they weren't really black.

The Europeans saw that the Tutsi ruled and decided that they were born to do so. They saw that the Hutu served and decreed that serving was their biological destiny. They didn't notice that only some Tutsi ruled, while others were as lowly as their Hutu neighbors, or that the two groups' ties of patronage and subjection were fairly recent, dating only to the 1860s. That was history, and the *abazungu,* the whites, didn't believe that Rwanda *had* history. It had race. And in the years that followed, their subjects came to think so, too. Under colonialism even the most wretched Tutsi prided themselves on their noble blood, while after independence an entire ideology sprang up around the importance of being Hutu. By the time of the genocide, the ranters of Radio Télévision Libre des Mille Collines were claiming that the Tutsi fighters of the RPF had tails, cloven hooves, and red eyes that shone in the dark, and many Hutu believed them.

Unlike any of the other groups that anthropologists recognize as ethnically separate, Hutu and Tutsi lived together, spoke the same language, observed the same customs, ate the same food. In addition, the two populations had been intermarrying for so long that they were often difficult to identify on sight. And since 1994, of course, the talk about race had come to seem not just unsound but sinister. In its place one now spoke of class, the word "Tutsi" designating aristocratic herdsmen and "Hutu" peasant farmers. The *mwami*, or divine king — the last of whom was deposed in 1961 — was a Tutsi,[27] as were most of his court, but elsewhere the social boundaries were said to be so porous that Hutu could become Tutsi by acquiring cattle and Tutsi who lost their herds "fell" into Hutu-dom. If the tribal model advanced the interests of the colonial authorities, the discourse of class served the purposes of the RPF. Because most of its leaders were Tutsi, the only way the new regime could pass for democratic was to blur distinctions between the rulers and the ruled.

For similar reasons it promoted the fiction that the two groups had lived together in prelapsarian harmony until the *muzungu* came slithering into the garden. Like the first serpent, he had tempted the garden's inhabitants with knowledge — not the knowledge of good and evil but the knowledge of Hutu and Tutsi. In postgenocide Rwanda it was bad form to use those labels; in some instances it was illegal. Now everybody was just Banyarwanda, or Rwandan. Foreign observers were saying so, too. An American journalist assured me that the difference between Tutsi and Hutu was no greater than that between people from Brooklyn Heights and those from Bensonhurst. "You can tell if somebody's from Bensonhurst just by looking at him, but that doesn't mean that Bensonhursters are their own ethnic group," he said.[28]

I tested this theory on a cabdriver named Alphonse. He was a Tutsi, who had escaped the genocide by fleeing to Burundi and returned to find that more than thirty of his relatives had been killed. "No, that's not right," he said briskly. "Tutsi and Hutu are different. Tutsi are tall, they're thin, they have long noses — *comme les blancs*," he added. "Hutu are short and very strong, and they like to eat a lot. Also they have flat noses with big nostrils." He flattened his own nose with a finger. "Their nostrils are ten centimeters wide!" Here I should add that Alphonse was quite short, no more than five foot six, and had a very broad nose.

What all this reminded me of was the old debate about Jews: were we a religion or a race? I used to brood about it as a child, not the actual question — none of the Jews I knew were all that troubled by phenomenological uncertainty — so much as the fact that some gentiles were so intent on classifying us. Even as a ten-year-old, I intuitively understood that classification was a kind of mastery and that it might be a prelude to other kinds that were less conceptual.

Having classified the Jews as a race (though not, as Goebbels liked to say, a human one), the Nazis snapped the constraints that had hampered the Inquisition and were free to destroy Jews who had never set foot in a synagogue, Jews who had turned Christian, and — in the case of children of gentile mothers — Jews who by Jewish standards had never been Jews at all. To know that goyim were still trying to figure out what we were after all that was to sense what a cow might feel if it were somehow to see a butcher's diagram of cuts of beef.

Many Tutsi I met felt a kinship with Jews. "The Tutsi and the Hebrews," a Pentecostal minister mused, as in his Range Rover we bumped down a paved road that wound around one of Kigali's hills, "two peoples who have suffered so much for such tiny countries." Once I was interviewing Benoit Kaboyi, a spokesman for Ibuka, an organization of Tutsi genocide survivors whose name means "Remember!" We were speaking at cross-purposes — every question I asked made him bristle — until it finally came out that I was Jewish and my father's mother had died in a cattle car on the way to Auschwitz. "Oh, then you understand," he said, with the peremptory triumph of a man who has just succeeded in getting his point across to someone very stupid.[29]

But of course I didn't. I had never known my grandmother or any of the other relatives who vanished in the camps. I had never seen my people rounded up for slaughter. I had never been forced to live next door to their murderers.

IN THE INITIAL interview, the police officer is deferential, while the subject speaks in monosyllables. Her voice is not just flat but oddly stifled, as if she were speaking through some obstruction — for example, a mask or a blanket that she has pulled over her head.

You understood your rights?

Yes.

OK, I'm going to read them to you again for the purposes of this tape recording, OK?

OK.

You have the right to remain silent and not make any statement at all and that any statement you make may be used against you and probably will be used against you at your trial. Do you understand that?

Yes.

Any statement you make may be used as evidence against you in court. Do you understand that?

Yes.

You have the right to have a lawyer present to advise you prior to and during any questioning. Do you understand that?

Yes.

If you are unable to employ a lawyer you have the right to have a lawyer appointed to advise you prior to and during any questioning. Do you understand that?

Yes.

And you have the right to terminate this interview at any time. Do you understand that?

Yes.

Are you willing to waive those rights that I've
just read to you and continue to talk to me about
this?

Yes [30]

This was June 20, 2001, at one in the afternoon. The interviewer was Sergeant Eric Mehl of the Houston Police Department; the subject's name was Andrea Pia Yates. She was thirty-six years old. In her mug shots she is thin, lankhaired, with a heavy jaw and a wide, sensitive mouth. She stares at the viewer so intently that her eyes seem lidless, and their expression is at once fearful — terrified, really — and grief-stricken, though it's possible that she was too dazed to feel much of anything. She may not have known what day it was or why she was being made, gently, by deferential Houston police officers, to stand in front of a wall chart marked with lines and numbers, first face-on and then sideways, while somebody took her picture.

My sense is that the police were treating her delicately, as one treats the victim of a particularly ghastly crime, but also with horror and even awe, which is not something policemen often feel. She may have sensed the complexity of the feelings that crackled around her. Maybe she thought she was in hell. She'd been thinking of hell a great deal, and she would later tell doctors that she had done what she had that morning with the purpose of saving her children from it.

Newspaper reports would describe her as a nurse, although it had been seven years since she'd last worked in a hospital. Since then she had devoted herself full-time to the care of her husband, Russell, a computer engineer for NASA, and their five children: Noah, age seven; John, five;

Paul, three; Luke, two; and Mary, six months. They moved around a lot. For one extended period they lived in a school bus in emulation of an itinerant pastor whom Rusty admired, a man known for his confrontational preaching style and his view of women as inheritors of "the sin of Eve." [31]

Rusty Yates was a deeply, if narrowly, religious Christian, who took certain scriptural injunctions literally, among them the ones concerning a man's dominion over his wife. Testimony suggests that it was he who wanted a large family and insisted that Andrea homeschool the children. Following the birth of her fourth child, however, she fell into a severe depression, refusing to eat or bathe or speak. She heard a voice commanding her, "Get a knife! Get a knife!" She had visions of someone being stabbed. [32] Twice she tried to kill herself. She was hospitalized and put on the drug Haldol, which relieved her symptoms, but her psychiatrist warned the couple that having another child could precipitate further episodes of what had been diagnosed as not just postpartum depression but psychosis. This was in August 1999.

In November 2000 Andrea Yates gave birth to a daughter, Mary. The following March her father died after a long illness, and her symptoms began to recur. Her mother-in-law found her agitated and unresponsive. "If I asked her a question, she often whispered a delayed answer or did not answer at all. She would stare into space. Her arm trembled. She would tap her foot and scratch her head until it was bald in spots. She bit her lip. She didn't eat." [33] Twice more she was hospitalized. A nurse who cared for her during one of these stays testified that Andrea was unable to feed herself and that when Rusty told her to hold her new baby during a family visit, the nurse had to mold her waxen hands so that the child could be placed in them.[34]

Rusty seemed to have trouble acknowledging how ill his wife was. Following her release, his one concession to her fragile state was to ask his mother to help with the housework and child care. "Something people really don't understand about someone who is psychotic is that you can look at them and if they are quiet, you know they appear normal," he later explained to an interviewer. "You know, an example would be, say, you are walking downtown and see a guy on the street corner and you assume he's sane until he starts singing some crazy song and then you are like well, that guy is insane." In the same interview he remarked, without any special emphasis, "Andrea didn't say ten words a day."[35]

On the morning of June 20, he left their house in Clear Lake for his job at NASA. Andrea was to stay alone with the children until his mother arrived. A while later she called 911 and asked the operator to send the police. She would not say what the problem was. Prosecutors would later cite this as evidence of a guilty conscience.

When officers arrived at the Yateses' one-story Spanish-style house on Beachcomber Drive, she was waiting for them, her hair wet and tangled. She ushered them into a bedroom. Four of her children lay side by side on a bed, their bodies covered with a blanket. One of the officers followed a trail of water to the bathroom, where the fifth child, Noah, was lying facedown in the bathtub.

> Um, after Rusty left, you filled the bathtub with water, is that correct?
> *Yes.*

How many bathtubs are in your home?

One.

OK, so it's just the, uh, the master bath I guess you would call it?

Yes.

OK, is it a regular sized bathtub or is it a big one?

Regular sized.

How far did you fill it?

About three inches from the top.

About three inches from the top, um, after you drew the bath water, what was your intent? What were you about to do?

Drown the children.

OK. Why were you going to drown your children?

[Here the transcripts reads, "Fifteen seconds of silence."]

Was it, was it in reference to, or was it because the children had done something?

No.

You were not mad at the children?

No.

OK, um, you had thought of this prior to this day?

Yes.

Um, how long have you been having thoughts about wanting, or not wanting to, but drowning your children?

Probably since I realized I have not been a good mother to them.

What makes you say that?

They weren't developing correctly.

Behavioral problems?

Yes.

Learning problems?

Yes.

So after you drew the bath water, what happened?

I put Paul in.

OK, and when you put Paul in the bath water, was he face down or face up?

He was face down.

And he struggled with you?

Yes.

How long do you think that struggle happened?

A couple of minutes.

And you were able to forcibly hold him under the water?

Yes.

By the time you brought him out of the water, had he stopped struggling?

Yes.

There was no more movement?

No.[36]

This happened four more times. Yates testified that only Noah tried to run from her. But the medical examiners found a strand of her hair in John's fist, which suggests that she struggled with him, too.

. . .

OEDIPUS IS KING of Thebes, a stranger raised to the throne by marriage to the widowed Queen Jocasta. Raised also by the people's acclaim, for it was he who rescued the city from the Sphinx, one of those Hellenic nightmare females, half lion and half human, by answering her riddle, which had defeated so many before him. Years later he is still proud of this:

> *I came by,*
> *Oedipus, the simple man, who knows nothing —*
> *I thought it out for myself.*[37]

And so when Thebes is stricken by plague, it's natural that his subjects should ask him to come to their aid once more, and he agrees — out of pride, certainly, but also because, like a good ruler, he shares in their misfortune:

> *I know that you are deathly sick; and yet,*
> *Sick as you are, not one is as sick as I.* (5)

Simone Weil was fascinated by classical anticipations of Christianity, but as far as I know, she never remarked on the parallels between Oedipus and Christ. Oedipus also takes on the burden of others' suffering. In time, of course, it becomes clear that the burden was really his all along, the suffering and the sin behind it. But in the beginning all he knows is that the plague is the result of a pollution, and soon an oracle declares that its source is the murder of the old king, Laios, who was killed around the time of Oedipus's arrival, by unknown persons who, it seems, are still present in the city. Up until then one might have wondered what Oedipus is supposed to do about the plague; he's not a physician. But now his fitness for the task is clear: "Once more I must bring what is dark to light" (9).

Oedipus Rex, then, is a detective story, probably the world's first. Its protagonist is both the investigator of a crime and its perpetrator, an unwitting perpetrator but no less guilty for that. The winding spool of the drama's suspense is the opposition between his desire to know and his desire not to know. Or between seeing and blindness, a metaphor the characters take turns blurting out like children charged with a grown-up secret: "Your own eyes must tell you" (4). "You cannot see the evil" (20). "But I say that you, with both your eyes, are blind" (22). As the shards of evidence cohere, Oedipus increasingly suspects that what he's piecing together is his own destruction. What could be simpler than just to stop seeking answers? Even the queen begs him to stop, but still he keeps asking, summoning witnesses from the ends of his realm, prizing answers from them. He needs to know, to see, just as having seen he will gouge out the eyes he saw with.

Much has been made about the psychology of *Oedipus Rex*. In our time he's the punch line of a shrink joke (a dated joke at that: shrinks don't believe in complexes anymore; they believe in neuroreceptors). Most such glosses place the emphasis on the hero's transgression. This, we're told, is what every man wants to do, deep down. But Sophocles will have none of it. Oedipus kills his father because he was fated to kill him. All his efforts to avert that fate have only brought it closer. And not just his efforts, but poor Laios's as well: this was his fate, too.

In Greek tragedy fate announces itself with omens, prophecies, the chorus's anguished warnings. Fate is the thing one sees coming but can't escape. The playwrights picture it as a force more powerful than the gods, who are known to quail before it. Human beings are even more vulnerable. Whatever they think or feel, whatever oaths they've sworn, whatever their obligations as kings or fathers or sons or wives, the tragic protagonists kill because they have to kill, out of a necessity as implacable as the laws of mathematics. They aren't always conscious of that necessity, and its compulsion doesn't always feel like compulsion. No force makes them pick up the dagger against their will. Rather, their wills are subverted, or maybe — because who can say how far in advance fate operates? — shaped from the beginning to serve fate's purposes. Laios's fear and pride, Oedipus's hot temper, Jocasta's loneliness, are the hilts by which fate will seize them up and wield them. Beside such necessity, morality counts for little.

This is why Christianity has problems with fate (and why Boethius pointedly demotes it to a subset of divine Providence). Fate reduces free will to the thrashings of a moth in a bell jar — a moth that thinks it is gliding through the open sky. And when free will is diminished, so is sin. So is guilt. We are in a moral universe where calamity is both random and inexorable, a heat-seeking missile that tracks its target through every evasive maneuver. In such a universe what can Oedipus be guilty of, and what is guilt at all except a kind of bad luck?

If I was created so, born to this fate,
Who could deny the savagery of God? (44)

The Talmud has a story in which God reproaches Cain for slaying Abel, and Cain defends himself by reminding God that he created him with the inclination toward evil. There's no mention of what God replies, which suggests that the Talmudists never meant Cain's argument to be taken seriously. Even back then the Jews believed in guilt because they believed in free will. (The Jewish worldview had no use for fate until Freud brought it up from the basement, webbed with dust, and started calling it the unconscious.)

This isn't to say that fate eliminates guilt. But it makes possible a more nuanced vision of human responsibility, allowing one to see it as an intricate bitmap of freedom and unfreedom in which there are many shades of doubt and pity. Cain murders his brother of his own free will, but God still shields him from the retribution of other men. Oedipus is compelled to slay his father and bed his mother, but ignorant and powerless as he is, he bears the consequences. He has the doubleness of somebody who is simultaneously innocent and guilty, and it makes him pursue the truth about Laios's death and shrink from it with that combination of drivenness and dithering that every neurotic knows so well. It's why, when he finally accepts the necessity of knowing what he did and suffering for it, he becomes heroic. To fully appreciate how heroic, try to recall the last time you heard of a criminal taking full responsibility for any crime — that is, without pleading for clemency or citing extenuating circumstances or promising that he's learned his lesson and is really, really sorry.

The question arises, who are the victims of Oedipus's crime? Put another way, who has been diminished by it? Laios, plainly, but at the play's outset he's been dead a long time. The king's survivors? That would be Jocasta, but she's come to terms with the death of her first husband and is happy with her new one. There are the surviving families of Laios's servants, whom Oedipus killed along with their master, but this story takes place before a servant's life was worth much, and by that token perhaps those who were so small to begin with could not be made any smaller. By the ancient standards of the blood feud, the case of Laios is settled. Rather, it is forgotten.

But the gods haven't forgotten. Years after the old king's death they still smell the mineral stench of his blood and demand justice, even if justice brings misery to the victim's entire line — his wife, his son, his grandchildren. What do they matter? Their lives are to the gods what the lives of servants are to kings. The story of Oedipus gives us a glimpse into the mythic past of the law at an intermediate stage between the indiscriminate savagery of feuding clans and the systematized intervention of society. And what it reveals is the reason for that intervention: not the anguish of victims but a principle that on close inspection turns out to be the wrath of the gods.

GÉRARD PRUNIER, THE most eloquent chronicler of the Rwandan genocide, notes that it, too, seems to have been fated.[38] (Certainly it had portents. In 1992 one of the country's numerous cheap political magazines ran a diviner's predictions of both the genocide and the death of the president.)[39] In the centuries before colonization, Hutu and Tutsi had a relationship that was partly exploitative and partly symbiotic. Under King Rwabugiri in the late nineteenth century the relationship tilted further toward exploitation. The Tutsi accrued more power, and the Hutu lost it. One or two days of every six they had to work without pay for their Tutsi overlords; Tutsi, of course, were exempt. First the Germans and then the Belgians, with not a little guidance from Catholic missionaries, wrote these inequalities into law. The Belgians introduced identity cards so that everyone would know who was Hutu and who Tutsi. The cards hardened ethnic categories that had formerly been elastic. Essentially, they determined their holders' futures. People who carried one kind of card got an education and a job in the civil service. Those who carried the other sort had to be content tilling their stony plots on those green hills as perfectly conical as the hills in a child's book of fairy tales. Both groups learned to see themselves the way their colonizers saw them: as clever, lordly, quasi-Caucasians or as stolid, pious, rather dim-witted sons of the soil.

Beginning in the 1950s, however, the authorities had a change of heart. Rwanda was to be democratic. Democracy meant majority rule. The Hutu were the majority, then as now some 85 percent of the population. Therefore they would rule. In preparation for that day, the Belgians ushered select Hutu into schools and government and encouraged the formation of Hutu political parties. The prevailing ideology of those parties could be summed up as this: Now it's our turn. It was understandable and in a more prosperous country might not have been a bad thing. But in Rwanda there was little to take a turn *at*, and so the ideology came to mean getting back at the old oppressors — not the Belgians, who were on their way out, but the Tutsi. The massacres started even before independence and continued at intervals throughout the presidency of Grégoire Kayibanda. One outbreak in 1963 claimed ten thousand victims in four days.[40] In 1973 the pogroms spread into the schools, where Hutu students killed their Tutsi classmates with impunity. A rescapé recalled how Kayibanda had brushed aside protests: " 'Oh, those are just children playing.' "

The man who told me this was named Isidore Munyakazi. He was a researcher who had come to the United States to do his postgraduate work in theology and peace studies. Physically he was an archetypal Tutsi — tall and thin even in middle age, with cautious, deep-set eyes. When I met him (fatefully enough, while I was raking leaves on my front lawn and he was canvassing the neighborhood for the phone company), he struck me as vain. He was going bald but disguised it with a sporty wool cap that he wore indoors and out. His people came from the east, near Kibungo. His father had owned a great many cows, the traditional measure of wealth, and used to spend hours standing on a lofty termite hill on his land, watching them graze below. But during the pogroms of 1973, Isidore told me, Hutu came and, not content with stealing cattle and beating the herdsman, destroyed the hill. "Destroyed it, for no reason. And I cannot forget the time that the chief of police came to our house and shot our dog. He did it only because it was a strong, brave dog. It would bark and bark to protect us. There was no other dog like this one. And so the chief of police" — he aimed an imaginary rifle — "shot him."[41]

I was struck by how calmly he could speak about what

he'd seen during the genocide. He described crouching in the pews of the Church of St. Paul, trying not to attract the attention of the Interahamwe death squads who were prowling its aisles in search of victims, and his tone was placid, even proud. He had survived a calamity that had swallowed almost a million other people. He had saved his wife and five children as well, partly through luck or providence but partly because of his courage and resourcefulness. Yet when Isidore spoke of the shooting of the family dog, his voice was filled with wondering grief. He sounded almost childlike. Maybe he sounded that way because the gratuitous meanness — the *spite* — of those attacks was enough to make any grown-up cry out in childlike incredulity. In mythological terms, Hutu and Tutsi often resemble warring twins; it's an odd coincidence that their traditional occupations, farming and herding, are the same, respectively, as Cain's and Abel's. Over the years the Hutu's hatred had become ingrown and baroque, but from time to time they reverted to slaps and pinches. And weak as these were, they still drew blood.

Isidore told me that his brother and the police chief were now neighbors and friendly. "They drink beer together, and my brother says" — his voice became teasing — " 'I still remember what you did to my father's dog; don't think I don't remember.' And the chief of police says, 'I didn't do this thing. They made me do it.' " I wondered where the chief had been during the genocide.

Juvénal Habyarimana, the army general who overthrew Kayibanda in a coup in 1973, cast himself as a protector of Tutsi. (In Hebrew school we used to learn about "good tsars" who sheltered the Jews.) He seized power on the pretext of restoring order after the pogroms, and during the early years of his presidency there were fewer outbreaks of violence. Relatively speaking, Rwanda prospered. But over time the economy deteriorated. The World Bank, which had loaned the country a lot of money during the good years, began its familiar disastrous tinkering in the social machinery, deepening inequalities and creating a new class of dispossessed and idle young people. These would eventually find employment in the ranks of the Interahamwe. In 1990 an army of mostly Tutsi exiles led by Major General Paul Kagame, invaded the country from neighboring Uganda. Seizing on the methods of its predecessor, the Habyarimana regime lashed out at the Tutsi under its control. Over the next four years a pattern emerged: ethnic massacres leading to defections to the rebels, whose advances justified further massacres.

As money dried up and the RPA pushed deeper into Rwanda, the Hutu power structure began to fracture. Moderates wanted an accommodation with the rebels. Hardliners wanted to crush the Inyenzi, or "cockroaches." The journal *Kangura* listed the "Ten Commandments of the Hutu." (Number 8: "Hutu must cease to have pity on Tutsi.")[42] Some of the factions acquired militias. A death squad called Réseau Zéro carried out massacres of Tutsi and hits on members of the Hutu opposition, receiving direction from a group of the president's notably ambitious in-laws, who were beginning to turn on their patron.

If Habyarimana had been content with a semitotalitarian Rwanda, the new extremists, in Prunier's formulation, aspired to "absolute power through absolute terror."[43] "In some societies," the philosopher René Girard writes, "whole categories of human beings are systematically reserved for sacrificial purposes in order to protect other categories."[44] Part of the awfulness of the genocide is that it emerged from a rivalry between Hutu factions. It was a ploy in that rivalry, as if someone, sensing that he is about to lose a high-stakes game of cards, were to take out a gun and shoot not the other player but a stranger at another table.

On the evening of April 6, 1994, the presidential jet was shot down shortly before it was due to land in the capital, killing Habyarimana and the newly elected president of neighboring Burundi. For all the mystery surrounding the assassination (furtive white men seen fleeing the vicinity; a 2004 French inquest that pinned the blame on Kagame), there's no question as to what it signaled. As soon as Isidore Munyakazi heard of the crash, he began telephoning foreign acquaintances to see if any of them would shelter his family. One man, a Belgian, agreed but shortly afterward called back to say that he couldn't come to fetch them; the city was already filled with roadblocks.

For the next three months Rwanda gave itself over to a single national project, the annihilation of the Tutsi and their Hutu "allies." The project was organized from above, its chief architect being Colonel Théoneste Bagosora at the Ministry of Defense, and its orders were passed down as if by a bureaucratic bucket brigade, from the Ministry of Defense and the presidential palace down through the prefectures and districts to the individual *cellules*, the smallest units of Rwanda's administrative system.[45] There were meticulously compiled lists of victims. There was a specialized killing apparatus. The militiamen who came to cull the refugees in the Churches of St. Paul and Ste. Famille came bearing signed authorizations. All this was in accordance with the country's reputation as the Switzerland of Africa.

Yet the genocide was also a popular project, one that enlisted — *implicated* — a broad swath of Rwandan society. It appealed not just to people's fears and resentments but to a spirit of license. Goaded by the Interahamwe, ordinary farmers became murderers, timid at first but increasingly skilled and enthusiastic. "The whole village would go out and come back, and the whole village would celebrate in the evening, and the whole village would split up the booty," a foreign researcher told me. "And the women would be eager for their men to come back and bring as much as they could. Suddenly they were rich. They could only do this for a while, because they could only leave the soil for one season. So instead of harrowing the soil, they harrowed humans." [46]

A prisoner interviewed in the book *Machete Season* recalled:

> We began the day by killing, we ended the day by looting. It was the rule to kill going out and to loot coming back. . . . Anyone who couldn't loot because he had to be absent, or because he felt tired from all he had done, could send his wife. You would see wives rummaging through houses. They ventured even into the marshes to get the belongings of the unfortunate women who had

just been killed. People would steal anything —
bowls, pieces of cloth, jugs, religious images,
wedding pictures — from anywhere, from the
houses, from the schools, from the dead.[47]

For the Tutsi, normal life ceased as if cut with shears. One
of the problems attending postgenocide legal proceedings is
that so few of the rescapés can compose a coherent narrative
of what they lived through, the typical survivor's story con-
sisting of a primal scene of blinding horror followed by
months of flight or hiding, the world shrunk down to the
dimensions of a false ceiling or a fetid bathroom where the
survivor and thirty others made themselves as small and
quiet as they could, knowing that even breathing too loudly
might draw the attention of people who had made it their
business to kill them. How to distinguish one day of this
from the next? Narrative does for time what geometry does
for space — it makes events make sense — but some events
will not be made sense of. A woman interviewed by the
filmmaker Anne Aghion remembers looking out her doorway one morning to see the people on the next hill methodically butchering their neighbors. "At first," she says, "you'd
think they were cutting down banana trees. People feel no
pity when they cut down a banana."[48]

From above the genocide was ordered, even logical; on
the ground it was chaos. This division is familiar from many
accounts of war. Generals see one thing and foot soldiers see
another, and before they lose the power of sight, the ones
the soldiers kill see something else again. Almost fifteen
hundred years ago Boethius struggled to reconcile the divine order that rules the universe with the heartless ran-

domness of the real, which was about to make him one of its casualties. He pictured a series of concentric circles with a tower rising from its center and God at the summit. Where the outer circles described their grinding revolutions, all was noise and motion and smoke. But at the center it was still; the air was clear. God, atop his tower, looked down on creation and, instead of mindless colliding and pullulating, beheld the stately working out of Providence. Perhaps that is how the genocide looked to its architects, its gods. Rwanda is a very small country with many high places, and you can imagine the génocidaires standing on a hilltop, surveying their work — the industry and ingenuity of the killers, the plenitude of the dead — and seeing that it was good.

I'm not a trained journalist, and I have to admit that it was a while before I could bring myself to ask Rwandans to talk about what had happened to them in more than general terms. I was afraid of sounding prurient and of making traumatized people excavate the traumatic past. Here is part of an interview with Beata M., a proud employee of the pharmaceutical company KiPharma and a volunteer gacaca judge, in her late fifties, dignified, softly wattled, with half-glasses dangling from a chain about her neck. It was difficult to picture her hiding above a false ceiling while Interahamwe storm troopers sacked her house and murdered the unlucky members of her family who remained below.

> It was evening, toward nine o'clock. We had closed up
> the house because we were afraid. . . . People came; I
> don't know who. They were Hutu. They told me,
> "Open up!" I asked them, "Are you Tutsi?" They

said, "Open up! If you don't open up, we'll do it our-
selves and then you'll see." Again and again I asked,
"Are you Tutsi?" Somebody tried to beat the door
down. My son, who was sitting in the living room,
they caught him. Then they tried to cut off the lights,
the electricity. The imbeciles, may their mother cut
out their hearts! They began to take things out of the
house. They broke things. My grandfather said, "Run
for your lives!" He yelled, yelled, yelled. But . . . they
killed my son. Later we heard noises. Maybe they
were climbing [up to the roof] *to pry off the tiles. I*
was agitated. . . . I told Giselle — the daughter of my
niece who was killed — "Be quiet, because they're
trying to pry off the roof tiles. Be quiet! They're going
to kill us all!" . . . They left around two in the
morning. . . . Finally we parted the curtains a little
and saw that there was nobody outside. They were
gone. The children went to the neighbors' house. I
also went to a neighbor's. But they'd killed him.[49]

When I listen to the tape, what leaps out at me are the
questions I failed to ask. When and how did the intruders
actually get in? Why did Beata's son stay downstairs in the
living room instead of climbing to safety in the rafters? Did
he sacrifice himself to protect his mother? Did she hear him
being killed or only discover his body later, when she came
down from her hiding place? What, I wondered, might this
woman consider a just outcome? The last question seemed
especially germane, since she was not just one of the genocide's myriad injured parties but one of its judges, whose

task it was to decide the fate of men like the ones who had butchered her son.

We conducted the interview in French, but toward the end Beata abruptly switched to English. I think it was because she was summing up and wanted to be sure I understood: "I can say that we have survived, but survived dead, because we are all the time dead."

NOBODY DISPUTED THAT Andrea Yates had killed her children, and so any defense would have to hinge on her sanity. Most observers agreed that she was severely mentally ill. For days on end she sat in her prison cell, seemingly unconscious of her surroundings. She shook, and picked at her scalp. She told her doctors that she wanted her hair shaved so that she could see the number 666 she believed lay branded beneath it.[50] To an examining psychiatrist, she amplified the explanations that had so plainly baffled Sergeant Mehl. The children had to die because she was a bad mother. She knew she was a bad mother because they kept misbehaving. "They didn't do things God likes," she said.[51] "They stumbled because I was evil. They were doomed to perish in the fires of hell."[52] The reason she knew that was because Satan himself had told her so. He had also told her that the only way to save them was by ending their corrupted lives. Then, presumably, the law would end hers. A doctor asked her if she was suicidal. She answered, "I cannot destroy Satan. Only the state can."[53] Here was somebody who wanted to die, wanted it so badly that she may have seen her children's murder simply as a means to that end. The psychiatrist Lucy Puryear, who diagnosed Yates as schizo-phrenic with postpartum psychosis, testified that she was the sickest person she had ever treated.[54]

In August, however, the Harris County district attor-ney's office announced its intention to charge Yates with multiple counts of capital murder and to seek the death penalty.

The State of Texas defines insanity in accordance with the 1843 M'Naghten rule, which excuses a defendant from criminal responsibility only if his mental impairment made him ignorant of the nature and quality of his act *at the time he committed it* or incapable of distinguishing right from wrong. It would apply to someone who stabbed a man to death thinking he was stabbing a wild beast or the devil or that the knife in his hand was a rose. It would apply to some-one who believed that there was no moral impediment to his stabbing anyone he pleased. It does not apply to most of the people we usually characterize as mentally ill.

The M'Naghten rule belongs to an age when insanity was simply the binary opposite of sanity and lunatics belonged to the same conceptual class as midgets and Siamese twins. In most of the country it has been replaced by more nuanced diagnostic standards. Texas is one of the few states that still use it. Texas law also stipulates that criminal defendants are sane and places on them the burden of proving otherwise. You might cite this as a further example of a judicial rigor that has made Texas the United States' perennial leader in executions. Between 1977 and 2005, the state killed 355 in-mates, more than the four runners-up combined.[55] You could also argue that Texas's attitude toward insanity re-flects an ethic of individualism that nails each person squarely to the cross of his actions. Among the nails used is a state law that bars a judge from informing a jury that a defendant it finds not guilty by reason of insanity may still be incarcerated for the rest of his life.

Still, even in Texas, seeking the death penalty for a woman — moreover, a white middle-class woman — was unusual and politically risky. Before filing charges, District Attorney Joe Owmby consulted not just other prosecutors but members of his church. Owmby is African American and goes to an African American church, where most of the people he canvassed, he says, "had this opinion: They had the suspicion that if Andrea Yates had been black, we wouldn't be *having* all this attention in the first place." His voice held a playful snap of impatience. Maybe he was enjoying twitting a white liberal — there was no use pretending I wasn't one — for his squeamishness. "The black people that I know are not opposed to the concept of retribution. A lot of them are opposed to the death penalty because of the way they feel it is *carried out,* but the principal underlying concept of the death penalty being right for certain crimes, not a lot of African Americans are opposed to that. And a lot of people I talked to strongly felt that justice would be served if Yates received the death penalty."[56]

During this time, Owmby told me, he'd been listening to a radio talk show in which most of the discussion had to do with the Yates case. One caller had said: " 'You know, I can understand how a mother can be under pressure psychologically and kill a child. I can understand that. But,' and he put it this way, 'I think she ought to be *coming to herself* around that third child.' His point was, what are we debating? This woman killed five children. Even a crazed person would have time to consider. And from the newspaper accounts, this wasn't some *frenzy*."

The Greeks, too, equated madness with frenzy, the violent overthrow of reason and the senses, usually inflicted by the gods. Frenzy is a volatile amalgam of ecstasy, terror, and rage. It blinds its victims so that they cannot distinguish between one thing and another, between one person and another, or between people and animals. In their delusion they become like animals themselves. Maddened by Dionysus, Queen Agave mistakes her son for a lion and, with her fellow Maenads, rips him to pieces as a lioness might. A deranged Heracles massacres his children, thinking they are his enemies. People in a frenzy do hideous things but are rarely punished for them. What punishment could be more terrible than Agave's realization (the blood on her hands, the dismembered corpse at her feet) that she has killed her son? Frenzy — or the dreadful awakening from it — is the punishment.

But Andrea Yates had killed her children methodically. "It takes a while to kill five children," Owmby told me, "and it takes some thought." Because she had thought, because she had waited to act until there was no one in the house to stop her, because she had drowned her children one by one instead of laying about her with a knife — an option she had considered but dismissed as too bloody — she couldn't be insane. Most criminal trials may be seen as a contest between two opposing sets of facts, but the Yates trial, which began eight months after the murders, was about two opposing definitions of madness. Yates's attorneys and psychiatrists cited her suicide attempts and hospitalizations, her catatonic symptoms, the satanic voice that taunted her with descriptions of her children's eternal torment. Owmby and his colleague Kaylynn Williford kept reminding the jury that Yates hadn't acted in a frenzy. And when the police came to her door that day, she didn't tell them that she had *saved* her children but that she had killed them.

"The State could say its whole case in one sentence: 'She knew it was wrong,' " Wendell Odom, one of Yates's attorneys, told reporters. "Our side of the case was much more complicated. We had to explain: 'If you know something is wrong but you're delusional, that's not the same thing as being sane.' "[57] If the prosecution insisted on defining insanity as a state like the Greeks' frenzy, the defense asked the jury to see it as being closer to the tragic model of fate. Yates's madness hadn't completely severed her from reality. Still, it had overwhelmed her moral judgment; it had made her do what it wanted.

I understood why this view might be inimical not just to district attorneys, but to anyone who believes that people are the masters of their actions and should be held responsible for them. "If they were your children, could you waste time thinking about her state of mind at the time?" someone posted on a newspaper's online discussion board. "The point is: whether she was insane or not doesn't matter. She killed them and that is true. She should be treated the same as her victims."[58] I encountered this desire for equivalence again and again, most drastically as a suggestion that the defendant be held underwater until she was almost dead four times in a row and the fifth time drowned for good. According to the author of the online posting, "Only then would justice be served."[59]

The prosecution's star witness was Park Dietz, a California-based forensic psychiatrist who had honed his reputation on Jeffrey Dahmer and the Unabomber, on which basis he was said to command a fee of $500 an hour. He claimed that Yates had been sane at the time she committed the crimes and had become psychotic only afterward: killing her children had driven her crazy. Throughout, she had known that what she was doing was wrong. Otherwise, Dietz argued, "I would expect her to try and comfort the children, telling them they are going to be with Jesus or with God."[60] She had not tried to comfort them. And afterward she had covered their bodies with a blanket, which the witness read as evidence of a guilty conscience rather than of maternal solicitude or a pathetic wish to turn dead children into sleeping ones.

The most damning piece of evidence was an episode of the TV show *Law & Order* that Dietz claimed had aired sometime before the killings. The plot concerned a woman who drowned her child in the bathtub and got off on an insanity plea. The prosecution suggested that Yates must have seen the episode and been inspired by it,[61] and this interpretation had a certain persuasiveness since, in addition to his other credentials, Dietz was one of the program's consultants. On March 12, 2002, after deliberating for three and a half hours, the jury found Andrea Yates guilty of three counts of capital murder.[62] But when Yates's lead counsel George Parnham tried to verify Dietz's claims before sentencing, he discovered that no such episode of *Law & Order* had ever been broadcast or even taped. Dietz conceded that he had been mistaken.[63] Parnham, whose air of gentle, somewhat baffled decency seems almost out of place in a criminal lawyer, asked for a mistrial. The judge refused to grant one. On March 15 the jury sentenced Yates to life in prison.[64]

What decided them in the end may not have been the contradictory and confusing assertions about the defendant's mental state, but the evidence of what the victims had suffered before they died. That did not have to be interpreted. Williford reminded the jury that it takes a drowning child some three minutes to lose consciousness. Noah had died in water that contained his siblings' vomit and feces. "Is this the act of a loving mother?" she asked.[65] One commentator shrewdly observed that this was the prosecution's covert theme, which made any debate about intent and insanity beside the point: Andrea Yates had been a bad mother.[66]

And in her closing argument, Williford repeatedly claimed to be acting on behalf of the children Yates had failed. She was demanding the justice they couldn't ask for, a justice whose central provision was that their mother be put to death. These claims were unverifiable, the children being dead. After the jury pronounced Yates guilty, the president of a victims' rights group called Justice for All told reporters, "I believe it was the absolute perfect verdict. In all of this, we didn't have someone to speak for the children. But [the prosecutors] spoke for the five children, and the jury heard them."[67]

If the prosecutors had wanted victims who could speak for themselves, they could have found them near at hand. There was Rusty Yates, compulsively playing Tetris on his PalmPilot and making himself available to reporters. Many onlookers found him hard to like, a coiffed, doll-like presence, at once overeager and oddly remote. Some felt that he was at least partly to blame for his children's deaths. As a columnist for the *Las Vegas (NV) Review-Journal* put it, "I couldn't understand how a man could repeatedly impregnate a mentally ill wife and force or allow her to home-school their children."[68] At the very least, Rusty had ignored the mounting evidence of his wife's psychosis. But his grief was unmistakable. His cluelessness made it more awful, the way a child's grief is, even if his cluelessness seemed *willed*. Also present was Andrea's elderly mother, who in two years had lost her husband and five grandchildren and was now faced with the prospect of losing her daughter. She was sometimes seen weeping alone outside the courtroom. Yet the prosecution chose not to speak of these people as victims. This was probably because neither of them — nor, for that matter, any of the other people directly affected by the children's deaths — wanted Andrea found guilty. Indeed, Rusty insisted that she was the case's real victim.

Well, what is a victim, and how should such a person be treated? The law often seems not to know. Not knowing, it treats victims like members of some fractious, well-connected minority, impossible to satisfy yet impolitic to ignore. Only in the past twenty-five years have federal and state governments passed legislation that funds counseling for crime victims and their families or gives them the right to be notified of a criminal's impending release — or, for that matter, the right to attend his trial. In the past the defense would often subpoena victims as witnesses solely to keep them out of the courtroom, where their presence might cast a shadow over the deliberations.

It's only lately that victims have been allowed to testify during a trial's sentencing phase so that their suffering may be taken into account when determining the fate of the condemned. Defense attorneys dread such testimony, which completes the circuit between criminal, crime, and victim, reminding juries that every major crime is a crime against *somebody*, that what has been violated is not just a penal code but a human being. "A criminal trial should be about the conduct of the defendant, not sympathy for the victim," a trial lawyer told me.[69] "Too much attention to the victim is going to take the jury's mind off its job."

Defendants' advocates sometimes argue that the campaign for victims' rights is actually a covert war on the rights of the accused, one waged, as it were, by irregulars, but prosecutors have their own problems with victims. And victims are often less than happy with prosecutors. Most DAs are pragmatists; their budgets and caseloads make them so. They want to get as many convictions with as little effort as possible. In practice, this means plea bargaining. Victims, however, are idealists. What they really want is something impossible: that their losses be undone. Failing that, they want verdicts and sentences that are commensurate with those losses — sentences that repair the shattered equality between the perpetrators and themselves. But this desire places victims radically at odds with most of what actually goes on in the courtroom. They are like pilgrims standing horrified in the marketplace where they expected to find a temple. Or maybe any temple will look like a marketplace to them. Because what kind of punishment is commensurate with the murder of the person you loved most in the world? With months of rape and sexual torture? With the extinction of an entire people?

A thousand years ago the Norse and Anglo-Saxons made

murderers pay wergild to the families of people they'd killed, a practice that was revived after World War II when Germany agreed to pay restitution to survivors of the Holocaust. My father received such wergild; my stepmother still does. But neither of them would say that it made good their losses or adequately punished the guilty.

On adjoining pages of a book called *Justice et Gacaca*, one finds two statements about the character of justice in precolonial Rwanda:

"The goal of the rule of law was not the repression of the guilty person, but his socialization."

"Vengeance was a religious obligation for every male." [70]

Rwandans I asked kept assuring me that the apparent contradiction was no contradiction at all; it was just the difference between microcosm and macrocosm. Minor disputes — say, quarrels over land or cattle — were brought before the village elders, who would hear out the claimants and, instead of ruling in favor of one side or another, try to work out a compromise both could live with. The disputed land would be divided, or one party would cede some of his land in exchange for a share of the other's crops. The elders made their deliberations while seated on the grass — hence, gacaca.

There was some disagreement about what the system covered. My translator Geneviève told me that gacaca were used in cases of rape, with the offender usually being pressured to marry his victim and the two families celebrating the union with a vow of friendship and ceremonial drafts of beer. But a Dutch anthropologist named Klaas de Jonge thought this would be true only if the victim were of low station: "If a Hutu man raped a Tutsi girl, there would be some killing."[71] In his view the gacaca had been Rwanda's equivalent of civil courts, and any genuine offense — in the language of Western law, any crime — could be resolved only by violence. It wasn't just honor that made this necessary; it was fear. The spirits of murder victims cried out for blood and if left unappeased might turn on their relatives. Every violent death was a debt that had to be repaid regardless of who had originally incurred it, and behind the culture of revenge lay the unspoken calculation that it was better to collect from the living than to pay their debts to the dead.

Sometimes the state, in the form of the mwami, or divine king, would intervene. Tharcisse Karugarama, one of the moving forces behind the new gacaca law, who since our interview has became Rwanda's Attorney General and Minister of Justice, told me that the mwami would hear the combatants' grievances and then grant the offended group leave to slay one of the offenders; this might not be the original killer but simply a kinsman of the same status as the murdered person. "They would come and bring somebody and make as if to kill him — take a spear and put it here." Fixing me with a hypnotic stare, he held an imaginary spear point against his throat. He'd once been a prosecutor and still knew how to create a sense of drama. "But they would not actually *do* the execution. They would go through all the *rituals* of killing, but they would not kill. They would do a *mockery* of killing. And the community would clap, cheer, beat their tom-toms, drink their gourd of beer, and say they have reconciled."[72]

De Jonge had doubts about the mockery part, but he was, after all, a European, afflicted with the European disease of skepticism. Most Rwandans preferred to believe that before the white man, justice had been relatively bloodless, a spear held briefly at someone's throat and then lowered while the onlookers laughed and shouted their approval. Over time I came to connect this with the belief that Hutu and Tutsi had lived together in harmony until third parties — colonialists or bad leaders — taught them to hate each other. There was some truth in this, though it struck me as odd that the people who blamed the genocide on their leaders passed over the fact that most of those leaders had been as Rwandan as themselves. I remember a young man who, when asked his thoughts about the catastrophe, declared, "Our politicians back then were very, very, very bad!" He spoke with the theatrical vehemence of someone scolding a child. But the génocidaires had been grown men.

The exact workings of the traditional justice system would be of mostly academic interest had that system not been refurbished to deal with the genocide. This became necessary because Rwanda's devastated criminal courts had proved incapable of dealing with it. By 1998 they had handed down only 1,274 judgments, out of more than 100,000 cases awaiting trial.[73] Each of those "cases" was a detainee sweltering in a prison so grossly overcrowded that the occupants had to sleep — and even sit — in shifts, and so scarce in amenities that they depended on their families to bring them food. Many of the people convicted had been tried without counsel. Some had been executed. "I had so many prisoners, the numbers were so high, and I was working very, very hard to process their files. And I thought I had failed," Karugarama recalled. "I couldn't move at the pace at which you were expected to render justice in a reasonable time, couldn't prepare the files in a reasonable period of time. I would never live to do the work; my children would never live to see it done."

People had higher expectations of the UN court, the ICTR. It enjoyed advantages Rwandan courts could only dream of, including a large staff of distinguished jurists and the cooperation of the international community.[74] It was also very well funded. By the beginning of 2003 it had spent $500 million. However, in the eight years since its inception, it had handed down only nine decisions. (In fairness to the tribunal, it provides defendants with attorneys. Moreover, it has succeeded in convicting some of the atrocity's chief planners, including former prime minister Jean Kambanda, the first head of state ever to be found guilty of genocide.[75] As of early 2008, though, the court had yet to rule on the guilt of Colonel Bagosora, whose trial had ground on for five years.)[76]

Most Rwandans I spoke with had little good to say about the ICTR. Even its location — not in Rwanda, but in Arusha, Tanzania — seemed like a breezy insult to them. Some of its staff had been exposed as génocidaires, including one man who took part in the massacres while working for the UN, which ended up compensating him for the pay he lost when he was finally fired.[77] Women testifying about being gang-raped had been harassed by defense counsel and ridiculed by judges. Women infected with HIV during their ordeals had been denied the antiretroviral drugs the court routinely gave HIV-positive defendants. "Where would we draw the line?" a spokesman explained. "If you want to treat one witness, you have to treat all the witnesses."[78]

When I asked Anastasie M. what she thought of the ICTR, she didn't hesitate. "Those people in Arusha, if a bolt could come down from heaven and destroy them all, it would be enough."

"You mean the planners, the big fish?" I asked.

"The big fish, the small fish, everyone." Her tone suggested that "everyone" included judges and attorneys, maybe even recorders and bailiffs. In her eyes, and I suspect in the eyes of many Rwandans, an institution set up to bring justice to the moral chaos of the genocide had instead become identified with that chaos, an insult placed on top of the obscene injury of the 800,000 like a party hat propped on a skull. The UN had failed them again — not just the UN but the entire legal edifice of modernity. Before the ICTR there had been the courts of the Kayibanda and Habyarimana years, which had declined to punish murderers of Tutsi, and before those there had been the courts of the colonial administration, which had allowed abazungu to treat Africans as they pleased. Who could blame Anastasie for seeing the apparatus of Western law the way so many westerners do: as a vast con game designed not to satisfy victims but to dupe them, its judges and attorneys only shells that when turned over are always revealed to be empty?

And so the country reached into the memory of its past, not worrying for the moment how reliable that memory might be. In September 1999 a group of officials held a workshop to determine the goals and procedures of an alternative justice system centering on gacaca jurisdictions. Such a system, they agreed, should uncover the truth of what had happened during Rwanda's murderous three-month fugue. It should punish all those who had taken part in the crimes — in another common phrase, "put an end to the culture of impunity." The new system would lighten the burden of the criminal courts so that neither victims nor detainees had to wait decades for their cases to be settled. Perhaps most important, the gacaca would be a participatory project, enlisting rescapés, witnesses, and even suspects in a debate whose goal was not only justice but reconciliation.

One practical consequence was that great value would be placed on confessions. Defendants who confessed promptly and with plausible remorse could reduce their sentences by half. At best, this was plea bargaining, and depending on how skeptical you were, you could see it as a tacit admission that without such confessions, the tribunals would be unable to convict anybody. Alternatively, you might see it as a grand gesture from the state to the detainees: confessing would be their way of taking an active part in the proceedings, of elevating themselves from the objects of justice to its subjects. Presumably, the subjects of justice would have an easier time accepting the courts' verdicts — accepting that these were in fact justice — than people who saw themselves as powerless, maltreated pawns. By the same token, the genocide's survivors might find it easier to forgive those who had acknowledged their guilt before them. I remembered what Anastasie had told me: "I want the one who raped me to understand that he's guilty. I want him to understand what he did — freely, without being forced. I want him to admit his blame." How closely the gacaca approximated this idea of justice would depend in part on what their various participants meant by "freely."

In March 2001 these principles were enacted into law. In many ways the most impressive thing about the law was its specificity, for in it the great amorphous body of the genocide was subjected to a Linnaean scheme of classification. At the top of this scheme were Category One offenders: those who had planned or organized the killings, those who had incited others to kill, those who had committed rape or sexual torture or murdered with "excessive wickedness." These would continue to be prosecuted in the magistrates' courts, which reserved the option of putting them to death. Beneath them, the law envisioned a second category of ordinary killers, people who had followed orders rather than given them. There was a category for manslaughterers and batterers; there was one for looters and vandals. Each of the lesser categories was subject to a different penalty, ranging from twenty-five years in prison for Category Two offenders to restitution and community service for those of Category Four.[79] Each level of crime would be tried in a different gacaca jurisdiction: Category Two offenders in the 106 district tribunals, Category Three in the 1,550 sectors, Category Four in the nation's 9,500 cells.[80]

The scheme's precision was surely practical, given the number of detainees awaiting trial and how loose and improvisational those trials were likely to be: the judges' instructions stipulated only eight rules.[81] But the gacaca also had a philosophical dimension. Genocide resists all ordinary kinds of apprehension. It has an impenetrable event horizon. Hannah Arendt describes the Nazi concentration

camps as "holes of oblivion," so shut off from the world of
the living that every report from them has an air of unreal-
ity and even their survivors doubt what they lived through.[82]
A perfect genocide would leave no surviving members of
the victim class. It would destroy the memory of that class
or poison it forever. This was why the Interahamwe infected
rape victims with HIV; it is why they didn't just cut off the
genitals of baby boys but buried the severed parts beneath
the door frames of burnt houses.[83]

In a perfect genocide, mass murder would become normal, unexceptional. This may be why the génocidaires enlisted the entire populace as accomplices. For as long as
there have been gangs, they have secured the silence of new
members by requiring them to make their bones. The idea
that somebody someday might attempt to bring so many
people to justice would probably have been enough to make
the genocide's planners burst out laughing. "Where all are
guilty," writes Arendt, "nobody in the last analysis can be
judged."[84] But the gacaca law insisted that judgment was
possible. It would count each victim, categorize every act; it
would name each perpetrator. Slowly, deliberately, it would
pace around Rwanda's hole of oblivion and measure its exact
circumference.

That October the country elected more than 250,000
volunteer judges called *inyangamugayo* — "persons of integrity." Under the law, they had to be of good character,
"exempt from the spirit of sectarianism and discrimina-
tion."[85] It went without saying that they could not have
taken part in the genocide. (To my surprise, they could be
genocide survivors. Of the handful of judges I interviewed,
two were rescapés who had lost several family members,

and one had fought in the RPA force that first marched into Kigali in July 1994, when the city still stank of the corpses stuffed into its latrines. "We called it the place of devils," he remembered.)[86] Before they began serving, the judges received thirty-six hours of training in gacaca procedures. It seemed like very little, considering that many of them were barely educated and the procedures had never been tried before.

Still, the inyangamugayo I met, four men and one woman ranging in age from late thirties to late fifties, appeared neither cowed nor jaded by their responsibilities. They didn't remind me of judges. Their gravity and modesty made them more like deacons in a church, members of the congregation who have been elevated to perform a sacred function — elevated, but not too high. When I asked them if they thought it would be hard to judge people who might literally be their neighbors, none displayed even a flicker of doubt.

The government had gone to great lengths to ensure a turnout at the trials, employing everything from radio talk shows to pop songs, as well as the sorts of veiled coercion that go unremarked in a society where the smallest administrative unit has its own "self-defense committee." I'd read Samantha Power's account of a preliminary gacaca hearing — she describes it as a cross between "the Salem witch trials and a Mississippi Christian revival"[87] — and so I thought I recognized villages where the tribunals were being held: the stream of foot traffic along the main road or in the narrow paths between fields; the men and women sitting patiently on hillsides so steep it would be risky for someone to doze off. Outside one village in the south, people stood in a great circle in a cow pasture. They were waiting for something, I thought, perhaps for the truck from the prison, with its cargo of pink-jumpsuited detainees. But in fact they were praying. And every other gathering I witnessed turned out to have a different purpose. With the exception of a few pilot jurisdictions in selected districts, in 2004 the gacaca were still in their pretrial phase and consisted solely of fact-finding sessions.

The most dramatic of these sessions was said to be a formal presentation of prisoners, at which those who wished to could confess and witnesses could exonerate those who'd been wrongly accused. But by the time I got to Rwanda, this stage of the proceedings was over. The first session I attended was held in a disused schoolhouse in Kigali's Kaciryu district, and the judges on the scene were just sorting dossiers, with no audience present. The persons of integrity sat in twos or threes on scarred benches, their folders stacked at their feet. The men wore clean shirts, the woman — it was Beata M., performing her civic duty on her one day off from the pharmaceutical company — a gay print skirt and head scarf. They were trying to decide whether a particular suspect had killed with intent or just in passing; whether another's crimes were so hateful as to place him in the first category to be transferred to the regular courts. A few weeks before, I'd interviewed a man who had confessed to killing three people in his village, two of them children, yet he had been classified as Category Two and released from prison after six years. The judges discussed their dossiers calmly. Even Beata, who had hidden in the rafters as her son was murdered in the room below, was calm. They were just dossiers.

This was the last of the pre-gacaca sessions. No one could

tell me when the actual trials would begin. In August maybe, or October. The system had entered a holding pattern.

AESCHYLUS'S *ORESTEIA* TELLS the story of a series of revenge killings. Clytemnestra kills Agamemnon to avenge his earlier slaying of their daughter Iphigenia, whom he sacrificed in order to secure a favorable wind for Troy; their son Orestes, with some prodding from the god Apollo, kills Clytemnestra. One pictures them — father, mother, and son — standing in a row, each poised to slay the one before him. Having murdered his mother, Orestes is pursued by the Erinyes, or Furies, abominable crones whose eyes weep blood, as if their wrath were a distorted form of sorrow. At length he seeks refuge at the temple of Athena and begs her to judge his case. There follows a murder trial, the world's first.

That Orestes has committed matricide is beyond dispute. That he has done so on Apollo's orders doesn't lessen his guilt so much as extend it to the god, who, appropriately, stands beside him in the dock. (Few things about this story are more alien to a modern religious reader than the idea of a guilty deity. One may believe in a god who dies for man's sins but what of a god who instigates them, a god who hands Eve the apple?) Instead, the trial hinges on whether it is permissible to kill one's mother in order to avenge one's father and, by extension, on which parent has a greater claim on a child's loyalty — which parent is the "true" one. Athena, who has no mother, having sprung from Zeus's forehead like a thought made flesh, casts the deciding vote in favor of the father. Orestes goes free.

Apart from its psychological undercurrents, its themes of father-love and mother-hate and mother-love deformed into hate, the *Oresteia* is a myth about the origins of justice. Justice comes into being to break what might become an unending chain of vengeance. Each of the killers in this drama is paying back an earlier killing; each claims to be righting a wrong. The violence extends deep into the past, to the primal atrocities of the brothers Atreus and Thyestes, and, with the arrival of the Furies, threatens to overflow the confines of the family and inundate the realm of the gods. René Girard observes that "as long as there exists no sovereign and independent body capable of taking the place of the injured party and taking upon itself the responsibility for revenge, the danger of interminable escalation remains."[88]

The Furies are old deities, residing not on Olympus but in the vaults and tunnels of the underworld. Nobody likes them. "No house is this to be approached by you," Apollo scolds them, when they invade his temple,

> But rather go where heads fall from the block,
> Where eyes are gouged, throats slit, and boyhood's bloom
> Blasted by gelding knife . . .
> Such festivals
> Are your delight and fill heaven with loathing.[89]

Yet even he and Athena, who, respectively, embody the powers of reason and wisdom, seem cowed by these infernal agents of pure, unreasoning retribution, and when Athena pronounces Orestes not guilty, she promises them their own shrine in her city, for fear of what they might otherwise do to it. In the formula made familiar by fairy tales, she has to repeat the offer three times before the Furies accept. Once they do, they are magically transformed into guardians of civil peace.

In this way the age of vengeance ends and the age of justice begins. Universal reprisal gives way to a single act of retribution, carried out against a person who has been judged guilty: a criminal. (And if, as in Orestes' case, that person is found not guilty, the aggrieved parties will just have to deal with it.) Like justice itself, the criminal is an invention, and in the beginning no one knows what to do with him, the court's deliberations being less concerned with what he has done than with what the victims or their families want as restitution. Aeschylus, the author of the *Oresteia*, devotes as much time to Athena's dickering with the Furies as he does to the debate over Orestes' guilt.

At the end of the negotiations, the Furies don't go away but remain in Athens to be honored by its people, under a new name — Eumenides, "the kindly ones." Justice doesn't banish vengeance but subsumes it. This may be why in most representations Justice bears not only scales but a sword. And perhaps her blindfold is necessary to disguise the fact that her eyes once wept tears of blood.

FOLLOWING SENTENCING, ANDREA Yates was transferred to the Skyview Prison Unit in Rusk, Texas, some 140 miles north of Houston. In the spring of 2004 she was being treated by two psychiatrists and getting a daily cocktail of antipsychotic and antidepressant medications. George Parnham told me that this was more or less the same treatment she'd receive in a state psychiatric hospital, the main difference being that her new home had bars on its windows and barbed wire on the walls below. The staff liked her, and the warden assured Parnham that she wouldn't be transferred into general population on his watch. "You want to know what he always tells me?" the attorney said. "He tells me, 'I don't know what that little girl was like before, but I can tell you she's not the same person today.' "[90] There was pride in his voice. He might have been speaking about a child of his own, a difficult one who'd caused him great worry in the past but was finally doing all right.

Rusty Yates was visiting Andrea every other week and making public professions of his continuing support. In July, as the third anniversary of the murders approached, Andrea took a turn for the worse. She stopped eating and lost thirty pounds. She seemed not to realize that her children were dead. Sometimes she thought she saw them crying for help.[91] She became so fragile that she was placed on suicide watch and rushed to Galveston prison hospital. There she responded to treatment, and a few weeks later she was judged well enough to return to Skyview.

Soon after, Rusty announced that he was seeking a divorce. The agreement, which was finalized a year later, granted Andrea $7,000 in cash, a nursing chair, and the right to be buried near her children.[92] This would be at Houston's Forest Park East cemetery, where the remains of Noah, John, Paul, Luke, and Mary Yates lie beneath a common headstone, a large slab of soot-colored granite whose somberness is peculiarly at odds with the row of portraits sandblasted into the stone. The portraits are highly realistic, probably copied from snapshots, and it doesn't take too much imagination to see the monument as an outsize refrigerator door, with the kids' pictures attached to it as if by magnets. Beside it, their mother's grave will probably seem very small and incidental, an afterthought.

What happened to Andrea Yates wasn't vengeance. Her victims' survivors viewed her not with anger and revulsion, or at least not primarily so, but with horror and pity, and they asked that she be treated as a sick person rather than a depraved one. Part of this, of course, was because they were her family. But maybe they also felt that there was no point in compounding her suffering. When I spoke with Parnham in 2004, he told me that he believed that one day Andrea would be cured. My immediate thought was that for her sake, I hoped not. For her to be cured would be for her to grasp, fully, what she did, to know what Oedipus knew. This may already have happened, briefly. She once told a visitor that what she found most painful was thinking of how her children must have felt when they realized that she was trying to kill them. A while after that, she retreated once more into psychosis, as Oedipus sought refuge in blindness.

Horror and pity, of course, are the classic responses to tragedy, the feelings it is supposed to arouse in spectators. As in tragedy, the killings of the Yates children were heralded in advance. One thinks of the warnings of the psychiatrist who treated Andrea after her suicide attempts. In addition, Andrea had once been a champion swimmer. The first time Rusty saw his future wife, she was floating on her back in a swimming pool with her long hair streaming behind her, looking so at peace that he would later describe her as "a person who was more graceful in the water than out of it." [93]

My own opinion is that Yates went to prison because of a principle. I'm not sure what the principle is; maybe, crudely speaking, it's that a mother shouldn't get away with killing her children. If in modern justice the state functions as a champion of victims, this is doubly true when the victims are children. Over centuries justice, like some very old people, has grown august and detached, serenely impersonal in its blindness. But sometimes, as when a child is murdered, it reverts to its earlier ferocity. The blindfold is removed; the eyes beneath weep blood. The Furies, we know from tragedy, are sharp-sighted and scry the guilty person no matter how far she may run. But the blood in their eyes may keep them from seeing the exact nature of her guilt, or from apprehending that, under certain circumstances, the perpetrator may herself be a victim.

Of course Texas may be right in asserting that justice is supposed to punish acts, not wring its hands over a killer's mental state. Every time Andrea Yates's attorneys brought up what was going on in her mind, Owmby and Williford had only to remind the jury what must have been going on in her children's. Underlying all modern judicial systems is the principle that certain acts are unequivocally wrong, regardless of who their victims are — or who their authors — and must be punished unflinchingly, not by outraged kinsmen but by a majestically impartial state. At times such impartiality can be heartless, as a machine is heartless. But who would wish it to be otherwise? The principle is all that stands between us and an eternity of universal vengeance, a hell in which we ourselves are the devils.

"Why do we seek justice?" District Attorney Owmby asked me. We were in a barbecue place near the court, a joint where lawyers on both sides roll up their sleeves to address heaped plates of ribs or smoked brisket. "Why do we hold people accountable for what they do? What right does Andrea Yates have to take away from us the potential of those children? We will never know what she has taken, but we know she's taken something. One of them was interested in insects; he wanted to be an entomologist. And I don't know what he would have discovered. I don't know what music she's taken, what literature she's taken, but she's taken something from society, and there's no justification for what she did. Through the ages we have always valued human lives, and this is what we will do to those who take them without justification. If you look, that is when we become more civilized. We have these punishments to stop Clan A from killing all the people in Clan B just because their brother was killed. That's where the death penalty comes from. So it's civilization that moves us toward the death penalty — not our uncivilized nature, but *civilization*."

Later I asked him if he ever applied what he heard in church in the courtroom. He chuckled. "I had one case, the defense argument was — and the defense attorney *opened* this line of argument — that Cain was exiled for murdering his brother, and that was enough. He was just exiled. And my response was" — he half-rose from his seat, as if making an objection — " 'That wasn't *capital* murder!' " In Texas capital murder is multiple homicide or homicide committed in the course of another crime — for instance, during a robbery or rape. Cain, of course, killed only Abel, in a moment of childish jealousy. And as far as the Bible lets us know, he lived out the rest of his days without harming another soul, set apart from his fellows by the mark God had placed on his forehead.

In the spring of 2004 the State of Texas tried another woman who'd killed her children, this time in Tyler. Her name was Deanna LaJune Laney, and her victims were her sons, eight-year-old Joshua and six-year-old Luke. She bashed in their heads with stones, a method she may have chosen for its biblical connotations. On this occasion, the M'Naghten rule came down on Laney's side. Owmby told me that her madness was evident even to a layperson. On the 911 tape her voice is a hair-raising singsong, and when the operator asks her to describe her emergency, she coos, "I killed my kids." She proudly told the investigating officers that she and Andrea Yates were messengers, and that they would meet in heaven. One of the expert witnesses who testified on Laney's behalf was Park Dietz. He told the jury that his client believed that God had commanded her to kill her children, and so naturally she'd obeyed him. Perhaps because of this, or because of the distorted affect that even the hard-nosed Owmby found so eerie, the jury found Laney not guilty by reason of insanity.[94]

The Laney case may have helped change the way Texans think about mental illness. (So, too, may George Parnham's impassioned efforts — a personal crusade mounted largely at his own expense — to heighten public awareness of postpartum depression.)[95] In January 2005 Andrea Yates's conviction was overturned, after an appeals court ruled that Dietz's false testimony could have affected the judgment of the jury, along with the "substantial rights of the appellant."[96] At the end of a month-long trial, Yates was found innocent by reason of insanity. "She needs help," one of her jurors said. "I think she'll probably need treatment for the rest of her life." Shortly afterward she was transferred to North Texas State Hospital in Vernon, where psychiatrists will periodically evaluate her to see if she is well enough to be released. Her new home is surrounded by guard towers and seventeen-foot-high wire fencing.[97] It really isn't much different from prison.

UP IN THE hills on the eastern edge of Kigali a group of *ex-détenus* and *rescapées* was building houses for the *rescapées* to live in. This was under the auspices of the Prison Ministry, whose executive director in Rwanda was a Pentecostal minister named Déo Gashagazi. He was tall and heavy and wide in the hips, ungainly-looking when he wasn't preaching, and his profile was almost Mayan, the fleshy nose forming a continuous line with a high, bumpy forehead. We drove to the site in a Land Cruiser, following a cobbled road that wound around the hillsides and narrowed as it climbed. Toward the summit the cobblestones gave way to hard-packed dirt. Most of the buildings in the neighborhood were made of earth, with thatched roofs and maybe a wooden door if the owner was better-off. Shops were identified by the minimal displays of merchandise arranged out front: three girls' dresses or a few cans of palm oil or a jumble of dusty machine parts. Churches had crosses on top; mosques had rickety plywood minarets. We passed children solemnly driving goats.

The Prison Ministry is an international organization

whose primary purpose is to spread the Gospel among the incarcerated, but its Rwandan affiliate was also playing an instrumental role in the justice system, encouraging suspected génocidaires to confess their crimes and repent, not just in the privacy of worship but before the law. The spiritual benefit to the detainees was matched by the practical advantage to the courts and gacaca jurisdictions. For this reason Déo and his fellow ministers had been given virtually free run of the prisons. Often they worked with prosecutors. Detainees who had seen the light would get their cell mates to confess, and they in turn would pass the message on to others. The penitentiaries were being swept by an epidemic of penitence. "These men," Déo said, "have lived with such a great weight on their spirits. Confessing is a relief for them." It could also be a reprieve. Detainees who had already spent eight or nine years awaiting trial had only to sign their confessions to be set free, time served.

If they were Déo's men, though, they had to build houses. The car stopped near the top of the hill, and we got out and began to climb. The slope was steep; once or twice I would have fallen if one of Déo's assistants hadn't steadied me. The house was maybe thirty feet up from the road, with others like it set farther up the slope. It was a shell of mud brick, no bigger than a one-car garage. A dozen men and and women were laboring inside. The men wore trousers and undershirts, the women wraparound skirts and head scarves, and all of them were daubed and spattered with mud, their hands caked with red mud to the elbows. Two or three men shoveled earth from the slope behind the house; some women soaked it with buckets of water. It was stirred into mud, scooped onto plasterers' hawks, and slapped onto the brick in handfuls. Both the men and women did this. The sound of slapping was ceaseless.

I assumed that all the women were rescapées and the men ex-détenus, but there was no way of being sure short of asking, and I'd been in Rwanda long enough to know better than to ask: one doesn't ask someone if he took part in the genocide. Déo had introduced his assistants, Didacien and Aloys, respectively, as a Tutsi who'd lost family in the killing and a Hutu who'd spent time in prison. He'd broken the etiquette of ethnic silence, and the men had allowed him to break it, to show me how the two groups could reconcile in Christ. By groups he meant Hutu and Tutsi but also, implicitly, perpetrators and victims.

Yet later it emerged that Aloys, a short man with thinning hair and a burst blood vessel in one eye, may not have been a perpetrator at all. He said he'd been railroaded into prison. Before the war he'd been a baggage handler at the Kigali airport, a good job, the kind you didn't throw away, especially not with eight children to feed. He'd always kept out of politics. During the trouble he'd stayed home like everyone else; everybody was afraid. It was only afterward, when it was all over, that somebody, a jealous coworker, said some things about him, for which he was arrested and sent to prison. Now he was free, he'd found God, he bore nobody ill will. That was the gist of it. Asked what the charges against him were, Aloys said that he was supposed to have killed people, though he wouldn't say what kind of people or under what circumstances he was supposed to have killed them. It was unclear whether he owed his freedom to having confessed or to a lenient judge. When he spoke of the events of 1994, he said "the war" or "the trouble" rather than "the genocide," which may or may not have been significant. And his claim that he'd stayed out of politics was disingenuous. People who stayed out of politics didn't get jobs as baggage handlers. The whole time we were together, I noticed, he kept exchanging looks with Didacien, who was sitting with us at the table, a man in his early thirties, as thin as a blade, with slightly bulging eyes.

Didacien had told his story earlier, using language almost as noncommittal as Aloys's. He'd worked at a hospital in Kigali. The Interahamwe had come to kill staff and patients. He'd hidden in a storeroom and then found his way to a church, where he'd stayed until the end of the trouble. I asked him if the church had been Ste. Famille, where many Tutsi had sought refuge, not always successfully, and he nodded, but a little too quickly.

I had a strong sense that the two men were in collusion, each assenting to the other's version of the past and abetting the other in his reticence. I could understand why Aloys would want to leave certain things unsaid, but Didacien's wariness perplexed me. Then I thought of something Geneviève had told me when I first met her: "There are people who accept what happened. They are healed. From their point of view ten years have gone by; they cannot keep crying forever. There are others who forgive but don't forget. And then there are those who *do not accept,* who will never accept. They will never recover. And they will not talk to you."

THAT WEEKEND I attended a service at Déo's church. The congregation was made up of genocide survivors, ex-détenus, and women whose husbands were still in prison. In its noise and exuberant melodrama, the ceremony was typically *nouvelle église*. When I entered, a parishioner was slapping time on a hand drum, while a small man who appeared to be blind — the meeting hall was dim, but he wore sunglasses with thick black lenses — led the worshippers in a hymn. He shouted the verses in a fierce, hoarse voice and hopped up and down to the beat of the drum, pumping his fists and thrusting out his chest like a swimmer breaking the surface of a pool. The congregation was infused by his energy, made reckless by it. Some even danced themselves, but the moment he stopped, they subsided into their seats and appeared to age ten years. The men's faces were gray and somber. Even the younger women in their bright headcloths looked fatigued.

They revived some when Déo began to speak. Even through the muffling arras of a foreign language, it was clear that he was a terrific preacher. He grabbed his listeners by the scruff of the neck and calmly transported them from one emotional state to another. A tiny girl named Juliet translated for me, so I know he told the story of the Fall, turning it into a parable of evasion, with Adam blaming Eve for giving him the apple and Eve blaming the serpent and neither of them asking for forgiveness. He told of a woman — he didn't say if she was Tutsi or Hutu — who was taken hostage by a militia, also unspecified, and asked if she wished to say anything before she died. "So she is telling him that she believes in God," Juliet whispered, " 'And now when I say it, it is fine if you kill me.' She is not afraid to die." But the woman's faith struck terror into her executioners. Déo popped his eyes and ran in place, as graceful as one of the massive comedians of the silents. Everyone in the room laughed, even the men who ten years before might themselves have belonged to militias and if so were unlikely to have asked their prisoners if they had any last words.[98]

The thrust of these parables was the importance of speaking out and taking responsibility for one's actions. It was a message tailored for an audience that was poised — or, more likely, braced — for a nationwide campaign of truth telling. The only way the gacaca will succeed is if Rwandans — or at least a preponderance of them — tell the truth. One assumes that the rescapés will do this, but they may not have much to say if they were in hiding, out of sight of the perpetrators but also unable to see them. Many detainees will confess, but some of their confessions will be suspect. I've heard of people pleading guilty to lesser crimes to avoid being prosecuted for more serious ones, and of persons already convicted taking the fall for relatives and friends, knowing that their sentences are unlikely to be increased. Because of the premium placed on confessions and the looseness of standards of evidence, innocents who refuse to speak may end up serving more time than chatty murderers. Of course, this has proved true elsewhere, as in the present-day United States.

The great unknown is the third parties, the Hutu who watched and saw and until now have remained silent. Reports from the pilot gacaca were unpromising, confirming a 2003 government survey which estimated that more than half of Rwanda's people wouldn't take part in the tribunals, or even attend them.[99] Part of the problem is that, from a practical perspective, the procedures are a nuisance. Most Rwandans are subsistence farmers who work every day in the fields. In addition, they have to contribute labor to the commune; they have to attend political lectures and go to church. Who would want to spend one or two more days every month squatting on the ground in the rain or sun, straining to hear people talk about the horror of ten years before, and knowing that you, too, may have to say something and that it will probably get you in trouble? Rwandan society is tightly enmeshed, with the ties between extended family members replicated in ties of social and political obligation. In such a society no one ever feels truly alone. The corollary is that no one ever feels completely free to tell the truth.

The other problem, according to Alison Des Forges of Human Rights Watch, is that the gacaca fail to address an entire category of crimes — the ones committed by the new government and its soldiers. Some of these offenses took place during the chaos of the war and others afterward, as the RPF was raking in the last chips on the table. Some of them could be attributed to the indiscriminate use of firepower, and a few were straightforward massacres of unarmed civilians. Almost all the victims were Hutu. The government has ruled that these killings qualify as war crimes or crimes against humanity, but not as genocide, and has declared them outside the gacaca's purview. A recent addendum to the law of 2001 fails to mention such crimes at all, effectively dropping nearly a hundred thousand victims into a juridical oubliette.

But in Rwanda, memory is reinforced by kinship. At every gacaca a certain portion of the witnesses have relatives whose deaths they blame on the state, which denies responsibility or insists that it must be determined elsewhere. Now that same state is asking these people to tell the truth about other deaths that it deems more important, the deaths of Tutsi. Des Forges gave me the strong impression that the reason for the system's frequent and lengthy delays is that witnesses aren't cooperating. In 2004 the government began to float rumors that it was about to charge a large number of new génocidaires, maybe as many as a quarter million. I asked Des Forges if this was a McCarthyesque ploy to terrorize people into testifying. She said it was an exit strategy. "The government will announce this preposterous figure and make noises about prosecuting them all. But really this is the government's way of admitting that it's impossible to try the lower levels of the genocide. And after a while it will throw up its hands and declare a general amnesty." [100]

If that happened, I thought, Rwanda would never know justice. The 800,000 dead would remain irremediably diminished, their survivors only a little less so. And while those who got the amnesty would never be big men — they had only *felt* that they were, back when they were engorged with killing — they would at least be free. They would come home to their farms and their loved ones, to houses that still had roofs on them, and those they had wronged would have to watch in silence.

In his version of the *Oresteia* story, *Electra*, Sophocles gives us the following exchange between Orestes and his sister:

ELECTRA: And yet you see but a small part of my pains.
ORESTES: And how could there be any more frightful
   to see?
ELECTRA: This: that I live among murderers. [101]

The sermon was nearing a close. Rwanda, Déo was saying, was like a truck loaded with prisoners. Some of the people on the truck were judging the others, saying, "This one has stolen. This one is a killer." But they, too, were in prison. He was serious now, his voice accusing. "In this room there are no killers," Juliet translated. "There are no thieves. There are only servants of God." I tried to ask her what he meant by that — it seemed to contradict everything he'd said earlier about responsibility — but the fierce little choirmaster burst out in another hymn.

The emotional high point of the service had occurred earlier. It was a laying on of hands. People who wanted to be saved went up to the front of the room, and one by one the reverend placed a hand on their foreheads and told the devil to leave. Sometimes he coaxed and sometimes he bullied. He pushed one docile man down the entire length of the aisle. At times he spoke, or shouted, in tongues: "Ra-ba-ba-ba, RA-ba-ba-BA!!" Juliet said that he was calling down fire from heaven.

Few people were immune to these ministrations. They rocked or wept silently or quaked with sobs. In the pews babies slept against their mothers' breasts. Abruptly one woman began to shriek. My immediate thought was that this was the appropriate — the correct — response to all that had happened in this country, but I soon realized that she wasn't just crying out of grief. Her shrieks grew louder and higher; she convulsed. She was in a frenzy. Déo went over to her and placed his hand on her head, but she was not comforted. She didn't want to be comforted, or the thing inside her didn't want to be. Her screams mounted, and Déo had to pray more loudly to be heard over them. Soon he was bellowing in her face: "RA-BA-BA-BA-BA!" The woman lunged away from him, was held back by other worshippers, broke free. She fell to the floor and thrashed there, still screaming, until some women ushered her to another room, where her cries grew fainter until they ceased.

Exorcism is an appropriate model for Rwandan justice, just as possession gives Rwandans a way of explaining the horror that befell them. The truth is that some of them designed that horror and inflicted it on others, but everyone prefers to speak of it as something that came from elsewhere, like a pestilence or a fire from heaven. Even Gérard Prunier, the most rigorous of judges, often speaks of "killer victims" or "victim killers."

Sophocles was right. For those who have escaped being murdered, the greatest anguish may lie in knowing that they live among murderers. (It's one reason so few Jews who lived through the Shoah returned to Germany.) This is the predicament of most surviving Rwandan Tutsi. And so many of them tell themselves that their neighbors were not murderers, not really. They tell themselves the same things the murderers themselves do: that those who killed, killed out of ignorance or fear. They blame the genocide on outside forces, if not on the abazungu, then on leaders who in the telling somehow cease to be Rwandans — *real* Rwandans like themselves — and if not on the leaders, why not on demons?

What happened in Rwanda will never be adequately punished. The ICTR may somehow get around to trying the entire pantheon of monsters, down to Bagosoras's lowest subalterns, but even if it succeeds in convicting them before the last of their surviving victims die, they will be vastly more comfortable in prison than most of their victims are in freedom. As for the ordinary people who *became* monsters, most of them, too, are beyond the reach of justice. There aren't enough jails; there aren't enough prosecutors. Even 254,000 gacaca judges may not be enough. Viewed against the enormity of the genocide, the crimes of Rwanda's new government might seem very small. However, in excluding those crimes from the sphere of justice, the government may end up shrinking the sphere's circumference to zero.

IN ONE OF Park Dietz's pretrial interviews with Andrea Yates, he asked why she thought it would be right to kill her children. "If I didn't do it, they would be tormented by Satan," she said.

"As you drowned each one," he continued, "did you think it was the right thing to be doing?" Andrea nodded yes. She explained that as she held the children under the water, she prayed that their souls would go to heaven. It was only afterward that she realized how her acts might be perceived by others. Satan had left her.

Dietz asked why Satan would leave her after she'd obeyed him. To this Yates replied, "He destroys and then leaves."[102]

IN THE SAME village where I met Jeanne d'Arc M. I was introduced to a murderer named Stefano K. Actually, the meeting took place in Jeanne d'Arc's house, which she'd consented to let Lola, the Dutch journalist, and me use for our interview. On the eve of the tenth anniversary of the genocide, such events had become routine. The rescapés got some money, the ex-détenus got some (less, ideally), the translators and facilitators got some, and so did the ministry that sold permits to foreign journalists and researchers. The payments violated the rules of both journalism and academic research, but some people made them anyway. We didn't ask Stefano into the house until Jeanne d'Arc had finished talking with us. He was forty years old, a small, wiry man in a soiled shirt that he wore unbuttoned, not out of sexual bravado but because it was hot and he'd been working. There were traces of red earth on his shirtsleeves. He came in slowly and looked over at Jeanne d'Arc, but when she avoided his gaze, he did the same and for the rest of the visit barely looked at her again. He didn't look at us much, either, but answered our questions while staring fixedly ahead, like someone giving an interview by remote hookup on the TV news. The TV people always warn guests to keep their eyes on the camera, and the inexperienced ones take that literally.

During the genocide Stefano had killed two children and a woman; the woman had been pregnant. He'd been arrested on his return from a refugee camp in Congo and spent six years in prison, winning an early release after he confessed at a pilot gacaca hearing. He was among the first beneficiaries of the new justice system, and he was grateful for it. Confessing had cleared his conscience. When he came home, people welcomed him, not just his family but rescapés, because they felt that justice had been done. The gacaca worked. People could live together without feeling afraid. "When you've committed a crime," he said, dropping his gaze from the imaginary news camera and looking at us, "you're filled with fear."

Lola asked, "If the government pressured you, would you kill again?" Stefano became agitated. "Look, even if it happened, the genocide wasn't our idea," he said. "It was the authorities — they gave us the idea and made us do things. If they gave the same orders again, I'd never obey them, because today I know it's wrong to kill a schoolchild." He sounded less guilty than exasperated, as if he'd put up with all the high-minded badgering he was going to take.

The whole time he was speaking, Jeanne d'Arc stared at the ceiling or at the floor or at her clenched hands in her lap. She, too, had been to a gacaca, to testify against one of the men who'd raped and murdered her sisters, but it had gone badly. She was alone; the defendant was related to the head of her cellule, and either for that reason or because he'd named other perpetrators, he was let go. A while afterward he'd come to her and asked for pardon. She shrugged. "I gave it to him. There was no choice."

Writing this, I imagine someone protesting that that's what the gacaca are all about: forgiveness and reconciliation. I think of Kigali's genocide memorial. It's divided into five zones. The first four are called "Before Genocide," "Warnings," "Genocide," and "Responses" and contain the sorts of exhibits their names suggest. A fifth section is labeled "Aftermath."[103] Originally, it was supposed to be called "Reconciliation," but rescapés insisted that its name be changed. An official of the Aegis Trust, the British charity that helped fund the memorial, said, "Survivors laughed at us when we raised the word."[104]

I also recall a scene from Anne Aghion's gacaca documentary, a conversation between two women who are peeling cassavas. One of them says, "I can still see how he grabbed my baby off my shoulder and flung it on the ground." She takes a piece of cassava from the basket at her feet and flips it across the room, making a trilling sound with her lips. "Then he beat it to death. And now he would come and tell me, 'Forgive me, because in fact I did you a big favor.' And I'm meant to reply, 'Thanks, I forgive you.' " [105]

At the end of the interview Stefano made to leave, but Geneviève stopped him. She's a handsome woman in her early fifties, with the soft, leonine features and world-weary voice of Simone Signoret. She and her family took no part in the genocide, but like millions of Hutu, they fled Rwanda in advance of the RPA and spent some time in a refugee camp in Congo. The camp was run by génocidaires, which didn't stop Geneviève from telling everyone she met that all Hutu were guilty of a great crime and should be praying for God's forgiveness. She continued to speak like this even when her life was threatened. Now she blocked Stefano's path and asked him something that he seemed to find astonishing. Ignoring his answer, she went on addressing him, her voice both teasing and scolding. Once or twice she touched him on the chest. When she was finished, she joined Lola and me outside by our hired taxi.

"I asked him," Geneviève explained, "if he had ever asked this lady Jeanne d'Arc to forgive him. He told me, 'Why should I ask her? I never did anything to her.' He is being a typical man; it makes me lose my patience. I told him, 'Only think of what this poor lady has been through! Put yourself in her place! If what had happened to her had happened to you, wouldn't you want her to say something? Now go to her.' And so he did." By now Jeanne d'Arc and her neighbor had left the house and were standing together in the shade of the thatched roof. They spoke hesitantly and often looked away from each other, but a half hour before, they'd seemed miserable at having to breathe the same air. Geneviève said, "I'm not sure, but I think I may have accomplished something."

I was grateful to her for not using the word "reconciliation." It was too early to say whether these people were reconciling. They might only be coexisting. Lion and antelope are known to coexist as well, beside water holes, in the brief interval before one pounces on the other.

Postscript: I first visited Rwanda in March and April 2004. It wasn't a long time to be there, and I count myself lucky in that at least one of the rescapés I spoke with lived not ten miles from me in upstate New York. When I returned in the fall of 2005, gacaca were proceeding. In parts of the country, the process was slow and grudging and riddled with injustice. The newspapers were full of stories of witnesses murdered by unknown parties. But elsewhere, especially in Kigali and Butare, people who had taken part in the genocide were being tried and convicted. Some were being sentenced, and not just symbolically.

At a gacaca in Kigali I watched as a man was condemned to thirty-five years in prison for the murder of eight people eleven years before. Two of his victims had been children. The defendant, a short, meager, sour man named Jonas, was unusual in that he refused to confess to any of the charges against him. Most defendants do; that's why their sentences are reduced. They may minimize their crimes, lowering the number of their victims or skipping over certain cruelties, but still they confess to *something*, and a grateful court rewards them.

Jonas, though, denied everything. A woman in an acid green head scarf testified that she had seen him swing a little boy by his arms into a pit and then club him to death. She imitated the way Jonas had held him, spreading her arms out and saying, "Like an airplane." His only reply was to ask, "When did you see me do this?" He asked it several times, but the woman ignored him. Only later did my translator explain the meaning of his question. The accuser was a Tutsi who during the genocide had lived in the home of a notorious Interahamwe. That was what had kept her from being killed. Still, even under her host's protection, she wouldn't have dared go outside, and so she couldn't have witnessed the things she claimed to have witnessed in the pit. She had probably heard the Interahamwe talking about them afterward over beer, the way working people talk about their work at the end of the day.

What remained unspoken was the reason for this woman's presence in the home of a dedicated killer of Tutsi. She had, Geneviève assured me, been a sex slave. She wouldn't speak of this; she couldn't bear to. And Jonas didn't dare question her any more directly because he had probably been one of the men who raped her. If this were to enter the official testimony, the gacaca would come to a halt and he would be remanded to the regular courts, where after a delay of many, many years, he might be sentenced to death. In the postgenocidal scheme of justice, rape is a Category One crime. From where I sat, it didn't much matter. Jonas was already in his fifties; he would die in prison.

Had this been a Western trial, with a defense attorney

ready to shout objections at the drop of a handkerchief, the witness's testimony would have been struck on the instant. Maybe the entire case would have been thrown out, and Jonas would have walked out of court a free man, looking jaunty in his pink jumpsuit. The thing is, he was almost certainly guilty. Other witnesses, many of them Hutu, broadly confirmed the woman's claims. And Jonas's defense was the defense of a guilty person. He rebutted one witness by insisting that he was mistaking Jonas for his son, who *had* been a killer, and to someone else he protested that he couldn't have killed on one of the days in question because he had hurt his foot. And finally he told the court that he couldn't have followed written orders because he didn't know how to read. He was pathetic. Many people in the courthouse — which was just a few rows of wooden benches shaded by corrugated plastic roofing — laughed in scorn.

Even knowing what I did, I was happy that the judges sentenced him to thirty-five years. And so were most of the spectators. Afterward the mood was one of calm satisfaction, as in a theater after the successful performance of an old and much-loved play. In the crowd I saw Beata M., the judge I'd spoken with the year before. Since then she had moved to another district and was no longer working for the gacaca, but she had come back to her former home for sentimental reasons, wanting to see justice done to the miscreants of that time. She pointed to the judges' table, where well-wishers were shaking hands with the trial's notables. "You see," she said, "all Rwandans want to reconcile."

Of course this left out Jonas and the other detainees, but by now they were being taken back to their prison, to serve out the remainder of their sentences or to await their turn at justice. All of them — the young ones and the old ones; the ones who had spruced themselves up for this public appearance, cleaning their pink uniforms as well as they could, and the ones who no longer bothered to care for themselves and stank of years of grime; the ones who strode past and the ones who shuffled — looked very small.

CHAPTER 4

Only Drowning Men Can See Them

What Does My Suffering Say About Me?
And What Does It Say About God?

When the twins were in the third grade, their teacher had them write an essay for Thanksgiving. The theme was "What I Am Thankful For." They handed in their papers, and after reading them the teacher told Kelly to show hers to her mother. Kelly was puzzled. Like her sister, Kate, she was a precociously gifted writer, used to getting her schoolwork back marked with A's. She was afraid she'd done something wrong. It wasn't until she read her paper to her mother that she learned what it was. She'd written that she was thankful not to be physically or mentally handicapped. Now Nancy Daley, who had been telling her children all their lives that they could do or be anything, explained to Kelly that she *was* handicapped.

I first heard this story from Kelly, with running commentary from Kate, and then again from Nancy, whose version of it was colored by embarrassment at the subterfuge and pride that the subterfuge had paid off and her children had had a few years in which they could think of themselves as normal, or, given the ambiguities surrounding that word, no different from anybody else. I was so taken by the story's charm that it didn't occur to me until later that even as eight-year-olds, the girls must have known they were different. None of their classmates came to school with various parts of their bodies heavily bandaged — their hands, most often, but sometimes their arms or legs or necks. None of them had to go to the hospital so often or stay home so long when they got out.

A possible answer was suggested by another story they told me. The summer after the Thanksgiving paper, Nancy and her husband, Chris, sent the girls to a camp for special children. They may have been trying to make up for their earlier deception by giving the girls a crash course in reality. Kate and Kelly met kids with Down syndrome and cerebral palsy, and a nosy girl in a wheelchair who kept asking them what was wrong with their hands, until at last Kelly asked her why *she* had to wear diapers. Kelly and Kate could walk; they could run and swim and use the bathroom on their own. At that point in their lives they could still change most of their dressings without too much help from a grown-up, sometimes holding a bandage in place with a nose. So strictly speaking, they weren't handicapped. Of course another possibility was that when she wrote her Thanksgiving essay, Kelly wasn't making a statement but asking a question: *Am I handicapped? Is that the word for the thing that makes me different?* By the time I got around to this hypothesis, there was no way to confirm it, since Kate and Kelly were dead. They died within two weeks of each other, at the age of twenty-seven.

Kate and Kelly Daley had recessive dystrophic epidermolysis bullosa, a rare congenital skin disease that is estimated to affect 2.5 people in a million.[1] (A more common, less severe variety is known as epidermolysis bullosa. Both conditions are known to their sufferers simply as "EB.") When the girls were born in 1979, doctors told their parents that there were only twenty-five cases like theirs in the United States. EB's effects have been compared to being burned every day of one's life. Its sufferers have abnormally fragile skin that is subject to severe and constant blistering. The blisters in turn develop into open sores, which frequently become infected. Not just the skin is vulnerable, but all the soft tissues. In some cases, nearly all skin surfaces and mucous membranes from mouth to anus are covered with blisters. The hands contract; the fingers and toes fuse. Even eating can be excruciating. Until fairly recently, EB was considered a childhood disease, because people who have it rarely live past thirty.

When you first met the twins, who usually went around together, your eye was guiltily drawn to the glaring stigmata of their illness: the sores and bandages, the blunt pawlike hands with fingers whittled to stubs by multiple surgeries and bone resorption. (For all that, they were pretty dexterous. Kelly was proud of being able to keep a cupcake balanced on top of her hand while she nibbled neatly around its edges.) After a while, though, their personalities asserted themselves, and their debility receded into the background; in time you barely noticed it.

They were in their late twenties but seemed younger, even childlike. It was why I always thought of them as girls. Part of it was that they were small and wispy — what women's magazines used to call "pixie-ish" — and dressed like Catholic-school girls, in high-necked sweaters and long skirts (though the first time I met them, at some friends' wedding, they were decked out in Goth formal, complete with long white half-gloves that disguised their tortured hands; the bandages visible below the short sleeves of their dresses might've been fashion accessories). Their body language, too, was childlike. When Kelly was amused, she'd hunch her shoulders, squeeze her eyes shut, and emit a soft, almost inaudible giggle. They still had the ardor and vulnerability that most young people shed in adolescence, or really scrape off like a despised skin, rubbing themselves raw against whatever experience they think will help them get rid of it.

But most EB sufferers are small, since every calorie they take in goes to healing. The few who live into middle age look like wizened children. Before Kelly and Kate had feeding ports, which they called their "buttons," surgically implanted in their stomachs at the age of thirteen, Kate weighed fifty-six pounds and Kelly sixty. They dressed the way they did to cover their wounds and keep their wrappings in place. Given a choice, they'd have worn tank tops and spaghetti straps. They'd have sunbathed naked. Kelly, who, had she been born twenty years earlier, would surely have been a hippie, was frustrated that she couldn't go about naked all the time. "We're more a mind than a body," she complained. And Kate sighed, "I so want to live as a body. It's my dream to live as a body!"[2]

Kate was smaller than Kelly and had a slight, endearing

lisp. Like many twins — like many people who've spent their lives together — the Daleys were used to finishing each other's sentences. And while they depended on each other's company, they were also a little bored with it and eager for other people's. In that way they reminded me of Chekhov characters. Kelly was more outgoing, Kate reserved, but in the presence of someone new and interesting, both girls would twitter and flirt competitively. They loved food. Few young women I've known were less preoccupied with carbs and calories; they could eat ice cream all day and not put on a pound. Because even a piece of toast could rupture the lining of their throats, they were restricted to soft foods, but there were plenty of those they liked. Kelly was wild for foie gras. "Not the pâté, the real thing," she specified, like an heiress ordering at Le Bernardin. "I have kind of a snobby palate. I'm a wistful hedonist. If I was healed, I'm afraid I'd be totally into the pleasures of the flesh."

Nancy Daley didn't know she was carrying twins. In 1979 ultrasounds weren't yet mandatory for expectant mothers, and the doctor didn't catch the second heartbeat. Kelly came out first, with a blister on her leg. But it was only when she saw Kate that Nancy realized that something was really wrong. From toe to hip, the baby's right leg had no skin. Kate and Kelly were whisked from St. Luke's Hospital in Newburgh, New York, to the neonatal intensive care unit at New York Hospital, where they remained for the next two months, nestled in an incubator, while the doctors tried to come up with a diagnosis. Nancy and Chris would drive down to New York a few times a week to gaze at them through the glass. They rarely got to hold them.

Only then did Nancy remember a dream she'd had years earlier, before she and Chris were married. At the time it had shaken her so badly that she couldn't go to her college classes the next day. She'd dreamed that she'd given birth to twins and wanted to tell Chris. But afraid of leaving the babies alone, she'd brought them to a girl she'd known in high school and asked her to watch them while she looked for him. She searched for Chris everywhere but couldn't find him, and at last she went back to her friend's. There was no sign of the babies. "What did you do with the twins?" she asked frantically, and her friend said, "They're in the oven." She opened the oven door to show her. The babies lay inside, covered with blisters.

At last the doctors found a name for the babies' condition, pronounced it incurable, and advised their parents to place them in an institution. Chris and Nancy refused. They may not have fully grasped how sick their children were or may have just taken it for granted that children belonged at home. They were young and inexperienced, and that made them stubborn. "They chose to live," Nancy said. "You could see it in their eyes."[3] The doctors suggested a compromise. Nancy and Chris could take one twin home and leave the other in care; Kelly always referred to this as "the Sophie's Choice option." Again the Daleys said no. The doctors shrugged. Nancy got a rushed lesson in bandaging a squirming infant, then she and Chris were on their own. The hospital didn't even give them a change of dressings.

This was long before the Internet gave ordinary people

access to the same information specialists had. The Daleys had to learn about their children's illness as it revealed itself, one fact at a time. One night, when the girls were still little, they woke up crying that they had "boo-boo eyes." They had developed spontaneous corneal abrasions. No one had warned Nancy that this was part of EB's repertoire. Kate's tongue would break out in blisters, which would cause it to adhere to her palate, and Nancy would have to carefully snip the adhesions with tiny surgical scissors before Kate's airway became blocked. Repeated procedures of this kind left Kate with a permanent lisp. Nancy would take the twins to family gatherings and on undressing them later find that the skin on their sides had broken open or slid down like a sweater because someone had picked them up under the arms — the way everybody picks up babies. The odd thing was that the children started crying only when they got home; all through the gathering they'd been quiet. "Tears wouldn't come to our eyes, we wouldn't say anything, because we didn't want to *not* get picked up," Kate remembered. "We wanted people to touch us."

The origin of the illness was a mystery. EB is an autosomal recessive condition, passed down by parents who each carry a copy of its gene but themselves remain disease-free. Neither Chris nor Nancy had a family history of EB, even in its milder forms. But Chris worked at the IBM plant in Fishkill, New York, where his job entailed frequent and prolonged exposure to chemicals. Over the years other IBM workers had children with severe birth defects, including microcephaly and other central nervous system malformations, bony anomalies, and vision problems. Because typically there was no family history that was remotely relevant, doctors often described these outcomes as being due to "spontaneous" mutations or simply of unknown origin, without ever considering chemical exposure as a factor. When the Daleys and other workers' families raised the question of chemical exposure with IBM, the corporation insisted that its employees' children had no higher incidence of birth defects than the general population.[4] Until Chris left IBM in 1993, Big Blue's health plan covered the girls' medical expenses; afterward they relied on Nancy's insurance at her job as a school medical assistant.

The expenses were staggering. In the course of their lifetime, Kate and Kelly each had thirty surgeries on their hands alone. Routine care required visits to specialists. Even with insurance, the family would have been bankrupted if Nancy hadn't overcome her natural shyness to take on health-care providers, insurers, and legislators in order to get the children the treatment they needed. In an average month the girls used more bandages than a small hospital, and for a while no one would pay for them. IBM told the Daleys to apply to Orange County; the county passed them back to IBM. Other families with the disease had to beg local facilities for their used bedsheets, which they would cut up and use as dressings.

In response, Nancy helped found the Dystrophic Epidermolysis Bullosa Research Association, or DebRA, an information and advocacy organization for EB sufferers and their families. One of her first accomplishments was to get the New York State handicapped children's program to include EB among the conditions it covered. After that the Daleys got their bandages — a term that encompassed such specialized products as fishnetlike contact layers, impregnated gauze, absorbent tape, and hydrofiber wound dressings — at a nominal cost. When I met Nancy, she was trying to get similar legislation enacted on a federal level. She's small and lean, with blue eyes whose gaze can be suspicious and dauntingly intense, and I wouldn't want to be the official who had to look into them while turning her down.

Actually, almost everything about EB was a mystery, and what little was known of the disease when Kate and Kelly were babies was overwhelmingly bleak. The most famous case was a young man known as "the Crisco Kid," because that was what his caregivers used to lubricate his dressings. He'd spent his life in institutions, where his days consisted of being bathed, wrapped, and unwrapped like some inert, suffering package. He had so little stimulation that he was thought to be retarded. Back then that was a common assumption about EB patients; even the people who cared for them had trouble telling the effects of the disease from the effects of the warehousing that passed for its treatment.

So the Daleys were understandably excited when they heard about a Romanian biochemist named Pavel Kozak who had developed an experimental therapy for skin diseases, including EB. Through the Kozak method, he had achieved cures dramatic enough to attract the attention of medical researchers in several countries, along with an international circle of devotees. One of these was a Canadian businessman who gave grants to the families of sick children. With his help Chris and Nancy took the two-year-old twins to Kozak's clinic in West Germany. They stayed for two months. Kate and Kelly were given mysterious medications — Kozak refused to disclose the ingredients or submit his results for peer review — and anointed with mysterious creams. They were fed a diet of freshly killed chicken, locally grown vegetables, and freshly caught fish from a nearby stream, with everything boiled twice for purity. Twenty-three years later, Kate swore that she could still remember how vile it tasted.

The clinic had the air of a religious encampment, a place holding its breath for a miracle. The Daleys were introduced to a child with EB whose fingers and toes had spontaneously unfused. While they waited for the treatment to take effect, the family stayed in a small room in a hotel attached to the clinic. At night, bored and half-crazy with hunger, Chris and Nancy would wait for the children to fall asleep so they could steal out to a restaurant across the street. Sometimes they had to crawl out the door on their stomachs in order not to wake them. Once, just as their dinner was being served, they were summoned to the phone. On the other end was a stony German nurse who ordered them to come back at once because "your daughters vill not stop screaming."

On the night before they were supposed to leave, one of Kozak's colleagues sidled up to Chris in the hotel corridor and offered to sell him what he insisted was the "real" medicine, which Kozak was keeping secret from all but a few "special" patients. It would cost a thousand dollars in cash. A big man with appraising, heavy-lidded eyes and the languid manner of a professional poker player, Chris suspected that he was being conned, but it was a risk he was willing to take. He and the contact met across from the restaurant at midnight and made the transfer, with a furtive solemnity more appropriate to the handover of a suitcase nuke.

The Daleys came back home, where after a while Kate and Kelly refused to eat the listless therapeutic fare and lost an alarming amount of weight. Nancy started letting them have ice cream. Their health, which had improved marginally, deteriorated. Although Nancy and Chris agreed that Kozak was a "snake," they also thought that he had something genuine, and for many years afterward they wondered if the girls might've gotten better if they'd stuck with his program. They could almost accept that their children wouldn't be cured as long as they could believe that a cure existed, somewhere, available to those who were strong or faithful enough to live up to its terms. It's hard to say who would have been strong enough to stick to the Kozak method. The few EB patients who passed through his clinics (he subsequently moved his practice to Spain, and today a Kozak clinic is operating in his native Romania) found it impossible to stay on his austere diet. As a young man from Holland said, "It was good for my skin but bad for my body."[5]

Kozak was the last authority the Daleys turned to. Rather, he was the last person they viewed as an authority, as somebody who knew more about EB than they did. From then on, they would continue to take the children to medical professionals but with a growing awareness of how uninformed and inept — and sometimes how cruel — those professionals could be. "We constantly hear, 'Hmm, what do you think?' " Kelly said. "They're always asking us what we think. The first time that happened, I was horrified. I'm thinking, 'Why are you asking me what I think? *I'm coming to you!*' " It came out as a wail whose anguish was only partly a joke.

When the girls were little, the EB clinic at Rockefeller University told Nancy to treat their sores exclusively with the antibiotic cream Bactroban, assuring her that they would never develop an immunity to it. When they were fifteen, the Bactroban stopped working, and Kelly lost 70 percent of her skin. Once, while the sisters were in college, Kate fell gravely ill, and a doctor had to make an emergency visit to her dorm room. Nancy was there changing her bandages when he arrived. "He went white and his jaw dropped," Nancy remembered. "And he started stammering, 'You n-n-need an expert! I-I-I d-d-don't know what to t-tell you. This is over my head.' And I grabbed him by the shoulders and said, 'I have no expert. I have you. And I need you to help me here.' " On still another occasion, Kelly had to be rushed to the hospital after fainting and falling on her hand only days after an operation. Her regular surgeon was off duty, and the covering doctor knew nothing about the Daleys and nothing about EB. He took one look at the children and threw his gloves across the room. "How could you let them get like this?" he hissed. It was one of the few times the girls saw Nancy cry.

"I was terrified my whole life," she says. "We were on our own to figure things out. There was nobody."

The practical consequences were that Nancy had to become an expert on EB by herself. She got so skilled at bandaging the girls after hand operations that the primary surgeon started referring to "the Daley method." Until they were thirteen and insurance began to pay for visiting nurses, she provided virtually all their care, spending as much as seven hours at a stretch bathing them, changing dressings, draining wounds, and applying ointment. To take off their bandages she'd have the girls soak in the tub until they floated loose, since removing them any other way would have meant tearing off inches of skin.

When Kate and Kelly were still babies, their parents would sing a song they made up as they worked on them: "They fly through the air with the greatest of ease; it's the Daley twins with the rare disease." It helped to have a sense of humor. It helped, too, that the girls were naturally resilient. After one especially gruesome hand operation — the surgeon had stripped off the girls' skin from elbow to fingertips — bits of dressing got stuck in the raw flesh, and Chris and Nancy had to pluck them out with tweezers. It took ten hours, and the only painkiller they had was Tylenol with codeine. "It was a bloody, gelatinous mess," Nancy recalled. "Their hands were shaking, their eyes were rolling in the back of their heads like they were going to pass out at any point. Ten hours of this, at four years old! And then we finally bandaged them all back up, and they looked at us and said, 'Are we going to get ice cream now?' "

Children first hone their intelligence on their immediate environment. They catalog its features; they figure out its rules. The puffy white shapes in the sky are clouds. Don't put your hand in the flame on the stove. Sugar, salt, and laundry soap look alike, but only one of them is nice to eat. Among the first things Kate and Kelly remembered learning were different kinds of pain. A superficial scrape hurt exquisitely and sharply and made you cry when Mama ran water on it. A deep sore on your hand hurt worse when you let the hand hang down. When Kelly was five or six, she told Chris that after operations she sometimes felt her hand going *Boom, boom, boom!* "I was astonished when he came up with an actual word for it: 'Throbbing,' " she would later write in her journal. "It was one of my first moments when I realized the thrill of finding the exact right word to describe an experience. It meant that if other people saw fit to find a word for it, then it must be a real feeling — it legitimized that pain."[6]

IN THE LATE 1990s, I spent five days listening to some Vietnam vets tell stories about their experience during the war and its sad, shameful aftermath — an aftermath that in the telling seemed to go on for decades without ever becoming ordinary postwar life. This was at a Buddhist retreat for Vietnam vets at a "holistic education center" in upstate New York, not far from where I live now. The retreat was part of a larger gathering that took place every two years, presided over by the revered Vietnamese Zen master and peace activist Thich Nhat Hanh. Only the Dalai Lama has greater stature within Buddhism or is more widely known outside it. As many as a thousand people would come to meditate and attend the master's dharma talks, while off to the side, in a bare one-room cabin with black zafus (meditation cushions) arranged in a wide circle on its industrial-carpeted floor, the vets hunkered. They were trying to heal. Thich Nhat Hanh had invited them. He always made a special place for vets at his retreats in the United States. It was a magnanimous and poetic gesture: a Vietnamese man of peace offering a refuge to American men of war.

I'd been invited to the retreat to help the vets write their stories. The goal wasn't aesthetic but spiritual and therapeutic. Many of the men had post-traumatic stress disorder (PTSD), whose treatment, according to many theories, hinges on the reframing of chaotic shards and splinters of memory as a coherent narrative. (For recovery to take place, writes the psychiatrist Judith Herman, "the survivor tells the story of the trauma. . . . This work of reconstruction actually transforms the traumatic memory, so that it can be integrated into the survivor's life story."[7] Hannah Arendt put it more simply: "All sorrows can be borne if you put them into a story or tell a story about them.")[8] I'd agreed to take part in this event, which I suppose was a kind of writing workshop, without considering how ill equipped I was to be a therapist or how many times I'd warned students against conflating writing with therapy: God forbid writing should make them feel good. By the time I did consider it, it was too late to back out.

I wanted to talk about my misgivings with the retreat's leader, a former marine sergeant turned Zen priest named Ted Fuller,[9] but when I got to the retreat, he wasn't there. Outside the cabin middle-aged men were pacing anxiously. They were dressed in outgrown fatigues or shapeless, gaily patterned jackets imported from Third World countries, as if they were simultaneously reenacting their service in the war and playing at being the hippies who'd marched against it. (Many of them, of course, had *become* hippies after they got home. They'd made war, and now they wanted their share of love.) They stayed close together, almost huddling, in a fug of cigarette smoke and looked narrowly at any stranger who approached too closely. They trusted only each other. Somebody told me that Fuller had had a recurrence of PTSD and wouldn't be coming to the retreat. Another vet, who was a counselor or facilitator of some kind, had stepped in to take his place, but it didn't make the men feel any better. They loved Fuller; he was their priest, their platoon leader and big brother, and with him gone you could sense their panic spreading in ripples. This was what had happened in Vietnam whenever a popular c.o. was killed. A new officer would take over his command, but the men were always unhappy. The fucking new guy wouldn't be any good.

Inside the cabin the fifty-odd participants sat in a circle on the floor. One by one, we introduced ourselves. Each named his branch, his unit, and the dates of his tour. The men said a little about their lives in the world. Many of them were estranged from their families. Statistically, Vietnam combat veterans are twice as likely to divorce as their civilian counterparts.[10] I was struck by how many belonged to religious communities — Buddhist, Hindu, or Christian ones such as the Bruderhof. Of all the men there, those with religious affiliations seemed to be the happiest, and I was reminded that in the Middle Ages many soldiers would enter monasteries on returning from the wars. The others struck me as haunted. This was true even of a man named Matt, who boasted of how much he'd loved killing gooks. He was playing the part of the jolly Vietnam psycho, but in repose his features were mournful and his mouth was crimped in a sneer of disgust. Only one of the vets was visibly injured, but all of them had the affect of injured people, a wincing inner stiffness. Amputees often experience pain at the site of the missing extremity; it's called phantom limb syndrome.

These men seemed to suffer from an odd inversion of it, as if an invisible limb had been lopped off and the rest of their being was flooded with the pain of its loss.

When my turn came, I felt obliged to say that as a teenager I'd been active in the peace movement, not the sweet-natured, flower-bearing peace movement, but the cussing, brick-throwing one. I'd once thrown a brick at Richard Nixon. (I didn't mention that I'd missed by a good fifty feet.) I wasn't ashamed of having opposed the war, only of having done so from dry high ground while boys a little older than I waded chest-deep through paddies that stank of the corpses rotting at the bottom and sometimes fell to join them. I was sitting on one of the zafus, and I felt both elevated and exposed. I half-expected to be driven out of the room.

I wasn't driven out of the room. Somebody laughed when I mentioned throwing a brick at Nixon, but otherwise the only response was "Thank you for sharing," and the vets said that to everybody. They were bitter about the war, but their bitterness was catholic. It made no distinction between the spoiled little pricks at peace marches and the old pricks at the legion hall. They resented everyone Vietnam had not happened to. That included parents, wives, and children. It may have been one of the reasons so few of them had families. Or perhaps their isolation represented another kind of phantom limb syndrome, in which they themselves were the severed extremities of some great, complacent body that from time to time was troubled by the distant twinges that emanated from them, and grimaced and patted at itself but could find nothing missing.

For all that, the mood of the retreat wasn't completely

somber. Once a younger attendee, a veteran of the 1991 Gulf War, called the Vietnam vets "a bunch of old fucks." He was skinny and haunted-looking, with a jaw hypertrophied from clenching, and he scowled around the circle as if daring somebody to make him take back his words. Instead the whole room cracked up, and afterward the young soldier became the group mascot, the kid who'd reminded them that they were just a bunch of old fucks.

I stayed at the nearby country home of one of the other writing instructors. Each morning we rose at five-thirty so we could join the men for the first meditation. Then we began work. The term "work" is probably a misnomer; so is "writing instructor." I didn't instruct anyone in anything. The vets were constantly showing me their writing, but early on I saw that it would be beside the point to critique it. That wasn't what they'd come for. It was the only time I've ever been asked to look at someone else's writing without him wanting to know if I thought he could get it published. Many men just told their stories, standing inside the circle of listeners, the shy ones sitting on its perimeter. In the end everybody did this.

The storytelling had a ritual quality that was heightened by the makeshift shrine the vets had set up at the center of the circle. It consisted of some Indian blankets on which they'd arrayed different objects: service medals, snapshots of their younger selves or buddies who hadn't made it back, Zippo lighters, flowers, cartridges, strings of beads, even one of those vicious Ka-bar knives that could be used for splicing a fuse or slitting a throat. I thought of them as offerings. You could say that they were the men's offerings to the Buddha or to the war, which had taken them in its mouth and spat them out. Before that, though, it had marked them with its teeth.

I remember a man named Harold, tall, thin, stooped, with a fringe of long hair around a glaring bald scalp. He was the saddest man I'd ever met. His sadness wasn't a feeling inside him. He was inside it, sealed in it like a homunculus in a beaker. During the war he'd been a conscientious objector, but the army had drafted him anyway. Then it magnanimously made him a corpsman so he wouldn't have to carry a weapon. Not long after he arrived in country, his unit got in a firefight. Everywhere Harold looked, men were dying. He saw men with their limbs blown off, men split open, the hot guts slithering out of them. Kneeling over one of the wounded, he discovered with horror that he was looking down at one of his buddies. He described frantically trying to stuff the man's — the boy's — entrails back inside him. That was what his training was good for.

After a while with this, he could no longer stand to just watch. When a man in front of him fell, he picked up his rifle and fired it and saw an enemy soldier go down. It didn't satisfy him, so he crawled up to the man and shot him in the face, then shot him several times more. With each pull on the trigger he screamed. I imagine that he was deranged with fury, not just fury at the enemy but at the forces that had turned him from an innocent, conscientious-objector kid into a killer. That was how he saw himself now.

As Harold told his story, I was afraid he'd start screaming again. He'd begun to speak in the high, pinched voice that is often a prelude to it. But instead of screaming he wept. The whole time he spoke, tears coursed down his face, and whenever I saw him in the next few days, his eyes were wet. If this had been a movie, the storytelling would have cured him and he'd have been free of his grief, able to smile again. But I never saw Harold smile. "The goal of recounting the trauma story is integration, not exorcism," Herman writes.[11] And the psychiatrist Jonathan Shay, author of two powerful and important books on combat trauma in Vietnam vets, warns, "There are no theatrical cures where the veteran screams, vomits, bleeds, dies, and is reborn cleansed of the war."[12]

Another man told us how he'd once killed two little girls. He'd been playing with them in a village when suddenly he heard a shot, dropped to the ground, and began firing wildly. So did everyone else in his squad; they were all terrified. When it was over, the children were lying dead before him; one girl had been cut in half. There was a man who'd assassinated civilians — my guess would be for the CIA, though he wouldn't say so directly. Even at the retreat there were things that couldn't be said. A chubby, soft-spoken man with the face of a kindly Bluto had been in charge of loading medium-range bombers at an air base, where one day he received orders to load some ordnance of an unfamiliar type. The shells were marked with the biohazard symbol. He and his crew refused to handle them, and for this insubordination he was busted in rank and put on a shit detail. A few weeks later he was caught in a rocket attack, in which he was badly wounded. All these years later he still walked with a cane. The Department of Veterans' Affairs, he said, was always trying to screw him out of his benefits. The other vets laughed. They all knew about the VA. It was like an insurance company that denied your claims after it had sent goons over to your house to saw off your arms and legs.

One of the things we are consistently told about trauma, by both sufferers and those who treat them, is that it is incommunicable. During World War I, psychiatrists were frustrated by their shell-shocked patients' inability to say what had happened to them. All they could do was reenact it, like the hypnotized soldier who "beg[an] to twist and turn on the couch and shout in a terror-stricken voice. He talk[ed] as he talked at the time when the shock occurred to him."[13] If trauma, as some experts believe, is recorded in an older, more primitive stratum of memory, in *pre*-memory, it may not be fully accessible to language. (Or perhaps the medium of recording isn't writing but crude pictures or the smears of a finger dipped in blood.) Hence the difficulty of telling a story about it, and the absolute imperative of doing so. A further complication is that even when the traumatized succeed in telling what happened to them, their testimony is often ignored or, alternatively, suppressed. Freud is thought to have disavowed his seduction theory because he couldn't accept the evidence that certain respectable Viennese burghers, men he smoked cigars with, were molesting their children.

That war can damage, even shatter, men's personalities has been known for almost a hundred years and on at least two occasions willfully forgotten. What we now call posttraumatic stress disorder was known as shell shock during World War I and as battle fatigue or war neurosis during World War II. In both instances, afflicted soldiers were initially accused of malingering before being diagnosed as mentally ill or, more accurately, mentally injured. But then the diagnosis fell out of fashion. By the early 1960s war neurosis had been purged from the *Diagnostic and Statistical Manual of Mental Disorders (DSM)* and most psychiatrists maintained that there was no such thing as a psychiatric war injury.

It wasn't until 1980, seven years after the last American troops had left Vietnam, that a new edition of the *DSM* included the diagnosis of post-traumatic stress disorder. Some of the delay was certainly due to clinical skepticism. Some of it can be traced to the politics of the VA, where insiders worried that the claims of psychologically injured Vietnam vets might "bankrupt the United States Treasury."[14] This is a recurrent fear. Even after a 2004 army study found that one in six soldiers in Iraq was reporting symptoms of a major psychiatric illness,[15] the Veterans' Hospital Association was said to be exploring ways of tightening its diagnostic criteria for PTSD so that fewer claims would be eligible.[16]

No bureaucracy could get away with tightening the diagnostic criteria for a severed arm. Trauma is different because it's invisible. We speak of it not as a wound but as a disorder, a label that Shay finds disingenuous: "We do not refer to a veteran who has had an arm blown off by a grenade as suffering from 'Missing Arm Disorder.' "[17] Trauma cannot be seen and resists being spoken of, and the people and institutions its victims turn to for help often resist hearing them. Perhaps this is why the traumatized can seem at once tongue-tied and overly vehement. Trying to make their injuries known, they flail, gesticulate, and stutter. A therapist who works with survivors of political torture told me about a client from West Africa who on entering her office pulled his pants down, wanting her to see the scars of his ordeal.[18] And perhaps the symptoms of trauma — the sleeplessness, the flashbacks, the detonations of rage, the self-entombment in drink or drugs — are also attempts at communication. In medieval paintings the martyrs are often depicted pointing to their wounds or to the instruments that made them: Saint Lucy holds her eyes on a plate, Saint Agatha a severed breast. Saint Lawrence displays his gridiron. Look, they say. See what they did to me.

AT FIRST THE other writers and I were the only civilians in the retreat house. But as the days passed, more outsiders joined us, admitted through some screening process that remained hidden from me. Uncharitably, I thought of them as voyeurs drawn by the vets' low-bottom charisma, the mud-dark mojo of their manly suffering. The sight of these tourists perched contentedly on their zafus irritated me. It made me feel less special. Further, it perplexed me that the men who had been so suspicious of strangers a few days before were now suddenly rolling out the carpet for them.

One day we heard from a German woman in her early forties. She was earnest as only a German can be, wanting not to be liked, as an American would, but to be approved of. She'd asked to join the group because her father was a veteran — that is, a veteran of the Wehrmacht. I mean Keitel's Wehrmacht, Hitler's. She didn't know what he'd done in the war; she'd never asked him. That was her problem. It wasn't that she was afraid of what she might find out. Her father was a good man, she was sure of this. But he was also in terrible pain, a pain he could not express, though she'd been conscious of it for as long as she could remember. It was a thing he wouldn't share with her, a burden but also a treasure. Speaking of her father's hoarded pain, she began to weep, and to my surprise many of the vets wept with her. I hadn't seen them weeping during Harold's story, though they were clearly moved by it. So why should they cry at a story told by a civilian, and a foreign civilian at that, a story whose true subject was not actual horror but inferred horror — what *might have* happened?

Perhaps hearing this story told by a woman gave the men license to feel more deeply and express what they felt with less restraint. Maybe the vets were reminded of their own daughters and moved to think of them being haunted by the pain they'd kept to themselves for so long. Or perhaps inference was somehow more powerful than experience, especially the experience of war, which is so often untrustworthy. Soldiers with combat trauma may only dimly remember the precipitating event or its aftermath. Shay notes that this is especially true if they became "berserkers," entering a trance of vengeful rage in which they piled up the enemy's corpses like sandbags, immune to pain, indifferent to death. Soldiers who have passed through a berserk state, Shay tells us, frequently can't remember the names or faces of the men they served with afterward. "No living human has any claim on [them], not even the claim of being noticed and remembered." [19]

By unveiling a sorrow from private life, a domestic sorrow as familiar as a cooking pot, the German woman had started a trend. She was followed by another civilian who, as far as I could figure out, had been admitted mainly because he was half Lakota Sioux and half Chicano. This gave him oppression on both sides of the family. I don't remember much of what he said. Soon the vets, too, were weighing in, telling stories about their alcoholism and defunct marriages, their brokenhearted parents and fucked-up kids. The stories were wrenching. Such yawning loneliness, so many lives stunted and ruined. Their whole time in Vietnam they had dreamed of coming back to the world, but when they did, they found that the world no longer had a place for them, or for what they'd become.

"What is wrong with you?" they were always being asked. Nearly all of them had heard it at one time or another. Their mothers asked them, their wives asked them, their bosses and drinking buddies asked them. Because they couldn't sleep or had dreams from which they woke covered in sweat, their hearts racing. (One man had woken with his hands around his girlfriend's throat.) Because they felt the wrong things — "irrational" rage, "inappropriate" grief. Or because they felt nothing at all. In Vietnam they had brushed off the deaths of their best friends. "Fuck it, they're dead," the refrain went. "Don't mean nothing."[20]

Listening to them, I was reminded of that stately Edwardian chiller "The Monkey's Paw." An elderly couple comes into possession of a charm, the monkey's paw of the title, that's supposed to grant its owner three wishes. Not believing it — more as a joke, really — the man wishes for two hundred pounds. Soon afterward a messenger comes with the news that their son has been killed in a factory accident, his body mangled beyond recognition. In restitution his employer is giving them two hundred pounds. Skeptics no longer, the parents wish that he be brought back to life.

And no sooner have they made their wish than they hear something tap softly at the door and then, more emphatically, knock: once, twice, three times, louder, always louder. The woman cries out the boy's name and totters to the door. By now the blows are deafening. "For God's sake, don't open it!" her husband warns her, but already she's drawing back the bolt. With nerveless fingers he clasps the monkey's paw and makes another wish, the last wish left to him, and at that moment the knocking stops. He remembered, you see, that he'd only wished for his son to be brought back to life, neglecting to stipulate that he be brought back whole.

Many of the vets' stories struck me as versions of that one, as it might be told by the son. They were the stories of dead men, or of men who saw themselves as dead. Shay reports that many of his patients think of themselves as having died in Vietnam, and people traumatized elsewhere often harbor similar convictions. I think of Beata M., the gacaca judge in Kigali: "I can say that we have survived, but survived dead because we are all the time dead."

But the horror of "The Monkey's Paw" resides not just in the fact that the son is dead but that he has been made unrecognizable. More than one hundred years ago, Pierre Janet, observing the bizarre "automatisms" of mental patients at the Salpêtrière, concluded that "the individual, when overcome by vehement emotions, is not himself."[21] In their most severe form, the traumatic disorders seem to smash the foundations of identity. Who am I to be possessed by a memory, not even a memory, but an image, a sound, a smell?[22] Who am I to be driven wild with fear because somewhere a door has slammed?[23] Who am I if I can no longer hold a job or sleep beside my wife or pick up my baby son without being afraid of what I might do to him? "Why I became like that?" one of Shay's vets wonders. "It was all evil. All evil. Where before, I wasn't. I look back. I look back today, and I'm horrified at what I turned into. What I was." Then he adds, "I brought it back here with me." [24]

But the vets' stories also contained an element of one-upmanship, or one-upmanship crept into them in the telling. If one man had walked out on his family, another had threatened his at gunpoint; one teller's alcoholism was trumped by another's drug addiction. The mood in the cabin became the mood of a high-stakes poker game, dry-lipped and avid. The stack of chips grew higher. At last Georgie — an older vet with an irate red face and shrewd blue eyes, who'd made a career lecturing on the war at schools and community centers and selling a video called *The Vietnam Experience* — stood up and announced that he was sick of talking about Vietnam. "Vietnam was bullshit," he said. "All these years I've been doing my Vietnam number, when I haven't even begun to touch my *real* pain. I'm talking about my *incest issues!*" Everybody stared at him. Was I imagining it, or did a look of triumph steal over Georgie's face? He had a royal flush, and he knew it.

The next day the vets retold their stories for an audience of visitors from the main retreat. At first only three or four men were supposed to do this, but after some complaints about elitism, the group voted to let anyone who wanted to get up and say his piece. The performance, for that was what it was, took place in a pavilion that could seat a hundred people, and sitting up front in a position of honor was Thich Nhat Hanh. People call him "Thay," Vietnamese for "Teacher." He must have been in his seventies and was said to be in poor health, but his carriage was sprightly, his face virtually without lines. His big ears and tentative, inward smile made me think of a dreamy kid spacing out at the back of the classroom. But he paid attention to everything.

As one vet after another got up to recite his toll of blood and guilt, many in the audience became restless. I was restless. The stories that earlier had welled with feeling now seemed shrill and false, a kind of chest beating. Of course the boy spilling out his life in Harold's arms would be his friend, the smoke would clear to reveal the corpses of children. I had a momentary fantasy that the men whose testimonies had moved me so a day or two before had been replaced by impostors. Thay kept his gaze fixed on each speaker in turn. He was scowling with what might have been disapproval or terrific concentration, as if he had never encountered such a phenomenon before and was trying very hard to make sense of it.

The following morning, the last of the retreat, we filed down to the main building to hear Thay's closing dharma talk. For the first time, he addressed the vets directly. He told them that it was time for them to give up their pain, to relinquish their special claim on it. The Buddha, he said, had given up an entire kingdom, with all its splendors and pleasures, so it shouldn't be too hard for them to give up their suffering. Instead they must go out into the world and tend to the suffering of others. The way he put it was, "You must become the flame on the candle."

Buddhism teaches adherents to dispel suffering by analyzing it, asking where it comes from, whom it really afflicts, whether, in the absence of a fixed self, it can be said to afflict anyone at all. In this way it may be transformed. The most useful — "useful" being the highest term of praise in Buddhism's pragmatic phraseology — transformation is that of suffering into compassion. I thought this was what Thich Nhat Hanh was trying to say. The brittle tinder of the self's proprietary hurt had to be set alight, that others might be comforted in the cold and the dark. Only then would the hurt be consumed. It seemed to me that a lot of the vets were already doing this — the ones in religious communities, for instance, or the man who returned to Vietnam every few years to help clear land mines. I imagined that they would find Thay's message encouraging.

But to my surprise, many of the vets were upset. They felt that they'd been accused of something. "He didn't get it," they kept saying afterward, as we sat down to talk one last time before heading our separate ways. "He's selling us out." They were like men frozen by a sudden slap, indignant but also shamed. They'd been sold out so many times, by so many people and institutions, that they saw the world through a lens of betrayal. Suffering was their big thing, their distinguished thing. For some of them it was the only thing, the only recognizable evidence of the sacrifice their country had never acknowledged. The problem was that their evidence often went unrecognized, since in most cases it had no outward sign, no stump or scar or lesion. That was why they kept pointing at it. If they didn't suffer, they might feel nothing. They might *be* nothing. From a Buddhist perspective, nothing's not such a terrible thing to be, but in America to be a nothing is to be a loser. And what could be worse than that?

We write to you, brethren, the story of the martyrs and of the blessed Polycarp, who put an end to the persecution by his martyrdom as though adding the seal. For one might almost say that all that had gone before happened in order that the Lord might show to us from above a martyrdom in accordance with the Gospel. For he waited to be betrayed as also the Lord had done, that we too might become his imitators.

— "Martyrdom of Polycarp"[25]

Read in its entirety, from Genesis to Revelation, the Bible tells the story of a supremely powerful, disembodied god becoming an embodied, powerless human being — choosing to become that being. In the beginning God has two primary ways of demonstrating his power. The first is creation, culminating in the creation of the first man and woman. But no sooner has God made them — one from mud, the other from a piece of bone — than the man and woman rebel. They rebel childishly, impulsively, seduced by a murmuring voice in the garden. But still they have to be punished, because into a world that was completely good they have brought evil.[26] And so God demonstrates his power a second time by afflicting them. He condemns the man to be broken in labor and the woman to be tortured in childbirth. He condemns them both to die. And all the generations after them.

No one has ever died before this, maybe not even the beasts over which God gave humans dominion but that he would not let them eat. So imagine the shock of this punishment, the rift it tore in creation: that what was quick and hot and breathing might suddenly become cold and still, with no light in its eyes; that the self that had been so full might be emptied, slowly or in an instant, its emptying usually accompanied by disfigurement, fear, and pain. And that, unlike all other creatures, human beings would know that it was their fate to be destroyed this way. Saint Paul is clear about the enormity of this event, and clear, too, as to whose fault it was: "Wherefore, as by one man sin entered into the world, and death by sin; and so death passed upon all men, for all have sinned" (Rom. 5:12).

So begins a pattern in which human beings trespass against God and God causes human beings to suffer. It's physical suffering, engraved on the tablet of the errant human body. (Curiously, though, the most literal of these inscriptions, the mark of Cain, is meant to protect the bearer from the violence of other men. Is this evidence that God is merciful or just that he views vengeance as his monopoly?) In a fast-forward of the Old Testament,[27] God drowns the world and razes Sodom and Gomorrah while incidentally turning Lot's wife into salt, stifles Egyptian babies in their cribs, and sends the sea crashing over Pharaoh's army. He plunges Korah into the earth. He consumes the sons of Aaron with "strange fire." He wastes Israel with plague. All these acts of injury are at once punishments and proof. What God punishes are doubt and disobedience, the sins that brought about the Fall. He does this by producing incontrovertible proof that he exists. The proof is the harm he inflicts on doubters' bodies.[28] Perhaps this is what Kafka had in mind when he wrote "In the Penal Colony," a story in which criminals are punished by being incised with the commandments they are guilty of breaking. The instrument of inscription is a hideous machine — half tattoo gun and half loom — that transfixes the victims' bodies, tearing them to shreds.

In the New Testament, particularly in the Gospels, God changes.[29] The biblical scholar Jack Miles says that he undergoes a crisis, occasioned by his earlier abandonment of his chosen people. Now Israel has been defeated and faces extinction at Roman hands, and God must choose whether to rescue it the way he has in the past, by leading it to victory over its persecutors. Instead, writes Miles, "he allowed himself and his people to suffer a still more catastrophic defeat; but before that doom descended, he joined them, suffering in advance all that they would suffer, and creating out of his agony a way for them to rise from the dead with him."[30] His omnipotence, his incorporeality, his violence, all these things he gives up. He becomes a man; not even a man at first, but a baby.

What could be more helpless than a baby, or more vulnerable, in a country where babies are being massacred? And although the baby will grow up and will become a man of some strength — he works as a carpenter, hauling lumber, driving nails — one of the things that strikes witnesses is his gentleness, or, better, his forbearance, his avoidance of obvious shows of power, especially the power to injure. Although he sometimes indulges in martial, even bloodthirsty, rhetoric, the only act of violence he permits himself is to drive money changers from the Temple. Offered kingship of the world, he refuses. (Many, many years later, when the Catholic Church adopted the doctrine of papal infallibility,

Dostoevsky wrote that in doing so it had "proclaimed a Christ who had succumbed to the third temptation of the devil.")[31] How then do people recognize that Jesus is divine? He heals them, beginning, of all things, with a Roman child, a child of the enemy.[32] What a strange way this is for a god to demonstrate his power. No wonder people don't get it. At no time in his earlier dealings with human beings has God healed anyone, with the possible exception of Moses, whom he cured of leprosy. But that was after he had made him a leper in the first place.

The final and greatest alteration in the divine identity is that Jesus dies, is put to death. If you accept that he goes to his death voluntarily — tarrying in the garden where he knows he will be seized, accepting the kiss of the one he knows will betray him, submitting to the lash and the barbed crown — then you know that you are witnessing God's suicide. As the philosopher Elaine Scarry points out, part of what is so radical about the Incarnation is that for the first time the Lord is visible.[33] "Thou canst not see my face," he once warned Moses, "for there shall no man see me and live" (Exod. 33:20). Now, however, it is God who dies, his face bare to the multitudes, while the people stand watching.

I once attended a Passion play in Jaffna, in the north of Sri Lanka. It's a Tamil city, and the actors were mostly Tamil Christians. Since Sri Lanka's Tamils are predominantly Hindu, they were a minority within a minority. Under other circumstances, a Passion play wasn't something I'd have gone to see. For centuries all over Europe, they were an occasion for anti-Semitic pogroms, a warm-up show for the popular entertainments of massacre, rape, and looting.[34] But this wasn't Europe, or even America, where not that long before, Mel Gibson had made an especially gruesome film of the Passion story, complete with a gloating, hand-rubbing Caiaphas. As far as I knew, Sri Lanka had never been the scene of violence against Jews. The Tamils I met, like some Tutsi I'd known in Rwanda, felt they were rather like Jews themselves. They, too, had been victims of institutionalized bigotry and pogroms. Unlike the Jews of Europe, though, they had struck back violently against their oppressors, or those they perceived as oppressors. The Liberation Tigers of Tamil Eelam had been the most feared terrorist group in Asia, the first anywhere to use suicide bombing as a tactic. Thanks to a 2004 cease-fire agreement, Jaffna was temporarily at peace, but you could tell that there'd been fighting there not long before. Many buildings in the town center were shell-holed Frankensteins stapled together with scaffolding and corrugated iron, and all along the beach there were signs warning you not to wander off the road that wound among the reeds and coconut palms because of anti-personnel mines. A year later the cease-fire would collapse and Jaffna would be at war again.

The play was slow, and never slower than during the final scenes. Bent beneath the cross, Jesus staggered across the stage, with apostles and helmeted Romans trudging behind him as if through mud. A man's voice keened over the loudspeakers. The music sounded ancient, except that it came from a synthesizer. The violence took place in slow motion. The men wielding the whips seemed to suffer almost as much as the god sagging beneath their blows. By the time the execution party arrived at the spot at stage right that was supposed to be Golgotha, the actor playing Jesus was drenched in stage blood, his meager torso as red as the devil's. There was a long interval in which he was trussed to the cross and the cross was raised and braced upright. Up until his final cry, he was silent. All his expressiveness resided in his body, in the heaving of his chest and the working of his sunken belly. In preparation for his role, the actor had fasted for four days.

The voice of the play belonged to an unnamed narrator, a stalwart, bearded figure who shadowed the action and interpreted it for the audience. Although he occasionally dropped to the back of a crowd scene, he was never offstage. At times he upstaged Jesus; he certainly had more lines. Early on I found him an irritating presence, but by the time the Crucifixion came around, he made sense to me. If God bore his agony in silence, the narrator spoke unceasingly. He lamented and accused. He railed at the executioners. He railed at Pilate and the Pharisees. He railed at the audience for its indifference — not just indifference to Christ's suffering, an English speaker beside me explained, but indifference to man's. Only a few years before, Jaffna's streets had been gutter-deep in blood, and who had tried to stanch it? Only eighty-four kilometers from this open-air theater, the tsunami had destroyed the town of Mullaittivu and thousands of its inhabitants, leaving the survivors to wander dazedly amid its wreckage. Who would shelter them? The God of the Old Testament was a god who spoke, a voice blasting out of the clouds to declare its mandate to a mute people. But in the New Testament the people have a voice as well: the narrator was its bearer.

The theater was packed. Behind me I felt the weight of

hundreds of spectators, the heat rising from their bodies in the hot night, and when I gazed about me, I saw their faces shining beneath the klieg lights. There were many families among them, and many, many small children. The kids were quiet, though I imagined that the sight of a man — or a god incarnated as a man — being tortured bloodily to death would be upsetting to a small child, even traumatic. But the mood in the theater was festive; the children's eyes gleamed with pleasure.[35]

Afterward the play's organizer, an urbane Catholic priest named Father N. M. Saveri who also heads the Centre for Performing Arts, Sri Lanka's largest arts organization, told me that many of the attendees were Hindus. I asked him if that was why the audience seemed cheerful rather than solemn, and he laughed. "I think our people are used to seeing suffering. They're not inured to suffering, but they are used to seeing it. Of course we have our Hindu idea of karma. And in our Christian background we see suffering as something that could be an instrument of purification, an instrument of peace."[36] He didn't say so, but I imagined that he was thinking of the tsunami, which had killed Sinhalese and Tamils with such evenhanded profligacy that it made the war between them seem like a petty quarrel. At least it was common to hear that sentiment as you went around the country, and for a while Sri Lankans hoped that the catastrophe might end the strife forever.

There are competing explanations for why Jesus had to be put to death. The Gospel of John blames the Jews. Theologically, Jesus's death fulfilled God's eternal plan for the redemption of a fallen humanity. If the first Adam had cast his descendants into sin and death, Jesus, "the second Adam," would lift them up in accordance with the prophecy of Isaiah 53:5:[37]

> But he was pierced for our transgressions,
> he was crushed for our iniquities;
> the punishment that brought us peace was upon him,
> and by his wounds we are healed.

Some contemporary scholars place Jesus among a series of nationalist messiahs who were trying to drive the Romans from Palestine, which would make the reasons for his execution political rather than religious.[38] What is certain is that within a few years of his death, many of his followers were meeting similar ends. Saint Stephen was stoned to death in A.D. 36. Around A.D. 67 Saint Peter was crucified in Rome, according to legend upside down. Saint Paul is said to have died in the same place on the same day. This is the Paul who had written, "From this time onward let no one trouble me; for, as for me, I bear, branded on my body, the scars of Jesus as my Master" (Gal. 6:17). Someone who died in this manner came to be known as a *martus,* or "witness," specifically a witness whose testimony is based on personal observation.[39]

What the martyrs were testifying to was the divinity of Christ, which they knew as intimately as if they had seen him step from his tomb. In time the term came to be used exclusively to denote those witnesses who died for their faith. It was a term of honor, and Christians strove to be worthy of it. A young man named Germanicus, who had been sentenced to be torn to pieces by wild beasts in the arena, so impressed the proconsul of Smyrna with his nobility that the official offered him a reprieve. Instead Germanicus seized one of the animals and dragged it toward him, "wishing to be released more quickly from [the pagans'] unrighteous and lawless life."[40]

One finds this story in the "Martyrdom of Polycarp" (A.D. 150–160), the earliest account of Christian martyrdom that is thought to be reliable. Polycarp was bishop of Smyrna in what is now Turkey. If not for the manner of his death, he would probably be best known for having heard the Gospel from John, which made him a member of the first post-apostolic generation, and for his ferocity in matters of doctrine. Although he aspired to unite all Christians in a universal church, he had no tolerance for the ones he regarded as deviants: "For every one who does not confess that Jesus Christ has come in the flesh is antichrist; and whosoever does not confess the testimony of the cross, is a devil."[41] Introduced to the heresiarch Marcion, who asked the bishop if he recognized him, Polycarp snapped, "Yes, I recognize you — firstborn of Satan!"[42]

In 155 Smyrna became the scene of grisly persecutions of Christians. The aforementioned Germanicus was killed before crowds that howled for his death. A man named Quintus would have followed him, but at the sight of the beasts he broke down and recanted. Cases like his were one reason early Christian writers cautioned would-be martyrs not to volunteer for the ordeal, lest by a failure of nerve they cast dishonor on their faith. Polycarp was eighty-six years old and wanted to stay in the city, but his followers persuaded him to take refuge at a farm in the countryside. There he prayed continually until he fell into a trance, in which the pillow beneath his head seemed to be on fire. On waking he said, "I must be burnt alive."

Soon after this the slaves who had been attending him were taken by the police, and under torture one of them revealed the bishop's whereabouts. "It was indeed impossible for him to remain hid," the narrator writes, "since those who betrayed him were of his own house, and the police captain who had been allotted the very name, being called Herod, hastened to bring him to the arena that he might fulfil his appointed lot by becoming a partaker of Christ, while they who betrayed him should undergo the same punishment as Judas."[43] One takes this to mean that the slaves were hanged.

What stands out in this portion of the story is its almost pagan sense of fate. Polycarp wishes to remain in Smyrna — whether to die or be delivered matters little to him; he is content to let destiny run its course. Instead he is pressured to flee. Still, fate catches up with him, announcing itself with a prophetic dream and the coincidence of the arresting officer's name. By these signs the reader understands that the saint's death is preordained. In classical theater fate is usually tragic, and that would seem to be true here. Except Polycarp welcomes his destiny, for he knows that in dying he will be partaking in Christ, sharing not just in his death but in his eternal life. Christianity's great innovation was to rob death of its terror by making it the antechamber to a beatific life to come. In this coincidence of death and life, the old pagan model of fate breaks down. To Sophocles, death was just death, as irreversible as the cutting of a thread. In "Polycarp" fate is less final but also, for the first time, explicitly moral, since it brings about a desirable end: the saint's death, his martyrdom.

Because of his age and piety, Polycarp's captors treat him with deference. The proconsul urges him to defend his beliefs to the people. He may be hoping that they'll be swayed and he won't have to preside over the old man's execution. "You I should have held worthy of discussion," Polycarp says, assuring him that Christians have no quarrel with temporal authority. But he declines to speak to the rabble. It's they — and especially the Jews among them (their appearance reminds us that Polycarp was a disciple of Saint John, whose Gospel is the foundational text of Christian anti-Semitism) — who are most eager for him to be killed. Between the victim and the official ordering his death, there is the mutual respect of men who recognize each other's worth, Polycarp's worth having been made evident by the voice that called from the sky as he was led into the arena: "Be strong, Polycarp, and play the man."[44]

It's a moment that marks the emergence of a new, and specifically Christian, model of nobility, one based not on birth but on the willingness to sacrifice one's life in witness to the truth. Such a sacrifice requires more than courage. The martyr has to overcome his human, even his creaturely, nature, for it's in the nature of every creature to preserve its life. Polycarp is someone who has overcome his nature; to what extent is made clear by his instructions to his executioners. As they make ready to nail him to the stake, he waves them away, saying, "Leave me thus, for He who gives me power to endure the fire will grant me to remain in the flames unmoved even without the security you will give by the nails." Even his reflexes have been cast aside.

> So they did not nail him, but bound him, and he put his hands behind him and was bound, as a noble ram out of a great flock, for an oblation, a whole burnt offering made ready and acceptable to God; and he looked up to heaven and said: "O Lord God Almighty, Father of thy beloved and blessed Child, Jesus Christ, through Whom we have received full knowledge of thee, the God of Angels and powers, and of all creation, and of the whole family of the righteous, who live before thee! I bless thee, that Thou hast granted me this day and hour, that I may share, among the number of the martyrs, in the cup of thy Christ, for the Resurrection to everlasting life, both of soul and body in the immortality of the Holy Spirit. And may I, to-day, be received among them before Thee, as a rich and acceptable sacrifice, as Thou, the God who lies not and is truth, hast prepared beforehand, and shown forth, and fulfilled." [45]

In death Polycarp undergoes a transformation. When the fire is lit,

> a great flame blazed up and we, to whom it was given to see, saw a marvel. And we have been preserved to report to others what befell. For the fire

made the likeness of a room, like the sail of a vessel filled with wind, and surrounded the body of the martyr as with a wall, and he was within it not as burning flesh, but as bread that is being baked, or as gold and silver being refined in a furnace. And we perceived such a fragrant smell as the scent of incense or other costly spices.[46]

The Buddhist monk Thich Quang Duc, who immolated himself on a busy Saigon street corner in protest against the Vietnam War in 1963, is said to have sat perfectly still as he burned, but the smell of his charred flesh was unmistakable and shocking.[47] Polycarp doesn't die the way most people do when they are set ablaze. His body does not shrivel and blacken, or give off the stench of burning flesh. The early Christians were curious about the next life. Some looked forward to the body's resurrection, while others were content to leave it in the grave. This story suggests that Polycarp has been freed of his physical body, leaving only a spiritual one, whose smell is as pleasing to the human witnesses as that of the burnt offering — the oblation — is pleasing to God. Perhaps he has risen to some intermediate state between flesh and spirit. The fire cannot kill him; someone must be brought to stab him with a dagger, an allusion to an earlier moment in sacred time, when a Roman centurion put an end to Jesus's agony by thrusting a spear into his side. At the moment the knife enters Polycarp, a dove flies from the wound, followed by a torrent of blood that quenches the fire so that "all the crowd marvelled that there was such a difference between the unbelievers and the elect."[48]

It's notable that throughout his ordeal, the old bishop remains silent. Such silence figures in almost all the accounts of martyrdom I have read, broken only by prayer or — in the case of Saint Lawrence, who was roasted alive — a joke: "This side is done, turn and eat."[49] The silence of the martyrs was one of the things that made them so impressive to onlookers. It thwarted the implicit aim of their executioners, which was not just to kill these "atheists" (how much effort, really, does it take to kill an eighty-six-year-old man?) but to make a spectacle of their deaths. The climax of that spectacle would come when the victims "reverted," in Scarry's words, to a "pre-language of cries and groans."[50] Such cries aren't even human, they're animal, and to hear them is to witness humans being turned into animals. By analogy, those who resisted that debasement seemed superhuman. This may be the true explanation of the miracles with which they are so often credited. Martyrdom evolved its own code of machismo, in which the ability to remain composed while being subjected to nightmarish physical torment demonstrated both the power of God[51] and the superiority of the elect. Their death was still a spectacle, but the theme of the spectacle — what its producers might have called its take-away — was no longer degradation: it was exaltation.

The silence of the martyrs represents the closing of a circle. In the beginning an invisible, incorporeal God — a god who was only a voice — made himself known by the damage he inflicted on speechless, sinful human bodies. The damage was freakish and unnatural, and with it the serene order that had prevailed in Eden came to an end, to be supplanted by a new order of transgression and dreadful retribution. Then the god became human. He chose to be one of the injured, the foremost of the injured, the first of the last, and in this way lifted the burden of suffering from humans. After the god died, his followers began to imitate him by re-enacting his suffering. Of course their sacrifice lacked the redemptive efficacy of the god's. Mankind could not be saved by any mere man's death, nor by the death of any thousand men. And since Christ had already given his life for man's sins, all further oblations were unnecessary, maybe even blasphemous. But the martyrs weren't theologians; they were enthusiasts, in the sense of being possessed by God. And so they suffered as their god had suffered, and their silence, too, was now godlike.[52]

Martyrdom is a powerful ideal. As a practice, though, it's problematic. How do you build a church when so many of its members are intent on dying grisly public deaths? "From the Third Century on, when Christianity changed from an outlawed cult to the official religion of the Roman Empire, there's a considerable expenditure of energy on the part of the Church Fathers to prevent outbreaks of enthusiastic martyrdom," says Bruce Chilton, Bell Professor of Religion at Bard College and the author of books on Jesus and Paul. "Martyrdom by that time had become such a widely accepted part of Christian practice and aspiration that people would pursue it even in the absence of official persecution."[53]

Saint Augustine may have been addressing this phenomenon when he wrote, "When they hear of the trials that are coming, some men arm themselves more and, so to speak, are eager to drain the cup. The ordinary medicine of the faithful seems to them but a small thing; for their part they seek the glorious death of the martyrs."[54] The suffering that had once been identified with sin had now been conjoined to the idea of holiness, had become holiness's outward sign. This idea is still current in Catholicism. Simone Weil, admittedly a very eccentric sort of Catholic, writes: "It is in affliction itself that the splendor of God's mercy shines, from its very depths, in the heart of its inconsolable bitterness."[55]

But dying for the faith becomes increasingly difficult as the faith becomes more widespread and institutionalized. So over time the literal, sacrificial death of martyrdom gave way to the figurative death of monasticism, called "white martyrdom." It was no longer the body that died but the senses and desires. The spiritual descendants of those who had stepped onto the pyres now mounted platforms in the desert or shut themselves up in caves. They subjected themselves to ordeals of hunger and sleeplessness. They scourged themselves until the flesh hung in tatters from their backs.

Yet even this model of holiness proved too stringent. By the fifteenth century, monasteries were so luxuriously endowed that they were no longer sites of holiness but of excess. They were like retreats where one could meditate and eat meals prepared by a five-star chef. Hence the stereotype of the dissipated monk. The Reformation began in a convulsion of austerity, a burning of icons and a stripping of gilded altarpieces. But in the ensuing centuries almost all the Protestant sects that issued from it further rejected suffering as an ideal. Christian virtue was no longer embodied by the martyr or the monk but by a somber burgher in his parlor. In America the burgher gave way to a televangelist with a Learjet and a church as big as a shopping mall.

This shift in styles of holiness reflects something basic in human nature. We don't want to suffer; our being shrinks from it. This remains true whether suffering is viewed as punishment or a sign of grace. In all of history very few people have volunteered to be tortured to death, and not many more have chosen to live in poverty and isolation. There are no Shakers anymore, and the Shakers at least were known to set a good table. Maybe this is why the model of God changed, too. Chilton says, "In modern Protestantism, especially in the U.S., Christ is no longer the substitute for man's sins but for his suffering. All the suffering you encounter in your life can be displaced onto Jesus. You do with your suffering what you do with your sin: you turn it over to Him."

In Catholic Europe the most common representations of Jesus depict him on the cross. The Crucifixions of the early Renaissance give him a body as attenuated as a wick and so white that it seems to have been drained of blood. But the cross that hangs on the wall of most Protestant churches is empty. This reflects a doctrinal emphasis on the Resurrection, but it may also speak of a visceral discomfort with the very idea of a god who suffers. The longer people live, and the more abundantly, the more insulated from hunger, war, and sickness, the greater this discomfort becomes. It reaches an apogee in the long-lived, abundant United States, where cities have passed laws barring the homeless from their centers.

In the World Prayer Center of the New Life Church in Colorado Springs, one of the largest and most powerful evangelical churches in the country, a visitor finds statues of warrior angels and Thomas Blackshear paintings "depicting gorgeous, muscular men — one is a blacksmith, another is bound, fetish-style, in chains — in various states of un-

dress." [56] One of the few paintings of Jesus shows him holding up a swooning man, who is more modestly proportioned
than the other figures in the room and, unlike them, fully
clothed. The man is holding a mallet, which suggests he may
be intended to be a modern counterpart of the carpenter
Christ. However, the relation between the figures and their
evident robustness suggest a man giving an assist to a neighbor who's gotten too much sun while working on his roof.
The painting is called *Forgiven*. [57]

Another contemporary image of Jesus appears in the end-
times thriller *Glorious Appearing*, the concluding volume
in the hugely popular Left Behind series, whose eleven previous installments sold more than forty million copies. [58]
Following the Rapture of true believers, the rise of the Antichrist (promoted from his old position as secretary-general
of the UN), and a barrage of catastrophic tribulations —
including a "Wrath of the Lamb earthquake" — the Son of
God returns to earth, stopping the Antichrist's Unity Army
as it advances on the last remnant of the faithful:

> Jesus' eyes shone with conviction like a flame of
> fire, and He held His majestic head high. . . . On
> His robe at the thigh a name was written: KING
> OF KINGS AND LORD OF LORDS. . . . "I am the
> Alpha and the Omega," Jesus said, "the First and
> the Last, the Beginning and the End, the
> Almighty." . . . And with those very first words,
> tens of thousands of Unity Army soldiers fell
> dead, simply dropping where they stood, their
> bodies ripped open, blood pooling in great
> masses. "I am He who lives, and was dead, and

behold, I am alive forevermore. Amen. And I have the keys of Hades and of Death." [59]

But who is Jesus if he doesn't suffer? He's Yahweh. The central paradox of much Christian fundamentalism is that for all its doctrinal rigor, its bristliness on matters ranging from relations with other faiths to the length of time between the Tribulation and the Last Judgment, it practices heresy. The Jesus it worships is more or less indistinguishable from the God in Numbers 16:49, the one who cuts down 14,700 Israelites for having grumbled against Moses. One might call him the Jewish God, except that in the later, post-Exilic books of the Old Testament, the Jewish God evolves dramatically, from a God of war to a God of justice and mercy. [60] Maybe the fundamentalists' God is that one's rough ancestor, come shambling back to wreak holy havoc on earth. Christ completed the godhead by manifesting what had been left out of it: flesh, weakness, affliction, death. American fundamentalism excises those traits once more, reducing (some, of course, would say "restoring") Christ to a wielder of power, an inflicter of wounds:

> The "goats" to Jesus' left beat their breasts and fell wailing to the desert floor, gnashing their teeth and pulling their hair. Jesus merely raised one hand a few inches and a yawning chasm opened in the earth, stretching far and wide enough to swallow all of them. They tumbled in, howling and screeching, but their wailing was soon quashed and all was silent when the earth closed itself again.

> . . . Rayford was spent. . . . Despite every horror he had witnessed during the Tribulation and the Glorious Appearing, the death and eternal punishment of millions overwhelmed everything else.
>
> "I know, Rayford," Jesus said. "Now rest your mind. My peace I give to you." [61]

Our gods shape our idea of what it is to suffer. Our ideas about suffering determine our choice of gods. In the end who can say whether the Jesus of *Glorious Appearing* reflects a vengeful, pitiless strain of American Protestantism or the same nondenominational fantasies of mayhem and invincibility on display in such horror movies and video games as *Saw, Halo,* and *Resident Evil*? Among the testimonies to come out of Abu Ghraib, one finds this account of an exchange between a Muslim prisoner and his American captors, who had allegedly forced him to eat pork, poured liquor down his throat, and made him thank Jesus that he was still alive. After that, the captive said, "they stripped me naked, they asked me, 'Do you pray to Allah?' I said, 'Yes.' They said, 'F— — you' and 'F— — him.' " Later, he continued, "someone else asked me, 'Do you believe in anything?' I said to him, 'I believe in Allah.' So he said, 'But I believe in torture and I will torture you.' " [62]

WHEN TALKING WITH Kate and Kelly, I'd sometimes catch myself appraising them for signs of post-traumatic stress disorder. It was something I always felt bad about. Nobody had to remind me that I was unqualified to make such assessments, and at those times when I tried to, I felt a clinical chill pass over the conversation, which was otherwise no different from the kind I might have had with any new acquaintances I liked a lot and wanted to know better, wanted to have as friends. Still, I couldn't help myself.

Did they have "recurrent and intrusive distressing recollections"? Did they display "persistent avoidance of stimuli associated with the trauma or numbing of general responsiveness"? Did they seem "detach[ed] or estrange[d] from others"? Were there "persistent symptoms of increased arousal"?[63] What I saw was inconclusive. The girls certainly recalled episodes of past pain, but I can't say if those recollections were intrusive, and their vividness and specificity may have owed something to the fact that their memories of pain were constantly being refreshed. To say that they avoided situations associated with trauma is only to say that they avoided ones in which they might be injured, especially since their bodies no longer healed as easily as they had when they were kids. (Kate kept a mental list of "Things That Would Kill Us," which included "all contact sports and wheels under our feet in the form of anything but a car.")[64] Wounds that in the past had quickly scarred over now stayed open and bubbling for weeks or months, or healed only as craters.

After a while I realized that the problem might lie in the definition of "trauma." Trauma is commonly thought to be an event whose elements of shock and violence constitute a blow to the organism. One commentator describes it as "the event par excellence, the event as unintelligible, as the pure impact of sheer happening."[65] Though the trauma may range in duration from an instant, in the case of a car wreck, to years — say, the years that someone like Viktor Frankl spent in concentration camps, famished, shivering, abased, and constantly in dread of being selected for the gas — it is still an event. It is finite and bounded. It has an end. More, it has a beginning. Even those psychoanalytic theories that argue for the ordinariness of trauma and award it a causative role in the formation of consciousness believe that before the original catastrophe, the child drifts in a state of self-adoring bliss or simple drowsy contentment that the trauma disrupts forever.

But Kate and Kelly had never known such a state. Or rather their earliest state had been a state of woundedness. They had been born without skin, and in the succeeding twenty-seven years they had never known an extended period in which they were whole and not in pain. In their case, it was useless to speak of trauma, for there had been no original bliss for trauma to bring to an end. It was useless to speak of post-traumatic stress disorder because for them there would be no *post*.

That was one way the Daley twins were different from the Vietnam vets I'd met. Another, of course, was that their wounds were visible, overwhelmingly so. There was no need to point at them. One of the things that strangers were always saying to them was "What's wrong with you?" The girls liked to sing it out in unison. They had made the question and the pitying or ghoulish or just naive curiosity that it sprang from part of their routine. A psychologist who'd worked with them called it "the Daley show." On one level the Daley show was the girls' way of concealing pain, or, rather, of minimizing it, of pretending that there was nothing wrong with them.

The paradox was that the routine also called attention to pain; it turned pain into the punch line of a bleak joke. They liked to quote a friend who, after Kelly invited him to give her a high five, squinted at her hand and said, "I'd call it what it is. It's a high four-and-a-half." "Give a card to the handicapped girl," one or the other would crack at family poker games, and grin when people got upset. It was the kind of joke Job might have made if God hadn't gotten around to restoring him. Its purpose was in part preemptive: better to make fun of yourself than let someone else do it. The girls' sense of humor had served them well in high school.

Another thing strangers kept telling them was that Jesus loved them. "I'm genuinely interested in why people are always trying to save us," Kelly mused. "I always say that our overt vulnerability allows other people to be vulnerable with us. People tell us the most amazing things. And we get to see their unabashed curiosity and bad manners. A lot of the time when people think that their religion tells them that they need to be proselytizing, they seek out people that look like they need a little help. And Kate and I — we just . . ." She paused, then dove in from a different angle. "My dad says we look like bait. Part of it is we're really wide-eyed and naive. And part of it is that people look at us and decide we need a little love. Everyone needs a little love. But I think our problems are so written all over us that they think somehow it's a license."

She told me a story. When she was twenty-two, she'd gotten pregnant by her boyfriend and, without telling Kate, went into the city to have an abortion. "I was on a train and I was terrified. It was my first time alone in New York City, and I was going to get an abortion. I had a lot on my mind. I was trying to navigate the train systems, and I was carrying all my luggage, and I was this lonely little girl in this huge, scary city, going to meet my boyfriend for the last time ever. And this girl keeps staring at me. I didn't want to make eye contact, but I accidentally did, and she came over and said" — she made her voice breathy and precise — " 'I have been debating whether or not to tell you this. But I just have to: Jesus loves you.'

"And I said, 'Thank you, I know.' I was hoping that would end it, but she sat with me for the entire ride. When she got up to leave she said, 'Thank you. Most people just tell me to shut up.' "

I found it momentarily unsettling to think of Kelly having sex, let alone getting pregnant, but EB is a progressive disease, and the girls' injuries hadn't been so evident when they were younger. From age eighteen to twenty-two, Kelly had a boyfriend with whom she was sexually active. Kate had one, too, but stopped short of intercourse, deterred by her Catholicism and, more to the point, her squeamishness about her damaged body. Her boyfriend, who seems to have been caught up in the romance of dating a young woman with a chronic disease, used to tell her that he wanted to help her change her bandages, and one night when he was sleeping over, she found a spot on her shoulder that needed a new dressing and almost asked him. She went so far as to bring the ThinSite and scissors into the bedroom. But at the last minute she lost her nerve and placed them out of sight, then spent the rest of the night lying tensely beside him. "I was not ready," she wrote, "for him to get elbow-deep into my bloody, gory care." [66]

After the girls died, one of Nancy's regrets was that Kate had never had a complete sexual experience, just as one of her lasting satisfactions was that Kelly had. What she wanted was for her children to lead normal lives, or at least full ones. Such lives might contain more moments of pain than the narrowly bounded kind that most people with EB lead — not just more injuries but more episodes of rejection, cruelty, and loss. But in the long run, Nancy thought, the pain would be balanced by pleasures that the Crisco Kid could barely imagine. "Most people live on the surface, never going deeper," she told me. "They worry about making their car payments, what movie they're going to see. We cry really hard, but we laugh really hard. We have a deeper sense of life."

Early on she decided that the girls ought to go to their neighborhood public school. The administration was afraid of what would happen if they got hurt on school property, so Nancy had to agree to work in the nurse's office, where she'd be able to care for them in emergencies. (The other unspoken benefit of the arrangement was that if anything did happen, it would be harder for her to sue.) She did this at every school the girls attended until they entered college. On the school yard Kelly would join in games (Kate, who was more timid, usually hung back) that left her literally flayed, and when she limped proudly into the infirmary, with blood squishing in her shoes, Nancy would force herself to stay calm while she bandaged her. That emotional self-mastery had a price. Throughout those years some part of Nancy's body always hurt, and she once looked down at her hands and realized that she couldn't recall a time when they hadn't been clenched in fists.

To smooth the girls' entry into school, Nancy decided to

give a talk on their illness at a PTA meeting. When she got there, she discovered that the meeting room was packed, with dozens of parents in attendance. "It took everything I had; I'm kind of a private person," she said. "Actually I was nauseous. I was telling all these personal things about our lives. But it had to be done so that the kids didn't go to school and have the other kids' parents saying, 'I don't want that person in your class. Is that catching?' "

Sometimes the girls felt she pushed them too hard. Because they lost weeks of school every year to surgeries and complications, Nancy wouldn't let them stay home for what she considered minor ailments, especially if only one child was sick. When Kelly got a corneal abrasion, she had to go to school — Kate would lead her between classrooms — and follow the lessons as well as she could with her eyes closed. Their mother's insistence that they soldier on could seem cruel, but its benefit was not just that they graduated on schedule. She also toughened them, and because they were tough, or at least seemed that way, they won the acceptance of classmates who might otherwise have made their lives wretched. Apart from a couple of incidents of name-calling and a home economics teacher who rhetorically asked the class, "Should people with open wounds on their hands be allowed to cook?" they glided through middle and high school on a cushion of stoicism and charm. It was the Daley show at its most polished.

At the heart of the show lay the stars' tacit agreement to keep outsiders from seeing the full extent of their pain for fear they might recoil in pity and revulsion. "When there's something *so much wrong* with you, you'll do a lot to please people," Kelly explained. "To kind of apologize." Along with the ability to conceal their suffering came an ability to dismiss it, even at times forget it. They were still the children who'd asked for ice cream minutes after their parents had finished debriding their mutilated hands. "People think of pain and pleasure as a spectrum, but at its midpoint they reside just over the border from one another, sometimes intertwining," Kelly wrote when she was older. "In my life they are less on a linear layout and more like concentric circles. Pain is the constant center, and pleasure has to build around it. Pain is the center of my Tootsie Roll pop. Or is it the reverse? Pleasure is at my center, that prized little nugget. But there's a lot of work to get there." [67]

I've seen relatively little written about the relationship between suffering and pleasure. I don't mean the complicated pleasure and ritualized suffering of masochism, but the kinds of pleasure that people seek out even in the greatest affliction, maybe especially in affliction. One thinks of Frankl's ladle of soup from the bottom of the pot, with its few extra peas. Perhaps because so many conduits of enjoyment were closed to them, the Daley sisters thought a great deal about the ones they had: meals, music, books, time with friends. They pursued them avidly and savored them in memory. On nights before they went to see friends, they'd be sleepless with excitement, and afterward they'd enshrine the visits' highlights in their journals: "Just bonding over a mutual love of marshmallow peeps and games with Noah and Lauren was ecstatic," Kate wrote of one couple. "The more serious conversation and treasured literary conversation is equally charged. Talking and giggling and crying with these people. These are the best parts of my life." [68]

They took pleasure in their feminine curves and especially in their breasts, for whose sake they'd consented to have the "buttons" implanted in their stomachs after Nancy warned them that without the extra nutrition, their bodies would never mature. After the operation, Kelly remembered, "I was obsessed. I strained in the mirror to see any change in my chest. I questioned my mom and Kate every day, 'Do you see a shadow?' That was my criterion. I wanted boob enough to cast a shadow. I also wanted to be able to place a pencil under a breast and have it hold. I worked for my tits, and I am proud of them."[69]

As the twins got older and Nancy started working full-time, they began to receive care from visiting nurses. These were the first strangers whom Kate and Kelly observed intently, maybe because they were so dependent on them and soon realized that they couldn't take their competence for granted. "It's not a job like other jobs," Kelly explained. "A nurse can walk in to a patient who's on a ventilator and know how to operate that ventilator. But with us, they've probably never heard of EB before, and the job is always changing. Our wounds are always healing and reopening somewhere else. You can't use the same bandages in every place; you constantly have to reassess and be inventive and be creative."

Nor could they always count on their caregivers' sensitivity, or even their goodwill. There were the ones who blasted them with Christian contemporary for the six hours they were trapped with them in the bathroom every day, a tooth-grinding ordeal for kids who relied on music to distract them from the misery of bandage changes but preferred the Foo Fighters and Natalie Merchant. There were the ones who helped themselves to their pain meds. There was one nurse who wanted to take pictures of the girls in lingerie to give to Chris "as a Father's Day present." They figured there'd been a hundred in all.

The nurse who ended up staying was named Barbara. She understood their baffling, protean disease, and she understood their bodies. Before long she could bandage them even better than Nancy could. "Give me a little baseball," she'd say, motioning Kelly to crouch forward so she could apply a dressing to her back. She had a genius for cutting ThinSite bandages into narrow strips that fit the curves and hollows of her charges' bodies, even their ears and armpits. And she loved them, although her love was colored by the fears and judgments of her literal-minded Catholicism. It was probably Barbara's influence that had Kate trying to drag herself to morning Mass because it was a holy day of obligation, even when she was shaking with fever. When the nurse came upon Kelly's cache of birth control pills, she was so angry that she wouldn't speak to her for a year.

In recollection Kate and Kelly's happiest time was college. They were so grateful for getting to go to one in the first place and to live in the dorms like ordinary students. Nobody with EB had ever done that. Even DebRA's director told Nancy to get her head out of the clouds when she brought up the idea. Undaunted, she found a school only five minutes from the house, close enough for her or Barbara to go over and change the girls' dressings before morning classes.

A student named Rachel[70] became their best friend. She was smart and defiant and had a theatrical self-destructive streak that both frightened and fascinated them. She cut herself, and on at least one occasion tried wrapping herself in the girls' bandages. Kate thought she was secretly envious of them, of the attention they got just by walking into a classroom looking the way they did. Maybe she was envious because what Kate and Kelly had wrong with them was so blatant and easily explained. What Rachel had wrong with her was more mysterious; it lay hidden beneath the unblemished skin that she kept slicing with razor blades and tattooed with the words "Sometimes you have to align yourself with the wound." A while after getting the tattoo, their friend committed suicide. I once asked the twins if they'd ever felt angry at her for trying, at least symbolically, to appropriate their illness, to turn it into a personal accessory. It was one thing, I thought, for *them* to align themselves with the wound and another for Rachel to do it, considering that her wounds were self-inflicted. But the question startled them. Rachel had made them happy.

For the Daleys, of course, happiness was always a relative state, the sweet nugget of pleasure encased in layers of sickness, disfigurement, and shame. It was something they experienced *in spite of*. During her freshman year, Kelly was deeply and unhappily in love with a boy in Albany. Her face broke out in an oozing infection that made even smiling painful. She couldn't sleep because the drainage would glue her face to the pillow. On the last night of the term she wrote a farewell note and took an overdose of prescription antihistamines. Cups of strong coffee had to be injected into her stomach tube to wake her. The next morning she found Chris lying miserably at the foot of her bed. "Are you going to hurt yourself again?" he asked. All she could do was groan. Her father sprang up. In the doorway he paused and said, "I just wanted to hear you say it. You couldn't fucking *lie*?"[71]

Most of Kelly's written account of her suicide attempt and hospitalization — she called it "My Stay in the Looney Bin" — has a whimsical tone, though the whimsy feels a little strained, in the manner of a student actor "doing" Holly Golightly. The other patients are lovable eccentrics. A cute guy tells her how beautiful she is. The only moment of real anguish occurs when her grandmother reproaches her. "Honey, why are you doing this to your family?" Kelly writes, "What I really felt like doing was dancing around, wildly waving my bandaged arms and tossing my scarred head and screaming, 'Do you see me? Do you think this is easy, my life? I'm surprised I made it this far!' "

Do you see me? Whenever I spoke with Kate or Kelly or read their journals, what struck me was their ambivalence about being seen, their dread of it and longing for it. They hated their concealing clothing yet were afraid to wear anything more revealing. When summer came and it got too hot for long sleeves and turtlenecks, Kate would become hysterical with discomfort and fight with her mother when she warned her that her wounds were more likely to get infected if they were kept warm and moist. Although both sisters loved shopping and treated trips to the supermarket like visits to an amusement park, in time they came to hate leaving the house; they were too conscious of people staring at them.

Once, a few years after they'd graduated from college, they were introduced to a current student, a boy prodigy named Akshar who wanted to interview them for a presentation on EB for his English composition class. Afterward he asked them to attend the presentation, and they agreed. It was a mistake. Neither Akshar nor the professor invited them to speak. The boy showed slides he'd downloaded from the Internet of EB wounds and deformities, and although none of those wounds was Kate's or Kelly's and they'd dressed for the visit with care, they felt wretchedly exposed. He passed around a sample of Kelly's handwriting, then had the girls hold up the stubs of their fingers and announced, "This handwriting comes from those hands!"

Kate could see the other students look at the images on the screen, then look at her and her sister, then look away. "We had no purpose," she decided. "We were mute human props. . . . We were nothing but our illness."[72] In her journal she quotes a passage from Pat Barker's *The Eye in the Door*, a description of some bombed-out buildings: "He saw the looped and trellised bedroom wallpaper that once only the family and its servants would have seen, exposed now to wind and rain and the gaze of casual passers-by." Underneath she wrote, "This is reminiscent to me of my blood (and my wounds) when it besmirches my clothes, my bandages. It is not, should not be, for all eyes. What was once private, what should remain private, now displayed for gawkers."[73]

And yet Kelly and Kate also wanted to be seen. In 2003 the twins were invited to appear on a segment of *60 Minutes* and were bitterly disappointed when Nancy vetoed it, fearful of the impact on the family's privacy. By the time I met them, they'd transferred their ambitions to *The Oprah Winfrey Show* because they'd heard that Winfrey was planning a segment on twins who'd overcome hardship. They thought they fit the description; I did, too. "My God, you'd be naturals!" I exclaimed. Kate picked up my excitement. "I don't just want to be on the show; I want to befriend her." She began to stammer. "I want — I really admire her and like her, and I think that she might possibly admire and like us." Abruptly my heart sank for her. What had I been thinking? The last guests Oprah would want on her show would be ones who weren't going to get better.

I tried pitching the Daleys' story to several women's magazines, but after an initial show of interest, the articles editor would ask me if EB was curable. When I said it wasn't, the feeler would invariably be retracted. It was William Dean Howells who said that "Americans love a tragedy as long as it has a happy ending."[74] Still, how could I blame Kate for wanting what she wanted? She and Kelly were members of the MySpace generation, and what made more sense than that two young women who had spent their lives being stared at for their injuries would want for once to be seen for their deeper, uninjured selves? Instead of objects of pity, they wanted to be objects of compassion.

I thought about the difference between those words, one of which appears so often in the literature and iconography of Catholicism — think of the *Pietà* — the other in those of Buddhism, as expressed in the Sanskrit word *karuna*. "Pity" connotes a gulf between its subject, the person who feels pity, and its object, the one who is pitied. It's the gulf that separates wholeness from sickness, satiety from starvation, the king on horseback from the legless beggar writhing in the dust. The gulf is vertical, which may be why pity is a little suspect in an egalitarian society. Today even desperate people are unlikely to cry out "Ah, pity me!" as they do in Shakespeare and grand opera. In "compassion," literally "feeling *with*," the distance between subject and object, viewer and viewed, is not vertical but horizontal, a distance between equal beings separated by circumstance. This distance can be bridged by feeling. Implicit in the word "compassion" is the recognition that all fortune is temporary, maybe even illusory. A Buddhist, of course, understands that the king may be reborn as a beggar in his next life.

For Kate and Kelly, I think the distinction was simpler. Pity might be the way strangers responded to the spectacle of their damaged bodies. Compassion might be how they responded to their character or souls. So might admiration. So might love.

It was the last they wanted most, and that kept eluding them. Kelly and her high school boyfriend had been about to get engaged when he abruptly broke it off, and she still believed he'd done so under pressure from his parents. Both girls were prone to feverish, sleep-devouring crushes that were all the more anguished because they knew the likely outcome. "I talk to all these guys online, and they love me," Kate wrote.

> They find me intelligent, adorable, witty, even cute (judging by a shadowy head shot). Even sexy. Guys I meet in the real world hardly see me, and if they do notice me, they never even think of wanting to date me. . . . My body — there's just so much ugliness. I told Kell she looked pretty tonight, and she said, "It's all a mirage." That's how I've been feeling too, though a mirage is not exactly right. A façade, perhaps, though my front — my clothes covering my bandages, my

bandages covering my wounds — isn't exactly false. I suppose "disguise" would be the best term. We can package ourselves to look presentable, even pretty sometimes, but underneath we're all purple and pink and scaly and rough or strangely smooth; we're bloody and open and wounded and gory and stinky. How will anybody love that?[75]

One reason they'd been so happy in college, I thought, was that they'd been around people who saw them as more than their illness. Since graduating they'd had no place where that could happen. They lived in a row house next door to their parents, who'd bought it for them so they could have some privacy. The EB, which grew more debilitating each year, made it impossible for them to work. They had many friends, but any trip outside their home was a logistical nightmare. If they were on pain meds, someone would have to drive them, and if they wanted to stay overnight, they'd have to bring along extra bandages and medications. In the fall of 2003 Kate went with some friends for a "women's weekend" in Vermont. By the time she got there, her throat was so swollen — another one of EB's side effects — that she could barely eat any of the delicious food that had been prepared for her. And after two days she "reeked of infection and unchanged bandages" and was relieved to return home.

The sisters loved to sing and did so at any opportunity. They had sweet, robust, flexible voices suited for everything from ethereal folk tunes to hollering rock and roll. They sang during care to take their minds off their pain and boredom or because it was better to sing than to scream. "Civilized screaming" was Kelly's name for the kind of singing she did on days when even Barbara's practiced touch was too painful to bear. They'd gotten confident enough to perform at open mike nights at local clubs and found that when they did, the noisy, half-drunken crowds almost always became quiet and attentive. "Part of it is that our physicality is arresting," Kelly explained. "It's the first thing that they notice. But after we have their attention, they give us more respect. And I don't think it's out of pity; it's out of genuine interest. After they get over their initial 'Wow, what's wrong with them?' "

They especially prized their friendship with the singer Natalie Merchant. It began as fandom; the girls often played her albums while they were being bandaged. Chris recalled taking them to one of Merchant's concerts barely a day after they'd come home from an operation and watching in horror as they plunged into the crowd, their hands cocooned in gauze and bristling with steel pins. He said he'd aged about five years. (Hearing him, Kate protested, "But we were holding our hands up!") An introduction was arranged. Merchant fell in love with Kate and Kelly's intelligence, warmth, and courage. When she realized how good their voices were, she began inviting them to sing occasional backup. They can be heard on one of her albums, on a song called "Henry Darger," after the reclusive outsider artist who created an entire mythology about a planet of endangered little girls:

Who'll save the poor little girl? Henry Darger.
Who'll save the poor little girl? Henry.

Who'll tell the story of her? Henry Darger.
Who'll tell it to all the world? Henry.[76]

There's a video of them singing at one of Merchant's shows a few years ago, before they became too ill for public appearances. Because the event was a benefit for DebRA, Kate and Kelly spoke to the audience about their disease. Kelly read a statement that she'd written. It began, "I live inside a cage of skin." They were charismatic speakers, and the sight of them, dressed in long, tie-dyed skirts and clinging tops, with their maimed hands and forearms plainly visible, must have been striking even to spectators who knew nothing about EB. For me the high point of the tape is watching them sing. For a little while they seem to forget their illness and their role as totemic patients. Their voices are almost too big for their bodies. They sound the way they must have sounded when they were singing in the bathroom, except that they have more room to move, and they do move, swinging their hips and tossing their heads, the moves practiced by backup singers since the Jordanaires. They move like young women who are filled with juice and sex and vitality, and know it.

And, of course, people are watching them.

Suffering has no "possessor,"
Therefore no distinctions can be made in it.
Since pain is pain, it is to be dispelled.
What use is there in drawing boundaries?

— Shantideva, *The Way of the Bodhisattva*[77]

Unlike almost every other religion, Buddhism has no presiding god, only a man who through various mental and ethical practices became like a god. He is godlike not in his power but in his freedom from suffering and the oceanic generosity that made him seek to impart that freedom to all living beings. Every religion has a central problem that furnishes the reason for its existence, and Buddhism's is suffering. The Buddha was the person who solved it.

He was born Siddhartha Gotama in the sixth century before Christ, in what is now Nepal. He belonged to the Shakya clan, for which reason he is called Shakyamuni — "Sage of the Shakyas" — to distinguish him from the Buddhas who came before him and the ones who will appear in future epochs, as well as the infinite number of Buddhas that some traditions believe are living in the world today. His father was a king. When the boy was five days old, a fortune-teller predicted two alternate destinies for him, either as a monarch who would sit on the throne of the world or as a Buddha who would win enlightenment.

These destinies are radical opposites: power or freedom, to turn the wheel of the world or to step off it. The choice between them is the same choice that Satan offered Jesus. Siddhartha's father wanted him to be a king, and to ensure this he acted on a second prophecy, which warned that one day his son would see four things — an old man, a sick person, a corpse, and a monk — that would lead him to renounce his inheritance. Against this eventuality, the king built a pleasure garden and posted guards at all its gates, instructing them to make sure that none of the four intruders ever entered. And then he bade Siddhartha live happily inside it.

Years passed. The prince married and had a son, whom he named Rahula, meaning "fetter." But in his twenty-ninth year, the prophecy came true. Eager for a Buddha to appear on earth, the gods took the form of an old man, a sick person, a corpse, and a monk and effortlessly slipped past the guards. Siddhartha saw the first three and was horror-stricken. He saw the last and was inspired, for he realized that the monk was the answer to the questions of old age, sickness, and death. Later that night he awoke in his bedchamber, surrounded by beautiful handmaidens who ground their teeth or muttered incoherently in their sleep and whose bodies, he now saw, were "slick with phlegm and spittle." He cried out, "How oppressive and stifling it is!"[78] Shortly thereafter he left the palace alone and on foot to take up the life of a religious mendicant.

Four of the world's religions begin in gardens, sheltered green spaces untroubled by pain or death. Adam and Eve leave Eden unwillingly, after their Father casts them out in punishment for their disobedience, and with that banishment all suffering begins. The Buddha walks out of his father's garden voluntarily when he realizes that outside it lies an entire world of beings who have been suffering since the beginning of time, and pledges to set them free. Perhaps the difference between these stories explains the difference in tone between the Middle Eastern religions and Buddhism, for what Judaism, Christianity, and Islam have in common is a tragic sense of human beings as exiled sinners and of suffering as their rightful punishment. That's part of what makes the Bible and the Qur'an so dramatic. In contrast, the Buddhist scriptures depict suffering with the same measured dispassion that a medical textbook would bring to bear on a common, pernicious disease. Suffering is a given, something that has always been here and happens to everything that has the capacity to feel.

The Buddha's story is the story of a long experiment regarding the means of attaining liberation from suffering. He tries various kinds of asceticism and rejects them. In the end he simply sits down beneath a bodhi tree. When he rises, he is a different person, a different kind of human being, that difference being summed up in the words with which he announces his transformation: not "I am liberated," but "It is liberated."[79] Something has vanished, maybe the self that was Siddhartha, maybe just the desires around which that self was organized. Something has been "blown out," the literal meaning of the Sanskrit word *nirvana* (in Pali, *nibbana*). As if a wind had shaken it, the bodhi tree showers the man beneath it with blossoms. The Buddha will live on for another forty-five years, transmitting what he learned to a growing number of disciples, but the great events of his life are over. At the age of eighty he dies peacefully in a grove of sal trees, whose blossoms fall onto his body.[80]

What the Buddha intuitively realized in his father's garden was the first of the Four Noble Truths: "Everything is suffering: birth is suffering, sickness is suffering, old age is suffering, death is suffering, union with a person one does not love is suffering, separation from the one whom one loves is suffering, not to obtain what one desires is suffering, the five aggregates of appropriation (which make up a person) are suffering."[81] For "suffering," Buddhist texts use the word *dukkha*. Some scholars say that a more accurate meaning is "unsatisfactory," "flawed," or "awry."[82] These latter words make it plain that suffering is not just physical phenomena — the catastrophes of old age, decrepitude, and death — but mental ones: the old person's unappeasable mourning for his lost youth, the healthy one's revulsion toward the sick, practically everybody's fear of death. Actually Buddhism views suffering primarily as a mental state, arising from *trishna*, "thirst," "desire," or "craving." This is the second truth. Because we cling to them, even pleasurable experiences can become occasions for misery. All that's necessary is that they pass away.

When the Buddha set out to free all sentient beings from suffering, he didn't mean that he was going to put an end to the physical conditions of old age, illness, and death.[83] He meant that he was going to find a way out of the mental straitjacket that causes us to desire youth over age, health over sickness, life over death, self over not-self, and that makes us scheme and grapple to possess one and throw up futile barricades against the other. "The first thing you've got to know is that Buddha's big thing is not suffering," says the Buddhist scholar Robert Thurman. "It's *freedom* from suffering. When the Buddha says 'life is suffering,' he means the *unenlightened* life is suffering. The enlightened life is blissful."[84]

Like Jesus five hundred years later, the Buddha became an object of emulation for his followers, who selected different aspects of his life and teachings as models. Some of them strode purposefully toward nirvana with the aim of winning a speedy release from further rebirths. Their goal was to become an *arhat,* a word that roughly translates as "saint." According to one early formulation, an arhat is a person "in whom the outflows have dried up, who has greatly lived, who has done what had to be done, who has shed the burden, who has won his aim, who is no longer bound to becoming, who is set free, having rightly come to know." [85]

But following his nirvana, the Buddha stayed in the world for another forty-five years to teach the dharma, moved by a compassion so great that it took in all living creatures, not just human beings but also animals, birds, insects, gods, and the devils in hell. This compassion became the basis for another form of practice, which predominates in the Mahayana tradition of China, Tibet, Nepal, Mongolia, and Japan. Its fulfillment is the *bodhisattva,* the "awakened being." The bodhisattva is a person who attains enlightenment but forgoes its most coveted reward. Instead of leaving the stream of birth and death, he vows to go on living, life after life, witnessing suffering and sometimes taking it on, until all sentient beings have been released.

> *And now as long as space endures,*
> *As long as there are beings to be found*
> *May I continue likewise to remain*
> *To drive away the sorrows of the world.* [86]

This is from the *Bodhicharyāvatāra (The Way of the Bodhisattva),* an instruction manual written by the Indian scholar Shantideva in the eighth century A.D. The book's tone is practical and optimistic, didactic and sometimes quite witty. It contains discussions of abstruse points of metaphysics and tips on etiquette:

> *When you spit and throw away*
> *Your tooth sticks, you should cover them.*
> *And it is wrong to foul with urine and with other filth*
> *The fields and water fit for public use.* (74)

But its principal subject is the cultivation of *bodhichitta,* "awakened heart," the intense longing to alleviate suffering, beginning with one's own but extending in due course to that of others, *all* others. The American Buddhist teacher Pema Chödrön reminds us that "all others" includes "those we'll never meet, as well as those we loathe." Bodhichitta is a generosity so radical that one is likely to agree with Chödrön when she calls its attainment "a sort of 'mission impossible.' " [87] Yet the book's nine chapters approach this undertaking in systematic fashion. The first three dwell on the initial dawning of bodhichitta, the next three on its preservation, the last three on its further development. The *Bodhicharyāvatāra* can be said to outline the steps by which an ordinary human being becomes a Buddha.

To Shantideva, all that's required in the beginning is a statement of intention: "the wish to drive away the endless pain of every living being" (34). That wish alone, he suggests, can alchemically transform the one who makes it, turning "impure flesh" (32) into the body of a Buddha. When one has fully committed to the bodhisattva path, one acquires merit even in one's sleep. This is a difficult notion for those of us raised in a tradition that distinguishes action from thought. But Buddhism treats intention as a species of action and when reckoning the karmic consequences of any act factors in both its effects and its underlying motives. For example, a contemporary Tibetan commentary on the *Bodhicharyāvatāra* specifies that it's permissible to kill an assailant if your aim is to save the lives of his other potential victims and to spare the assailant himself the anguish of being reborn in a hell world, as he certainly would be were he to commit murder.[88] A more realistic interpretation is

that any intention, when sufficiently strong, has a transforming effect on the mind. Because vows formalize intention, they are especially powerful. When the Buddha vowed
to go on sitting beneath the bodhi tree until he attained nirvana, the earth trembled.[89]

Of course Shantideva understands that vows can be re-
neged on, and he forecasts grave consequences for those
who do so. But since suffering is primarily a mental phenomenon, the work of ending it also is chiefly mental work,
the work of undoing the mental habits — and especially the
"afflictions" or "defilements" — that cause us to suffer and
inflict suffering on others: greed, aggression, ignorance,
jealousy, pride, all the things that in other traditions are
known as sins. Sometimes these afflictions, or *kleshas* in
Sanskrit, are personified as malign enemies, and their undoing is portrayed as a kind of swashbuckling combat.

> *Proud but wretched rivals, destined all to suffer when*
> *they die,*
> *Will draw the battle lines and do their best to win,*
> *And careless of the pain of cut and thrust,*
> *Will stand their ground refusing to give way.*(58)

But Shantideva stresses that the most effective antidote to
defiled emotions is simply not to act on them.

> *When the urge arises in your mind*
> *To feelings of desire or angry hate*
> *Do not act! Be silent, do not speak!*
> *And like a log be sure to stay.* (68)

Staying like a log is a good metaphor for meditation, the main component of Buddhist practice, though the log in question would have to be alive and supremely conscious. And meditation is a valuable refuge for those given to acting on impulse, both because it demands *in*action and because it directs the mind's attention to its own unexamined contents, the thoughts and feelings that flit beneath the surface of consciousness and the ones sunk in the green ooze at the bottom.

> *Examine thus yourself from every side.*
> *Take note of your defilements and your pointless efforts.*
> *For thus the heroes on the Bodhisattva path*
> *Seize firmly on such faults with proper remedies.* (69)

Sri Lanka's prison authorities may have had this in mind when they invited the Buddhist NGO Sarvodaya Shramadana to hold meditation workshops in the country's penal institutions. The one I attended was held at Colombo's Welikada prison, a Dickensian warren of stained, crumbling brick buildings built in 1844 and designed to house twelve hundred prisoners. In 2005 it held five thousand. They wandered the grounds in limp white trousers or dhotis; some of them slept in the dust, squeezing themselves into the narrow shade of the cell blocks that had no room for them. The mood of the place wasn't angry, like that of prisons in the States. It was listless. Still, most of the men I sat with inside an open cinder block building seemed alert and happy. Hundreds more, I was told, were waiting for a place in the workshop to open up.

The meditations were held two weekends a month and went on for three days. Participants sat for thirty minutes, then spent fifteen minutes in walking meditation and the rest of the hour on break. This went on for six hours a day. The building was hot, and I could feel the hardness of the cement floor even through a cushion. The walls were decorated with posters of scenes from Buddhist and Hindu mythology as brilliantly colored as a pimp's wardrobe. A teacher murmured instructions into a microphone: "Think of your body as the trunk of a tree that is straight from top to bottom." He sounded like a flight attendant telling passengers how to put on their oxygen masks. "Release your negative thoughts." Some two hundred men sat before him on thin mats, their eyes meekly lowered, hands folded in their laps or propped on their knees with thumb and forefinger touching.

There wasn't a single guard inside. If the inmates had gotten it into their heads to take a visitor hostage, no one could have stopped them. But since the program's introduction four years earlier, I was told, violence at Welikada had dropped dramatically. The prison's general population had a 40 percent recidivism rate; among graduates of the meditations it was zero. Practitioners spontaneously gave up drugs and alcohol; they quit smoking; they stopped eating meat. After the tsunami many had volunteered to have their rations cut so that the money saved could be sent to survivors.

I was introduced to a prisoner named Chandraratna.[90] He was big and slow moving, with a shaved head, a thick mustache, and heavy-lidded eyes, one of which had a scar beside it. His manner was gentle and abashed. At one time he'd been a policeman, but out of greed and thwarted ambition he'd taken part in a kidnapping, for which he'd been sentenced to eighty-four years, reduced to forty on appeal. "When I came into prison, I was afraid of the other prisoners," he told me through an interpreter. "Before the meditations started, there were a lot of rowdy people here. Now they're calm. And I'm becoming a good person; my mind is coming to tranquillity. I pray for mercy and kindness to all living things. I pray to be freed of anger and jealousy."

Another man came up to me. His name was Jayasinghe, and he'd killed his girlfriend after discovering that she'd cheated on him. The case had been famous in Sri Lanka, covered in all the papers. He was a handsome man — his nose was strong and beaked — and in his face you could still see a propensity for violence. But he said that meditation had changed him. Even his victim's family had seen it and was no longer angry with him. "Before I started meditating, I was obsessed with revenge," he said. "I wanted to kill the people who'd testified against me. Meditating kept me from acting on those feelings, and little by little it's taken them away." At the close of our interview, he arranged himself ceremoniously on his mat and asked me to take a picture of him sitting. I snapped it and showed him the image. But he shook his head sternly. I'd cut off his feet. And so I took a second shot, from farther back, and this time Jayasinghe was happy.

The rhetoric of the *Bodhicharyāvatāra* alternates between grand exhortations to virtue and specific instructions as to how to achieve it. In the course of time — "time" in a Buddhist context can mean eons — a bodhisattva may have to make the most extreme self-sacrifice.

For all those ailing in the world,
Until their very sickness has been healed,
May I myself become for them
The doctor, nurse, and medicine itself.

Raining down a flood of food and drink,
May I dispel the ills of thirst and famine,
And in the aeons marked by scarcity and want,
May I myself be drink and sustenance. . . . (54)

This body I have now resigned
To serve the pleasure of all living beings
Let them ever kill, despise, and beat it
Using it according to their wish. (55)

The value of such sacrifices isn't substitutive. Unlike Jesus, the Buddha didn't give up his life in exchange for humankind's. Rather, his sacrifice was to continue living when nirvana lay within his grasp, in order to point other beings along the path to enlightenment. The same is true for a bodhisattva. He suffers in solidarity with other creatures to teach onlookers something about the nature of suffering, perhaps only that nobody is exempt from it. When asked why he has fallen ill, the bodhisattva Vimalakīrti replies, "For the bodhisattva, the world consists only of living beings, and sickness is inherent in living in the world. Were all living beings free of sickness, the bodhisattva would also be free of sickness."[91]

If a bodhisattva lays down his life, it may be to demonstrate that one's life is not such a terrible thing to part with. Or it may be for the same reason that a handful of men and women stayed behind in the World Trade Center on September 11: not for the sake of dying but to save other people who couldn't get out on their own. Such feats of radical selflessness seem to belong in the same category as the miracles attributed to Christian martyrs in the arena. But according to Shantideva, by far the greater part of the bodhisattva's practice consists of curbing his natural, creaturely selfishness. The method is perfection by increments.[92]

> *Our guide instructs us to begin*
> *By giving vegetable greens or other little things,*
> *That later, step-by-step, the habit once acquired,*
> *We may be able to donate our very flesh.* (100)

To sacrifice one's life for the benefit of other beings is a monumental undertaking, but it may be even more difficult to will that certain of those beings, the ones we really dislike, get the love and admiration we want for ourselves. Although Shantideva speaks of the extreme forms of suffering, including that of hell, the misery he writes about most eloquently is the kind he is likely to have experienced himself. Like the Buddha, he was a king's son who took up a monastic life. Instead of becoming a mendicant on the open road, however, he entered the monastery at Nālandā. There the other residents are said to have treated him with disdain, calling him Bhusuku because he seemed to do nothing but eat (*bhuj*), sleep (*sup*), and stroll around (*kuti m gata*).[93] So it's especially poignant to hear this teacher addressing the agonies of envy and resentment that fester in monastic communities, as they do in grad schools and corporate head offices.

He's the center of attention. I am nothing.
And, unlike him, I'm poor without possessions.
Everyone looks up to him, despising me,
All goes well for him; for me there's only bitterness.

All I have is sweat and drudgery,
While he's there, sitting at his ease.
He's great, respected in the world,
While I'm the underdog, a well-known nobody. (129)

For twelve more verses Shantideva gnaws on this injustice and thinks of ways to avenge it. Then abruptly he shakes himself.

Happiness, fulfillment: these I give away.
The pain of others: this I will embrace.
Inquiring of myself repeatedly
I will thus investigate my thoughts.

When others are at fault, I'll take
And turn the blame upon myself.
And all my sins, however slight,
Declare, and make them known to many.

The fame of others I will magnify
That it might thus outshine my own. (132)

The call to abandon life comes along rarely in the United States today (unless you're a soldier in Afghanistan or Iraq). It's one reason that the stories of the Christian martyrs seem so remote from us. But we *do* know what it's like to feel unappreciated and neglected; we know what it's like to seethe while others claim the rewards that ought to be ours. And so we can anticipate the internal rending it would take to wish sincerely that our rivals get what they want, all of it, including the right to have it, so that we forfeit even the wormwood pleasure of feeling wronged.

The latter feeling is something one rarely comes across in Buddhist literature. The Buddha never warns his followers that they will be hated of all men for his sake, or even that they will suffer for it. Part of that is because the Buddha intended his method to be an *antidote* to suffering. And part of it is because the Buddhist view of karma more or less does away with the idea of unwarranted injury. All dukkha has an origin, and the origin always lies in the self. If some of the glamour of martyrdom resides in the victim's innocence, Shantideva recognizes that innocence is an illusion, and so for that matter is the victim. Victim and perpetrator exist only in relation to each other and to the suffering that connects them. The wronged person must remind himself that

> . . . *in the past*
> *It was I who injured living beings.*
> *Therefore it is right that injury*
> *Should come to me their torturer.*
>
> *Their weapons and my body —*
> *Both are causes of my torment!*
> *They their weapons, I my body brandished;*
> *Who is then more worthy of my rage?* (83)

With only a slight distortion, this might be Louise Hay or any of the other smiling New Age scolds who tell their unhappy followers that they chose their AIDS or abusive parents. Those scolds, of course, are usually peddling a debased version of karma. Buddhism does teach that what goes around comes around and that somebody who causes suffering in one life is likely to receive it in the next. But karma is more complex than that. Because someone who harms another being is reborn in a hell, his victim is, in a sense, the agent of his future suffering. Because suffering is often instructive, an oppressor can become a teacher.

The danger of this worldview is that it can seem to minimize gross misery and injustice. While the Buddha accepted disciples of all castes, for example, he never explicitly questioned the caste system, under which one baby was born to be exalted and another to be loathed and downtrodden. Asked to explain those babies' different circumstances, Buddhism, like Hinduism before it, would invoke the unerring sorting mechanism of karma. Of course there's no way to challenge that, for who knows what any baby did in its previous life? "All that has washed in has washed out," the Venerable Bhante Piyatissa told me when I asked him about the deaths from the 2004 Boxing Day tsunami, and he may have meant babies, too.

On the other hand, the elder may only have been speaking about the provisional character of life itself, the ease with which it takes root, the ease with which it is uprooted and swept away. A truly Buddhist response to any injustice would be to look very closely at the line that divides victims from perpetrators, so closely that it blurs. Then one might see that the line was arbitrary from the beginning, a boundary marker drawn on an ocean of suffering. So, for that matter, is the line that distinguishes one individual from another.

Underlying the *Bodhicharyāvatāra*'s doctrine of extreme selflessness is the conviction that there is no self — none, at any rate, that is stable and enduring or separate from all the other selves that mill around it. Shantideva takes a methodical inventory of the parts that make up a human being, examining each to see if the self resides there. Bones, blood, flesh, skin, hair, nails, lymph, phlegm, lungs, liver, breath, warmth, even consciousness — each is held up beneath the loupe and then returned to its numbered bin. It would be easy to dismiss this as sophistry if it weren't for Buddhism's conviction that the origin of all suffering is the self's delusional belief in its separate existence, and the craving — a psychoanalyst would say the anxiety — that makes it cling to anything that will ratify that delusion, including its misery.

One edition of the *Bodhicharyavātāra* includes two meditations from a nineteenth-century Tibetan commentary. The first is called "Equalizing Self and Other," the second "Exchanging Self and Other."[94] Jesus commanded us to love our neighbors as ourselves. Shantideva puts it less equivocally: Our neighbors *are* ourselves. So are our enemies.

The martyr and the bodhisattva gaze at each other like figures carved on facing sides of an arch, each a prototype of sacred suffering. One reenacts the sacrifice of a god, the other that of a man. The martyr's agony is literally spectacular: from the time the first Christian was delivered to the lions, his wounds were meant to be seen. The bodhisattva's wounds are invisible, as is the weapon that makes them. One sacrifices himself by dying; the other does so by living. Curiously, in most representations neither seems to be suffering greatly. The most famous paintings of Saint Sebastian, to name just one martyr, show him looking somber, melan-

choly, even ecstatic. And paintings and statues of the bodhi-
sattvas frequently show them smiling.

A few months after the Vietnam vets' retreat, I finally
met Ted Fuller, the monk who'd originally invited me. The
occasion was the screening of a documentary about an in-
terfaith retreat at Auschwitz-Birkenau. Fuller had been one
of its leaders, and he appeared throughout the film, looking,
with his shaved head and large, protuberant eyes, like a
somber Jiminy Cricket as he talked about the special suffering of killers. He believed that this was what soldiers were
at bottom: killers, all of them, to a man. When speaking to
groups, he often introduced himself by saying, "I'm just like
Ted Bundy." It grabbed people's attention.

The film's high point was a meditation in the camp's main
yard, where during the Shoah inmates had lined up in the
morning and where some of them had been selected for
the gas. Dozens of people took part in the meditation: Buddhist monks, Catholic nuns, priests, rabbis, and laypersons
of every faith. In the intervals between sittings, they would
read the names of the one million people who'd died there.
Someone mentioned that this included officers and guards.
Afterward, when the lights in the theater went up, a man in
the audience rose; he was white with rage. By reading the
names of prisoners and guards together, the Buddhists, he
felt, had made a mockery of Auschwitz. They had thought-
lessly erased the line that separated victims from perpetrators. The line wasn't just conceptual; it was a trench filled
with real blood and real ashes. By reading those names together, by ladling their undiscriminating compassion over
the murderers and the murdered alike, the Buddhists had
declared they were the same.

Of course the angry moviegoer was right. Never have categories like perpetrator and victim, or, for that matter, good and evil, had a greater objective reality than they did at Auschwitz. But I also understood why the Buddhists who came there fifty years later (and not just Buddhists but Christians and Jews as well) would insist on ignoring those categories. Suffering is greater. It is greater than anything that can be said about it. And, the Buddhists might have added, categories like good and evil were part of what had made Auschwitz possible. The Nazis, too, had boxes marked "good" and "evil"; they just filled them with different people. And when the box marked "evil" was filled to the bursting point, they pumped it full of gas.

THE ADJECTIVE BOTH Kate and Kelly used to describe EB was "Sisyphean." It was constantly upping its ante. The blisters turned into sores, and the sores got deeper and healed more slowly. The infections multiplied and grew more resistant to drugs. The surgeries that had once salvaged the twins' hands for a few months were futile now. The tendons there were too short; their health was too frail to withstand major surgery. They were getting tired. Once they'd believed that they would somehow beat EB, fending off its worst ravages until a cure was found. But increasingly they understood that they would not.

"All our lives people have been saying" — Kelly began, then she and Kate finished the sentence in unison — " 'three to five years.' "

"That's how long they keep saying it'll be until they come up with a cure," Kelly went on. "And in the last few years it's seemed increasingly possible scientifically, with gene therapy. But as possible as it's started to seem, it also seems really far away, far enough away that I don't think it will happen for me. And besides, there's already been so much damage that's irreversible that . . ." She paused self-consciously, perhaps out of embarrassment, perhaps out of fear. "It would be an incredible boon if they could stop the disease process right now, but . . . The vision I always had was of me being restored to a perfect body." She gazed down at her hands. "And that's fantasy."

"My biggest dream is to take a shower," Kate told me. "Or go to the beach in a really small bikini and feel comfortable." She thought for a second. "Although most people don't feel comfortable. Well, some people do.

"I think it's sort of ironic. I have a nicely shaped body, but I hide it all the time. I have to. I feel like it's almost a requirement. I feel like my bandages and my sores are a confrontation. People are afraid to — people don't want to — see them. I don't want them to see them."

In the last year of their sickness, Kate and Kelly stopped going out almost entirely. They stopped returning phone calls. They wrote only sporadically in their journals. Their days crawled past, isolated moments looming out of a haze of morphine and OxyContin, then dissolving back into it. They needed several pills just to get them through their morning care, and even with pills, they often screamed in pain for hours on end. It wasn't the first time that they'd spoken with their parents about dying, but they did it more often now and more matter-of-factly. Chris hated those conversations. He'd been diagnosed with lymphoma and would say, only half-joking, that if anything happened to the girls, it would kill him. (He would die in September 2007, ten months after his daughters.) It was Nancy who told them, "If you really get to the point where you can't deal anymore, then I don't want you to take any more than you think you can."

In 2006 both sisters were having trouble swallowing and had to be taken to the hospital to have their throats dilated. An EB patient's throat is considered dangerously narrow when it shrinks to ten centimeters. Blistering and scarring had constricted Kate's to one. The procedure bought them a few months. That November, though, Kelly's hemoglobin level plummeted, and it became hard for her to breathe. Chris and Nancy took her back to the hospital. In the emergency room, the staff scrambled to intubate her. Someone said she needed an iron infusion for anemia. Kelly begged to be left alone; the infusions were especially painful. But the resident and nurses insisted on treating her.

Later Nancy learned that a small boy had died in the ER earlier in the day and the traumatized staff couldn't bear to lose another patient. When Kelly asked what would happen if she refused treatment, she was told, incorrectly, that she'd drown in her own fluids. So she agreed to be hydrated and infused. Then her parents took her home. "Do you know how it hurts our hearts to have to put a patient through this?" a nurse confided in Nancy. The father of the dying boy had insisted that they do everything to save him, long after it became clear that everything wouldn't be enough.

When they got home, Nancy reminded Kelly that the choice whether to go on living was hers. "If you want to fight, I'll roll up my sleeves and fight for you. And if you don't . . ." She left the sentence unfinished. Kelly chose to die. It took her four days. Although their rooms were next to each other, Kate was too ill and weak to visit her more than once. "I can feel her pain. I mean, I feel it!" she told her parents afterward. She touched the port in her stomach. "Even my button starts to hurt." Nancy asked her if she had any last things she wanted to say to Kelly. "Mom, we've always told each other everything. We never held anything back." She didn't see her sister again. In the following days Nancy rarely left Kelly's side. After she died, she carefully unwrapped her daughter's bandages until she was as naked as on the day she came into the world. Then she zipped her into a red dress that Kelly had bought years before but had never had the courage to wear because it showed too much skin.

"I don't know what words to use," Nancy said later. She sounded almost giddy. "None of them feels right. I'm so grateful that I got to have her for twenty-seven years, but 'Thank you' doesn't feel like enough. There ought to be different kinds of thank-yous, like a thank-you for opening the door for me. And there'd be another kind of thank-you for Kelly. I don't know, maybe it's just because I'm in shock, but what I feel right now is . . . acceptance. I'm like, 'I get it, God. I get it. I have no control over anything.' Maybe I'll feel different later."

This was a day or two before Kelly's funeral. I'd come down to pay my respects. When I visited Kate in her room, she was lying in her hospital bed. She couldn't have weighed more than eighty pounds. It was the first time I'd seen her without clothes, wrapped only in the contact layers that Kelly had once compared to fishnet stockings. Her body was like a bundle of twigs twisted into an effigy. Her hands were stubs. Her head looked unnaturally large. In repose her mouth and cheeks drooped like those of an unhappy old woman, and behind her thick glasses her eyes were enormous.

"Oh, honey," I blurted out when I saw her, "you must be so lonely."

"Yes, I am," she said. She couldn't sit up, and so I gave her juice from a carton, feeding the straw into her small, pursed mouth. Her voice was very soft. She was grateful to me for coming, grateful that I'd taken an interest in her. All her life she'd wanted to be seen. She'd wanted that even as she'd drawn back from it, fearful of how her maimed body would appear to others. On leaving I kissed my hand and pressed it to her forehead. "Be at peace," I said. We looked at each other, then she closed her eyes.

She died early on the morning of November 23, Thanksgiving Day. She'd been in increasing pain since Kelly's death, as if the portion that her twin had relinquished had passed to her. Nancy was injecting morphine directly into her wasted leg, but no amount of the drug seemed to help. "I'd look at her," Nancy said, "and I'd see these morphined eyes looking at me in pain. You know, how you can tell if someone's in pain? And Chris and I were going out of our minds trying to find something. One of my girlfriends told me about a homeopath nearby. And I was ready to do anything. If you'd told me to rub myself with shit and roll around in the yard, I'd have done it."

She called the homeopath and he came over and gave Kate some arsenicum. "And from that time on, she took nothing. No drugs. Except right at the end she got frightened, and I gave her some Ativan." Some friends of Nancy's came: Maureen Markel, who'd taught the girls in college, a woman named Sharon from Canada, who'd met the Daleys at the Kozak clinic twenty-five years before, when she'd brought her son there for treatment. He had died years earlier, at the age of fourteen. Barbara was there, and Nancy's best friend, Shirley Ponder. Kate's death became a ceremony of women.

Once Nancy caught Barbara trying to give Kate electrolytes through her feeding tube. "She needs them," the nurse protested. "Otherwise she'll die."

Nancy refrained from saying that that was the point. "If Kate asks for something to drink, you give it to her," she said. She held up a paper cup. "You give it to her in this. Otherwise, leave her alone." She poured some electrolyte solution into the cup and handed it to Barbara, then poured a cup for herself and tapped the cups together in a toast. "This is for us. We're the ones who need it. Now drink up."

It had been days since Kate's bandages had been changed, and they smelled terrible. They gave her fluids with a syringe and a moistened sponge. It was how Nancy had fed her when she was a baby. "I'd come full circle," she said later. Kate passed in and out of consciousness. Nancy and Chris sat by her during the night, while the other women spelled them during the day. Sometimes they read to her, or sang. Sometimes Nancy sat and read quietly from her daughter's journals. "Do you know how incredible that was, to read her life while she was dying? She was three-quarters in the next world."

Kate kept telling her that she wanted to die, and Nancy could see her struggling to let go, but something was holding her back. At last she realized what it was: Kate was afraid of going to hell. She put her hand on her daughter's heart. "Honey, you and Kelly never sinned," she told her. "You made some mistakes. Every human being makes mistakes. But you never sinned. You'll be with your sister in heaven. What loving God would banish his children to hell?" She told me this story on the phone, and when she was done, I could hear her take a drag on her cigarette. Then she said, "I had to get her past all that Catholic shit." Soon after that, Kate's heart stopped beating.

On one of their daughter's last nights, the Daleys and their company were sitting down to dinner when someone knocked at the door. Outside stood an elderly black man. His eyes were red-rimmed and filmy, and he smelled of liquor. He said that his arthritis was bothering him; his feet hurt too much for him to walk. He asked if he could come in. Nancy's first impulse was to say no, but when the man asked a second time, she shrugged and opened the door. On joining them at the dining table, he asked for vodka, but Nancy told him that he had to eat first. He was already drunk. Once he started drinking after dinner, he became quite loud, and the Daleys worried about Kate. At last Nancy got up quietly and called a neighbor. When she described the man, the woman recognized him as a former local police officer named James Watkins.[95] Over the years alcoholism had gotten the better of him, and he'd been forced to retire. He often wandered around Newburgh, seeking refuge in strangers' homes. Nancy asked her friend to call the police and have them come pick him up. "But ask them to come without sirens," she begged her. "I've got a sick girl here." The police came and politely took Watkins home.

Afterward the Daleys broke up laughing. "If anybody had come and seen us laughing like that while our daughter was dying upstairs, I don't know what they would've thought," she said. "But that's what our lives were like always. One minute we were crying, the next we were laughing. Even today, when we called up the funeral home, we said we'd come over, but the director said no, he'd come here, no problem. I started to say, 'No, no, don't bother. We'll come.' But then I figured that he's the only guy who's not swamped with customers the day after Thanksgiving. We're the only people shopping for caskets today.

"I was in awe of my children. How many parents can say that? Our children taught us what they needed. And they taught us how to live. I was so grateful to have had them as long as I did. I was so grateful to be able to be with them at the end. Missing that would've been like missing a meteor shower. How awful to miss a meteor shower because I forgot to look up."

I THINK BACK to a conversation I had with the girls one of the first times I visited. We were talking about Kate's church-going, which back when they were in college had been at its peak, and about the expectations that lay behind it.

"It used to upset me," Kelly admitted. "Because she went to church every day, and every day I knew that she was praying to be healed and she kind of expected it."

Kate said, "And every day I woke up and I wasn't, I was really disappointed." She seemed almost amused by the memory.

"I used to get really angry at her because she was setting herself up for a fall," Kelly said. "And that's a big fall, every day to have that kind of disappointment."

Kate recalled, "There was a chapel downstairs from me in

the dorm, and I used to go down there when I was . . . *over-wrought* and sit in front of the Eucharist and just cry and scream at God. Sometimes I would sing to him. It was a sort of communion. But I just became . . . I don't know. There was no great event that suddenly disillusioned me. But just living all of these years with more pain and suffering, I stopped getting comfort from that. I still pray every night, though."

I asked her what she prayed for.

"I stopped praying for healing pretty much," Kate said. "I pray for peace. Barbara was always telling me to offer my suffering up, and I never knew what that meant. But I kind of realized the meaning of it a few years ago, which was that Jesus suffered and died for us, and when we suffer we're kind of . . . we're kind of joining our suffering with his. So I do that."

"She's always telling me to do that," Kelly complained. "I just don't understand how. You say, 'Offer up your suffering.' I'd think God would want your joy, but I just can't see how somebody else *wants* your suffering. I don't get that."

It was one of the few times I got to see the antagonism that sometimes crackled between them. It made me uncomfortable, and as much to change the subject as anything else, I asked Kelly if there was anything that she used in lieu of prayer to comfort herself.

"I've always had a sort of detachment from myself, like I'm watching myself experience things," she said. "Not all the time, but very often. Very often I'm looking at my life like it's a story to be told and I'm narrating it in my head. And that's what keeps me going. I want to know what happens. Sometimes it's the only thing that keeps me going."

CHAPTER 5

The Faces in the Hold

What Do I Owe Those Who Suffer?

The first symptoms may have appeared as far back as 1986, when his posture, which had been notably erect, became stooped. In the early 1990s observers noted a tremor in his left hand.[1] His gait grew stiff and shuffling, and he walked with such a pronounced forward list that he often seemed to be in danger of falling. By the beginning of the new century it was clear that he was very ill, though the Vatican would issue no official statement about what was wrong with him. His symptoms worsened. Even so, he continued in office, perhaps conscious that in the preceding two thousand years only nine popes had left it while they were still alive. He brushed aside suggestions that he retire, scornfully asking, "Did Christ come down from the cross?"[2] He refused to make concessions to his debility. He had always been known for his physical vigor, his love of hiking and skiing. And he understood that much of the power of his papacy derived from his personal charisma, which required that he show himself to his people. Since becoming pope, he had traveled more than all his predecessors combined. And so he went on traveling even now that he was dying, slowly and in pain.

Pope John Paul II had Parkinson's disease, a neurological condition named for James Parkinson, the physician who first identified it. His 1817 treatise, "An Essay on the Shaking Palsy," remains a chillingly accurate description of the disease's creeping progression:

> So slight and nearly imperceptible are the first inroads of this malady, and so extremely slow its progress, that it rarely happens, that the patient can form any recollection of the precise period of its commencement. The first symptoms perceived are a slight sense of weakness, with a proneness to trembling in some particular part; sometimes in the head, but most commonly in one of the hands and arms. These symptoms gradually increase in the part first affected; and at uncertain period, but seldom in less than twelve months or more, the morbid influence is felt in some other part.

In time, Parkinson writes,

> the tremulous motion of the limbs occur[s] during sleep, and augment[s] until they awaken the patient, and frequently with much agitation and alarm. The power of conveying food to the mouth is at length so impeded that he is obliged to consent to be fed by others. . . . The trunk is almost permanently bowed, the muscular power is de-

cidedly diminished, and the tremulous agitation becomes violent. . . .

As the debility increases and the influence of the will over the muscles fades away, the tremulous agitation becomes more vehement. It now seldom leaves him for a moment; but even when exhausted nature seizes a small portion of sleep, the motion becomes so violent as not only to shake the bed-hangings, but even the floor and the sashes of the room. The chin is now almost immoveably bent upon the sternum. The slops with which he is attempted to be fed, with the saliva are constantly trickling from the mouth. The power of articulation is lost. The urine and faeces are passed involuntarily; and at the last, constant sleepiness, with slight delirium, and other marks of extreme exhaustion, announce the wished-for release.[3]

Today Parkinson's is recognized as a common illness of old age, with 1.5 million patients in the United States and 50,000 new cases diagnosed every year.[4] It remains incurable, but its symptoms can be managed by drugs such as levodopa and apomorphine hydrochloride. In the later stages of his disease, the pope was treated with both. Earlier, though, he is said to have refused medication on the grounds that it "would interfere with his suffering."[5] Clues to his reluctance may be found in his apostolic letter *Salvifici Doloris*, written in 1984, two years before the onset of his symptoms. In it the pontiff affirms the special relationship between human suffering and Christ. That relationship might be compared to the relation between a lump of coal and a diamond, or to the pressure that transforms the first into the second.

"Christ wishes to be united with every individual, and in a special way he is united with those who suffer," John Paul writes. "In so far as man becomes a sharer in Christ's sufferings — in any part of the world and at any time in history — to that extent *he in his own way completes* the suffering through which Christ accomplished the Redemption of the world." [6] In submitting to the ravages of his illness, the pope was in a sense reenacting the sacrifice of the martyrs nineteen centuries before, obeying Christ's summons to suffer with him and for him. Moreover, because he had declared the church to be the champion of life — especially the marginal lives of the unborn and the terminally ill, which are so often ended under the pretext of alleviating suffering — the pope's ordeal had a pedagogical value. The lives of the unborn and the dying might weigh very little on the scale of Western conscience; the life of a pope would even things out a bit. In the words of Cardinal Joseph Ratzinger, the guardian of church doctrine who would succeed John Paul as pontiff, "To suffer is a special way of preaching." [7]

But preaching requires a congregation, and so the Holy Father put his suffering on display. This was one reason that he continued to travel even as the disease extended its dominion over his body. Everybody saw it, not just Catholics but those of other faiths. They, too, lined the streets by the thousands when he came to their cities and shouted his name as he waved to them stiffly from the specially designed car whose top was a bubble of bulletproof glass. (More than twenty years earlier, as his car — which was open back then — rolled slowly through St. Peter's Square, a would-be assassin had shot him three times with a 9-mm pistol, nearly killing him.) He let them see his hobbling gait, and when he could no longer walk, he consented to be rolled out at audiences in a wheeled throne like an effigy in a religious procession. Sometimes it seemed that that was what his sickness was turning him into. Trying to describe Parkinson's for a layman, a doctor said, "Imagine yourself encased in armor." [8]

The pope may have conceived of his suffering as a symbolic sharing in the cross, but it had neither the hieratic dignity nor the swooning languor one finds in classical representations of the Crucifixion. His suffering was commonplace, and it was grotesque. On a visit to Canada in 2001, he was presented with a bouquet of flowers by a little girl who, when he bent painfully forward to take it from her, ran sobbing from the stage because, as one observer speculated, his stiffened features may have made him look "angry, or ill-meaning, or sad." [9]

The press's coverage of this long Calvary was respectful, often reverent. The international edition of *Newsweek* featured a cover story titled "The Pope's Pain," the headline printed beside a close-up of the face that had made a little girl burst into tears. It peered up as if from the bottom of a well, the lips compressed in a way that suggested that the person trapped behind it was trying to form a word. Nothing in the story suggested what that word might be. "This pope is not doing a job," the reporters explained. "He is carrying out a divine mission, and his pain is at its core." [10]

National Review amplified that idea: "The principal task of the pope is not the effective management of the Church bureaucracy — it is to serve as an effective witness for Christ in the world. John Paul does this most eloquently today through his silent suffering. . . . He has a mystical relationship with his suffering, offering it up for us, and for the whole world." [11] The conservative columnist Peggy Noonan recounted attending a papal audience at the Vatican in 2003: "After seeing him, I thought: *I saw a saint at sunset.*" As the Holy Father sang to the congregation, softly, "like an old man sitting in the sun," she told a friend, "We are hearing a saint singing." She continued, "I breathed it in, let the sound enter my ears. I wanted to put my hands over them and hold the sound in my head." [12]

Rarely had the long dying of a single man been the object of such hushed attention, especially given that the man was old and dying of natural causes.

AT ABOUT THE same time, a city was dying, though nobody knew it yet. It had been dying for some time, and its symptoms were so like those seen in other cities that they passed for life, or a particular kind of life, and were not recognized as the spasms of the mortally ill. To this add the fact that when the city died, it would be because of a blow, and the blow had not yet fallen. The city's public face was the face of pleasure, combining features of the musician, the clown, and the whore. People came from far away to drink in its bars, eat in its restaurants, listen to music in its clubs, cheer the gilded, feathered revelers at its Mardi Gras, hoot at the naked dancers in its strip joints. Tourism was the principal source of income, generating $5 billion a year. [13]

Yet New Orleans was also a poor city, the poorest city in

the second-poorest state in the richest country on earth. More than 103,000 of its people — 23 percent — lived in poverty, nearly 50,000 of them in neighborhoods where the poverty rate approached 40 percent[14] and per capita income might be little more than $10,000 a year.[15] In those neighborhoods, which not so many years before had had dirt roads and open drainage ditches running through them, four in every ten people had no job. Most children lived with one parent, who fed them rice and red beans or junk food and bought their clothes at the thrift shop. Close to 57 percent of the city's old people were disabled. Nearly one in four of its citizens had no access to a car.

New Orleans's schools did not teach: fewer than half the city's residents could read and write.[16] Its police didn't protect the citizenry. Many of them supplemented their municipal salaries with bribes; some worked as muscle for drug dealers. In the early 1990s four New Orleans police officers were charged in separate murders.[17] One of them gunned down her former partner and two other victims while holding up the restaurant where the partner was moonlighting as a security guard.[18]

Overall, the city's homicide rate was ten times the national average,[19] and one neighborhood, the Lower Ninth Ward, was said to be fifteen times more crime-ridden than New York City.[20] In 2005 only 12 percent of the people arrested for homicide in New Orleans were convicted.[21] The housing projects lay in thrall to drug gangs armed with AK-47s, whose top earners could make $50,000 a week. The corner convenience stores sold crack packaged in bubble gum wrappers.[22] The inevitable turf wars produced a harvest of the dead: young gangstas and younger corner boys and the small, hapless casualties who were called "mush-rooms" for their unlucky habit of popping up in the cross fire. In the early 1990s an installation by the local artist Dawn DeDeaux re-created one such housing project in miniature.[23] Visitors passed through its trenchlike corridors into a small room to watch a video monitor on which a bizarrely old-looking young woman recalled looking out her kitchen window one afternoon to see her son being shot dead in the courtyard below. In another room, one could watch a video of a small boy in an oversize suit tap-dancing for tourists' change.

Of course things like this were happening in almost every city in America. In New Orleans they just took more extreme, more hopeless forms, their hopelessness thrown into relief by the nonstop party in progress less than a mile away. And New Orleans also had nature to worry about. Only Los Angeles and San Francisco were so completely at its mercy. Surrounded by water — the Gulf of Mexico, the Mississippi River, and Lake Pontchartrain — the city lay an average of six feet below sea level. Thanks to the destruction of the surrounding wetlands, it was sinking a little more every day.[24] It was situated on a meteorological bull's-eye, exactly where the storms that come lashing up from the Caribbean were most likely to make landfall. Floods and hurricanes had devastated it repeatedly since its founding. Yet the levees that had been built to protect the city were old and in disrepair, and there were frequent reports of leaks.[25] In 2005 New Orleans didn't have a single shelter certified by the Red Cross, the Red Cross being reluctant to set up shelters that, given the lack of high ground, were in imminent danger of themselves being submerged.[26] For years experts had been warning of a disaster. In 2002 the *New Orleans Times-Picayune* forecast that a major storm "would turn the city and the east bank of Jefferson Parish into a lake as much as thirty feet deep, fouled with chemicals and waste from ruined septic systems, businesses and homes. Such a flood would trap hundreds of thousands of people." [27]

In August 2005 that was what happened. The storm hit, the levees breached. Overnight, New Orleans became the stage for a vast spectacle of natural disaster and institutional collapse. All the world saw it: the inundated neighborhoods where rooftops protruded above the water like capsized arks; the families clinging to those rooftops and waving frantically for rescue that didn't come; the thousands of people packed for days without food or water into the reeking hulls of structures designed to entertain a fraction of their number for a few hours; the body of an emaciated woman propped in a wheelchair with a plaid blanket draped over her in someone's attempt to shield her dignity, the normal dignity-shielding measure of a prompt burial being unavailable to her, as it was to some thirteen hundred others who died in Hurricane Katrina and its aftermath. [28] Where the dead were concerned, New Orleans post-Katrina was a grotesque inversion of New York post-9/11. Instead of vanishing into air, the bodies were everywhere, bloated and drifting on the stagnant water; they were part of the city's shame. Pointing to the dead woman in the wheelchair, one onlooker snorted. "I don't treat my dog like that. I buried my dog." [29]

The press was there to record the spectacle and interview its victims and marshal the public's outrage on their behalf. It was in the disaster area days before the first FEMA buses arrived on the scene; it stayed on the streets after the police abandoned them. It reminded viewers that these scenes of ruin and squalor weren't taking place in Sri Lanka or Rwanda but in America, that the victims were Americans,[30] and that the officials charged with protecting them — "He's the most powerful man in the world and all he wants is to make sure I'm safe" — were not. The press did such a good job that one tended to forget that up until Katrina, it had paid little attention to New Orleans. What was happening in New Orleans had gone virtually unnoticed outside the city itself. Jon Donley, an editor at NOLA.com, the *Times-Picayune*'s Web site, says that crime and scandal aside, New Orleans was generally the subject of one big press story a year. Usually it had something to do with Mardi Gras. "Other than that," he summed up, "we're pretty much out of sight, out of mind."[31]

Along with being a poor city, New Orleans was predominantly black: 68 percent of its people were African American.[32] They were the descendants of slaves. New Orleans was once a slave port, and slavery had been the mainspring of its economy. It's a queer coincidence that the first slave ship built in America was called the *Desire*, the same name as one of the city's most famous streets and one of its most ravaged housing projects. Nothing I've read indicates whether the names are related. *Desire* is, at any rate, an apt name for a ship designed for the trade in human beings. The ship made its maiden voyage from Salem, Massachusetts, in 1638 and returned carrying a cargo of "cotton, tobacco, salt and negroes," the negroes being considered so unimportant that not even their number was recorded.[33]

Throughout history certain categories of suffering have

been given attention, while others have been ignored. Those who suffer may be valued so little that their suffering is taken for granted. It passes beneath the radar of our recognition, without ever being seen for what it is. Thus ships' outfitters in the slave ports of the South filled their shop windows with eye-catching displays of chains, leg irons, and thumbscrews, as a farm store displays its cattle prods and branders.

By July 2005 the predicament of New Orleans was no longer considered newsworthy, maybe because the bloody, senseless deaths of young people in the Desire houses had been eclipsed in public consciousness by the bloody, senseless deaths of young people in Baghdad. That it had ever been newsworthy probably had less to do with white viewers' compassion, say, for a poor black woman who had seen her son gunned down in her project's courtyard than with their fear of the young black men — boys, really, but armed with AK-47s — who had killed him and whose violence might conceivably spill out of Desire and into the neighborhoods where those viewers lived.

A cursory scan of the TV news was enough to learn the names of the most murderous gangs, their weapons and hand signals, their derisive terms of art, but one could watch forever and not learn other things. You wouldn't learn, for instance, that out of every one thousand African American babies born in Louisiana in 2005, fifteen would die before their first birthday; in Sri Lanka, harrowed by tsunami and civil war, the infant mortality rate was only thirteen per thousand.[34] Or that black youths in Harlem, central Detroit, and the South Side of Chicago had the same probability of dying by age forty-five as whites *nationwide* did of dying by age sixty-five, not of violence but of illness. Or that the rates of diabetes, heart disease, asthma, and cancer among poor inner-city blacks and Latinos were so staggeringly high that they led one commentator to wonder "whether there is something deadly in the American experience of urban poverty itself." [35]

Of course asthma and diabetes are hard to translate into the visual language of television, but so are "sick houses" and E. coli outbreaks, and television had told stories about them; they'd made everybody hysterical. From this you could conclude that it was the identity of the victims that eluded representation, or defied it, maybe because as recently as 2005 there was a tacit assumption in this country that the suffering of poor people of color — and, to a lesser extent, that of poor whites — was not exceptional. It was business as usual. They were designated sufferers.

People may be designated to suffer for sacred reasons, like the divine kings whose coronations were the prelude to their ritual murder,[36] or for economic or political ones. The suffering of the first category is intrinsic and intentional; that of the second is incidental. Its members suffer because value is being extracted from them, as gold is extracted from the earth. Those who extract that value may bear the afflicted no more malice than the miner bears the rock he drills. One of the paradoxes of slavery is that its chattels were simultaneously valuable and valueless.[37] African slaves in North America were shackled and flogged, or had their ears cropped or their noses slit, for the same reasons that white indentured servants had been treated similarly a generation or two earlier: it was that era's version of worker motivation. And their descendants were treated as they were — which is to say mostly with neglect and occasionally with the sanctioned brutality of the law — because they had been exhausted of value (nobody owned them, and nobody could envision profiting from their labor) but could not, for reasons both practical and humane, be destroyed. That is the difference between a devalued human being and a tapped-out gold mine.

The origins of this system may have been pragmatic, but over time it came to seem sacred, the victim's suffering the punishment for a fall too ancient to be remembered: *And he said, Cursed be Canaan; a servant of servants shall he be unto his brethren* (Gen. 9:25). It is astonishing to realize that this single verse provided the theological pretext for an entire system of humans owning humans. From an economic perspective, the wretchedness of slaves, or of a slave class, is substitutive, securing the well-being of others.[38] But so, from a spiritual perspective, was the suffering of the scapegoats that Israel sacrificed each year to redeem its sins. And so was that of Christ.

One way to tell that a population has been designated to suffer is when its suffering goes unremarked. Another is when the victims are blamed for their suffering. The eighteenth-century Jamaican planter and historian Edward Long justified the maltreatment of slaves on the Middle Passage as a necessary measure against mutinies: "The many acts of violence they have committed by murdering whole crews and destroying ships when they had it in their power to do so have made these rigors wholly chargeable on their own bloody and malicious disposition."[39] Alongside the many blistering press accounts of Katrina are others that are more equivocal. They're the ones where the observer scratches his head at the victims' failure to evacuate neighborhoods they had been warned would soon be underwater — "Why didn't they leave?" — implicitly suggesting that the people stranded on those rooftops were too lazy or passive or stupid, or perhaps too dependent on government handouts, to do the obvious.

There's the AP photo of a young black man wading through chest-deep floodwater "after looting a grocery store in New Orleans," and a similar one of a white couple wading through more or less the same water and carrying more or less the same items, acquired in the same manner, "after finding bread and soda from a local grocery store." From this one could derive the rule that during Katrina, the difference between the races came down to the difference between looting and finding.[40]

There were the feverish reports of robberies, carjackings, and murders, of snipers shooting at rescue helicopters, of small children raped in the Superdome. Most of these reports turned out to be false.[41] Of the six people who died in the Dome, four died of "natural causes," that is, of heat and dehydration; one overdosed on drugs; and one committed suicide by plunging from an upper deck, as despondent Africans once plunged from the decks of the ships transporting them to the New World.[42] The gangs that were said to be terrorizing the Superdome and the Morial Convention Center may in fact have been keeping order. "They were the ones who were getting juice for the babies," an eyewitness at the convention center said. "They were the ones getting clothes for the people who'd walked through that water, and they were the ones who were fanning the old people. . . . And they're calling *these* guys animals."[43]

Responding to charges that the catastrophe had revealed the persistence of America's racial divide, the TV pundit Bill O'Reilly insisted that Katrina wasn't about race; it was about class:

> You can't rely on government. If you're poor, you're powerless, not only in America but everywhere on earth. You don't have enough money to protect yourself from danger. Danger is going to find you. The aftermath of Hurricane Katrina should be taught in every American school: If *you* don't get educated, if *you* don't develop a skill and force yourself to work hard, you'll most likely be poor, and sooner or later you'll be standing on a symbolic rooftop waiting for help. Chances are that help will not be quick in coming.[44]

Uttered by somebody else, the last sentence might have been an indictment of a society that condemned its poor to death by drowning. But O'Reilly sounded pleased, as people are when a long-neglected principle is triumphantly reasserted.

Of course few people who watched the disintegration of New Orleans approved of what they were seeing. Even President George W. Bush, who at the height of the crisis had been shown on television clowning with a guitar, later declared that "the results are not acceptable."[45] There are moments in history when the suffering of the neglected and despised is seen for what it is, as if the hatch of the slave ship had been thrown open, forcing those above decks to gaze down at the faces in the hold and meet their eyes. The trouble with such moments is that the feelings they inspire — outrage, revulsion, shame — may be too easily dispelled. The normal human impulse is to look down into the hold, then avert one's gaze. Perhaps this is the secret meaning of the refrain of "Dixie": "Look away, look away."

ON SEPTEMBER 6, 1781, the ship *Zong* left São Tomé off the coast of West Africa for Jamaica, carrying 440 slaves and a white crew of 17. Before it made landfall on December 22, 60 slaves and 7 crewmen had succumbed to the bloody flux, the descriptive name then given to dysentery. (This is only a little above the English Privy Council's estimate of 12½ percent as the average mortality rate on the Middle Passage.)[46] Fearing that the remaining cargo might be too weak to sell and knowing that if they died of illness, the loss would fall on the vessel's owners, Captain Luke Collingwood proposed an alternative: "It would not be so cruel to throw the poor sick wretches into the sea as to suffer them to linger out a few days under the disorders to which they were afflicted."[47] The latter remedy had the advantage of being covered by insurance. On November 29 the captain selected 133 sick Africans, and the initial "parcel" of 54 was promptly hurled overboard. He caused an additional 42 to be jettisoned on December 1. When it came time for the last group, the majority were handcuffed and flung straightaway into the sea, but 10 others resisted and held off the crew for a while. Then they leapt overboard and vanished in the waters.

After making landfall and selling the remainder of his cargo, Collingwood returned to England, where his employers filed for thirty pounds indemnity for each of the jettisoned slaves. The underwriters refused to pay. The case was brought to court, where the jury found for the owners, on the grounds that no more wrong attached to disposing of an ailing slave than to putting down a horse with a broken leg. The insurers appealed, and a second trial ensued in the Court of Exchequer. At its conclusion the magistrate acknowledged that the law supported the owners of the *Zong.* But citing a "higher law," he ruled for the insurers. The case was a watershed: for the first time an English court had decreed that slaves could not be treated as mere merchandise.[48]

Still, it would be another quarter century before slavery was banned in England and its territories. In the United States it would be another eighty years, and it would take a war.

I MET GAY at a New Year's Eve party in 1976, in a fifth-floor walk-up on Thompson Street in New York City, where I was living with my girlfriend. The room in which the party took place was a tiny cube wallpapered in itchy burlap that was meant to contain the disintegrating plaster behind it. During the lulls in the music you could hear a continuous anxious rattle like the prelude to a landslide. Gay was the only person there who was dressed up, in a blue blazer and a freshly ironed pink shirt that set off his narrow blue eyes and pink skin. The effect was at once correct and ironic. These turned out to be the two poles of his attitude toward a lot of things.

He had a fussy, Waspish regard for certain proprieties.

Once, during a weekend at a horsey bed-and-breakfast in Vermont, he got truly angry at me for not having brought along a dinner jacket. Yet he also liked to tweak the rules. He might show up at another party — I mean a real one, in an apartment where not a single room was covered in sacking and waiters in black tie made obeisance to the guests with trays of drinks and hors d'oeuvres — wearing a sport coat over a T-shirt decorated with two rows of latex dog's teats. He'd made the T-shirt himself, having learned to cast latex while working as a fabricator of dildos. This was a real job he'd had, and the company he'd worked for really was called Ram-It.

His name really was Gay. It wasn't short for anything. It went back in his family at least three generations, its origins lying in an era when the primary meaning of the word was "happy." Of course the name must have been an occasion for torture when he was in high school. He wasn't any more homophobic than the next straight fellow, certainly no more than I was, but when I first knew him, if I referred to someone as gay, he'd snap, "You mean *homosexual!*" and I'd say, "Sorry, homosexual," only to find out that his indignation had been a joke. At least he said it was.

I looked up to him. He was older than me; he knew how to do things — ride a motorcycle or stretch a canvas. He could hang by his feet from a parallel bar. He could cast a dildo. Even if I didn't believe in dressing up — the only dinner jacket I owned back then was one my father had bought for me, for "occasions" — I was still impressed that someone would know when you could wear seersucker. It was the 1970s. Officially, nobody wanted to be a man anymore. Men started wars and oppressed women. They didn't get laid all that much either. What people wanted to be was a boy. Yet secretly manhood retained some of its lost, dark glamour. Gay was a boy who dressed up in his father's clothes and drank his father's martinis. He shook them up in his father's silver cocktail shaker, scowling in concentration, and laid out a line of speed to boost the high.

He lived near the meat markets, which were still meat markets then. Sections of cows hung from hooks in their doorways, scarlet flesh iced with thick white suet. The only restaurant was a coffee shop where the cutters ate with bloody fingernails. But the neighborhood was changing. Men fucked each other on the piers and in trucks parked in the medieval shadows under the highway. Cars from the boroughs jolted along the cobbled streets, their drivers cruising for prostitutes and yelling insults at fags. It drove Gay wild. He was a little bit of a prude, and he had a snob's disdain for tourists. The first time I went to his apartment, he asked me if I wanted to help him make tank traps. On his worktable he had boxes of twopenny nails, wire, and a soldering gun. "It'll be fun," he said. He showed me how to solder three or four nails into a steel asterisk, and after we'd made a few dozen, we went out and strewed them about the streets, then slouched beside a lamppost waiting for some johns to come along and blow out their tires. We must have done something wrong. A few cars barreled down the street and passed by unharmed. One driver slowed and offered to suck Gay's dick. He threw up his hands in disgust, and we went back to his loft. Secretly we were both relieved.

The loft was on the top floor of a yellow brick artists' housing project that towered over the empty streets like a fortress dominating a steppe. The floor space wasn't that great, but Gay had taken advantage of the eighteen-foot ceilings by stacking on two extra levels — a raised platform by the windows that served as a sitting area and a gallery above that for sleeping. The bathroom was up there, too. You could look up from the pot and see the vast shining loneliness of the Hudson and an immense sky filled with light, the blazing, martial light of a summer morning or a soft, dreamy, lilac twilight out of Chekhov. It was the kind of view that makes you clap your hand to your mouth or over your heart, the way people do during the national anthem.

He lived there with his wife, a sweet-tempered woman named Molly with vast, pale, hopeful eyes, who supported them working in finance, leaving Gay to paint and keep house. It seemed like a sensible arrangement. Gay was a fine painter — when I first knew him, he was doing romantic, almost Pre-Raphaelite portraits of women posed against dark, allegorical-looking backgrounds — and when he was on speed, he liked to clean and to cook plain, heavy dinners of roast beef and mashed potatoes and vegetables that he wouldn't eat. He hated vegetables, like any eight-year-old, but included them on the menu for balance: I mean aesthetic, not nutritional. What mattered to him was how things looked.

When he wasn't painting, he was collecting Depression glass or Rockwood vases or old brass diving helmets. Years later he traveled to Indonesia with me because he'd heard you could get them cheap there, which, as it turned out, you could, though the cost of bringing back half a dozen diving helmets weighing eight or ten pounds apiece must have taken a bite out of his profit when he sold them in New

York. But then he never really wanted to sell anything he bought. He liked arranging his finds around him the way a magpie arranges objects in its nest, or assembling the smaller ones into nosegays that he gave as gifts. You could tell when he was trying to make up to Molly after a quarrel, because there'd be an offering for her laid out on the dining table, say a pink glass candy dish filled with marbles and fishing lures and a twenty-year-old packet of hair rollers.

But his freedom haunted him; some dogs like to be kenneled. He'd oversleep and spend the better part of the day walking his dogs and visiting friends and shopping in the antique stores on Hudson Street, so that by the time he started work, it was almost time for Molly to get home, and of course when she got home, he'd break for cocktails and dinner, which then left him the choice of painting through the night or going to bed and blaming her for keeping him from working. Often enough he'd blame her anyway. It was his least attractive trait. All she had to do was call down from the bedroom to ask him to turn down the stereo — he liked to play old rockabilly records while he worked, as if he weren't painting but driving a rig down a highway — and it was proof that she was trying to stifle him. Still, this sense of opposition, of embattlement, may have been what he needed. He painted a lot in those days, and a lot of it was good.

He had his big show in the early 1980s, at a gallery-restaurant in Soho just as the neighborhood was being inundated by the money that would soon sweep it away. The fact that it was in Soho was enormously exciting to all his friends. I think even Gay was excited, though, typically, he pretended not to be. He'd passed through his Pre-Raphaelite period and was doing big canvases, six feet by six feet, eight by ten, inspired by the lurid covers of the 1950s paperbacks he'd started collecting. They had titles like *Naked on Roller Skates* and *The Brimstone Bed*. The titles were what he bought them for, and of course the cover art: a man yanking a woman into his arms, another man firing a gun at a woman sprawled despairingly on an unmade bed, endless tableaux of sexual combat, as stylized as sumo wrestling. Gay's new paintings magnified those images but softened their edges and colors so that they were like stills from dreams. For all their overt violence, their mood was one of longing.

We had hopes for the show. A lot of people came to the opening — women with hypnotic cleavage and hair piled into ironic spires. A famous novelist spilled his drink on me. But there were no reviews and very few sales, and when the show closed, Gay was convinced it had been a failure and was angry at everyone who'd talked him into having it. He continued to paint, but without his old fervor and concentration. He was like someone plinking out a tune on a piano, note by disheartened note. And after a while the notes stopped.

Around the time of the show, the overpass of the highway collapsed. It had been the source of the neighborhood's protective shadow, and with it gone the whole meat market felt harshly exposed, like a dark room filled with friendly moans and rustling in which some killjoy has suddenly turned on a light. Around that time people started coming into emergency rooms with the symptoms of what was then being called GRID (gay-related immune deficiency). The revelers on the piers kept screwing, but fewer yokels crossed the rivers to bait them. Word gets around; they may have been scared of catching something. I remember the first guy I knew who died, a meek little jeweler named Marvin, whom Gay used to find old settings for. "What the fuck did *he* ever do?" Gay wondered afterward. Marvin's death outraged him. "He just liked to watch old musicals on TV and go to the baths once in a while. The poor son of a bitch was scared to tell his mother."

I asked him, "What would *you* tell your mother?"

"I'd tell her I had a heart condition."

We didn't yet know the joke that had started going around — Q: What's the hardest thing about having AIDS? A: Convincing your parents you're Haitian — but I told it plenty of times later on, even after more people I knew started dying and I realized that I myself was at risk. I wasn't tough-minded, just stupid and cosseted enough to think of myself as immune. I didn't share needles and sterilized my points in a folding vegetable steamer, not realizing that for the procedure to work, I would have to do it for twenty minutes, by which time the syringes' plastic collars would have melted. I didn't realize that sharing a cooker — which I did all the time, drawing up heated water from a bottle cap calcified with the residue of other people's blood — was the same as sharing a needle.

Because of who I was — or more accurately *what* I was, a white man of middle-class upbringing living in the most powerful and privileged nation on earth — my primary experience all my life had been one of safety, a safety like the warmth beneath a down comforter pulled up over my head. As a child, of course, I didn't realize this. I believed what my parents told me. Outside, they said, it was cold, black. You could hear the wind howling, and maybe other things.

In the Russia of my father's childhood, people were deathly afraid of wolves, and in the countries where he lived afterward, they were afraid of men who had become wolves.

The safety in which I was raised was fraught with agonized attention to the threats that might destroy it: germs, accidents, hoodlums, anti-Semites. Predictably, as soon as I was old enough, I began to seek out threats, the glamorous kind that a prosperous country makes available to its young. By now I was convinced of my safety, and again and again my experience confirmed that I was safe: safe from war, safe from want, safe from storm and flood, safe even from crime, unless you counted the times I was ripped off by people who knew a mark when they saw one.

Once I was held up at gunpoint in Bed-Stuy. I told friends about it afterward. Two men jumped me and, pressing a gun to my head, asked me over and over, "Do you want to die, motherfucker?" Apart from the fact that they were black and in their twenties, I couldn't have described them; all my attention was on the gun, that eerily significant toy with a muzzle as deep as a well. I didn't plead for my life, something I remain stupidly grateful for even now. I muttered, "Not especially," and handed over my money, and then followed the robbers' instructions by walking slowly down the street and into a vacant lot strewn with bricks and refuse. They told me not to turn around, and I didn't. If I was going to be killed, I didn't necessarily want to see the face of my killer. I understood that I might be killed, but I was too shocked to be scared, and too upset at the thought of not getting what I'd come down there for. What I didn't tell friends was that an hour later, my hands started trembling and my heart was pounding so hard that I could feel it slam against my breastbone, and I had to go out and cop again, only this time in a "safe" neighborhood.

Gay thought I was an idiot for shooting dope. He said it was an affectation. He may have been right, though even today I can barely remember what it was like not to need dope, as you might need an organ that had been ripped out of your body and left on a block of ice on the other side of town. After I finally cleaned up, he'd scoff, "Oh, get real! You never had a problem!" Maybe he was angry at me for things I'd done in the past. He knew that I'd once OD'd in his loft while he and Molly were traveling. A friend of ours had let it slip, and I might've forgotten to clean up some of the blood I'd squirted from my syringe onto the bathroom mirror.

Sometime during the first months of my new life, he and Molly went on another trip, and he asked me to watch the dogs for them while I was in town. It was a tacit show of trust, and I was grateful. On my first evening there, I noticed the row of buttons on the telephone, a clunky office model that Gay had scavenged from his neighbors' trash. Each button had a name written beside it on a piece of paper, and one of the names was "Junky." When I pushed the button, the phone dialed a number, and after an interval I heard the outgoing message of my answering machine in Baltimore.

I never asked Gay to explain why he had me down as "Junky." It may have been another of his jokes. I wouldn't be at all surprised to learn that he changed the label from "Peter" just before I came over, knowing that I wouldn't be able to resist pushing the button to see who "Junky" was. In which case the joke was on me.

Only now is it clear to me that in all the time I knew him, he was always using something. He migrated from substance to substance according to his mood and the drug's availability. Back when we first knew each other, it was speed and quaaludes, and for a while it was coke. For a long time he did not become physically habituated, which was why he could view addiction as a weakness or, as in my case, an affectation. He didn't like junkies or sloppy drunks. He thought a gentleman should be able to stay upright.

Later, after the series of catastrophes that broke his life apart, he started taking Valium and Klonopin. He got them from doctors or from friends who went to doctors, and he didn't take them to get high. He took them to get through the day without weeping or shaking uncontrollably, and in such high doses that you'd sometimes catch him drooling. I knew that the drooling embarrassed him, but I didn't see that by then he had passed over a threshold.

When Simone Weil was six years old, she refused to eat sugar, in solidarity with the soldiers at the front, who were not getting any in their rations. This was in France during World War I. Her parents were assimilated Jews — her father a doctor, her mother an indefatigable household manager, whose chief project seems to have been the rearing of geniuses, toward which end she banned toys and dolls from the children's nursery. By the time Simone's older brother, André, was nine, he was solving complex mathematical problems; by the age of twelve he had taught himself classical Greek and Sanskrit. Simone didn't master the first language until she was in her teens and learned the second only as an adult. It was one of the reasons she thought of herself as a failure.

Weil sometimes blamed her inadequacy on having been poisoned by her mother's milk in infancy.[49] All her life she was preoccupied with food and eating. Not surprisingly, many commentators think she was anorexic. She was very thin and ate like someone suffering from toothache, as if every bite were painful. She hoped that science would find a way to nourish human beings on sunlight.[50] The metaphor of eating recurs throughout her writing, where it is associated with both greed and grace: "The great trouble in human life is that looking and eating are two different operations. . . . It may be that vice, depravity, and crime are nearly always . . . in their essence, attempts to eat beauty, to eat what we should only look at."[51] "The beauty of the world is the mouth of a labyrinth. The unwary individual who on entering takes a few steps is soon unable to find the opening. . . . If he goes on walking, it is absolutely certain that he will finally arrive at the center of the labyrinth. And there God is waiting to eat him."[52]

When, at the age of twenty-nine, Weil experienced a religious awakening, it was after reading George Herbert's poem "Love," which concludes with an image of the despondent soul given succor at a supernatural feast:

> *My deare, then I will serve.*
> *You must sit down, sayes Love, and taste my meat:*
> *So I did sit and eat.*[53]

And when she died in an English sanitarium in 1943, the cause of death was starvation. She was thirty-four. The coroner's report concluded, "The deceased did kill and slay herself by refusing to eat whilst the balance of her mind was disturbed."[54]

Her life was marked by tragedy and grotesque comedy, genius and ineptitude, not in alternation but simultaneously, as if at the very moment that she made her noblest gestures, they were being parodied by a mocking shadow. In school she was known for her brilliance and otherworldliness. One of her teachers called her "the Martian," thinking of the ones H. G. Wells wrote about, who were all eye and brain.[55] After receiving her diploma at the École Normale Supérieure, where she had scored first in the national entrance exams, she began teaching at girls' lycées.

She was gifted, and her students were devoted to her. But her radical politics got her in trouble. She kept getting transferred. Wanting to better understand the circumstances of their laborers, she took a long leave of absence to work in factories. For this she proved unsuited because of her awkwardness and frail health, since she suffered from respiratory ailments and migraines, the latter of which caused the slightest sounds to fall on her like blows. In 1936 she went to Spain to fight on the republican side, joining the militia of the anarchist trade union movement. Within a week of reaching the front, she stepped by accident into a pot of boiling cooking oil and was burned so badly that she had to be evacuated. Shortly after her return to France, her unit was caught in an ambush and all of its women members killed.

Throughout, Weil wrote. Her essays, on subjects ranging from the conditions of labor to classical tragedy, appeared mostly in intellectual journals. What reputation she had spread by word of mouth. Increasingly she was drawn to Christianity, going to Mass and having long, earnest discussions with priests, but she would not speak of converting. As far as she was concerned, she had been implicitly Christian for as long as she could remember; she had only lacked the name for it. Still, to others she was a Jew, and when France fell in 1940, her family had to flee the German advance and take refuge in the Vichy-controlled south. There she worked on a farm and as an occasional courier for the Resistance. She tried to go back to teaching, but her request for a position was met with silence, the new regime having banned Jews from most professions. Within two years it would begin rounding them up and transferring them into German hands.

By then the Weils had managed to book passage to New York, a piece of good fortune that certainly saved their lives. Simone lived with them only a little while before traveling to England, hoping to be sent back across the Channel to work for the Resistance. Instead, to her chagrin, she was given a civilian post in the Free French government in exile. She began formulating her ideas for postwar French society in a book that was posthumously published as *L'Enracinement* (*The Need for Roots*). In it she rejected the notion of human rights that had been enshrined in French political thought since the eighteenth century. Instead she spoke of obligations. It is part of what gives her thought its medieval cast.

Her guilt at leaving France and her inability to return filled her with despair. She refused to eat more than the meager rations her countrymen were getting. It was as if she were reenacting her childhood fast on more radical terms, depriving herself not just of sugar but of all nourishment, in communion with her entire nation. She collapsed and was taken to the hospital, where she was diagnosed with tuberculosis.

In spite of the efforts of her caregivers, she still refused to eat, though she thought of food with longing. One of her last pieces of writing dwells on the ritual value of certain dishes: "Christmas turkey and candied chestnuts — Candlemas cakes at Marseilles — Easter eggs — and a thousand local and regional customs (now almost vanished). The joy and the spiritual significance of the feast is situated *within* the special delicacy associated with the feast." [56]

A few days later she died.

She could do nothing right, and she was probably more than half-crazy. She was a Jew who flung away Jewishness with the revulsion of an anti-Semite. She was a leftist who held Marxism to be a form of the Great Beast, an anarchist who believed in the spiritual necessity of hierarchies. She was a Christian who insisted on remaining outside the church, standing on its threshold to mediate between it and everything that it excluded. "I do not want to be adopted into a circle," she wrote the priest who vainly tried to persuade her to be baptized, "to be among people who say 'we,' and to be part of an 'us,' to find that I am 'at home' in any human *milieu* whatever it may be." [57] Perhaps the best way of describing her is as a constitutional — a physiological — heretic, but a heretic who valued obedience above all else.

Because she distrusted the social realm, the realm of churches and political parties and the devil, she could be obedient only to God. It was a hard obedience. God as Weil understood him didn't issue commandments, or did so only in secret. He wasn't given to interventions. He had removed himself from the world not out of anger or disappointment but out of love, knowing that nothing else could exist in a world in which he was fully present. The Kabbalists believed this, too. God had once covered the earth like an ocean but then withdrawn to make room for his creation. It was our fate to live on the dry seabed, not knowing when God would roll back and submerge it once more. Perhaps he would do so at such time as we were completely ready to be submerged by him. In the meantime we could only wait. To Weil this waiting, without hope, without even the desire for something good to follow, was obedience.

A sufferer herself, she was acutely sensitive to the suffering of others. She understood the different forms that suffering could take, and she understood that abysmal state — a state that bears the same relation to ordinary suffering as truth does to opinion — that she calls affliction. She describes it this way: "Affliction is an uprooting of life, a more or less attenuated equivalent of death, made irresistibly present to the soul by the attack or immediate apprehension of physical pain."[58] A tacit distinction between affliction and ordinary suffering is that the former is prolonged, the result not of a single blow but of many, even a lifetime of blows.

By "physical pain" Weil meant pain both actual and potential — she uses the example of a condemned prisoner who is made to gaze for hours at the guillotine that will shortly cut off his head — and also pain whose source may not be physical but which is nonetheless experienced in the depths of the body. Anyone who has lost a loved one knows that heartache isn't a metaphor. Anyone who has been humiliated has felt his whole organism surge up under the insult and quiver at the effort of holding itself in check. To understand the rage and hopelessness of certain populations, say of Jews in the Soviet Union or Tibetans under the Chinese or African Americans in much of the United States, consider what it must be like to have to hold yourself in check during any encounter with the police, no matter how arbitrary or abusive, and to have to do so not just on isolated occasions, but regularly, for years, so that one of the first lessons you teach your children is how to live with humiliation rather than be killed surging up against it.

The other component of affliction, as intrinsic to it as pain, is social degradation. Some categories of sufferer are recognized and even honored. (In France in Weil's time, it would have been the wounded veterans of the Great War, who made up a staggering percentage of the male population.)[59] But the afflicted receive no recognition, only fear, incomprehension, and contempt. Operating in tandem like the jaws of pliers, pain and degradation seize the individual and reduce him to the condition of a stripped screw or a rusted bolt: the condition of a thing. ("You'd think they were cutting down banana trees," says one of Anne Aghion's Rwandan eyewitnesses. "People feel no pity when they cut down a banana.")[60]

In time the afflicted become things to themselves. The "I" within them is crushed. "They will never find warmth again," Weil writes. "They will never believe any more that they are anyone."[61] This may be why they are so often complicit in their misery, unable to lift its spell, resisting all outside efforts to help them lift it. They may resist passively or with the flailing energy of a defective mechanism shaking itself to pieces. They turn on their benefactors. Although Weil followed a long tradition of Catholic thought about suffering, she was trailblazer in her explicit acknowledgment that certain kinds of suffering make their victims self-destructive, perverse, unpleasant.

Anyone who works in an emergency room knows this; shrinks and social workers know it. They tell about the honor roll student who surrenders to the gravity of the street and, after a run of bad decisions and bad luck, fatally shoots himself in the lobby of his ex-girlfriend's apartment building.[62] They tell about the teenage girl, placed in a group home to protect her from a battering mother, who curses out the social worker who gave up her day off to attend parents' day at her school. They tell about the clinging and imperious sick, the undeserving poor. They tell about the people who seem to have nothing wrong with them except an infallible tropism for misfortune, a chattering inner voice that always urges them toward the wrong choice and the false move; who spend their lives reeling from one closed door to the next, pounding to be let in, though on the rare occasions a door opens, they are likely to peer inside and then slam it in disgust, not having found what they wanted. But they cannot tell you what they wanted. They may not remember what it was, they may never have known. And so how can one help them?

At Calcutta's Nirmal Hriday, the Home for Dying Destitutes founded by Mother Teresa and maintained today by members of her order, the Missionaries of Charity, a small, bustling nun explains, as she mops between the closely spaced beds, that they have to keep a strict eye on the people they let in to die. So many of the ones with AIDS are drug addicts and steal from the other patients, from the sisters themselves. Even on the deathbed they steal. Just thinking about it makes her fume. "They are naughty people!"[63]

This is a far cry from Mother Teresa: "The poor are great people, most lovable people."[64] If Simone Weil thought about the afflicted, the Albanian nun spent most of her life working with them, feeding them, bathing them, tending them while they lay dying. In Calcutta — or Kolkata, to call it by its new, official name — even many Hindus regard her as a saint. A painting of her in prayer on the side of a building near the Kalighat Temple may be the single largest image in the city.

Still, in all her years of ministering to Calcutta's poor, she seems never to have encountered bad behavior ("I have never heard the poor grumble or curse, or seen them dejected with sadness"),[65] only patience, gratitude, and faith. Maybe this is because Mother Teresa wasn't ministering, strictly speaking, to *people*. Or, rather, her people were something more than people. "The lepers, the dying, the hungry, the ones sick with AIDS: they are all Jesus," she said.[66] Her charitable work was a sacrament, its suffering beneficiaries stand-ins for a suffering god — not just stand-ins, but God himself, become flesh in their multitude. Their suffering was holy because Christ's had been holy. This may be why the home for the dying didn't give out painkillers.[67]

Many religions treat human beings as instances of the divine. The greeting *namaste*, common throughout India, is said to mean "I greet the god in you." It's a powerful notion that suffuses all humanity with an otherworldly glow and makes any violence against another person, even the basest murderer, a crime against God. Of course this notion is anathema to those who believe in the irreducible distance between god and man, like the fundamentalist Christian blogger who denounces Mother Teresa as a closet pantheist.[68] But in this idea of holiness, there is also danger: that the merely human will be subsumed by the divine, hollowed out by it, until the individual is no more than the god's vessel, valued only because of what he contains. Woe to him if what makes him godlike is his suffering.

Weil thought that it is false to love our neighbors for God's sake; the very expression is an oxymoron. She writes, "God is not present, even if we invoke him, where the afflicted are merely regarded as an occasion for doing good. . . . A man has all he can do, even if he concentrates all the attention of which he is capable, to look at this small, inert thing of flesh lying stripped of clothing by the roadside. It is not the time to turn his thoughts toward God."[69] If she believed in the remoteness of the divine, she also insisted on the immanence of the human, its absolute, urgent claim on our attention.

God needs nothing from us, other people a great deal. Charity is insufficient to their needs; Weil had contempt for it. Someone who gives charity knows that he is under no obligation to do so, and so, having given, he is pleased with himself; he thinks he has a right to be pleased. (Such self-flattery may be what motivated the rich and powerful people, including gangsters and a despot or two,[70] who paid court to Mother Teresa in the latter stages of her career.)

But we are obligated to other human beings for no other reason than that they are human and need something from us. This isn't charity; it is justice. Unlike charity, justice is unconditional. We can't choose its occasions or recipients.

"To no matter whom the question may be put in general terms," Weil says, "nobody is of the opinion that any man is innocent if, possessing food himself in abundance and finding someone on his doorstep three parts dead from hunger, he brushes past without giving him anything."[71] Should that supplicant be the descendant of slaves, should he bow down to a different god or to no god at all, should he be guilty of heinous crimes, should he have arrived on the doorstep illegally, the one who gives nothing is not absolved.

Because Weil was a social ethicist as well as a religious one, she wanted to define the kinds of things our human obligations entail, beginning with food, shelter, medical care, and freedom from violence, and extending to the spiritual needs of order, liberty, obedience, responsibility, equality, "hierarchism," honor, and punishment. Some of these are seemingly contradictory. Many lie beyond the scope of what any individual can give. Only a society can provide them. Our own does not. The United States is not yet so hard-hearted as to brush past the starving on its doorstep (there are food banks), but it is less and less inclined to shelter the homeless or give medicine to the sick, and it is looking more narrowly at *who* is on its doorstep in the first place, wanting to know how they got there and how they can be driven back to where they came from. Americans pride themselves on their charity but have a dim view of obligation. In my memory no one has been elected president who said he would raise taxes.

To talk about the kind of society Weil had in mind and how our own might come to resemble it would take another book. If I'm honest, I'm not sure I would want to live in such a society. I don't like obligations any more than the next person does, even the obligation to do the right thing. (It's a queer and revealing peculiarity of the American language that "do-gooder" is an expression of disdain, while its nearest opposite, "evildoer," is not.) Looked at closely, most of Weil's prescriptions are mysterious and perhaps impossible. She favored justice over charity, but to her justice was "behaving exactly as though there were equality when one is stronger in an unequal relationship."[72] How does one do that? How does a nation?

Judged by Weil's standard, America's treatment of the survivors of Hurricane Katrina was anything but justice, the inequality between strong and weak being underscored by everyone from the Gretna police, who fired at refugees as they tried to cross over to the more prosperous suburb from New Orleans, to the President's mother, who, after a goodwill visit to a shelter in a Houston sports stadium, remarked that since so many of its occupants were "underprivileged anyway," their new arrangements were working out very well for them.[73]

An evacuee named Denise Moore recalled the despondency that came over her as she and hundreds of other displaced people at the Morial Convention Center were made to line up over and over for buses that didn't come: "We're talking about old people in wheelchairs, women with babies, in line, waiting for busses that you know goddamn well aren't coming — like they were playing with us. . . . We were left there without help, without food, without water, without sanitary conditions, as if it's perfectly alright for these 'animals' to reside in a frigging sewer."[74]

No inequality is greater than the one that separates human beings from animals. Weil writes, "There is no difference between throwing a stone to get rid of a troublesome dog and saying to a slave, 'Chase that dog away.' "[75]

Inequality is marked by one party's failure to see the other. One doesn't look at a troublesome dog except for the purpose of taking aim at it. After the initial frenzy of media attention, the flotsam of Katrina was allowed to drift from view, to be reeled back at intervals for follow-up stories. One such story, aired on National Public Radio as the hurricane's second anniversary approached, concerned a FEMA trailer park in southern Mississippi called Scenic Trails that housed some one hundred displaced families, most of whom appeared to be white. At such parks, we're told, the rate of attempted suicide was seventy-nine times the region's average. Suicide seemed to be on the mind of everyone the reporter interviewed at Scenic Trails, including a distraught woman who, a while before, had announced to her eleven-year-old son that she was leaving him to go kill herself. "I picked up the gun and said, 'I got to get out of here, if you need anything go next door.' And I got in the car and I left." She calmed down a little. "And you know it's stupid, 'cause you know you're not going anywhere and you don't want to die, you want to make your life better." But a moment later her voice speeded up, drew taut and thin as wire, and she began to cry. "And every day you're, 'Oh God, stop, take me. I can't handle this!' "

Elsewhere in the camp a man with one leg complained that he had to crawl around his trailer because it was too small to admit his wheelchair. His wife couldn't sleep at night for fear that one of their neighbors would break in and kill their dog. Somebody at the park had been poisoning pets with antifreeze. Apart from its general level of misery, the lack of work, the drugs, the violence, Scenic Trails' most striking feature — so striking that I keep thinking of the place as "Hidden Springs" — was its isolation. It's tucked away in the backcountry, thirty minutes from the nearest town and, presumably, from hospitals or schools or jobs that pay more than minimum wage. More than thirty minutes if you don't have a car. Many of the residents didn't. As the reporter prepared to leave, a disheveled man knocked on her car window. When she rolled it down, the man handed her a box of apricots and said, "Take this to the outside world."[76]

We don't have to see suffering if it's hidden from us. We don't have to mourn dead soldiers whose coffins cannot, by government decree, be photographed. We won't be appalled by the shoddy treatment given wounded ones if they're sequestered in the derelict, mold-infested outbuilding of an army medical center. We needn't weigh the guilt or innocence of uncounted, unnamed enemy combatants rendered to black locations for undisclosed reasons, or feel squeamish about the coercive techniques with which secret information is twisted from them, the techniques also being undisclosed and, it goes without saying, unseen. We won't be troubled by the poor when they no longer occupy the centers of our cities, only their flyblown margins, where nobody goes. "All the people that don't fit society's standards are in little camps now," said a minister who was trying to help residents at Scenic Trails. "And people are seeing it."[77]

But they aren't seeing it.

That may have less to do with strategies of concealment than with the seemingly infinite human capacity to deny or rationalize suffering that lies in plain sight. The abject, naked figures in the Abu Ghraib photos aren't being tor-

tured but "hazed," and in any case probably deserve whatever was done to them. As the senator said, we know they
aren't there for traffic violations. The prisoners who hanged
themselves in their cells were demonstrating their utter dis-
regard for human life.[78] The man jerking in the throes of
Parkinson's is exaggerating his symptoms. The innocents
killed in the tsunami may not be that innocent. Maybe they
had the wrong livelihoods; maybe they worshipped the
wrong gods. In certain circles the immediate response to the
news that someone has cancer isn't an exclamation of sympathy but probing questions about what the sick person ate
or drank or smoked. The sympathy comes later. After intervening in a number of suicide attempts, the minister at Scenic Trails had become hardened. "He's wanting something,"
he said of one caller, "and most of it's pity. The government's
come in and give a helping hand, people in the churches
around has come in and give a helping hand, so what's the
problem? The person."[79]

Some of the people who say these things are cosigners of
torture; some are selfless benefactors of their neighbors. But
even the best-intentioned of them are to some degree like
Job's comforters. I've always found it mysterious that the
men who harass and defame Job are called that. Of course
their first impulse *was* to comfort him. That is why they
wailed and tore their garments and sat down silently beside
him in the dust. Inasmuch as was humanly possible, they
acted as if there were no inequality between them and their
friend.

Then their sense of justice faltered and they begin to
comfort themselves, manufacturing reasons why Job should
suffer and, implicitly, why they should not. The reasons

were like the bricks in a wall raised to keep out the plague. That they were imaginary was beside the point. Back then people had yet to understand that walls are useless against plague. From a historical perspective, the book of Job represents the first moment that any religion recognizes the inadequacy of walls — that is, of the measures religions have traditionally employed to protect their congregants from evil.

To quarantine the suffering, it isn't strictly necessary to blame them for their misfortune. We can also praise them for it. This is what Mother Teresa did when she declared that the poor and sick are Jesus. It's why strangers kept telling the Daley sisters that they were angels. It's why the Jewish characters in popular representations of the Shoah are always righteous. There are no cheats or philanderers in the camps; nobody sells out his fellows for an extra scrap of bread or claws out a few more months of life by serving as Sonderkommando. Every age has its designated sufferers and also its exceptional ones, whose anguish inspires shock and pity and even reverence. They are the human counterparts of the sacrificial animals offered to the Lord. Leviticus specifies that such animals must be without blemish.

Sometimes a class of designated sufferers will be raised into the ranks of exceptional ones. When a thirteen-year-old boy with AIDS was barred from attending his school in Indiana in the 1980s, his patient, dignified struggle for the rights guaranteed every other child in the United States effectively rehabilitated the disease and its despised victims. That Ryan White's ordeal acquired a sacred dimension is suggested by the fact that after his death in 1990, his personal effects were put on display in the Indiana State Museum, like the relics of a saint. White could have the transformative effect he had because he was a child, and a white child at that. In his person the unexceptionable suffering of AIDS — the suffering of gay men and drug addicts and the promiscuous — became the heartrending suffering of a child, and in time the compassion people felt for him extended to the other victims, too.

It's often said of exceptional victims that they are just like us, but they aren't. They're *better* than us — braver, nobler, more sweet natured and forbearing. Because they're better, they reassure us in the same way that their outcast counterparts do, and of the same thing: that what has happened to them will not happen to us. For the true horror of another's calamity is the prospect that it may strike us, too. As Weil puts it,

> To acknowledge the reality of affliction means saying to oneself: "I may lose at any moment, through the play of circumstances over which I have no control, anything whatsoever that I possess, including those things which are so intimately mine that I consider them as being myself. There is nothing that I might not lose. It could happen at any moment that what I am might be abolished and replaced by anything whatsoever of the filthiest and most contemptible sort." [80]

The just treatment of suffering begins with seeing. This holds true for both societies and persons. I don't mean that we should learn to see each suffering person as an individual. That is certainly beyond our powers. It takes time to see anybody as an individual, especially when that person is a stranger: a woman, no longer young and poorly dressed, bent double in a plastic chair in an emergency room, moaning too loudly; a strangely rigid man hectoring people at a shopping mall, not begging but wanting to tell them something; perhaps only an inert "thing" of flesh lying by the side of the road, that we pass by.

Even people we know and love become strangers when they suffer. I think of my father on his deathbed, his moans so weak they were almost inaudible. He had always had a bad back, and as a little boy I used to sit by his bedside and watch in pity as he lay staring miserably at the ceiling. But his pain now inspired not just pity but horror; it was cracking open his personality, his humanity, and exposing those things as brittle shells. I tried to look at what was pulsing among their shards but couldn't bear to for very long, and so I looked away.

Maybe the best we can do is see the other's face. "It is always starting out from the face," says the philosopher Emmanuel Levinas, "that justice appears."[81]

To do even that much, however, we have to give up the stories we tell about suffering and sufferers, all the occluding narratives of sin and dysfunction, drunkenness and sloth, redemption and damnation. They aren't really sick. They don't want to work. They're being punished. They're happier this way. They're just depressed. Jesus loves them. It's making them stronger. They must have done something.[82] Only those who suffer are entitled to tell such stories, including even the stories that seem punitive and crackbrained. They have paid for the privilege, and the stories may make their sorrows easier to bear. It lessened Kate

Daley's unhappiness to feel that she could offer her suffering up to God, though it only made her sister angry. All those stories do for the rest of us — the whole ones, the healthy ones, the ones who have enough, the ones who've been spared — is distract us from what we should be looking at.

When I went to Calcutta in 2005 to research this book, I expected to be overwhelmed by its people's misery, as if by the torrent from a broken hydrant. This is partly why the city is ambivalent about Mother Teresa. She helped the poor a great deal — though not as much as many unsung local charities have — and gave the world a false picture of Calcutta as a cesspit. Of course it was really the foreign press that did this, and the picture owed as much to Kipling as it did to Mother Teresa. In the early 1980s the picture was exemplified by a popular book called *The City of Joy.* People in publishing used to refer to it as "The City of Oy."

By 2005, however, Calcutta (no one I met there ever called it "Kolkata," except ironically) was, if not prosperous, striving and alive. The subway stations were no dirtier than the ones in New York and were filled with young people dressed for business or university. Presidency College remained one of the most prestigious academic institutions on the continent. In coffee shops and gentlemen's clubs people conducted exuberant, brainy conversations known as *adda,* shouting opinions at each other in air blue with cigarette smoke — in Calcutta the intellectuals still smoked.

Still, there was misery: the rickety slum buildings that leaned over narrow streets strewn with every kind of waste; the half-naked people who slept on the curb and splashed themselves with water from the gutters. To get anywhere on foot meant navigating through ranks of beggars, mostly women, with thin babies hanging from their breasts, but also children of both sexes, the very old, and the maimed. The women smiled as they came up to you; the others usually didn't. On the sidewalk outside the Indian Museum on Jawaharlal Nehru Road, a man with stunted flippers for limbs rocked on his belly and moaned for alms, which you were supposed to drop in a little bowl before him. To their needs I allocated four hundred seventy rupees, about ten dollars a day. Before leaving the hotel in the morning, I'd ask the cashier to give me that much in small change, and I'd parcel it out as I went about my rounds until it was gone. Usually it took less than an hour. For the rest of the day I'd skulk around the city, my gaze averted from every supplicant. I was ashamed and, I suppose, afraid, though what did I have to fear from a scowling child or an old man squatting on thin haunches with a stare as expressionless as wood?

After a while it came to me that what was shameful wasn't my failure to give but my failure to look at the people I refused, for I was, tacitly, refusing them. So I made a resolution that the next day I would try to maintain eye contact with every person who asked me for money, regardless of whether I gave or not. Looking at the ones I gave to was easy, even pleasurable. It's pleasurable to see that a small action of yours has made another person happy, or at least, briefly, content. But it was hard to look into the faces of the others, the unrequited ones. And I'm sure it was confusing to them. They probably saw eye contact as a signal that I was about to give them something.

One morning, after attending Mass at the motherhouse of the Missionaries of Charity, I came upon a cluster of beggar women on the street nearby. It was still early. The air was not yet hot. I gave money to three or four women and bought a fifth some powdered milk for her child, but then my small money was gone. Still, I looked into the black eyes of the mendicant who came after her and, trying to smile kindly, told her, "I'm sorry, I don't have anything for you." She didn't understand. "Uncle, money for baby!" The greeting was meant to be respectful, but I found it repulsive. I said "I'm sorry" again and spread my hands to show that they were empty.

Now she looked at me with perplexity, and a moment later with anger. I was playing with her. Her eyebrows bristled. A vein in her forehead twitched. "Money for baby. Uncle, you give!" I stepped past her, but she was not to be put off and followed me down the street, with other women trailing after her, even some of the ones I'd given alms to. They wanted to express their solidarity with her, their outrage at a rich foreigner who was mocking the old code of largesse and also the code of hard-heartedness, for the hard-hearted aren't supposed to give you a soft look and a smile. "Uncle, you give!" In the end I broke my promise to myself and gave the woman some money. It was a large bill, I remember, and I was angry at her and myself, at myself more than her. I can't say whether she was pleased to get it, for I dropped it into her hand without looking at her.

Afterward I tried to resume the exercise but found it all but impossible. It had been poisoned for me. Had the exercise been spiritual at all, or was it just a thoughtless experiment conducted at the expense of needy people?

I brought my confusion to Swami Prabhananda, the elegant, humorous, and learned secretary of the Ramakrishna

Mission Institute of Culture in Gol Park. The swami wore scarlet robes but had the clipped speech and austere jollity of an Oxford don, the kind who enjoys making puns in Sanskrit but would never in a thousand years commit the gaffe of laughing at them. On entering his study, the visitors in front of me prostrated themselves before him and shyly touched his foot, and when my turn came, I did the same. It seemed to amuse him. But when I explained my problem, his expression grew severe, the lines around his small mouth deepened. "Please, you must not let yourself be taken advantage of!" he said. "Some of these beggars are scoundrels. Do you know that they borrow those children?"

WHEN TEACHING WRITING workshops, I often begin with E. M. Forster's dictum: " 'The king died and then the queen died' is a story. 'The king died, and then the queen died of grief' is a plot." I think I know the story of Gay's life, but I'm not sure about the plot. Grief had a part in it, certainly, but also talent and stubbornness and bad judgment and an almost defiant will to fail. Drugs, surely. Trauma came into it, and so did mental illness, which Gay didn't believe in and I didn't take seriously. Not, at any rate, in his case.

In the mid-1980s, a few years after the disappointing show, he got involved with another painter named Karen. Her cushiony sex appeal disguised a dogged nature, and the affair quickly became obsessive. He went to Costa Rica for a while to let things cool down, but Karen showed up there, too, and when Gay came back to New York, Molly knew and wanted nothing more to do with him. He was sick with remorse; years later he was still berating himself for what he'd put her through and insisting that she was the only woman he'd ever loved.

He was broke, of course, and for much of the next year he lived at his mother's house in the Washington suburbs, buying and selling bits of odd junk to get by. Once he spent his last $200 on a rectifier, an antique weather instrument similar to a barometer. "Does it work?" I asked him. He sputtered at me. To ask a practical question was to commit treason. "It's *old!*" Selling it may have netted him a hundred dollars. From then on, this was how he earned his living, though never a very good one. People in the business — which wasn't the antique business but the junk business, the trade in things used and discarded — all said he had a great eye. He could walk into any darkened shed and, feeling his way through the gloom, pick out the one object that might be worth something.

But he was a dreadful businessman. When he worked the flea markets, he showed up early and arranged his merchandise with care. He teased and flattered the customers, and his dog — he always had a dog and took it with him everywhere — charmed them. Even his bib overalls inspired confidence. The problem was he couldn't bargain. It was a lack of nerve. Someone would point to an old dresser he'd painstakingly stripped and refinished and ask what he wanted for it. He'd say $300. The customer would say, "That's ridiculous." It was what the customer was supposed to say, and what Gay was supposed to say next was "Okay, $250." Instead, he'd seem to forget his line. His shoulders would sag, and a panicked look would come into his eyes; he'd try to hide it by staring down at his feet. "How about fifty?" Afterward he'd be furious, not so much with himself as with the customer — for cheating him. And the customer, too, would feel cheated.

He moved back to New York. For all that had happened between them, Molly ceded their old loft to him. "Be his friend," she asked me. This was after I'd cleaned up; very few people would have suggested it before. "He needs somebody to watch out for him." Once people loved Gay, they tended to go on feeling that way. He reestablished himself in his old home, and a while afterward Karen moved in with him. A few years after that, without any ceremony, they married. It was a mistake, but I can't say how many mistakes had come before it or how many would follow. I'm not even sure "mistake" is the right word, since it implies a choice, the idea that one could act — could have acted — differently. Some misfortune confounds any attempt to impose order on it, to separate causes from effects, to attach blame. At a certain point the line between bad luck and character becomes invisible.

From the first they quarreled, usually over money, about which Gay was still cavalier. But anything could serve as a pretext. At last, hoping that a change of scenery and a low mortgage would help, they moved to a small town on the Eastern Shore of Virginia, situated amid tidal flats, where clouds of biting insects hung in the air, waiting to be walked into. They bought a house, and Gay sublet the loft to me. I paid him $1,000 a month over the nominal rent and knew I had a good deal. In the beginning of the arrangement, he came up every other weekend to work the flea markets and get away from his marriage. He had his own little sleeping alcove, which we referred to as "the dog room." A morning's entertainment was to sit smoking and drinking coffee on the roof, looking out at the river and arguing. It was how we got along. People could always tell I'd been spending time with him because I'd be hoarse from yelling.

We'd argue about politics, art, religion; about psychiatry, which he dismissed as an unscrupulous cult; about my girlfriends and his wife. I thought he treated her badly. When I scolded him for it, he'd rub his face in frustration. "You don't know what she's like!" Once a woman I was seeing, who'd listened to him unscroll his long indictment of Karen, counseled him, "Just give her what's hers." She said it with patience, even tenderness, and he seemed to hear that. For a moment he lifted his head like a dog hearing a faraway whistle. Then he said, "But she thinks everything's hers." Still, he refused to leave. He was scared that if he did, Karen would get the house and he'd be left with nothing.

After a year or two the trips to New York became less frequent. Gay was getting absorbed in the life of the shore — the long days of fishing, the nights playing poker with old farts who hadn't been north of Pocomoke City since the Reagan presidency. Neither he nor Karen painted anymore, but he'd started writing a novel set among the yard sales and flea markets of his new home. The characters were gleeful distortions of the locals he knew; the plot was an endless piling up of events. A lot of it was very funny, but Gay wasn't a natural writer. His sentences buckled beneath their narrative load. Still, he was a fast learner. His second draft was much better than his first and his third an improvement on the second.

But he was staking too much on getting the book published. He needed money, and he wanted to show people — Karen, Molly, the audience of friends who'd been waiting thirty years for him to do something astonishing — that their confidence hadn't been misplaced. He barely went to the fleas anymore, just holed up in his shed and wrote and called up friends to read pages to them over the phone. Karen was unhappy. She wasn't thrilled to be married to someone who was bringing in only a few hundred dollars a month and spent all his time writing a novel. "I tell the bitch, 'Just be patient!' " he'd say, taking another tortured swipe at his face. "Once I sell this thing, I'll pay her back and we'll never have to see each other again." Looking back, I'm shocked I didn't see how awful it must have been — I mean, awful for both of them, the awfulness of spoiled love, of being trapped, the latter misery made worse by the fact that they had built the trap together with their eyes open. But I was newly remarried, and happy, and like many happy people, I thought that happiness was accessible to anyone who wanted it. You just had to make up your mind.

In the summer of 2002 they were fighting worse than usual. Once, Karen told me, he fired a gun at her, though Gay said he'd only fired it out the window. Still, it was a gun, and he'd fired it. Afterward he made a half-assed attempt at killing himself by tying a plastic shopping bag over his head. He told me about it shamefacedly, which made me think he was being funny. A shopping bag. I laughed; he did, too. He may have been relieved that I hadn't seen the depth of his despair, had mistaken an abyss for a basement rec room, and so he pretended that he was in fact in the rec room, pay no attention to that echo.

A few months later, Gay came home from fishing one afternoon to find that Karen had taken out a protection order against him. It was posted on the front door, like an eviction notice, which in a sense it was. He had the presence of mind not to go inside the house. Instead he crossed the street to the house of one of her friends, not realizing that Karen had taken refuge upstairs and that his action could be construed as an attempt to make contact with her. Later he was sure the whole thing had been a setup.

Hearing him outside, she or the friend called the police, and they came and arrested him. They weren't amused by his outraged sputtering, and he didn't make a good impression on the judge. Within hours he was in a cell at the Accomack County Jail. His friend Larry tried to bail him out, but it was summer and the court was in recess. A week later there was a hearing at which Gay was briefly brought forth, a scrawny middle-aged man with vacant eyes, drooling down the front of an orange jumpsuit that was much too big for him. The guards were giving him Thorazine. A month passed before they let him out.

Afterward Gay's time in jail became another one of the ghastly, outlandish episodes that people who knew him shook their heads and laughed about. The laughter had sorrow in it, even horror. Still, his misery had become our entertainment. When someone suggested that we take up a collection to pay for him to go into therapy, Larry said that then he wouldn't be Gay anymore. But Gay wasn't who he had been. He could barely drive for fear of being pulled over, and the sight of a police cruiser — not just in the rearview but anywhere on the road — would make him start shaking.

He never said exactly what had happened to him while he was incarcerated. He'd try but would become incoherent and start raving about torture and fascism. The lights in the cell were kept on all the time; he could barely sleep. At least once he was beaten. Only later did I find out why the guards had been drugging him. He'd tried to hang himself with a bedsheet. I wouldn't be surprised if he was raped. Someone might have done it just to humiliate him, intuitively realizing that that was what Gay was most afraid of. Because, of course, he was already humiliated, deeply, irremediably, and had been for some time. ("Men have the same carnal nature as animals," Weil observes. "If a hen is hurt, the others rush upon it, attacking it with their beaks.")[83]

In the summer of 2005 he returned to New York, with little in the way of property but some suitcases, his manuscript, and a dog called Razz — a beautiful, silent husky who'd spent the first year of his life tied to a tree in a yard on the Eastern Shore until Gay came along, disentangled him from his rope, and bought him from his owner. The dog conferred some of his magisterial calm on him. The only time Gay seemed at ease now was when Razz was nearby, gazing into the distance with dark, slanted eyes. He moved back into his loft. Actually, it was now Larry's loft — to raise cash Gay had illegally sold him the lease — but I was still paying the rent.

The last time I came to visit, I found the place in chaos. Some of that was because it now had five rotating occupants, including Larry's wife and mine. There were air conditioners in every window and at least three DVD players, their clocks set a few minutes apart, arrayed around what was essentially one vast room. But much of the chaos reflected Gay's mental state. Cigarette ashes powdered the floor. You couldn't walk five feet without barking a shin on one of the plastic crates in which he kept the junk he was still selling, for less and less money. The table was hidden beneath drafts of the book. I couldn't tell which was the most recent. I'm not sure Gay could either. He was dead broke and living on boiled potatoes, liverwurst, and store-bought doughnuts. His face was like an old wallet that had been turned inside out for its small change. He was fifty-nine.

He was angry at Larry, convinced he meant to kick him out of the loft. I tried to reassure him. "Come on, he's your friend."

He mopped a hand across his face. The gesture no longer seemed comical, only hopeless. It was as if he wanted to tear his face off the way certain animals, when caught in a trap, chew off their paws. "You don't understand."

"He tried to bail you out when you were stuck in that jerkwater pen. That's more than anybody else did for you."

"But he didn't get me out, did he?" He anticipated my objection. "Okay, he hired a lawyer, but the lawyer he hired was no good, and why was that? Why is it that everything Larry does for me is fucked-up? You don't know him; he's not like us."

I didn't ask what he meant by "like us," what we had in common that Larry lacked. Maybe he meant that Larry had done all right by himself and we hadn't. I was better-off than Gay — almost anybody was — but I was going through a hard stretch, too. In another month, I told him, I'd have to stop paying the rent. "You know I'd keep doing it if I weren't broke. I just don't have it anymore."

"It's okay; you did what you could."

"Maybe your sister can help you?"

"She's helped me enough already." He shut his eyes.

That's how I remember him most vividly at that time — not closing them, as you do when thinking, but shutting them, squeezing them shut, the way a baby clamps his mouth shut when rejecting the spoon.

"Then you've got to ask Larry to carry you for a while. What's he going to do, kick you out?"

He scowled. "I'll tell you one thing, I'll kill myself before I let him take this place from me."

I almost yelled at him. In Rwanda not two months before, I'd spoken with people who'd seen their children cut to pieces before their eyes. Six months before that, I'd been counting tsunami orphans in Sri Lanka. *Those* people, I wanted to say, had a right to talk about killing themselves, and not because they were "depressed." But I remembered that Gay wasn't just talking; he'd already tried to kill himself twice. And so I told him that it was his right to end his life if he wanted to, it was anybody's right, but he was going to die anyway one of these days, probably not too long from now, given his age and his smoking. "In the meantime," I said, "you've got a book to finish."

He looked dully over at the desk where the manuscript was. I wasn't lying — the book needed to be finished — but I doubted he'd be able to sell it, and he knew I doubted it. Quickly I added, "And you've got a dog to take care of." Razz looked up at me. His eyes might have been made up with kohl. "Right now that's your job." I said it like a king out of Tolkien, and Gay seemed to accept it. "It's not like I want to *kill* myself," he explained. "I just want to wake up dead." Afterward I was pleased with myself. If the people who cared for Gay could just marshal their resources to get him through the next few months, I thought, he'd be all right.

That was a week before Christmas. Early in the new year I got a call from Rocky, the woman who worked for the gallery in the next loft. "We've got a situation here," she said. She sounded like a cop, except her voice was shaking. "It's not good." She'd seen Gay over the weekend; they'd hung out on the roof the two lofts shared. That had been Saturday. On Tuesday she saw Razz out there by himself, pacing silently, sniffing the air. Gay had left the window open. He often did that; he wasn't afraid of burglars. The dog looked hungry, and she put out some food for him. On Wednesday the same thing happened. She called Gay's cell and got his voice mail. That evening Razz bumped his snout against her office window. Rocky fed him again. She went out on the roof and called Gay's name a few times. But it was January, the wind was shrieking the way it does along the river, and he might not have heard her.

A little anxious now, she let herself in through the open window. A light was burning on the upper platform, and this reassured her that he was in bed, asleep. She knew he worked odd hours. It was only when the dog returned the following morning that she felt her stomach sink — in moments of dread it's not the heart that sinks but the stomach — and called the management office to ask a porter to come up to the thirteenth floor. This time she didn't want to go in alone. They found Gay on the sofa, with a plastic shopping bag over his head. Snaked inside it was the hose from a shop vac whose other end was hooked up to the propane tank of the gas grill on the roof. By the time I got there the cops had removed the hose.

A detective from the Sixth Precinct asked me to take him through the premises and point out anything that seemed out of place. He showed me a note on the dining table. It was taciturn, little more than a set of instructions. Even these, however, were marked by a sense of failure: "THE VAN IS PARKED ON ~~BANK~~ WASHINGTON ST. ~~IN FRONT OF THE COURTYARD~~. HERE ARE THE KEYS. BUT I'D JUST LET THEM JUNK IT." And "MY BOOK IS ON DISKS AND THE COMPUTER. ANYONE WHO WANTS CAN FINISH IT AND HAVE IT. THE END-ING IS BRIEFED IN THE LONG SYNOPSIS. PROBABLY NOT WORTH THE EFFORT."

The detective asked me to confirm that the handwriting was the deceased's. I said it was. So were the characteristic misspellings: Razz, for instance, was "Raze." I wanted to check the address book on Gay's computer so I could start letting people know, but the cop wouldn't let me turn it on; he said it might be rigged. We circled the loft. The low winter sun lanced through the windows, filling the room with golden light that had the paradoxical effect of making everything it touched look squalid — the begrimed floors, the table strewn with crumbs and cigarette ashes, the shape abandoned on the sagging couch that I only then realized was Gay's body. It seemed incredible that I hadn't noticed it before. Maybe I had and then disavowed what I'd seen.

It — he — was lying on his back, with one arm dangling over the side. He was wearing jeans and a flannel shirt, clothes I'd seen him in dozens of times. His boots were on the floor by the armchair, where he must have sat as he took them off. The police, as I said, had removed the hose from his mouth but placed a cushion over his face, or replaced one that Gay himself had put there when he lay down. The cushion, which was stained with some brownish fluid, gave the figure the appearance of a dummy.

The loft had to be sealed until the police were satisfied that Gay was a suicide and not a murder victim, so weeks passed before I was allowed back in. The dummy was gone, of course, but everything else was still there, down to the pair of boots. Up until then I'd been angry at him, furious, as you would be at someone who asks you to clean an apartment he's trashed — not in a night of shit-faced jollity, but systematically, over years — and while you're at it, pay the back rent, too. Why had I ever agreed to it, or kept such a person as a friend? Why had I cared about him? But I had. And when I walked in, I could imagine what Gay might have felt in the last hours of his life. I saw what he must have seen: the filthy rooms he'd once shared with a woman he loved, the worthless chattel strewn about them, the unsold paintings, the book he couldn't finish and whose different versions he could no longer sort out. He'd made beauty and no one had noticed it. His love had turned to gall. Strangers had beaten him and stifled his cries with drugs. Of course he'd killed himself, I thought, looking around me. Another hour of that life would have been insupportable, and he didn't know how to change it.

THE LAST TIME I saw Gay alive was the day after Christmas, when he came up to visit my wife and me in the country. Christopher, a sad, listless little boy we'd gotten to know through the Fresh Air Fund, was staying with us, too, and we hoped that he and Gay might cheer each other up. Although Christopher viewed most grown-ups with suspicion or disdain, he thought Gay was the coolest guy on earth. It had snowed a few days before. Gay took Christopher sledding in the town park. It was probably the first time in his life Christopher had done that. There was no park in his neighborhood in East New York. The hill was steep and icy, and although Christopher liked the downhill part, he didn't want to climb back up. If it had been just the two of us, I'd have gotten impatient and raised my voice, but Gay knew how to humor him, and was able to coax him into going up and down several times.

Afterward we walked over to the frozen playground. Chris said that he was tired.

"Tired? You're *tired?*" Gay cried. "What've you got to be tired about? You're just a kid."

"That's why I'm tired," Chris said. "I'm just a kid."

"Oh, yeah?" Gay replied. We were standing under the parallel bars. With one jump, Gay caught them and swung himself up, then over. He was upside down. Chris goggled at him. "Now watch this." He had on padded thermal overalls, work boots, and a heavy denim coat, the kind road crews wear. Still upside down, Gay lifted his legs and hooked the toes of his boots over one of the bars. Then he let go, so that he was hanging just by his feet. His cap fell off, and his thin hair fell around his scalp. His face turned red. "I'm fifty-nine years old, kid. I'm an old man. But look at me." He let out a whoop. Behind him the sun shone palely through the clouds. "Look at me!"

I THINK OF Gilgamesh, watching his friend quake in his fever, wiping the sweat from his limbs. For twelve days and twelve nights he has held him. One day Enkidu's breathing was fast, the next slow and groaning, as if he were lifting a great burden. Now it rasps in his throat. Abruptly his eyes, which have been closed for days, snap open. Gilgamesh feels a stab of hope. But no sooner have they opened than they roll back until only the whites show, and it is plain that they see nothing. Froth spills from Enkidu's mouth; his breathing ceases. My friend whom I loved has become like unto mud. And I, must I too, lie down like him and never rise again?

Was there something wrong with him? Was it always there, and did I just not see it? Was it something he did? Was he just a fuckup? How did I fail him? Suffering is as common as death, and like death, it resists all attempts to explain it. Perhaps it is worse than death. We long for the dead to speak to us, but who wants to hear the suffering, even when they return, as they sometimes do, from the land of pain? Who wants to know what they know? All the stories that we tell about suffering are only afterthoughts. In the moment of calamity, when the great wind comes out of the wilderness and smites the corners of the house, killing all inside it, we do what Gilgamesh does; we do it even if we cannot take a step.

We run.

NOTES

Epigraph

1. Anton Chekhov, "Gooseberries," in *The Tales of Chekhov*, vol. 5, *The Wife and Other Stories*, trans. Constance Garnett (New York: Ecco Press, 1985), 283.

Introduction

1. *The Book of Kindred Sayings* (English translation of the *Samyutta-nikāya*), Pali Text Society. Quoted in James W. Boyd, "Suffering in Theravada Buddhism," in *Suffering: Indian Perspectives,* ed. Kapil N. Tiwari (Delhi: Motilal Banarsidass, 1986), 146, n. 5.
2. David Hume, "Dialogues Concerning Natural Religion," in *God and the Problem of Evil,* ed. William L. Rowe (Oxford: Blackwell, 2001), 41.
3. Simone Weil, *Simone Weil: An Anthology,* ed. Siân Miles (New York: Grove Press, 1986), 16.
4. *New Larousse Encyclopedia of Mythology,* trans. Richard Aldington and Delano Ames, new ed. (London: Hamlyn, 1968), 66.
5. Ibid., 71–72.
6. Theodore J. Lewis, "CT 13.33–34 and Ezekiel 32: Lion-Dragon Myths," *Journal of the American Oriental Society,* 116, no. 1 (January–March 1996): 34.
7. *The Epic of Gilgamesh,* trans. Maureen Gallery Kovacs (Palo Alto, CA: Stanford University Press, 1989), 107.
8. *The Five Books of Moses: Genesis, Exodus, Leviticus, Numbers,*

Deuteronomy, ed. and trans. Everett Fox (New York: Schocken, 1995), 502.

9. Jon Lee Anderson, "Ill Winds: Tomahawks, Bunker Busters, and Dust Storms Afflict the Iraqi Capital," *New Yorker,* April 7, 2003, 39.

10. Primo Levi, *Survival in Auschwitz,* trans. Stuart Woolf (New York: Touchstone, 1996), 113–15.

11. Viktor E. Frankl, *Man's Search for Meaning: An Introduction to Logotherapy,* 3rd ed. (New York: Touchstone, 1984), 86.

CHAPTER I. YOUR EYES ARE UPON ME, AND I AM NOT

1. Spinoza, *Ethics,* ed. and trans. G. H. R. Parkinson (New York: Oxford University Press, 2003), 173.

2. Fergus Shiel, "Wasted by War, Now Crushed by a Mountain of Water," *Sydney Morning Herald,* January 13, 2005.

3. Paul Wiseman, "Wave Cuts Off War-Ravaged Town's Revival," *USA Today,* January 2, 2005.

4. In Mullaittivu, by contrast, some twenty-two thousand refugees were sheltering in eighteen camps, and all evidence suggested that they would be there for a long time (ibid.). Sri Lanka's long civil war was temporarily in abeyance, but the Sinhalese-dominated government may still have seen Mullaittivu, most of whose inhabitants were Tamil and which was controlled by the LTTE, as enemy territory and deliberately held back aid from the town and its surrounding region. An alternate explanation is that it was the Tigers themselves who were impeding the flow of aid in the interest of keeping Tamils disaffected from the state. In the camps under their control, they were said to be warning residents that the food shipped from Colombo was poisoned.

5. Dolitha Ranchagoda, author interviews, Indurawa, Sri Lanka, March 4–5, 2005.

6. Alexis de Tocqueville, *Democracy in America,* trans. Henry Reeve (Project Gutenberg, 1997), bk. 2, chap. 19, http://www.gutenberg .org.

7. Christmas Humphreys, *A Popular Dictionary of Buddhism* (New York: Citadel Press, 1961), 105–6; *The Long Discourses of the Buddha: A Translation of the Dīgha Nikāya,* trans. Maurice Walshe (Boston: Wisdom Publications, 1995), 34–35.

8. *Dhammapada, Wisdom of the Buddha,* trans. Harischandra Kaviratna, online ed. (Pasadena, CA: Theosophical University Press, 1980), v. 165, http://www.theosociety.org/pasadena/dhamma/ dham-hp.htm.

9. Venerable Bhante Piyatissa, author interview, February 1, 2005.

10. "The Shorter Instructions to Malunkya," in *Majjhima Nikaya,*

trans. Thanissaro Bhikkhu, no. 63, http://www.accesstoinsight
.org/canon/sutta/majjhima/mn-063-tb0. html.

11. Eric Lichtblau and Wayne Arnold, "For Indonesian Survivors,
Constant Reminders of Havoc," *New York Times*, December 30,
2004.

12. Amy Waldman, "Faith Divides the Survivors and It Unites Them,
Too," *New York Times,* January 12, 2005.

13. Ibid.

14. Bishop Joseph Vianney Fernando, Catholic-Hierarchy.org, http://
www.catholic-hierarchy.org/bishop/bfejv.html.

15. Barbara Bradley Hagerty, "Analysis: People of Different Faiths
Interpret the Tsunami and Its Devastation in Different Ways,"
Morning Edition, National Public Radio, January 10, 2005.

16. Waldman, "Faith Divides."

17. Ibid.

18. Ibid.

19. Sri Shiva Swami, author interview, Batticaloa, March 15, 2005.

20. Lichtblau and Arnold, "For Indonesian Survivors."

21. Stephen Bates, "Religions Strive to Make Theological Sense of
Disaster," *Guardian Weekly,* January 7–13, 2005.

22. Ibid.

23. Hagerty, "Analysis."

24. Harold S. Kushner, *When Bad Things Happen to Good People*
(New York: Avon, 1981), 134.

25. Hagerty, "Analysis."

26. Kushner, *When Bad Things Happen,* 4.

27. Almost the same thing had happened 250 years earlier, following
the 1755 Lisbon earthquake, in which some 100,000 people died. It
may be the only natural disaster to have played a significant role in
an intellectual movement — the Enlightenment. Several thinkers,
most prominently Voltaire, cited the quake as graphic evidence that
human beings were not living in an orderly world ruled by a benevolent God.

28. Emil G. Hirsch et al., "The Book of Job," *The Jewish Encyclopedia,*
http://www.jewishencyclopedia.com/view.jsp?artid=331&letter
=J&search=JOB. See also Cynthia Ozick, "Preface to the Book
of Job," in *The Book of Job* (New York: Vintage Spiritual Classics,
1998), xi, and Moshe Greenberg, "Job," in *The Literary Guide to
the Bible,* ed. Robert Alter and Frank Kermode (Cambridge: Harvard University Press, 1990), 283.

29. In the Talmud one reads variously that Job lived at the time of
Abraham; at the time of Jacob, whose daughter Dinah he married;
and during the Babylonian captivity. Different commentators identify him as a Jew and as a gentile. In the *Sefer Ha-Yashar* he is said

to have been a counselor of Pharaoh's who advised his patron to murder the Hebrews' firstborn sons. Other rabbis claim that Job was the only member of Pharaoh's retinue who urged him to heed the Word of God and release the Hebrews from captivity. Emil G. Hirsch et al., "Job," *The Jewish Encyclopedia,* http://www .jewishencyclopedia.com/view.jsp?artid=330&letter=J& search=Job.

30. Timothy K. Beal, *Religion and Its Monsters* (New York: Routledge, 2002), 40.

31. For a definitive analysis of his different roles, see Elaine Pagels, *The Origin of Satan: How Christians Demonized Jews, Pagans, and Heretics* (New York: Vintage, 1996).

32. Ray Krone, author interviews, June 28, 2005; February 6 and 7, 2008. All quotations from Krone in this chapter are from these interviews unless otherwise indicated.

33. Robert Nelson, "About Face," *Phoenix* (AZ) *New Times,* April 21, 2005, 2, http://www.phoenixnewtimes.com/2005-04-21/news/ about-face/2.

34. Ibid., 5–6.

35. Hans Sherrer, "Twice Wrongly Convicted of Murder, Ray Krone Is Set Free After 10 Years," *Justice Denied,* 2, no. 9, http://www.fore justice.org/wc/ray_krone_JD_vol2_i9.htm.

36. Henry Weinstein, "Death Penalty Foes Mark a Milestone; Arizona Convict Freed on DNA Tests Is Said to Be the 100th Known Condemned U.S. Prisoner to Be Exonerated Since Executions Resumed," *Los Angeles Times,* April 10, 2002.

37. Richard L., author interviews, January 17 and 24, 2005.

38. Surveillance, Epidemiology, and End Results (SEER) Program (www.seer.cancer.gov) SEER*Stat Database: Incidence-SEER 9 Regs Limited-Use, Nov 2006 Sub (1973–2004), National Cancer Institute, DCCPS, Surveillance Research Program, Cancer Statistics Branch, released April 2007, based on the November 2006 submission.

39. Daniela Cihakova, M.D., "Hashimoto's Thyroiditis," Johns Hopkins Medical Institutions Autoimmune Disease Research Center, http://autoimmune.pathology.jhmi.edu/diseases.cfm?systemID=3 &DiseaseID=22.

40. *Hildegard von Bingen: Lyrics in Latin and English,* trans. Rupert R. Chapelle, http://irupert.com/HILDEGRD/hildegard.htm.

41. Greenberg, "Job," 283–286, 299.

42. See Kushner, *When Bad Things Happen,* 37. The propositions (A) God is infinitely powerful, (B) God is infinitely just, and (C) The innocent suffer (sometimes paraphrased as "Evil exists"), which date to the pagan philosopher Epicurus (341–270 B.C.), are known

in apologetics as "the inconsistent triad," because they seem to stand in intractable opposition. "Epicurus' old questions are still unanswered," Hume concludes in "Dialogues Concerning Natural Religion." "Is he [God] willing to prevent evil, but not able? then he is impotent. Is he able but not willing? then he is malevolent. Is he both able and willing? whence then is evil?" (David Hume, "Dialogues Concerning Natural Religion," in *God and the Problem of Evil*, ed. William L. Rowe [Oxford: Blackwell, 2001], 43). Job's critics focus on what they perceive to be the triad's weakest leg — the human one.

43. Ray C. Stedman, "The Test," in *Let God Be God* (Palo Alto, CA: Discovery, 1995), http://www.raystedman.org/job/3540.html.
44. Ted Wade, "Job 1," The Bible Explained, http://www.bible explained.com/other-early/Job/job01.htm.
45. John H. Ogwyn, "Seven Lessons from the Book of Job," Living Church of God, http://www.lcg.org/cgi-bin/lcg/studytopics/lcg-st.cgi?category1&item=1122911276.
46. Yehezkel Kauffman, "Commentary on Job," in *The Book of Job* (New York: Vintage, 1998), 91–92.
47. Sherrer, "Twice Wrongly Convicted of Murder."
48. Christopher J. Plourd, J.D., "Wrongfully Convicted — the Clue 'Saving Ray Krone,' " *CACNews*, 3rd Quarter 2005, www.cacnews.org/pdfs/3rdq05.pdf., 19.
49. *State of Arizona v. Kenneth Phillips*, Superior Court of Arizona, Maricopa County, CR 2002-007255 (June 29, 2006), and *State of Arizona v. Kenneth Phillips*, Superior Court of Arizona, Maricopa County, 2002-007255 (August 18, 2006).
50. Weinstein, "Death Penalty Foes Mark a Milestone."
51. Beth Defalco, "Phoenix OKs $3 Mil Krone Settlement," *Arizona Republic*, September 28, 2005.
52. "Critique of D[eath] P[enalty] I[nformation] C[enter] List ('Innocence: Freed from Death Row')," http://www.prodeath penalty.com/DPIC.htm#_ftn2. The DPIC gives the figure as 128 as of April 4, 2008; Justice for All gives the total as 102.
53. Emily Bernard, author interview, March 25, 2005.
54. Nancy Ramsey, "The Horror of Beslan, Through Its Youngest Survivors," *New York Times*, September 1, 2005.
55. John Hick, "Soul-Making Theodicy," in *God and the Problem of Evil*, ed. William L. Rowe (Oxford: Blackwell, 2001), 265–81.
56. Per a Google search on February 7, 2008, using the keywords "I asked God to spare me pain."
57. See Susan Sontag, *Illness as Metaphor* (New York: Farrar, Straus & Giroux, 1978), esp. 21–24, 40–42.

58. Katherine Russell Rich, *The Red Devil: To Hell with Cancer — and Back* (New York: Crown, 1999), 132.
59. Eric Konigsberg, "Letter from Nebraska: Prairie Fire," *New Yorker,* January 16, 2006, 55.
60. According to Midrash, God created two leviathans on the fifth day but slew the female, fearing that if they were allowed to breed, they might destroy the world. Emil G. Hirsch et al., "Behemoth and Leviathan," *The Jewish Encyclopedia,* http://www.jewishencyclo pedia.com/view.jsp?artid=275&letter=L&search=Leviathan.
61. "Demands of French Protesters Include Freedom for Ngawang," France-Tibet Association Loi, October 20, 1999, http://www.inch .com/~shebar/ngawang/20oct99.htm.
62. Philippe Broussard and Danielle Laeng, *La Prisonnière de Lhassa: Ngawang Sangdrol, religieuse et résistante* (Paris: Livre de Poche, 2002), 127. Most of the preceding chronology of Sangdrol's arrests and incarcerations is derived from this work, which was recommended to me by its subject.
63. Phuntsog Nyidron et al., "Songs from a Tibetan Prison: 14 Nuns Sing to the Outside World," TIN News Review, April 26, 1994, 18–21, http://www.columbia.edu/itc/ealac/barnett/pdfs/link17 -nunssong.pdf.
64. Philippe Broussard and Danielle Laeng, *La Prisonnière de Lhassa,* 156–161.
65. "Drapchi: A History Written in Blood," *Tibetan Envoy,* 6 (2002): 19. Posted on the Web site of the Gu-Chu-Sum Political Prisoners Association, http://www.guchusum.org/NewsCampaigns/ TibetanEnvoyMagazine/tabid/63/Default.aspx.
66. See, for example, *The Tibetan Book of the Dead: Liberation Through Understanding in the Between,* trans. Robert A. F. Thurman (New York: Bantam, 1994), 10.
67. Simone Weil, "The Love of God and Affliction," in *Waiting for God,* trans. Emma Craufurd (New York: G. P. Putnam's Sons, 1951, 1979; New York: Harper Perennial, 2001), 70. Citations are to the Harper edition.
68. Quoted in Susan Sontag, "Regarding the Torture of Others," *New York Times Magazine,* May 23, 2004.
69. Weil, "The Love of God," 70.
70. Paul Ciholas, *Consider My Servant Job: Meditations on Life's Struggles and God's Faithfulness* (Peabody, MA: Hendrickson, 1998), 46.
71. See, for example, William M. Ramsey, *Westminster Guide to the Books of the Bible* (Louisville, KY: Westminster John Knox Press, 1994), 151.

72. Tertullian, "To the Martyrs, I–IV," in *The Christianity Reader,* ed. Mary Gerhart and Fabian E. Udoh, trans. Rudolph Arbesmann et al. (Chicago: University of Chicago Press, 2007), 246.

73. Greenberg, "Job," 298.

74. Stedman, "The Test," in *Let God Be God* (Palo Alto, CA: Discovery, 1995), http://www.raystedman.org/job/3540.html.

75. Carl G. Jung, "Answer to Job," *The Portable Jung,* ed. Joseph Campbell (New York: Viking, 1971), 542.

76. Jack Miles thinks so. See his *God: A Biography* (New York: Vintage, 1995), 318–24.

77. The few Islamic ones I'm acquainted with scarcely mention the devil at all. "But in Islam," says Karen Armstrong, "Satan is a much more manageable character than he became in Christianity. The Koran tells us that he will be forgiven on the Last Day, and Arabs frequently use the word 'Shaitan' to allude to a purely human tempter or a natural temptation." *A History of God* (New York: Knopf, 1993), 148.

78. Miles, *God: A Biography,* 329–30.

Chapter 2. A Place to Be Heartbroken

1. Sally and Donald Goodrich, author interviews, May 6, 2005, December 4, 2006, March 25, 2007. All quotations from the Goodriches in this chapter are from these interviews, or from phone conversations and e-mails.

2. The Goodriches got this macabre piece of information from Jon, who had gotten a phone call from a reporter at one of the news networks, who apparently hoped for his thoughts on having his product used for this purpose.

3. Quoted in Sally Goodrich, Peter M. Goodrich Memorial Foundation Web site, http://www.goodrichfoundation.org/index .php?post=s1123959086.

4. National Commission on Terrorist Attacks, *The 9-11 Commission Report: Final Report of the National Commission on Terrorist Attacks Upon the United States* (New York: W. W. Norton, 2004), 7–8.

5. Yuval Neria, Ph.D., et al., "The 9/11 Grief Survey" (paper). Made available through the courtesy of Donald Goodrich.

6. Carol Paukner (NYPD), interview, American Folklife Center, Library of Congress, http://www.loc.gov/exhibits/911/911-folklife .html.

7. Daniel Mendelsohn, "September 11 at the Movies," *New York Review of Books,* September 21, 2006.

8. Boethius, *The Consolation of Philosophy,* trans. Victor Watts (New

York: Penguin, 1969), 31. The capitalization used in the original has been retained.

9. Quoted in Victor Watts, preface to ibid., xv.

10. At least the church claims him as one, although it's suggestive that the name of Jesus appears nowhere in the *Consolation,* nor does any reference to the Christian doctrines of the Incarnation and grace.

11. Quoted in Watts, preface, xxiiii.

12. Boethius, *The Consolation of Philosophy,* 4.

13. Ibid., 5.

14. Ibid., 36.

15. Ibid., 7.

16. Ibid., 35.

17. Farinaz Amirsehi, author interviews, November 6 and 7, 2004.

18. Jonathan Shay, M.D., *Odysseus in America: Combat Trauma and the Trials of Homecoming* (New York: Scribner, 2002), 87–88.

19. Two days after the attacks only eighty-two bodies had been recovered. Dan Barry, "After the Attacks: The Search; A Few Moments of Hope in a Mountain of Rubble," *New York Times,* September 13, 2001.

20. Dan Barry, "A Nation Challenged: Survivors; As Sept. 11 Widows Unite, Grief Finds Political Voice," *New York Times,* November 25, 2001.

21. James Glanz, "Fresh Kills Journal; Mountains of Twisted Steel, Evoking the Dead," *New York Times,* October 1, 2001.

22. Patricia Yaeger, "Rubble as Archive, or 9/11 as Dust, Debris, and Bodily Vanishing," in *Trauma at Home: After 9/11,* ed. Judith Greenberg (Lincoln: University of Nebraska Press, 2003), 188–89.

23. Dan Barry, "For One 9/11 Family, Five Waves of Grief," *New York Times,* September 10, 2003.

24. James Tatum, "An American War Experience," in *The Mourner's Song: War and Remembrance from the* Iliad *to Vietnam* (Chicago: University of Chicago Press, 2003), 22–32.

25. Since the fall of Saigon, there have been 1,914 firsthand reports of Americans in Southeast Asia. Of these 69.02 percent were identified as POW returnees, missionaries, or civilians jailed for violations of Vietnamese law; 2.35 percent were related to wartime sightings of military personnel or civilians who remain unaccounted for; and 27.52 percent were fabrications. There are only seventeen (0.89 percent) reports of Americans in country that remain unresolved. The Vietnam-Era Prisoner-of-War/Missing-in-Action Database, Library of Congress, http://lcweb2.loc.gov/frd/pow/Nov0701.html.

26. See Robert C. Doyle, "Unresolved Mysteries: The Myth of the Missing Warrior and the Government Deceit Theme in the Popular

Captivity Culture of the Vietnam War," *Journal of American Culture,* 15, no. 2 (June 1992): 9–11.

27. Homer, *The Odyssey,* trans. Robert Fitzgerald (New York: Vintage, 1989), 200.

28. Malcolm W. Browne, "Vietnamese Also Extending the Search for Their M.I.A.'s," *New York Times,* May 20, 1994.

29. Philip Shenon, "U.S. and North Korea Agree on Joint Search for Missing," *New York Times,* May 10, 1996; Michael Sullivan, "Looking for American Remains in Vietnam," *All Things Considered,* National Public Radio, June 8, 2005, http://www.npr.org/templates/story/story.php?storyId=4694997.

30. *The Epic of Gilgamesh,* trans. Maureen Gallery Kovacs (Palo Alto, CA: Stanford University Press, 1989), 69.

31. Although Stephen Push, one of the group's first directors, lost his wife at the Pentagon. Don Goodrich, e-mail message to author, July 23, 2006.

32. David Firestone, "Threats and Responses: The Investigation; Kissinger Pulls Out as Chief of Inquiry into 9/11 Attacks," *New York Times,* December 14, 2002.

33. Lisa Belkin, "Just Money," *New York Times Magazine,* December 8, 2002, 69.

34. Aircraft Operator Security; Final Rule, 66 Fed. Reg. 37330, 37353 (July 17, 2001). See also Aircraft Operator Security; Proposed Rule, 62 Fed. Reg. 41430, 41746 (August 1, 1997).

35. "Caps on Non-Economic Loss Damages Would Unfairly Penalize Women, Minorities, Elderly," press release, State University of New York at Buffalo, July 17, 2003.

36. David W. Chen, "Worst-Hit Firm Faults Fairness of Sept. 11 Aid," *New York Times,* September 17, 2002.

37. Belkin, "Just Money," 68.

38. Ibid., 73.

39. Stephanie Strom, "Ground Zero: Charity; A Flood of Money, Then a Deluge of Scrutiny for Those Handing It Out," *New York Times,* September 11, 2002.

40. Steve Fishman, "The Dead Wives Club, or Char in Love," *New York,* May 31, 2004, http://nymag.com/nymetro/news/sept11/features/9189/index3.html.

41. James Barron, "Behind Relief to 9/11 Families, a Man's Flaws," *New York Times,* April 3, 2006.

42. Boethius, *The Consolation of Philosophy,* 104.

43. In this context, one thinks of Simone Weil's dictum: "I cannot conceive the necessity for God to love me. . . . But I can easily imagine that he loves that perspective of creation which can only be seen from the point where I am." Quoted in Robert Coles, *Simone Weil:*

A Modern Pilgrimage (Woodstock, VT: Skylight Paths, 2001), 2. Perhaps there is a vista accessible only to the abject, and it is one that God especially prizes.

44. Boethius, *The Consolation of Philosophy,* 104.

45. Ibid., 108.

46. "God Carries Out His Divine Plan: Providence," *Catechism of the Catholic Church* (Mahwah, NJ: Paulist Press, 1994), 83, n. 312.

47. Boethius, *The Consolation of Philosophy,* 110.

48. Jeff Sharlet, "Soldiers of Christ: Inside America's Most Powerful Megachurch," *Harper's,* May 2005.

49. Boethius, *The Consolation of Philosophy,* 137.

50. In the aftermath of 9/11 the only feeling not subject to counterfeit may have been fear. All over America, people were feeling that. It was just that the fear was often disproportionate to any actual threat. Five years later it would emerge that the Department of Homeland Security was spending vast amounts of money safeguarding targets such as the Old MacDonald's Petting Zoo in Woodville, Alabama; the Amish Country Popcorn factory in Berne, Indiana; and Columbia, Tennessee's Mule Day Parade. Eric Lipton, "Come One, Come All, Join the Terror Target List," *New York Times,* July 12, 2006.

51. John Tierney, "Mourning in America," *New York Times,* June 10, 2006.

52. Quoted in David Carr, "Deadly Intent: Ann Coulter, Word Warrior," *New York Times,* June 12, 2006.

53. Alessandra Stanley, "Florida, an Electoral Prize, Is Awash in a Sea of Ads," *New York Times,* October 29, 2004.

54. Peter Brooks, "If You Have Tears," in *Trauma at Home: After 9/11,* ed. Judith Greenberg (Lincoln: University of Nebraska Press, 2003), 50–51.

55. Janny Scott, "The Silence of the Historical Present," *New York Times,* August 11, 2002.

56. Glenn Collins, "Memorial Unit at Ground Zero Lists Donors," *New York Times,* June 2, 2007.

57. David W. Dunlap, "Blocks: Plans for a Random List of Names Anger Families," *New York Times,* February 19, 2004.

58. Kirk Johnson, "In Bereavement, Pioneers on a Lonely Trail," *New York Times,* September 8, 2002.

59. Walter Benjamin, "Theses on the Philosophy of History," quoted in Shoshana Felman, *The Juridical Unconscious: Trials and Traumas in the Twentieth Century* (Cambridge: Harvard University Press, 2002), 264 n. 42.

60. Judith Butler, *Precarious Life: The Powers of Mourning and Violence* (London: Verso, 2004), xiii.

61. Andrew C. McCarthy, "It's *All* About 9/11," *National Review,* June 29, 2005, http://www.nationalreview.com/mccarthy/mccarthy200506290912.asp.

62. Linda Feldman, "The Impact of Bush Linking 9/11 and Iraq," *Christian Science Monitor,* March 14, 2003.

63. Joan Didion, *The Year of Magical Thinking* (New York: Knopf, 2005), 37.

64. Quoted in Elizabeth Kelley Kerstens, "Victorian Death Ritual," *Ancestry,* September–October 1999.

65. Cited in W. Stroebe, M. Stroebe, and H. Schut, "Does 'Grief Work' Work?" *The Forum* (Newsletter of the Manchester Area Bereavement Centre), vol. 7, no. 4, Winter 2004. http://www.mabf.org.uk/newsletter_archive.asp?archive=74.

66. Carolyn Jaffe and Carol H. Ehrlich, "Only God Knows When," originally published in *All Kinds of Love: Experiencing Hospice* (Amityville, NY: Baywood Publishing, 1997). Broadcast on *The End of Life: Exploring Death in America,* National Public Radio. http://www.npr.org/programs/death/readings/essays/jaffe.html.

67. Neria et al., "The 9/11 Grief Survey."

68. Viktor E. Frankl, *Man's Search for Meaning: An Introduction to Logotherapy,* trans. Ilse Lasch (New York: Simon & Schuster, 1962), 86.

69. Primo Levi, *Survival in Auschwitz,* trans. Stuart Woolf (New York: Simon & Schuster, 1998), 29.

70. Frankl, *Man's Search for Meaning,* 27.

71. Ibid., 29.

72. Ibid., 32.

73. Jean Améry, *At the Mind's Limits: Contemplations by a Survivor on Auschwitz and Its Realities,* trans. Sidney Rosenfeld and Stella F. Rosenfeld (Bloomington: University of Indiana Press, 1980); quoted in Giorgio Agamben, *Remnants of Auschwitz: The Witness and the Archive,* trans. Daniel Heller-Roazen (New York: Zone, 2002), 41. I am indebted to Agamben for most of the ideas in the paragraph that follows.

74. Zdislaw Ryn and Stanislaw Klodzinski, *"An de Grenzen zwischen Leben und Tod. Eine Studie uber die Erscheinung des 'Mussel-manns,' "* quoted in Agamben, *Remnants of Auschwitz,* 42.

75. Levi, *Survival in Auschwitz,* 90.

76. Frankl, *Man's Search for Meaning,* 50.

77. Agamben, *Remnants of Auschwitz,* 51.

78. Ibid., 77.

79. Frankl, *Man's Search for Meaning,* 25.

80. Ibid., 68.

81. Ibid., 49.

82. Ibid., 50.
83. Boethius, *The Consolation of Philosophy*, 29.
84. Elizabeth Rubin, "Taking the Fight to the Taliban," *New York Times Magazine*, October 29, 2006, 82.

CHAPTER 3. THE PURPOSE OF THE BLINDFOLD

1. Lt. Gen. Roméo Dallaire, *Shake Hands with the Devil: The Failure of Humanity in Rwanda* (New York: Carroll & Graf, 2005), 305.
2. Anastasie K., author interview, Polyclinic of Hope, outside Kigali, March 23, 2007. Her name, like those of other Rwandans interviewed for this book, has been changed. All quotations from Anastasie K. in this chapter are from that interview.
3. "Country Health Systems Fact Sheet, 2006: Rwanda," World Health Organization, http://www.afro.who.int/home/countries/facts_sheets/rwanda.pdf.
4. Jean Hatzfeld, *Machete Season: The Killers in Rwanda Speak*, trans. Linda Coverdale (New York: Farrar, Straus & Giroux, 2005), 77–78.
5. A 1997 study found that 60 percent of women sexually violated during the genocide had been deliberately contaminated with HIV. Françoise Digneffe and Jacques Fierens, eds., *Justice et Gacaca: L'expérience rwandaise et la génocide* (Namur, Belgium: Presses Universitaires de Namur, 2003), 107.
6. Consolée Mukanyiligira, author interview, March 15, 2004.
7. Actually, a lot of bones were being claimed by the ruling Rwandan Patriotic Front, without much consideration of whom they'd originally belonged to. When government workers opened a mass grave in Gisozi, the site of the future genocide memorial, they dug up tons of skeletons, leaving behind the identity cards that had been buried with them. Witnesses who sorted through the cards afterward said that many of them designated their bearers as Hutu. It didn't matter. When the bones were later put on display, they were all identified as Tutsi.
8. Ervin Staub, "Genocide and Mass Killing: Origins, Prevention, Healing, and Reconciliation," *Political Psychology*, 21, no. 2 (2000): 379.
9. Quoted in Martha Minow, *Between Vengeance and Forgiveness: Facing History After Genocide and Mass Violence* (Boston: Beacon Press, 1998), 4.
10. Gérard Prunier, *The Rwanda Crisis: History of a Genocide* (New York: Columbia University Press, 1995), 341.
11. Jeanne d'Arc M., author interview, March 10, 2004.
12. According to Arendt, the judges who sentenced Adolf Eichmann cited the explanation that "punishment is necessary 'to defend the

honor or authority of him who was hurt by the offence so that the
failure to punish may not cause his degradation.' " Hannah Arendt,
"Eichmann in Jerusalem," in *The Portable Hannah Arendt*, ed.
Peter Baehr (New York: Penguin Putnam, 2000), 378–79.

13. Pierre Richard Prosper, "U.S. Announcement of Campaign to Capture Fugitives Indicted by the International Criminal Tribunal for
Rwanda," http://www.gov.rw/government/061302_2.html.

14. Sean Sinclair Day, "Felicien Kabuga in Kenya: Eluding Justice,"
African Affairs, July 12, 2006, http://africanaffairs.suite101.com/
article.cfm/f_licien_kabuga_in_kenya.

15. "Father Nsengimana Pleads Not Guilty" (press release, International Criminal Tribunal for Rwanda, April 16, 2002),
http://69.94.11.53/ENGLISH/PRESSREL/2002/315e.htm.

16. International Criminal Tribunal for Rwanda, Case No. ICTR-
2001-66-I, The Prosecutor Against Athanase Seromba,
http://69.94.11.53/ENGLISH/cases/Seromba/indictment/
seromba.pdf.

17. Marlise Simons, "Rwandan Pastor and His Son Are Convicted of
Genocide," *New York Times*, February 20, 2003.

18. Jody Ranck, author interview, February 25, 2004. Ranck is an anthropologist and human rights worker.

19. Mark Lacey, "Since '94 Horror, Rwandans Turn Toward Islam,"
New York Times, April 7, 2004.

20. Rory Carroll, "In Memory of Murder," *Guardian*, March 24, 2004,
http://arts.guardian.co.uk/features/story/0,,1176333,00.html.

21. Helen Nyambura, "Accused Rwanda Genocide 'Kingpin' Defiant,"
Reuters, November 13, 2005; "In Depth: Roméo Dallaire," CBC
News Online, October 24, 2003, and March 9, 2005, http://www
.cbc.ca/news/background/dallaire/.

22. Johan Pottier, *Re-imagining Rwanda: Conflict, Survival and Dis-
information in the Late Twentieth Century* (Cambridge: Cambridge University Press, 2002), 155.

23. Quoted in William Safire, "On Language: Alone with 'Alone,' or
What 'Is' Is," *New York Times*, October 11, 1998.

24. Prunier, *The Rwanda Crisis*, 268.

25. Ibid., 8.

26. Pottier, *Re-imagining Rwanda*, 22.

27. Although an old Rwandan proverb states, "The mwami is not a
Tutsi or a Hutu; he transcends Tutsi and Hutu."

28. Peter Landesman, author interview, February 16, 2004.

29. Benoit Kaboyi, author interview, Kigali, March 16, 2004.

30. "Andrea Yates Interview with Sergeant Eric Mehl" (transcript,
Houston Police Department, June 20, 2001), http://www.click2
houston.com/news/1247698/detail.html.

31. Anne Eggebroten, "A Biblical Feminist Looks at the Andrea Yates Tragedy," *EEWC Update: Newsletter of the Evangelical & Ecumenical Women's Caucus,* Winter 2001–2002.
32. Timothy Roche, "The Yates Odyssey," *Time,* July 26, 2006, http://www.time.com/time/magazine/article/0,9171,1001706-1,00.html.
33. Carol Christian, "Heat Felt by Yates' In-Laws at Trial," *Houston Chronicle,* March 6, 2002.
34. Peggy O'Hare and Dale Lezon, "Nurse Says Yates Acted Overwrought as a Mother," *Houston Chronicle,* July 8, 2006, http://www.chron.com/disp/story.mpl/special/drownings/4032430.html.
35. Russell Yates, interview, *Larry King Live,* CNN, March 18, 2002, http://transcripts.cnn.com/TRANSCRIPTS/0203/18/lkl.00.html.
36. "Andrea Yates Interview with Sergeant Eric Mehl."
37. Sophocles, *Oedipus Rex,* in *The Oedipus Cycle: An English Version,* trans. Dudley Fitts and Robert Fitzgerald (New York: Harcourt, 1949), 22. All further page references are indicated inside parentheses in text.
38. Gerard Prunier, *The Rwanda Crisis,* 346.
39. Christopher C. Taylor, "Deadly Images: King Sacrifice, President Habyarimana, and the Iconography of Pregenocidal Rwandan Political Literature," in *Violence,* ed. Neil L. Whitehead (Santa Fe, NM: School of American Research Press, 2004), 81.
40. Digneffe and Fierens, *Justice et Gacaca,* 25.
41. Isidore Munyakazi, author interviews, February 2004, May–June 2004. All quotations from Munyakazi in this chapter are from these interviews.
42. "Ten Commandments of the Hutu," *Kangura,* December 1990, www.stanford.edu/class/psych165/10comm.doc. Other commandments include: "All Hutu must know that female Tutsi, wherever they are, work in the interests of their Tutsi ethnicity. Because of this, any Hutu is a traitor who marries a Tutsi woman; makes a Tutsi woman a concubine; makes a Tutsi woman his secretary or protégé," and "All Hutu must know that our Hutu women are more dignified and more conscientious in their role as woman, wife and mother of the family. Aren't they beautiful, good secretaries, and more honest!"
43. Prunier, *The Rwanda Crisis,* 169.
44. René Girard, *Violence and the Sacred,* trans. Patrick Gregory (Baltimore: Johns Hopkins University Press, 1977), 2.
45. Alison Des Forges, *Leave None to Tell the Story: Genocide in Rwanda* (New York: Human Rights Watch, 1999), 175–87.
46. Georg Weiss, author interview, Kigali, March 14, 2004.
47. Hatzfeld, *Machete Season,* 86.

48. Anne Aghion, *Gacaca: Living Together Again in Rwanda?* (Gacaca Productions, 2002).
49. Beata M., author interview, March 21, 2004.
50. Roche, "The Yates Odyssey."
51. "Psychiatrist Testifies About Yates," *Click2Houston*, February 25, 2002, http://www.click2houston.com/news/1250287/detail.html.
52. Timothy Roche, "Andrea Yates: More to the Story," *Time*, March 18, 2002, 1.
53. Associated Press, "Former Nurse Testifies Yates Was Psychotic," *USA Today*, June 3, 2006, http://www.usatoday.com/news/nation/2006-06-30-yates_x.htm.
54. Katherine Ramsland, "Andrea Yates: Ill or Evil?" *Crime Library: Criminal Minds and Methods*, http://www.crimelibrary.com/notorious_murders/women/andrea_yates/index.html.
55. Tracy L. Snell, "Capital Punishment, 2005," Bureau of Justice Statistics Bulletin, December 2006, 1, http://www.ojp.usdoj.gov/bjs/pub/pdf/cp05.pdf.
56. Joe Owmby, author interview, May 26, 2004. All quotations from Owmby in this chapter are from this interview. Mr. Owmby's views are not necessarily those of the Harris County District Attorney's office.
57. Paul Burka, "It's Crazy: Andrea Yates and the Insanity of the Insanity Defense," *Texas Monthly*, July 2002.
58. Posted on Andrew Cohen, "Bench Conference: Justice for Andrea Yates," *WashingtonPost.com*, July 26, 2006, http://blog.washingtonpost.com/benchconference/2006/07/justice_for_andrea_yates.html.
59. Ibid.
60. Roche, "Andrea Yates: More to the Story," 2.
61. Associated Press, "Insanity Remains Focus in Yates' 2nd Trial," *New York Times*, June 18, 2006.
62. The prosecution had charged her with killing only three of her children, and some observers speculated that it was holding the other two deaths in reserve in the event of an acquittal. Jim Yardley, "Friends and Family Ask Jury to Spare Texas Mother's Life," *New York Times*, March 15, 2002.
63. Associated Press, "Woman's Convictions on Drowning Children Are Overturned," *New York Times*, January 6, 2005.
64. "Yates Sentenced to Life in Prison," CNN.com, March 15, 2002, http://archives.cnn.com/2002/LAW/03/15/yates.sentence/index.html.
65. Roche, "Andrea Yates: More to the Story," 2.
66. Anne Taylor Fleming, "Ideas and Trends: Crime and Motherhood; Maternal Madness," *New York Times*, March 17, 2002.

67. Ed Asher and Melanie Markley, "Victims' Rights Group Praises Verdict/Yates Backers: Mental Illness Misunderstood," *Houston Chronicle*, March 13, 2002.

68. Barbara Robinson, "Rusty Yates Is Culpable, Too," *Las Vegas (NV) Review-Journal*, March 22, 2002, http://www.commondreams .org/views02/0322-02.htm.

69. This was told to me by a trial lawyer who wishes to remain anonymous, during a telephone interview on May 14, 2007.

70. Digneffe and Fierens, *Justice et Gacaca*, 16–17.

71. Klaas de Jonge, author interview, March 10, 2004. De Jonge is affiliated with Penal Reform International.

72. Tharcisse Karugarama, author interview, March 11, 2004. All quotations from Karugarama in this chapter are from this interview. For his new position, see Sulah Nuwamanya, "Rwanda: Gacaca Courts to Get More Powers," *Weekly Observer* (Kampala), March 6, 2008, http://www.allafrica.com/stories/200803060759.html.

73. Digneffe and Fierens, *Justice et Gacaca*, 75.

74. An example of that cooperation, provided to me by the former ICTR prosecutor James Stewart, involved the case of Jean Bosco Barayagwiza, a founder of Radio Télévision Libre des Mille Collines and one of the chief instigators of the genocide. After the downfall of the old regime, he took refuge in Cameroon, which refused Rwanda's request to extradite him. Two days later, the ICTR made the same request, and Cameroon agreed. He was convicted in 2003. James Stewart, e-mail, April 20, 2008.

75. Samantha Power, "Rwanda: The Two Faces of Justice," *New York Review of Books,* January 16, 2003, 2.

76. "World Briefing, Africa: Rwanda: Genocide Trial Finishes After Five Years," *New York Times,* June 2, 2007; International Criminal Tribunal for Rwanda, "Bagosora, Théoneste (Colonel)," ICTR 96–7, http://69.94.11.53/ENGLISH/cases/Bagosora/index.htm. Clicking on "Trial Chamber Decisions" yields a complete chronology of the court proceedings. The last entry, dated June 1, 2007, ends, "The Trial Chamber has not fixed a date for delivery of the judgment. However, due to the length of the case and the testimony, observers expect delivery of the judgment towards the end of 2007 or early in 2008." As of April 2008, however, the succeeding heading, "Judgement and Sentence," was conspicuously grayed out, a strong indicator that none had yet been handed down.

77. Jane Perlez, "Rwandan Accused in Genocide Wins Suit for U.N. Pay," *New York Times,* August 8, 2004.

78. Power, "Rwanda: The Two Faces of Justice," 5.

79. Digneffe and Fierens, *Justice et Gacaca*, 56–63.

80. Ibid., 90–91, 97–102.

81. Ibid., 113. My rough translation follows:
    1. Anyone who wishes to take the floor must ask to do so.
    2. The president of the court is responsible for recognizing those who wish to speak.
    3. Precedence in testifying is given to those who have come from far away, to the elderly, and to those who have difficulty rising or sitting.
    4. The witness must be animated by the desire to tell the truth.
    5. It is forbidden to interrupt someone who has the floor.
    6. Violence, abuse, and threats are forbidden.
    7. It is preferable not to speak too long so that others get the chance to take the floor.
    8. Witnesses may speak only on the subject for which the court has been called into session.
82. Hannah Arendt, "The Origins of Totalitarianism," in *The Portable Hannah Arendt*, ed. Peter Baehr (New York: Penguin Putnam, 2000), 119–26.
83. The intention of this gesture was to blight the future: to cut off the line of Tutsi and curse their habitations forever. It was magical genocide.
84. Arendt, "The Origins of Totalitarianism," 150.
85. Digneffe and Fierens, *Justice et Gacaca*, 89.
86. Winston H., author interview, Kigali, March 21, 2004.
87. Power, "Rwanda: The Two Faces of Justice," 6.
88. Girard, *Violence and the Sacred*, 17.
89. Aeschylus, *Eumenides*, in *The Oresteia*, trans. George Thomson (New York: Everyman's Library, 2004), 101.
90. George Parnham, author interview, May 26, 2004. All quotations from Parnham in this chapter are from this interview.
91. Associated Press, "Insanity Remains Focus."
92. Associated Press, "Andrea Yates's Husband Files for Divorce," Fox News, August 3, 2004, http://www.foxnews.com/story/0,2933, 127850,00.html; Associated Press, "Russell Yates Finalizes Divorce," Fox News, March 17, 2005, http://www.foxnews.com/ story/0,2933,150755,00.html.
93. Roche, "The Yates Odyssey," 1.
94. John Springer, "Jury Accepts Insanity Defense for Mother Who Killed Sons," CNN.com, April 5, 2004, http://www.cnn.com/ 2004/LAW/04/05/laney.
95. "Attorney Given Jefferson Award for Postpartum Health Fight," *Click2Houston*, May 3, 2007, http://www.click2houston.com/ jeffersonawards/13253293/detail.html.
96. Associated Press, "Woman's Convictions on Drowning Children Are Overturned," *New York Times*, January 6, 2005.

97. Associated Press, "Yates Found Innocent by Reason of Insanity," *New York Times*, July 26, 2006.

98. Prunier (*The Rwanda Crisis*, 260) tells of a *milicien* who was so moved by the faith of a Catholic lay worker that he asked her to pray for his soul before he shot her. Still, he shot her. And more often you hear of Interahamwe telling their captives, with gloating thoroughness, precisely how they were going to kill them.

99. National Unity and Reconciliation Commission (NURC), Republic of Rwanda, "Opinion Survey on Participation in Gacaca and National Reconciliation," January 2003, 10–11.

100. Alison Des Forges, author interviews, March 3 and September 8, 2004.

101. Quoted in Simone Weil, "The Laments of Electra and the Recognition of Orestes," in *Intimations of Christianity Among the Ancient Greeks* (London: Routledge, 1957), 14–15.

102. Roche, "Andrea Yates: More to the Story," 2.

103. Carroll, "In Memory of Murder."

104. Rory Carroll, "Rwanda: Peace but No Reconciliation," *Guardian*, April 5, 2004, http://www.guardian.co.uk/world/2004/apr/05/rwanda.rorycarroll.

105. Aghion, *Gacaca: Living Together Again in Rwanda?*

CHAPTER 4. ONLY DROWNING MEN CAN SEE THEM

1. Dr. Peter Marinkovich, M.D., "Epidermolysis Bullosa," http://www.emedicine.com/derm/topic124.htm.

2. Kate and Kelly Daley, author interviews, May 31, June 5, and December 3, 2005; January 21, 2006. All quotations from Kate and Kelly in this chapter are from these interviews or from the Daleys' journals and other writings.

3. Nancy Daley, author interviews, June 5 and December 3, 2005; January 21 and November 28, 2006; October 14, December 3, 2007; January 5, 16, and 29, 2008. All quotations from Nancy Daley in this chapter are from these interviews.

4. Amanda Hawes, Alexander Hawes LLP, e-mail message to author, February 1, 2008. Ms. Hawes is the Daley family attorney.

5. "Geen Standaard Mens" (No Ordinary Man), De Penne van Swenne, http://www.dpvs.nl/GeenStandaardMens.htm.

6. Kelly Daley, "Minutiae of EB" (journal, n.d.), 4.

7. Judith Herman, *Trauma and Recovery* (New York: Basic Books, 1992), 175.

8. Quoted in Shoshana Felman, *The Juridical Unconscious: Trials and Traumas in the Twentieth Century* (Cambridge, MA: Harvard University Press, 2002), 106.

9. His name, like those of all other participants at the vets' retreat, has been changed.

10. Jonathan Shay, M.D., *Achilles in Vietnam: Combat Trauma and the Undoing of Character* (New York: Touchstone, 1995), 179.

11. Herman, *Trauma and Recovery*, 181.

12. Jonathan Shay, M.D., *Odysseus in America: Combat Trauma and the Trials of Homecoming* (New York: Scribner, 2002), 169.

13. Ruth Leys, *Trauma: A Genealogy* (Chicago: University of Chicago Press, 2000), 100–101.

14. "Post-Traumatic Stress Disorder," *All Things Considered*, National Public Radio, August 19, 2003, http://www.npr.org/templates/story/story.php?storyId=1401789.

15. Scott Shane, "A Flood of Troubled Soldiers Is in the Offing, Experts Predict," *New York Times*, December 16, 2004.

16. Or so I was told by a counselor at a V.A. facility in Maryland who wishes to remain anonymous. E-mail to author, May 12, 2007.

17. Shay, *Odysseus*, 40.

18. Farinaz Amirsehi, author interview, November 17, 2004.

19. Shay, *Achilles*, 86.

20. Ibid., 37.

21. Pierre Janet, *L'automatisme psychologique* in *A History of Psychology in Autobiography*, vol. 1, ed. C. A. Murchison (Worcester, MA: Clark University Press, 1930), 1607; quoted in Bessel A. van der Kolk and Onno van der Hart, "Pierre Janet and the Breakdown of Adaptation in Psychological Trauma," *American Journal of Psychiatry*, 146, no. 12 (December 1989): 1530–40, http://www.trauma-pages.com/a/vdkvdh-89.php.

22. An anthropologist who'd been caught up in a political riot in North Africa, during which he'd seen a man shot to death in front of him and then been seized and tortured by government paramilitaries, told me that during flashbacks his mouth would be flooded with the taste of human brains: his captors had forced him to eat some of the dead man's. Jody Ranck, author interview, June 2, 2005.

23. Herman, *Trauma and Recovery*, 86.

24. Shay, *Achilles*, 33.

25. Kirsopp Lake, trans., "Martyrdom of Polycarp," in *Apostolic Fathers*, Vol. II, Loeb Classical Library (Cambridge: Harvard University Press, 1912), 313.

26. "The intention of the Adamic myth is to separate the origin of evil from that of good. In other words, to posit the radical origin of evil distinct from the more primordial origin of the goodness of all created things: man commences evil but does not commence creation." Paul Ricoeur, quoted in Samuel E. Balentine, "For No Reason," *Interpretation*, 57, no. 4 (2003): 354.

27. Or of its earlier books. As the Old Testament progresses, God be-comes more temperate. See, for example, Jack Miles, *God: A Biography* (New York: Knopf, 1995), chaps. 9–13.

28. For the previous discussion, I am greatly indebted to Elaine Scarry, *The Body in Pain: The Making and Unmaking of the World* (New York: Oxford University Press, 1985), chap. 4.

29. Though periodically he changes back. As Bruce Chilton points out, an undercurrent of violence, both implicit and explicit, persists throughout the New Testament, as in Mark 13's prophecy of the Great Tribulation and Revelation's gleeful elaboration of same. E-mail messages to author, January 22, 2008.

30. Jack Miles, *Christ: A Crisis in the Life of God* (New York: Knopf, 2001), 244.

31. Fyodor Dostoevsky, *Demons*, trans. Richard Pevear and Larissa Volokhonsky (New York: Knopf, 1994), 249.

32. Miles, *Christ*, 76–77.

33. Scarry, *The Body in Pain*, 210–15.

34. James Shapiro, *Oberammergau: The Troubling Story of the World's Most Famous Passion Play* (New York: Vintage, 2001), 57–58.

35. Similar thoughts had troubled me a week earlier while watching a troupe of young volunteer performers present a dramatic dance about the tsunami at a refugee camp in Batticaloa, on Sri Lanka's east coast. They performed their movements to a sound track of crashing waves that grew steadily louder until, at the piece's climax, they were practically deafening. Only the accompanying music re-minded me that I was listening to a sound track. The dancers thrashed as if caught in churning water, clutched one another in ter-ror, and at last crouched and grieved silently over a small, limp child who was meant to stand in for an entire populace of the dead. I looked anxiously about the audience, which was largely made up of the disaster's survivors, many of them children of the same age as the "drowning victim." "Isn't it too soon for them to be seeing this?" I asked the show's director, a local man who, like his young per-formers, was a volunteer. It was mid-March, and the tsunami had hit Batticaloa on December 26. "Oh, no," he assured me. "All enjoy."

36. Father N. M. Saveri, author interview, Jaffna, March 19, 2005.

37. Cited in the *Catechism of the Catholic Church* (Mahwah, NJ: Paulist Press, 1994), 155.

38. See Marvin Harris, *Cows, Pigs, Wars, and Witches: The Riddles of Culture* (New York: Vintage, 1989), 179–203; Israel Knohl, *The Messiah Before Jesus: The Suffering Servant of the Dead Sea Scrolls* (Berkeley: University of California Press, 2000); Michael O. Wise, *The First Messiah: Investigating the Savior Before Christ* (San Francisco: HarperSanFrancisco, 1999).

39. "Martyr," *The Catholic Encyclopedia,* http://www.newadvent.org/cathen/09736b.htm.

40. Kirsopp Lake, trans., "Martyrdom of Polycarp," 317.

41. F. J. Bacchus, "St. Polycarp," *The Catholic Encyclopedia,* vol. 12 (New York: Robert Appleton, 1911), http://www.newadvent.org/cathen/12219b.htm.

42. Elaine Pagels, *Beyond Belief: The Secret Gospel of Thomas* (New York: Vintage, 2003), 80–81.

43. Kirsopp Lake, trans., "Martyrdom of Polycarp," 319–321.

44. Ibid., 323.

45. Ibid., 331–333.

46. Ibid., 333.

47. David Halberstam, *The Making of a Quagmire* (New York: Random House, 1965), 211.

48. Kirsopp Lake, trans., "Martyrdom of Polycarp," 335.

49. Saint Ambrose, *De Officiis,* quoted in Fr. Francesco Moraglia, "St Lawrence: Proto-Deacon of the Roman Church," http://www.vatican.va/roman_curia/congregations/cclergy/documents/rc_con_cclergy_doc_19022000_slaw_en.html.

50. Scarry, *The Body in Pain,* 6.

51. See, for example, Pagels, *Beyond Belief,* 85.

52. Of course the god who died on the cross wasn't completely silent. In the depth of his agony, Jesus cried out to his Father, "Why have you forsaken me?" Simone Weil writes, "The martyrs who entered the arena singing as they went to face the wild beasts were not afflicted. Christ was afflicted. He did not die like a martyr. He died like a common criminal, confused with thieves, only a little more ridiculous." Simone Weil, "The Love of God and Affliction," in *Waiting for God,* trans. Emma Craufurd (New York: Harper Perennial, 2001), 73.

53. Bruce Chilton, author interview, January 5, 2006. All quotations from Chilton in this chapter are from that interview.

54. Saint Augustine, Sermon: "On Pastors." Cited in Neil MacDonald, "Suffering and the Call to Christian Leadership," *Olive Leaf Journal,* undated, http://www.peace.mb.ca/01.Suffering/xneil01.htm.

55. Simone Weil, "Letter VI: Last Thoughts," in *Waiting for God,* trans. Emma Craufurd (New York: Harper Perennial, 2001), 44.

56. Jeff Sharlet, "Soldiers of Christ: Inside America's Most Powerful Megachurch," *Harper's,* May 2005, 46.

57. Ibid., 41.

58. Tim LaHaye and Jerry B. Jenkins, *Glorious Appearing: The End of Days* (Wheaton, IL: Tyndale, 2004), flap.

59. Ibid., 203–4.

60. See Miles, *God: A Biography,* 231–302.

61. LaHaye and Jenkins, *Glorious Appearing,* 380–81.
62. Andrew Sullivan, "Atrocities in Plain Sight," *New York Times Book Review,* January 13, 2006.
63. American Psychiatric Association, *DSM-III-R: Diagnostic and Statistical Manual of Mental Disorders,* 3rd ed. (Washington, DC: American Psychiatric Association Press, 1987), 250.
64. Kate Daley, "Kate Journals: Mid-2001 to Mid-2004," 16.
65. Felman, *The Juridical Unconscious,* 179.
66. Kate Daley, "Journals," 22.
67. Kelly Daley, "Minutiae of EB," 3.
68. Kate Daley, "Journals," 28.
69. Kelly Daley, "Minutiae of EB," 6.
70. A pseudonym.
71. Kelly Daley, "My Stay in the Looney Bin" (n.d.), 9.
72. Kate Daley, "Journals," 9–10.
73. Pat Barker, *The Eye in the Door* (New York: Penguin, 1995), 18; quoted in Kate Daley, "Journals," 14.
74. Quoted in David W. Blight, "The Shaw Memorial in the Landscape of Civil War Memory," in *Beyond the Battlefield: Race, Memory, and the American Civil War* (Amherst: University of Massachusetts Press, 2002), 157.
75. Kate Daley, "Journals," 10.
76. Natalie Merchant, "Henry Darger," Indian Love Bride Music, 2001 (ASCAP). Used by permission.
77. Shantideva, *The Way of the Bodhisattva: A Translation of the Bodhicharyāvatāra,* trans. Padmakara Translation Group, rev. ed. (Boston: Shambhala, 2006), 123. All further page references are indicated inside parentheses in text.
78. Karen Armstrong, *Buddha* (London: Penguin, 2004), 33.
79. Ibid., 85.
80. "Mahāparinibbāna Sutta: The Great Passing," in *The Long Discourses of the Buddha: A Translation of the Dīgha Nikāya,* trans. Maurice Walshe (Boston: Wisdom Publications, 1995), 262.
81. *The Book of Kindred Sayings* (English translation of the *Samyutta-nikāya*), Pali Text Society. Quoted in James W. Boyd, "Suffering in Theravada Buddhism," in *Suffering: Indian Perspectives,* ed. Kapil N. Tiwari (Delhi: Motilal Banarsidass, 1986), 146, n. 5.
82. Armstrong, *Buddha,* 23.
83. Or not directly. What the Buddha did set out to end was the chain of cause and effect that produces those phenomena. In "The Great Discourse on Origination," he puts it this way:

    If asked: "What conditions ageing-and-death?" you should answer: "Ageing-and-death is conditioned by birth." . . . "What conditions birth?" ... "Becoming conditions birth." ... "Clinging conditions becoming." ... "Craving conditions clinging." ... "Feeling conditions craving." ... "Contact conditions feeling." ... "Mind-and-body conditions contact." ... "Consciousness conditions mind-and-body." ... If asked, "What conditions consciousness?" you should answer: "Mind-and-body conditions consciousness." "Mahānidāna Sutta," in *The Long Discourses of the Buddha: A Translation of the Dīgha Nikāya*, trans. Maurice Walshe (Boston: Wisdom Publications, 1995), 223.

84. Robert Thurman, author interview, April 27, 2005.
85. Edward Conze, *Buddhism: Its Essence and Development* (New York: Harper, 1965), 93–94.
86. Shantideva, *The Way of the Bodhisattva*, 171.
87. Pema Chödrön, *No Time to Lose: A Timely Guide to the Way of the Bodhisattva* (Boston: Shambhala, 2005), xiii.
88. Bardor Tulku Rinpoche, *Shantideva's Bodhicharyāvatāra*, trans. Lama Geshe Gyamtso, pt. 12 (Woodstock, NY: Namse Bangdzo Bookstore, 2005). CD 1 of five-CD set.
89. Armstrong, *Buddha*, 89.
90. Author interviews, Colombo, March 26, 2005. All the prisoners' names have been changed.
91. *The Holy Teaching of Vimalakīrti*, trans. Robert A. F. Thurman (University Park: Pennsylvania State University Press, 1976, 2003), 43.
92. A monk I spoke with at a Tibetan monastery in upstate New York suggested that for someone who was especially resistant, a beginning might simply be visualizing picking wild herbs from the roadside and giving them to a stranger. Tsultrim Oser, author interview, May 10, 2007.
93. Shantideva, *The Way of the Bodhisattva*, 175–77. Pema Chödrön puts it more entertainingly as "eating, sleeping, and shitting." Chödrön, *No Time to Lose*, xi.
94. Shantideva, ibid., 182–94.
95. A pseudonym.

CHAPTER 5. THE FACES IN THE HOLD
1. Christopher Dickey and Rod Nordland, "Precious Suffering," *Newsweek*, February 28, 2005, international edition.
2. Ibid.
3. James Parkinson, "An Essay on the Shaking Palsy" (1817), reprinted in *Journal of Neuropsychiatry and Clinical Neurosciences*, 14 (May 2002): 223–36, http://neuro.psychiatryonline.org/cgi/content/full/14/2/223. Used by permission.

4. "About Parkinson Disease," National Parkinson Foundation, http://www.parkinson.org/NETCOMMUNITY/Page .aspx?pid=225&srcid=201.

5. Marc A. Thiessen, "The Blessed Sounds of Silence," *National Review,* March 31, 2005, http://www.nationalreview.com/comment/ thiessen200503311119.asp.

6. Pope John Paul II, *Salvifici Doloris* (papal letter, February 11, 1984), http://www.vatican.va/holy_father/john_paul_ii/apost_ letters/documents/hf_jp-ii_apl_11021984_salvifici-doloris_en .html.

7. "He's Preaching with His Suffering, Says Cardinal Ratzinger: John Paul II 'Shares in the Passion of Christ,' " ZENIT News Service, March 1, 2005, http://www.zenit.org/article-12388?1=english.

8. Dickey and Nordland, "Precious Suffering."

9. Peggy Noonan, "Victim Soul: What John Paul II Is Teaching Us Through His Suffering," *OpinionJournal: The Wall Street Journal Editorial Page,* February 10, 2005, http://www.opinionjournal .com/columnists/pnoonan/?id110006271.

10. Dickey and Nordland, "Precious Suffering."

11. Thiessen, "The Blessed Sounds of Silence."

12. Noonan, "Victim Soul."

13. Douglas Brinkley, *The Great Deluge: Hurricane Katrina, New Orleans, and the Mississippi Gulf Coast* (New York: William Morrow, 2006), 29.

14. Michael Eric Dyson, *Come Hell or High Water: Hurricane Katrina and the Color of Disaster* (New York: Basic Civitas, 2006), 5–8.

15. Brinkley, *The Great Deluge,* 258.

16. Some other statistics: nearly fifty thousand New Orleans schoolchildren cut classes every day; 50 percent of black ninth graders wouldn't graduate in four years; Louisiana's schoolteachers had the third-lowest salaries in the United States. Dyson, *Come Hell or High Water,* 5–8.

17. Bob Herbert, "In America; Killer Cops," *New York Times,* September 15, 1995.

18. News Services, "Policewoman Guilty of Killing 3," *Washington Post,* September 12, 1995.

19. Brinkley, *The Great Deluge,* 22.

20. Ibid., 45.

21. Ibid., 49.

22. Ibid., 47.

23. Dawn DeDeaux, "Soul Shadows: Urban Warrior Myths," Baltimore Museum for Contemporary Art, Baltimore, 1992.

24. It was the poorer neighborhoods that lay farthest below the water level, but this seems to be true in most cities. A suburb with the

word "heights" in its name is usually wealthy, or supposed to sound
that way. There are obvious material factors that make high ground
desirable, starting with safety from floods and including relief from
noxious miasmas and mosquitoes and the relative ease with which
the terrain can be defended against incursions from below. Over
time such advantages acquire moral, even spiritual, connotations: to
live on the heights is to be exalted. The corollary is that to dwell on
lower ground is to be abased. "It was a place of ever-present fever,
and there was swampy mud even in summer," writes Chekhov, describing the impoverished, low-lying village setting of
his story "In the Ravine." "There was always a smell of factory
waste. . . . The water in the river often stank on account of the tan-
nery; the waste contaminated the meadows, the peasants' cattle suffered from anthrax." (In *Stories*, trans. Richard Pevear and Larissa
Volokhonsky [New York: Bantam, 2000], 383–84.) After Katrina,
an Israeli military contractor hired to guard the wealthy — and
elevated — gated community of Audubon Place noted that the
floodwater had stopped just at the rear gate and shrugged. "God
watches out for the rich people, I guess." (Jamie Wilson, "Mercenaries Guard Homes of the Rich in New Orleans," *Guardian*,
September 12, 2005, http://www.guardian.co.uk/katrina/
story/0,16441,1567656,00.html.)

25. Brinkley, *The Great Deluge*, 195–97.
26. Ibid., 17.
27. Ibid., 14.
28. Ibid., 620–21.
29. Associated Press, "Unrest Intensifies at Superdome Shelter," *New York Times*, September 1, 2005.
30. Actually, the victims themselves did that. "We are American," a woman at the convention center told the news cameras, her voice crackling with anger. Michael Ignatieff writes: "She — not the governor, not the mayor, not the president — understood that the catastrophe was a test of the bonds of citizenship, and that the government had failed the test." "The Broken Contract: It Was Not Blacks or the Poor but *Citizens* Whom the Government Betrayed in New Orleans," *New York Times Magazine*, September 25, 2005.
31. Jon Donley, author interview, June 14, 2007.
32. Dyson, *Come Hell or High Water*, 5–8.
33. Daniel P. Mannix and Malcolm Cowley, *Black Cargoes: A History of the Atlantic Slave Trade* (New York: Viking, 1965), 61.
34. Nicholas D. Kristof, "A Health Care Disaster," *New York Times*, September 25, 2005.
35. Helen Epstein, "Enough to Make You Sick?" *New York Times Magazine*, October 12, 2003.

36. Sir James George Frazer, *The Golden Bough: A Study in Magic and Religion,* abr. ed. (New York: Macmillan, 1969), 309–29.

37. Until the 1840s slave traders had an estimated average annual profit of between 15 and 30 percent; after that profit rates went down to a still respectable 15 percent. Peter Kolchin, *American Slavery, 1619–1877* (New York: Hill & Wang, 1993), 98.

38. This was what a planter named James Henry Hammond had in mind when he wrote, "In a slave country every *freeman* is an aristocrat." Quoted in Kolchin, *American Slavery,* 195. For more on Hammond, see ibid., 119–23.

39. Quoted in Mannix and Cowley, *Black Cargoes,* 111.

40. "Black People Loot, White People Find?" *Boingboing: A Directory of Wonderful Things,* August 30, 2005, http://www.boingboing .net/2005/08/30/black-people-loot-wh.html; quoted in Dyson, *Come Hell or High Water,* 164.

41. Jim Dwyer and Christopher Drew, "Fear Exceeded Crime's Reality in New Orleans," *New York Times,* September 29, 2005.

42. Brinkley, *The Great Deluge,* 193.

43. "After the Flood," *This American Life,* Chicago Public Radio, September 9, 2005, http://www.thislife.org/Radio_Episode .aspx?sched=1097.

44. Ibid.

45. Brinkley, *The Great Deluge,* 544.

46. Mannix and Cowley, *Black Cargoes,* 125.

47. Ibid., 126.

48. Ibid., 125–27.

49. Francine du Plessix Gray, *Simone Weil* (New York: Penguin, 2001), 7.

50. Ibid., 164.

51. Quoted in Leslie Fiedler, introduction to *Waiting for God,* by Simone Weil, trans. Emma Craufurd (New York: G. P. Putnam's Sons, 1951, 1979; New York: Harper Perennial, 1973, 2001), xxxi. Citations are to the Harper edition.

52. Gray, *Simone Weil,* 226.

53. Quoted in Fiedler, introduction, xviii.

54. Gray, *Simone Weil,* 212.

55. Ibid., 21.

56. Ibid., 211.

57. Simone Weil, "Letter II: Same Subject," in *Waiting for God,* trans. Emma Craufurd (New York: G. P. Putnam's Sons, 1951, 1979; New York: Harper Perennial, 2001), 13.

58. Weil, "The Love of God and Affliction," in *Waiting for God,* trans. Emma Craufurd (New York: G. P. Putnam's Sons, 1951, 1979; New York: Harper Perennial, 1973, 2001), 68.

59. Elaine Scarry, *The Body in Pain: The Making and Unmaking of the World* (New York: Oxford University Press, 1985), 113.

60. See ch. 3 n. 48.

61. Weil, "The Love of God and Affliction," 73.

62. Patrick J. McCloskey, "The Rough Side of the Mountain," *New York Times*, April 11, 2004.

63. Nun at Nirmal Hriday, Calcutta, author interview, March 31, 2005.

64. Mother Teresa, *Love, a Fruit Always in Season: Daily Meditations from the Words of Mother Teresa*, ed. Dorothy S. Hunt (San Francisco: Ignatius Press, 1989), 63.

65. Mother Teresa, *No Greater Love* (Novato, CA: New World Library, 2001), 153.

66. Mother Teresa, *Mother Teresa: In My Own Words* (New York: Random House, 1997), 41.

67. Alternatively, it may be because none of the sisters who worked there was certified to dispense medication. "We are not social workers, not teachers, not nurses or doctors," Mother Teresa famously insisted. "We serve Jesus in the poor." "Mother Teresa R.I.P.," obituary, *Commonweal*, September 26, 1997, http://findarticles.com/p/articles/mi_m1252/is_n16_v124/ai_20158998.

68. Tim Challies, "The Myth of Mother Teresa," http://www.challies.com/archives/articles/the-myth-of-mot.php.

69. Weil, "Forms of the Implicit Love of God," *Waiting for God*, trans. Emma Craufurd (New York: G. P. Putnam's Sons, 1951, 1979; New York: Harper Perennial, 2001), 93.

70. See, for example, Christopher Hitchens, *The Missionary Position: Mother Teresa in Theory and Practice* (London: Verso, 1995), 1–12, 64–70, 82–83.

71. Simone Weil, "The Needs of the Soul," in *Simone Weil: An Anthology*, ed. Siân Miles (New York: Grove Press, 1986), 89.

72. Weil, "Forms of the Implicit Love of God," 87.

73. Brinkley, *The Great Deluge*, 466.

74. "After the Flood."

75. Weil, "Forms of the Implicit Love of God," 87.

76. Alix Spiegel, "Stuck and Suicidal in a Post-Katrina Trailer Park," *All Things Considered*, National Public Radio, August 8, 2007, http://www.npr.org/templates/story/story.php?storyId=14331157.

77. Ibid.

78. James Risen and Tim Golden, "3 Prisoners Commit Suicide at Guantanamo," *New York Times*, June 11, 2006.

79. Spiegel, "Stuck and Suicidal."

80. Simone Weil, "Human Personality," in *Simone Weil: An Anthology*, ed. Siân Miles (New York: Grove Press, 1986), 70.

81. Emmanuel Levinas, "Philosophy, Justice, and Love," in *Entre*

Nous: Thinking-of-the-Other, trans. Michael B. Smith and Barbara Harshav (New York: Columbia University Press, 1998); quoted in Shoshana Felman, *The Juridical Unconscious: Trials and Trauma in the Twentieth Century* (Cambridge: Harvard University Press, 2002), 1.

82. An extreme version of the last explanation appears in a *New York Times* story on a monument in Duluth, Minnesota, that commemorates the lynching of three African American circus hands eighty years ago. Fixing the memorial with a baleful gaze, a white woman grumbled, "Those men wouldn't have been killed if they hadn't done nothing, would they?" Monica Davey, "It Did Happen Here: The Lynching That a City Forgot," *New York Times*, December 4, 2003.

83. Weil, "The Love of God and Affliction," 71.

ACKNOWLEDGMENTS

This book has accrued many, many debts. I can acknowledge only some of them here:

My thanks to Ray Krone, Ngawang Sangdrol, Sarah and Donald Goodrich, Isidore Munyakazi, Anastasie K., Beata M., Jeanne d'Arc M., and Kate, Kelly, Christopher, and Nancy Daley, who told me their stories with such unstinting generosity, and sometimes allowed me to watch them unfold.

I thank my agent, Kathleen Anderson, and Asya Muchnick, who worked harder than any editor should have to. My thanks as well to Michael Pietsch, Geoff Shandler, Eric Wolff, Peggy Freudenthal, and Barbara Jatkola at Little, Brown.

My gratitude to the Whiting Foundation for its support. I am also grateful to Bridget Hughes and Fiona Maazel at *A Public Space*, Meehan Crist at *Columbia*, Pat Towers at *O*, Ann Marie Gardner and Agnes Greenhall at *T: The New*

York Times Travel Magazine, and Binyavanga Wainaina at *Kwani?*

For telling me what they knew, in language I could understand: Farinaz Amirsehi, Ole Anthony, Laurel Blossom, Ariane Brunet of Droits et Democracie, Bruce Chilton, Bob Coen; Jim Cusack, Jim Tischer, Matt Ryan, Ken Lavery, Les McCandless, and their clients at Veritas Villa, whom I leave unnamed only out of respect for their privacy; Dawn DeDeaux, Rick Derby, Tom Donley, Erin at the American Cancer Society, Andrea Esquer at the office of the Arizona Attorney General, Pete Evans, Ellen Furnari, Denise Gordon, Amanda Hawes, Carroll Huffman, Leonard Jacobs, Irene Kacandis, Erik Kalkurst, Peter Landesman, Starling Lawrence, Ruth Leys, Lhamo at the International Campaign for Tibet, Elissa Love, Jack Mattair, Anna McLellan, Myra Mniewski, Yuval Neria, Tsultrim Oser, Joe Owmby, Emily and Rachel Paine, George Parnham, the Venerable Bhante Piyatissa, Jody Ranck, Katherine Russell Rich, Frank Romaniello, Elaine Scarry, Jeff Sharlet, Jonathan Shay, James Stewart, Robert Thurman, Leonard Todd, Joy Warren, and Geraldine Winter. Thanks as well to the Death Penalty Information Center.

In Capetown: The members of the Bambanani Women's Group: Noloyiso Baltintulo, Niedeka Mbune, Thozama Ndevu, Nomawethu Ngakmani, Bulelwa Nokwe, Cordelia Nozomela, Nomonde Rundayi, and Zoelwa Somlayi; Cleopatra Eland, Siyamthemba Kazaka, Richard Mason, Sifiso Mazibuko, Nadine Moodie, Jonathan Morgan, Omwaba Nkayi, and masters and staff at Wynberg Boys' High School.

In Kolkata: Amitabh Bhattasali and Subir Bhaumik at the BBC, Dr. Krishna Bose, Suman Chattopadhay, Swami Parameshananda of Bharat Sev Ashram, Swami Prabhananda at the Ramakrishna Mission Institute of Culture, Rakhi Sarkar and Pratiti Sarkar at the CIMA Art Gallery, and Neil Trevithick.

In Rwanda: Anne Aghion, Mary Balikungeri of the Rwanda Women's Network, Professor Emmanuel Bugingo, Michael Cavanaugh of National Public Radio, Christophe, Chantal, and their colleagues at the Hotel Iris in Kigali, Alison Des Forges of Human Rights Watch, Lee Ann Fuji, Gerard Gahima, Rev. Deo Gashagazi of the International Prison Ministry, Jean Bosco Higiro, Klaas de Jonge of Penal Reform International and his colleague Jean Charles Paras, Benoit Kaboyi of Ibuka, Peter Karasira of the National Service of Gacaca Courts, His Excellency Tharcisse Karugarama, Rwanda's Minister of Justice, David Mugarura, Geneviève Mukandekezi, Consolée Mukanyiligira of Avega Agahozo, the late Albert Mutaganda, Casimir Nkuzi, Jean Bosco Ntwali, Rakiya Omaar of African Rights, Kim Pease at USAID, Luwei Pearson, Innocent Ruzigana at the National Unity and Reconciliation Commission, Julius King Rwahurire, Rev. John Ngabo Segasinde of the Fraternité Évangelique de Prison, Juliet Umurerwa, and George Weiss of Radio La Benevolencija Humanitarian Tools Foundation.

In Sri Lanka: Dr. A. T. Ariyaratne, Richard Brooks, and Charika Marasinghe of Sarvodaya Shramadana; Venerable K. Dharmashoka Nayaka Maha Thera; Felician at the Mangrove Psychosocial Support and Coordination Network in

Batticaloa, Sri Krishna Swami, K. W. Lenora and her sons Dazun and Lakmal, the members of the meditation group at Welikada prison, as well as welfare officer W. A. F. Luxman, Commissioner Rummy Marshook, and S. Lakshman Silva, Superintendent of Sri Lanka prisons; Johnson Rajkumar, Dolitha Ranchagoda, Helaena Rathore, Ravi, Achini Samendika, Sandiya Sandamali, Rev. Father Paul Satkunanayagam; Rev. Father Prof. N. M. Saveri and Frances Solomentine of the Centre for Performing Arts in Colombo, along with Mr. Walluwan and his talented volunteers in Batticaloa, N. H. Thilani, and Ven. Prof. K. Vajira. Thanks as well to Varuni Hewarithrana and Merlin Rajakaruna at the Sri Lankan consulate in New York.

In St. Petersburg: Resa Alboher, Grigory Alexandrovich Popov, Violetta Pavlovna Ryabchikova at the State Memorial Museum of the Defense and Siege of Leningrad, and Ekaterina Vodopyan.

Thanks go to those who read early versions of this book, in part or whole: Jeff Allen, Jack Barschi, Jo Ann Beard, Rebecca Berlant, Fergus Bordewich, James McCourt, Eileen Myles, Nicca Ray, and Binyavanga Wainaina. Thanks, too, to the friends who sustained me while writing it. Most of all, I thank my wife, Mary Gaitskill.

I honor the memory of Linda Corrente and Gay Milius; Kate and Kelly Daley and their father, Chris; and Peter Morgan Goodrich.

COPYRIGHT ACKNOWLEDGMENTS

Peter Trachtenberg is a recipient of a Whiting Writer's Award, the Nelson Algren Award for Short Fiction, and a NYFA Artist's Fellowship. He is the author of *7 Tattoos: A Memoir in the Flesh*. His essays and short stories have appeared in *The New Yorker*, *Harper's*, *BOMB*, and *A Public Space*, and his commentaries have been broadcast on NPR's *All Things Considered*. He has taught at the New School, Media Bistro, and Summer Literary Seminars in St. Petersburg, Russia. He lives in upstate New York with his wife.